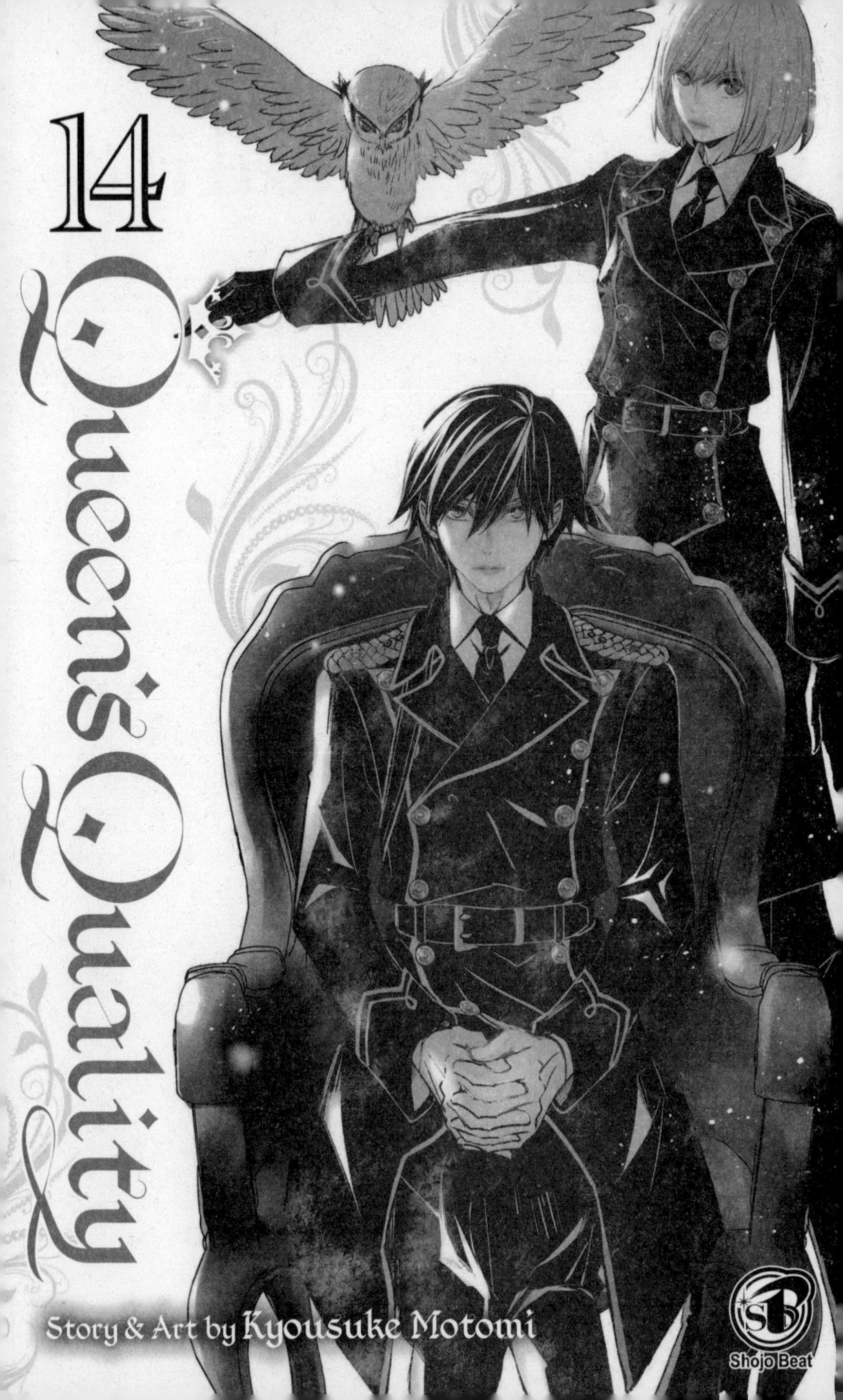
14
Queen's Quality
Story & Art by Kyousuke Motomi
Shojo Beat

Queen's Quality

CONTENTS

14

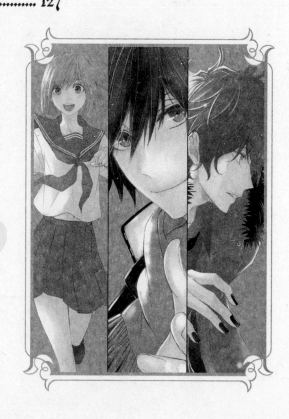

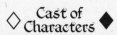
◇ Cast of Characters ◆

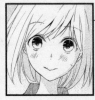

Fumi Nishioka
An apprentice Sweeper with the powers of a Queen, this second-year high school student dreams of finding her very own Prince Charming.

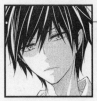

Kyutaro Horikita
A mind Sweeper who cleanses people's minds of dangerous impurities. Although incredibly awkward with people, he and Fumi are now dating.

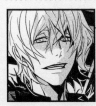

Ataru Shikata
A former bug handler who uses bugs to manipulate people. Saved by Fumi and Kyutaro, he has joined the Genbu Clan.

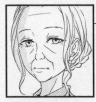

Miyako Horikita
The prior head of the Genbu Gate Sweepers. She can be both strict and kind, and she watches over and advises Fumi.

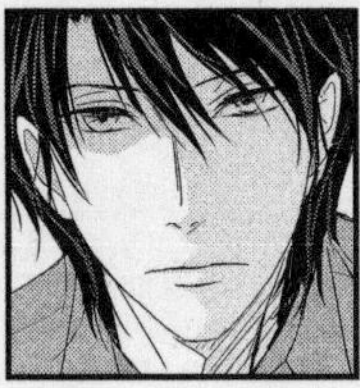

Koichi Kitagawa
The chairman of the school Fumi and Kyutaro attend. He's a Sweeper as well as being Kyutaro's brother-in-law.

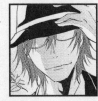

Takaya Kitahara
One of the Genbu Clan, he was originally a member of the main Byakko Clan. He's an expert with suggestive therapy and is actually Fumi's uncle.

◇ Story Thus Far ◆

The Horikitas are a family of Sweepers—people who cleanse impurities from human hearts. After seeing Fumi's potential, they take her on as an assistant and trainee. Within Fumi dwells the power of both the White and the Dark-Gray queens, both of whom have the ability to give people immense power.

Having both paid the compensation demanded by the White Queen and completed their training in Seichi, Fumi and Kyutaro are now in a relationship! Soon after, when it becomes clear that a snake is dwelling within Kyutaro, Fumi defeats the snake and attains the powers of the True Queen.

Kyutaro and his snake form a pact and defeat the Seiryu snake while Fumi and the others help save the Seiryu Clan. Peace has barely descended when disaster strikes again—Yanagi of the Suzaku Gate, the mastermind behind the recent crises, steals Ataru's spirit away!

CHAPTER 62

MONTHLY BETSUCOMI SALE DATE NOTICE ON TWITTER AND INSTAGRAM

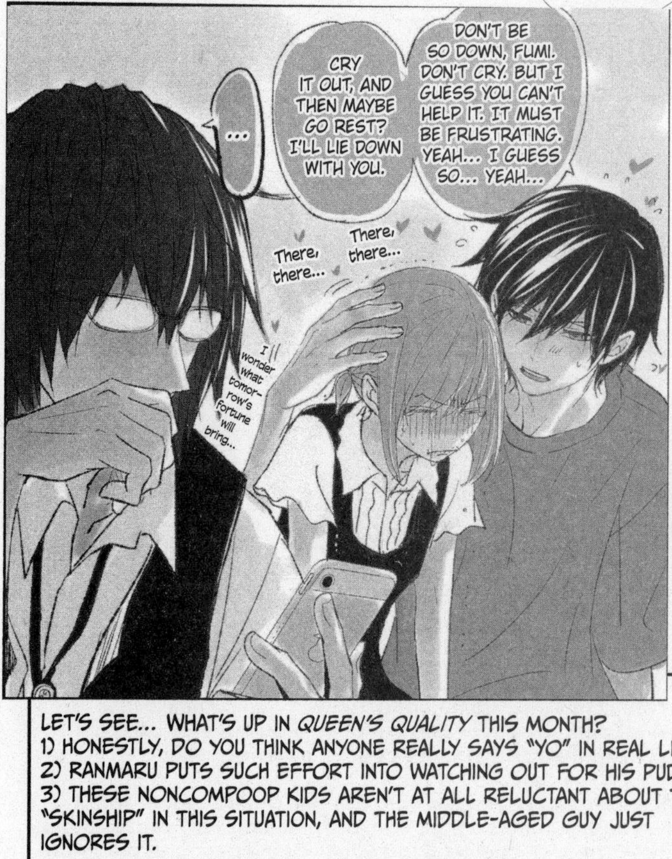
DON'T BE SO DOWN, FUMI. DON'T CRY. BUT I GUESS YOU CAN'T HELP IT. IT MUST BE FRUSTRATING. YEAH... I GUESS SO... YEAH...
CRY IT OUT, AND THEN MAYBE GO REST? I'LL LIE DOWN WITH YOU.
...
There, there...
There, there...
I wonder what tomorrow's fortune will bring...

THE LINE FORTUNE SERVICE IS GREAT. I'VE REGISTERED WITH THEM.

LET'S SEE... WHAT'S UP IN *QUEEN'S QUALITY* THIS MONTH?
1) HONESTLY, DO YOU THINK ANYONE REALLY SAYS "YO" IN REAL LIFE?
2) RANMARU PUTS SUCH EFFORT INTO WATCHING OUT FOR HIS PUDDING.
3) THESE NONCOMPOOP KIDS AREN'T AT ALL RELUCTANT ABOUT THE "SKINSHIP" IN THIS SITUATION, AND THE MIDDLE-AGED GUY JUST IGNORES IT.

EVERYONE FROWNS HEAVILY IN THIS OUTRAGEOUS CHAPTER!

I SEND OUT TWITTER UPDATES LIKE THIS EVERY MONTH. YOU CAN READ SOME OF MY OTHER MUTTERINGS THERE TOO.

@motomikyosuke

I'VE STARTED AN INSTAGRAM ACCOUNT TOO! (kyosukemotomi)

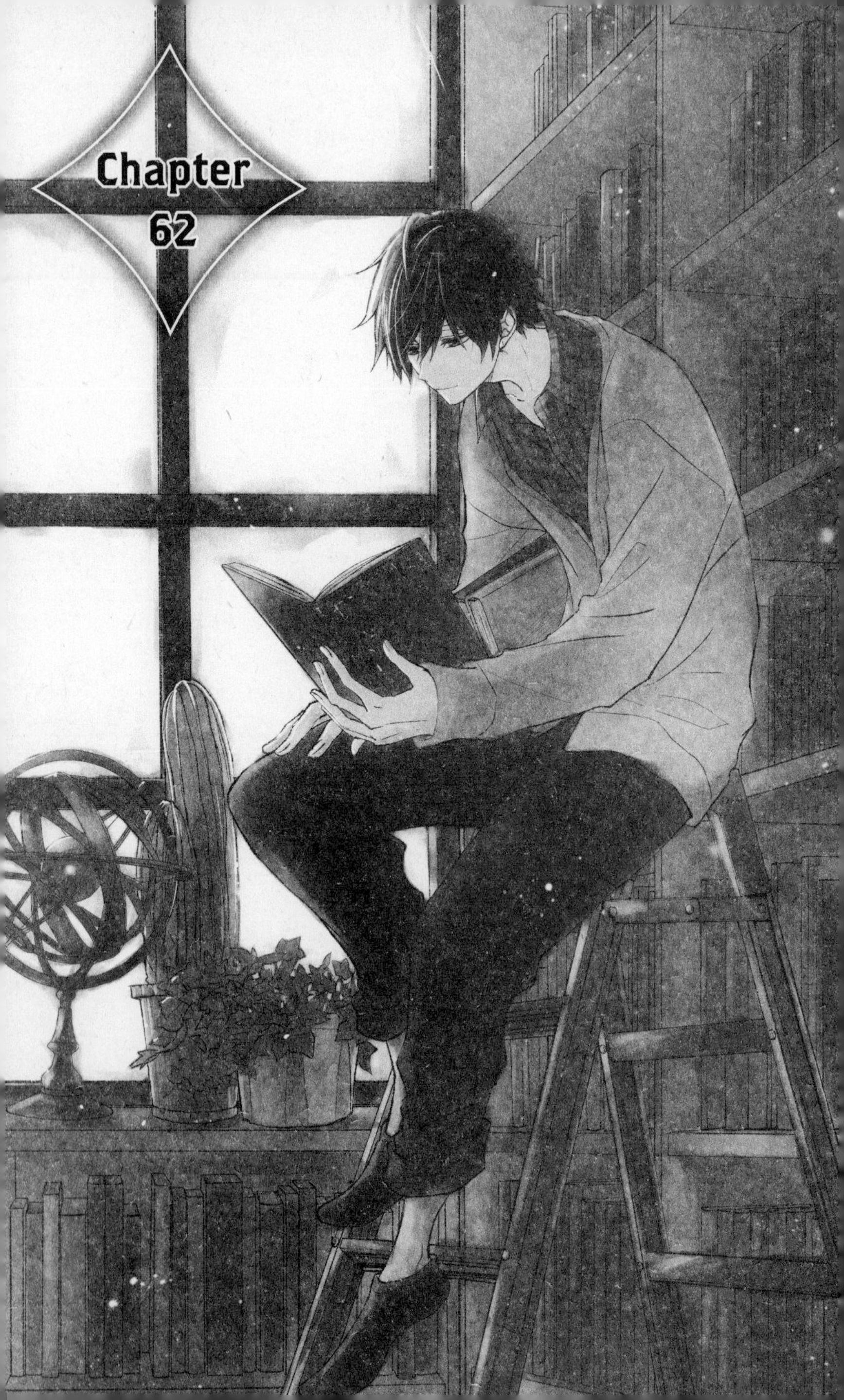
Chapter
62

Queen's Quality

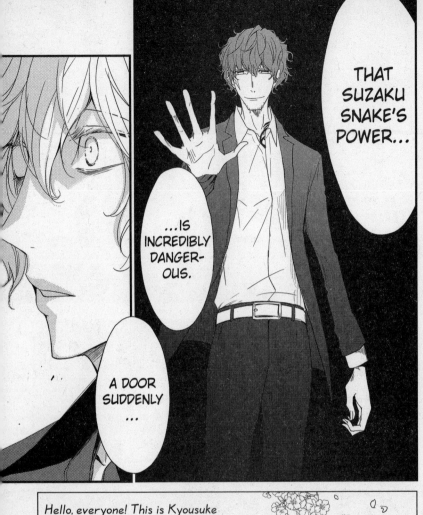

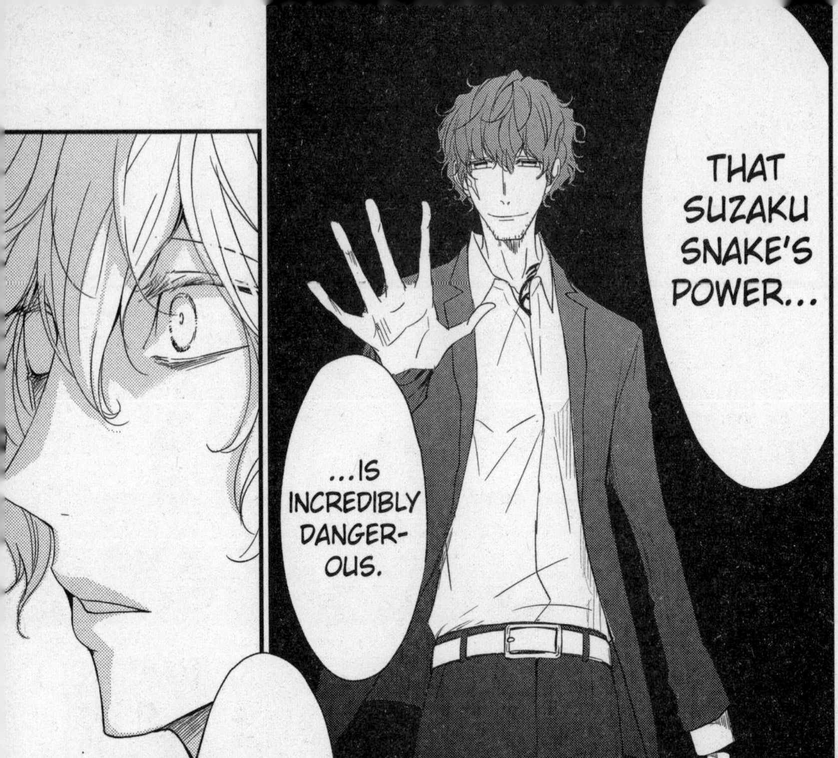
THAT SUZAKU SNAKE'S POWER...
...IS INCREDIBLY DANGER-OUS.
A DOOR SUDDENLY ...

Hello, everyone! This is Kyousuke Motomi. Thank you for picking up volume 14 of *Queen's Quality*.

As I'm working on this volume, cherry blossoms are in bloom outside. It's so exciting. Volume 14 is filled with action (and people too). I hope you enjoy it.

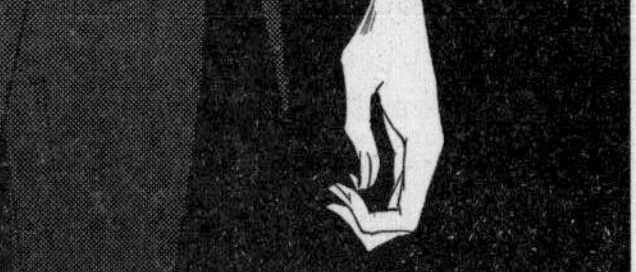
Soon I'll be able to wear my straw hat! I'm so glad!

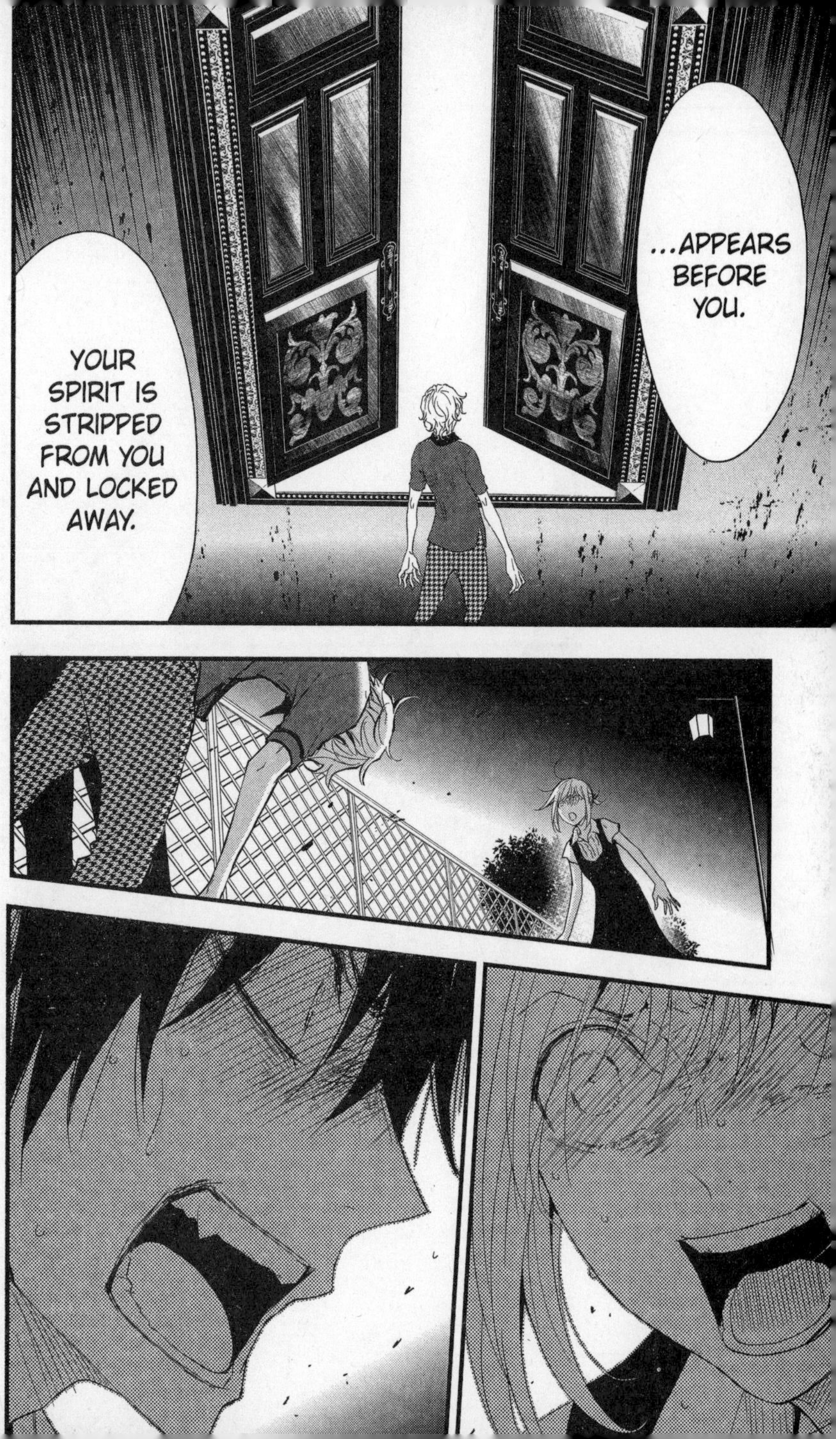
...APPEARS BEFORE YOU.
YOUR SPIRIT IS STRIPPED FROM YOU AND LOCKED AWAY.

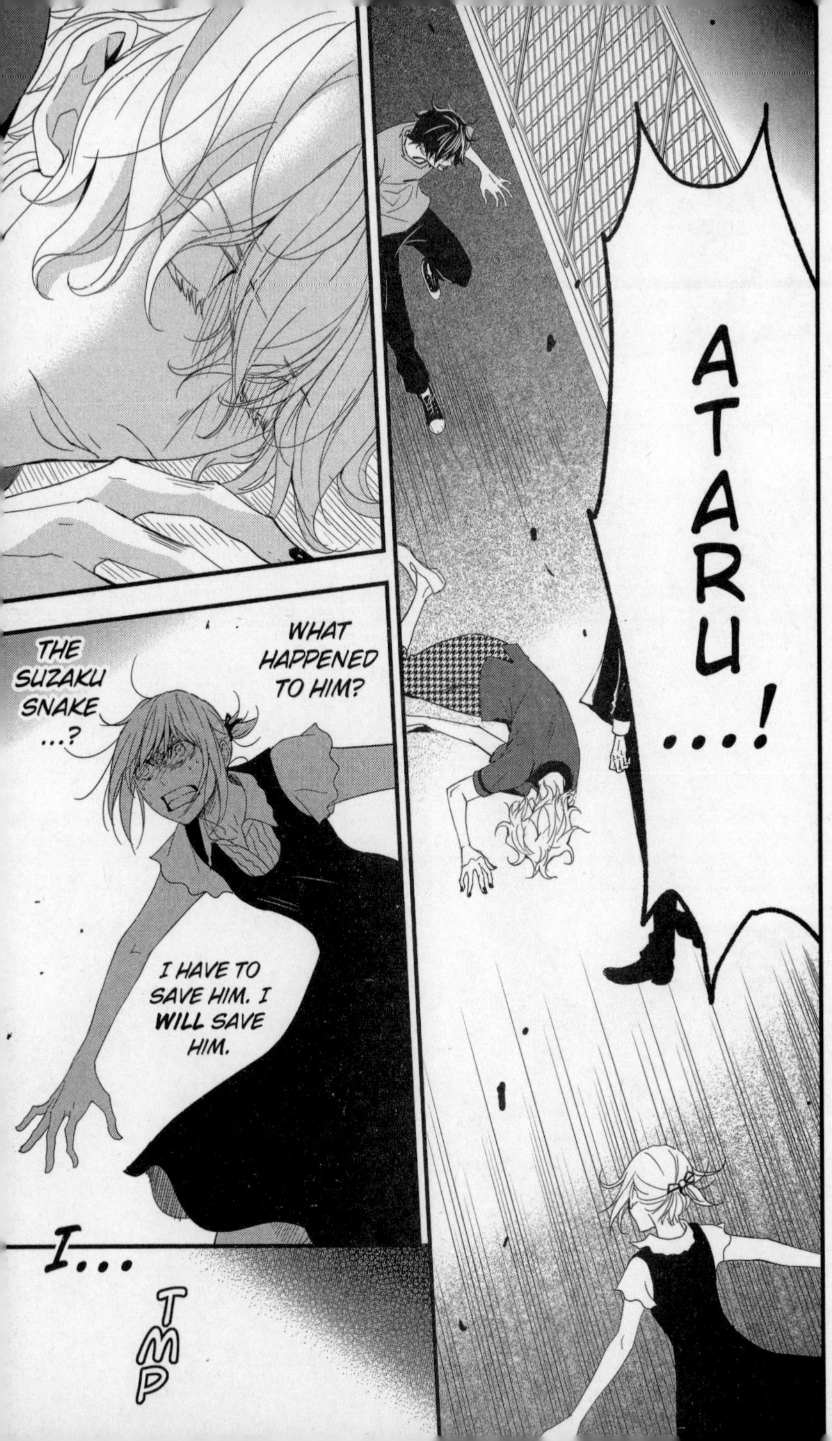
ATARU...!
WHAT HAPPENED TO HIM?
THE SUZAKU SNAKE ...?
I HAVE TO SAVE HIM. I WILL SAVE HIM.
I...
TMP

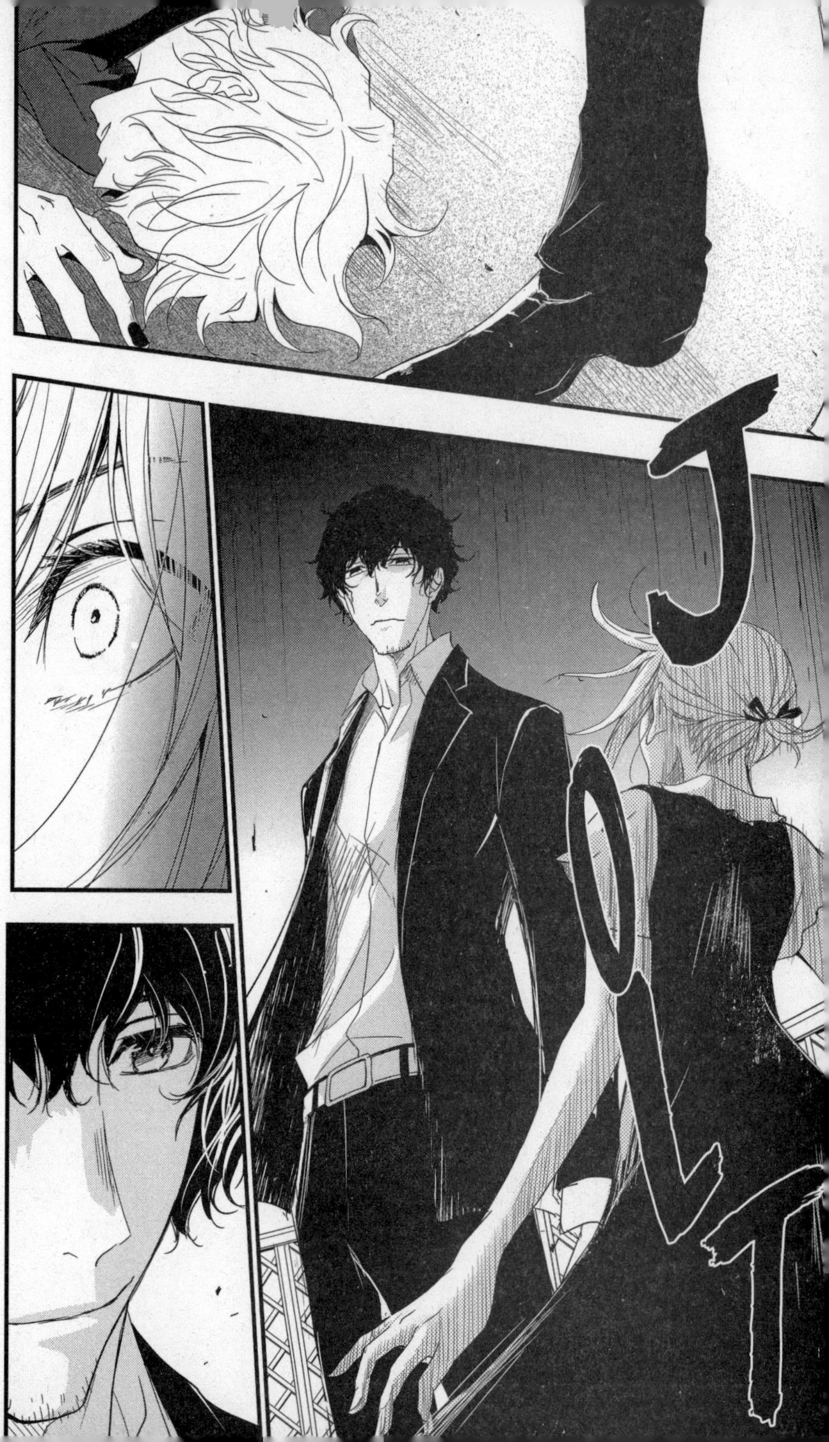
JOLT

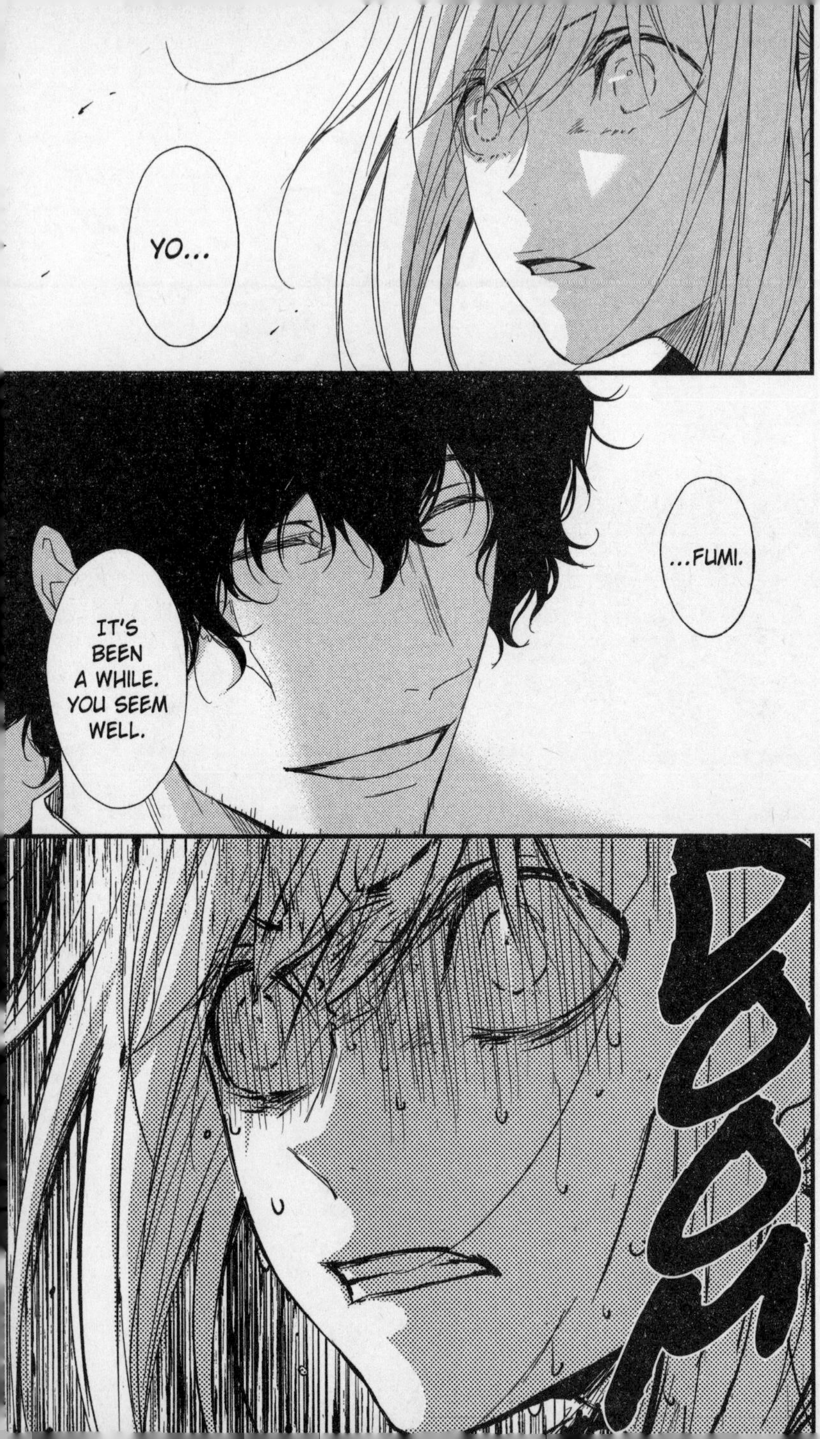
YO...
...FUMI.
IT'S BEEN A WHILE. YOU SEEM WELL.

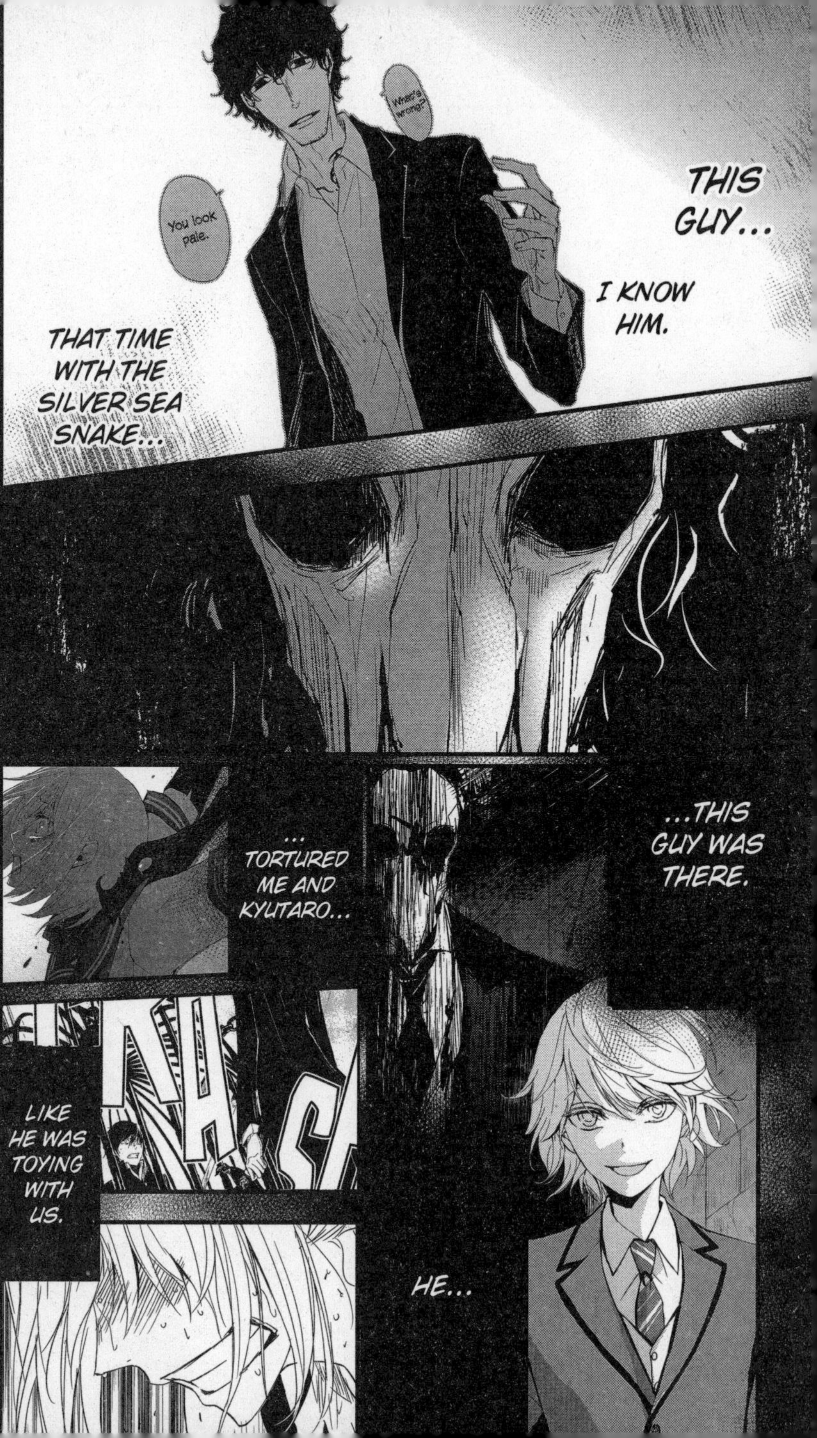
THIS GUY...
I KNOW HIM.
What's wrong?
You look pale.
THAT TIME WITH THE SILVER SEA SNAKE...
...THIS GUY WAS THERE.
... TORTURED ME AND KYUTARO...
LIKE HE WAS TOYING WITH US.
HE...

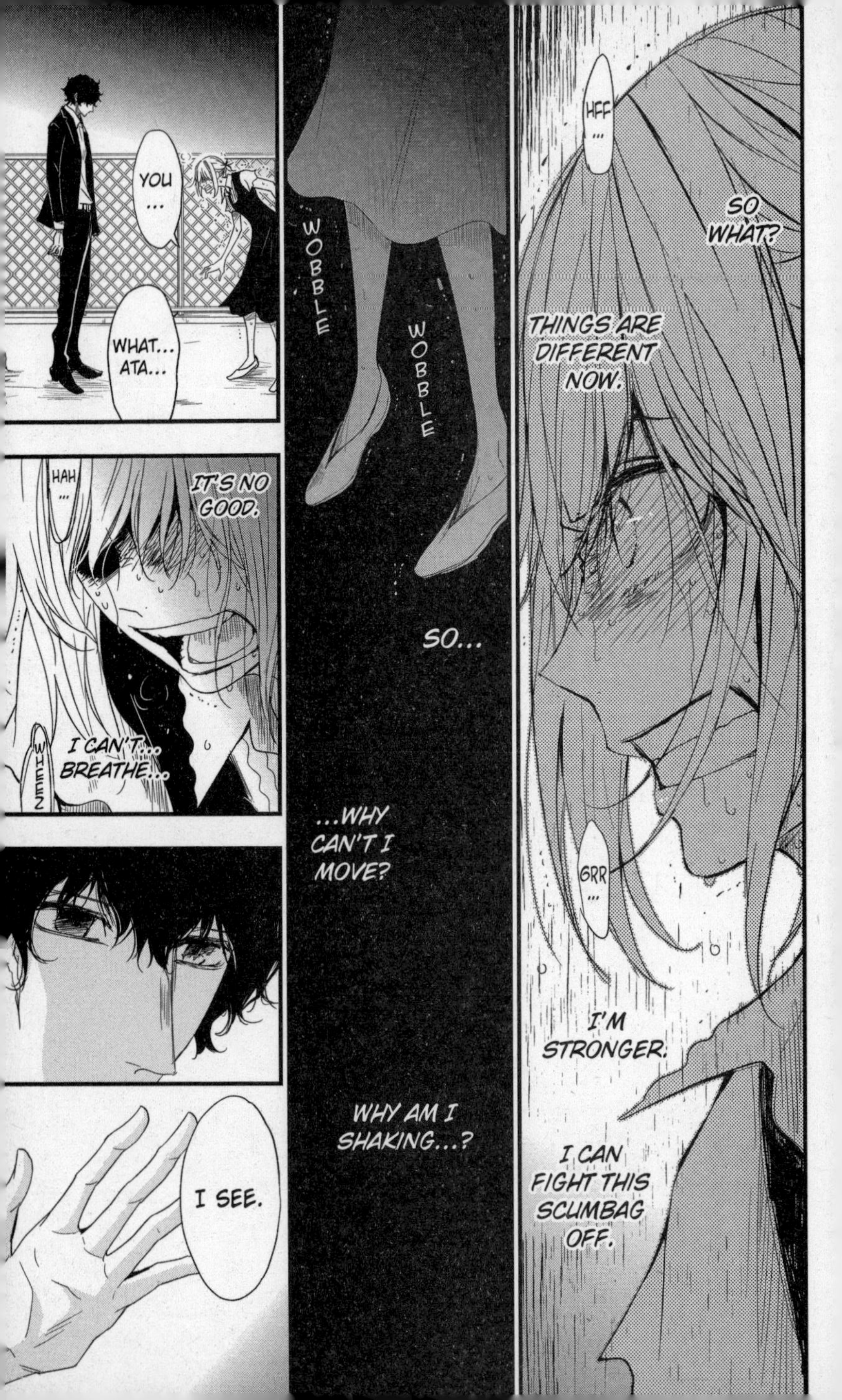
HFF...
SO WHAT?
THINGS ARE DIFFERENT NOW.
GRR...
I'M STRONGER.
I CAN FIGHT THIS SCUMBAG OFF.
WOBBLE
WOBBLE
SO...
...WHY CAN'T I MOVE?
WHY AM I SHAKING...?
YOU...
WHAT... ATA...
HAH...
IT'S NO GOOD.
I CAN'T... BREATHE...
WHEEZ
I SEE.

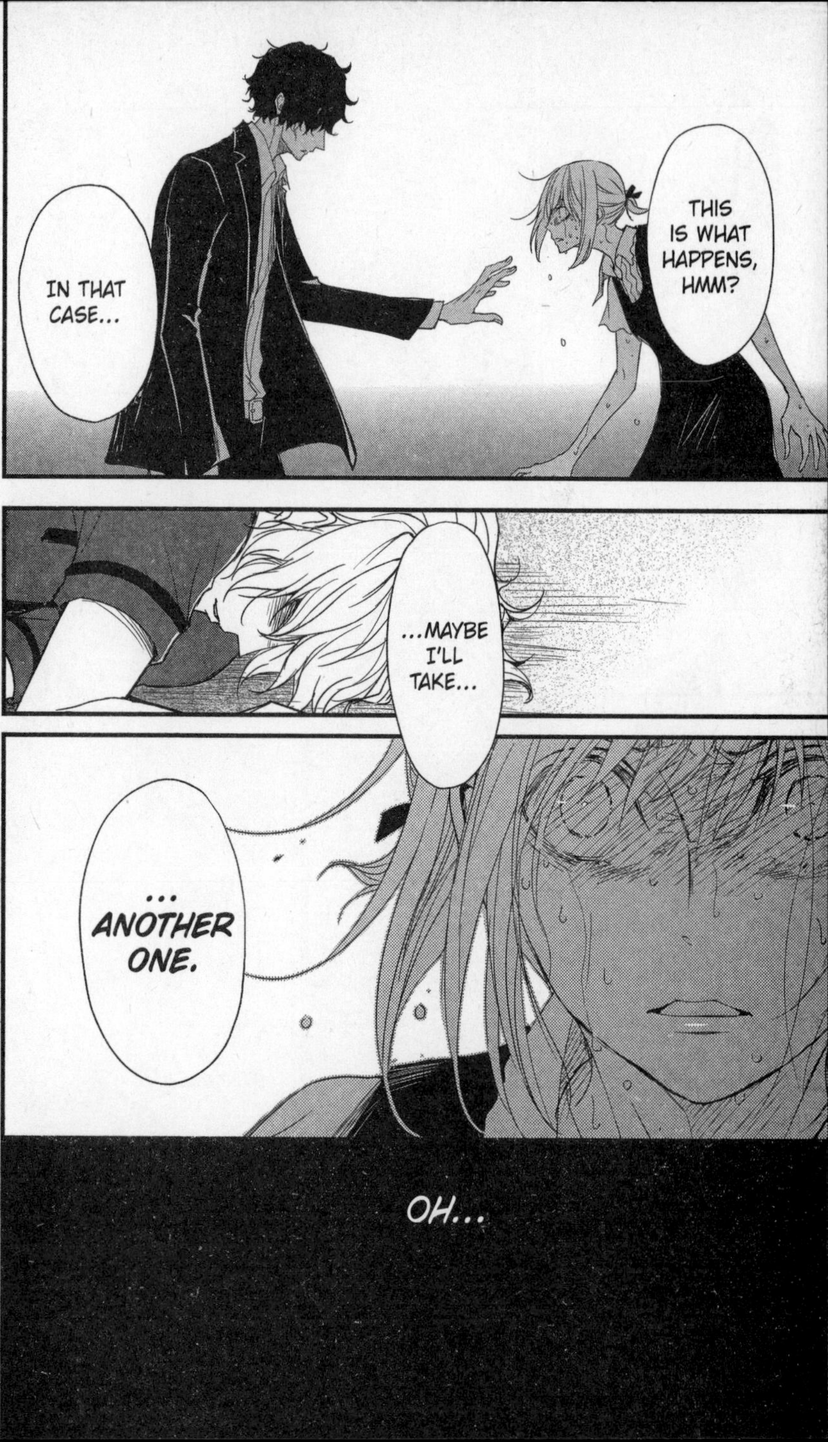
THIS IS WHAT HAPPENS, HMM?
IN THAT CASE...
...MAYBE I'LL TAKE...
... ANOTHER ONE.
OH...

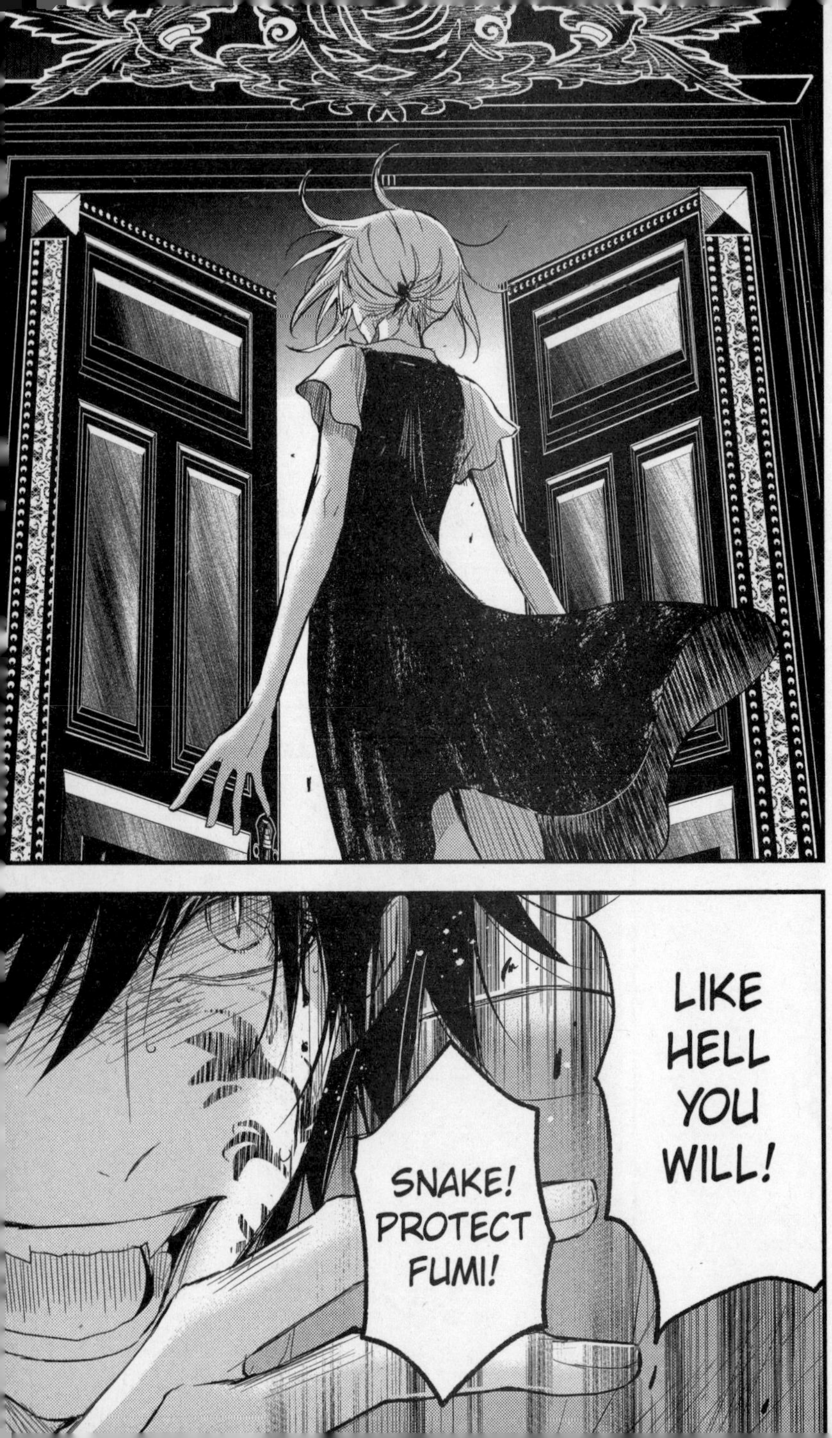
LIKE HELL YOU WILL!
SNAKE! PROTECT FUMI!

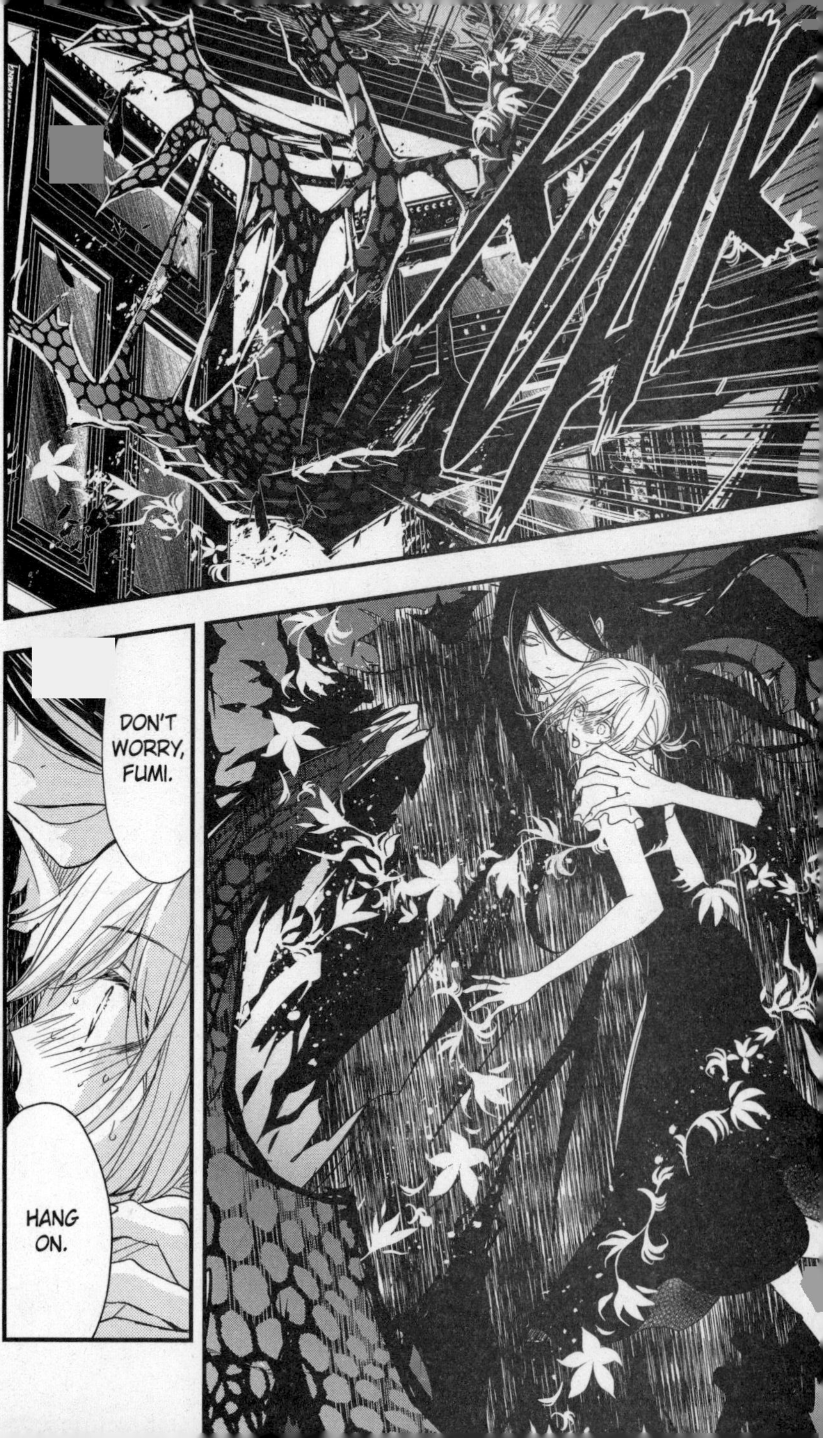
DON'T WORRY, FUMI.
HANG ON.

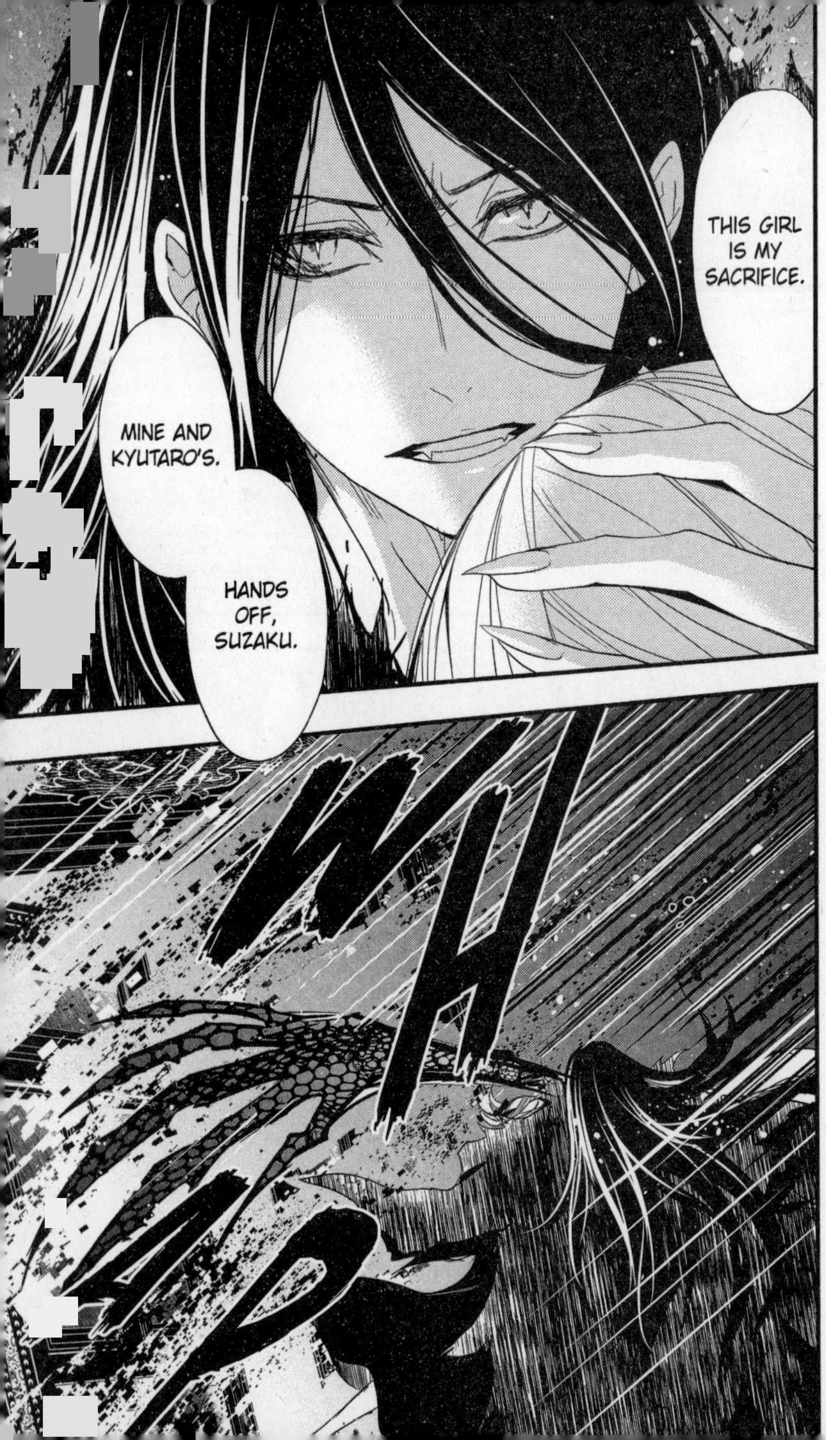
THIS GIRL IS MY SACRIFICE.
MINE AND KYUTARO'S.
HANDS OFF, SUZAKU.

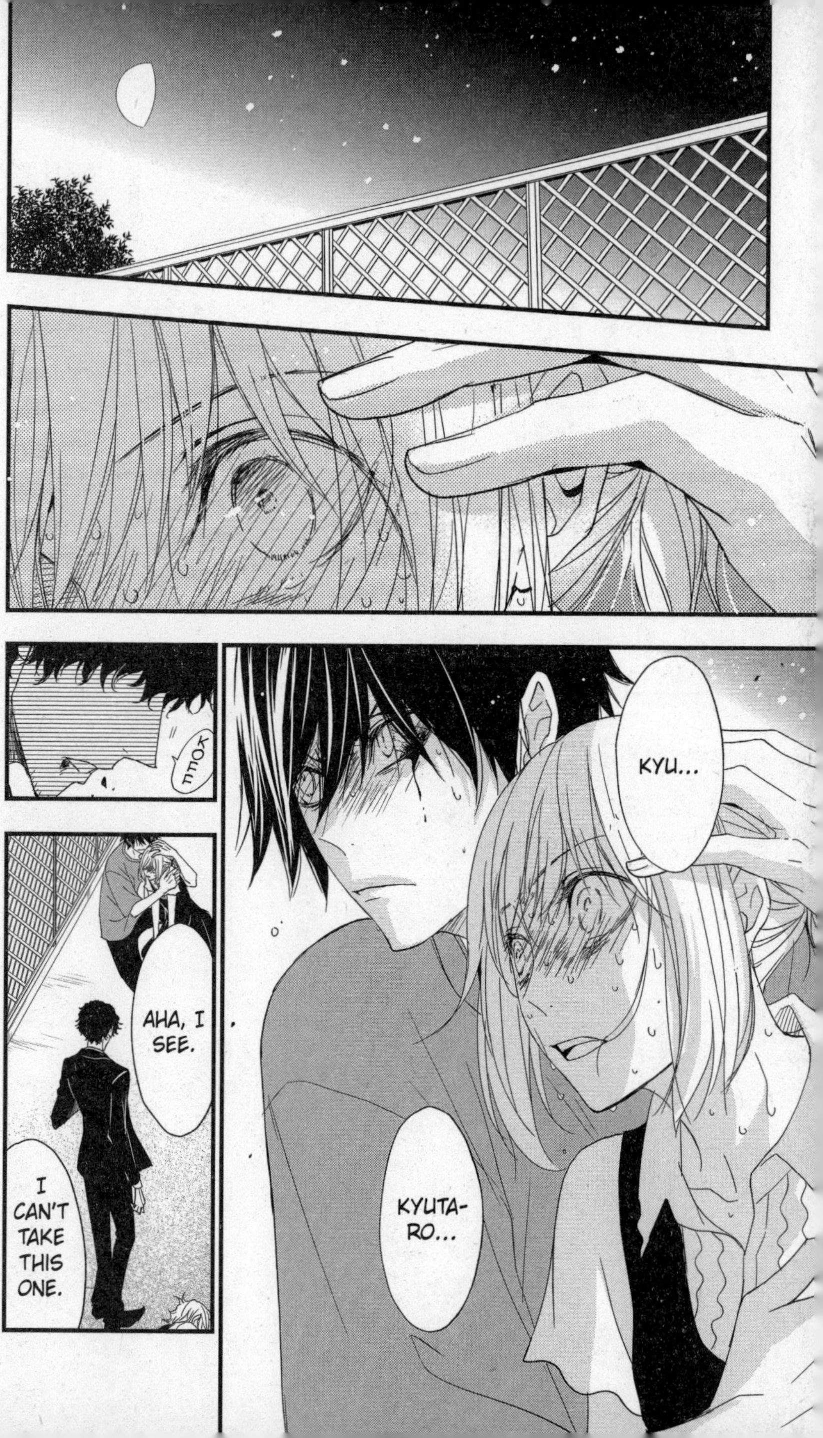
KYU...
KYUTA-RO...
KOFF
AHA, I SEE.
I CAN'T TAKE THIS ONE.

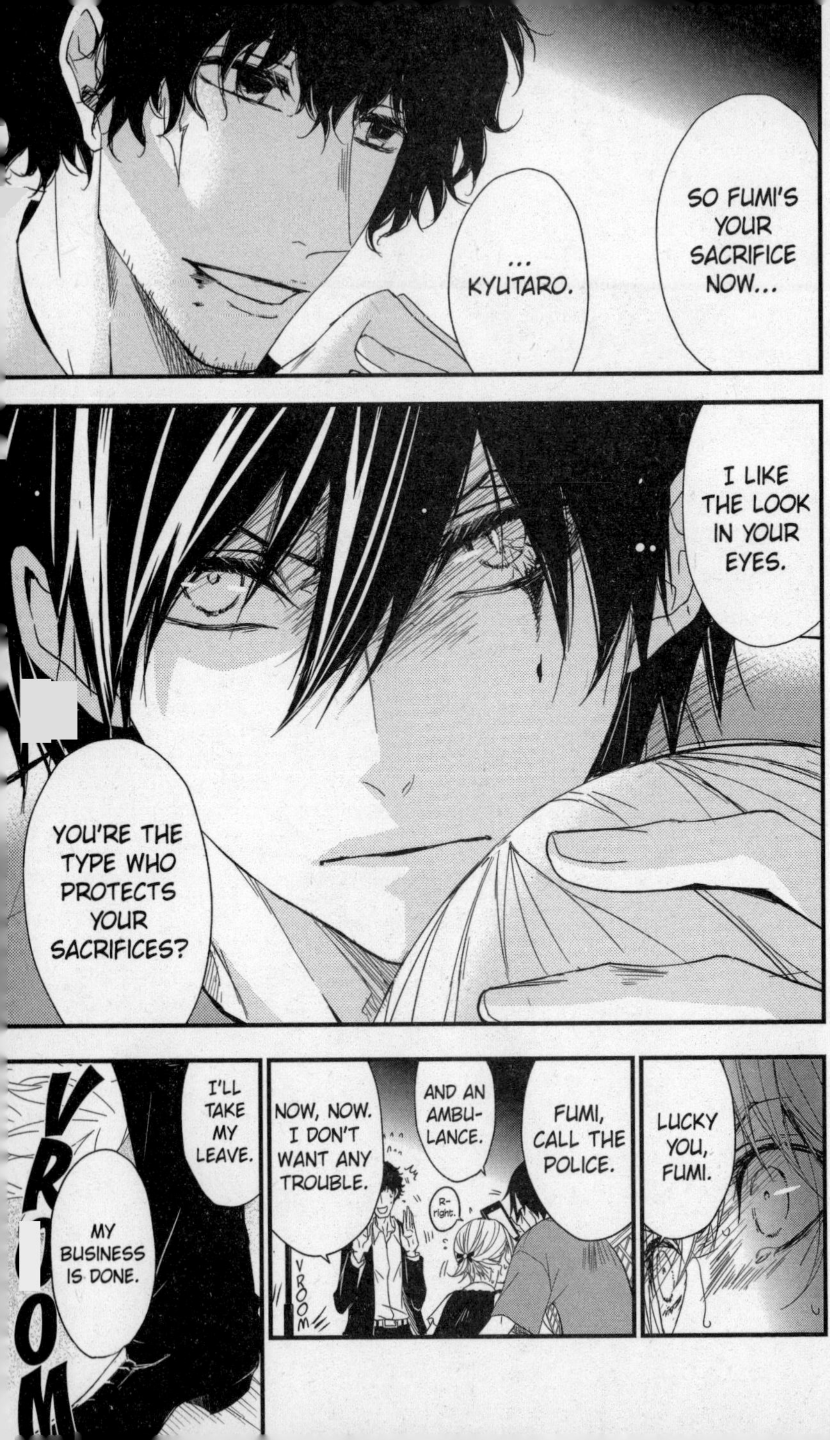
SO FUMI'S YOUR SACRIFICE NOW...
... KYUTARO.
I LIKE THE LOOK IN YOUR EYES.
YOU'RE THE TYPE WHO PROTECTS YOUR SACRIFICES?
LUCKY YOU, FUMI.
FUMI, CALL THE POLICE.
AND AN AMBULANCE.
R-right.
NOW, NOW. I DON'T WANT ANY TROUBLE.
VROOM
I'LL TAKE MY LEAVE.
MY BUSINESS IS DONE.
VROOM

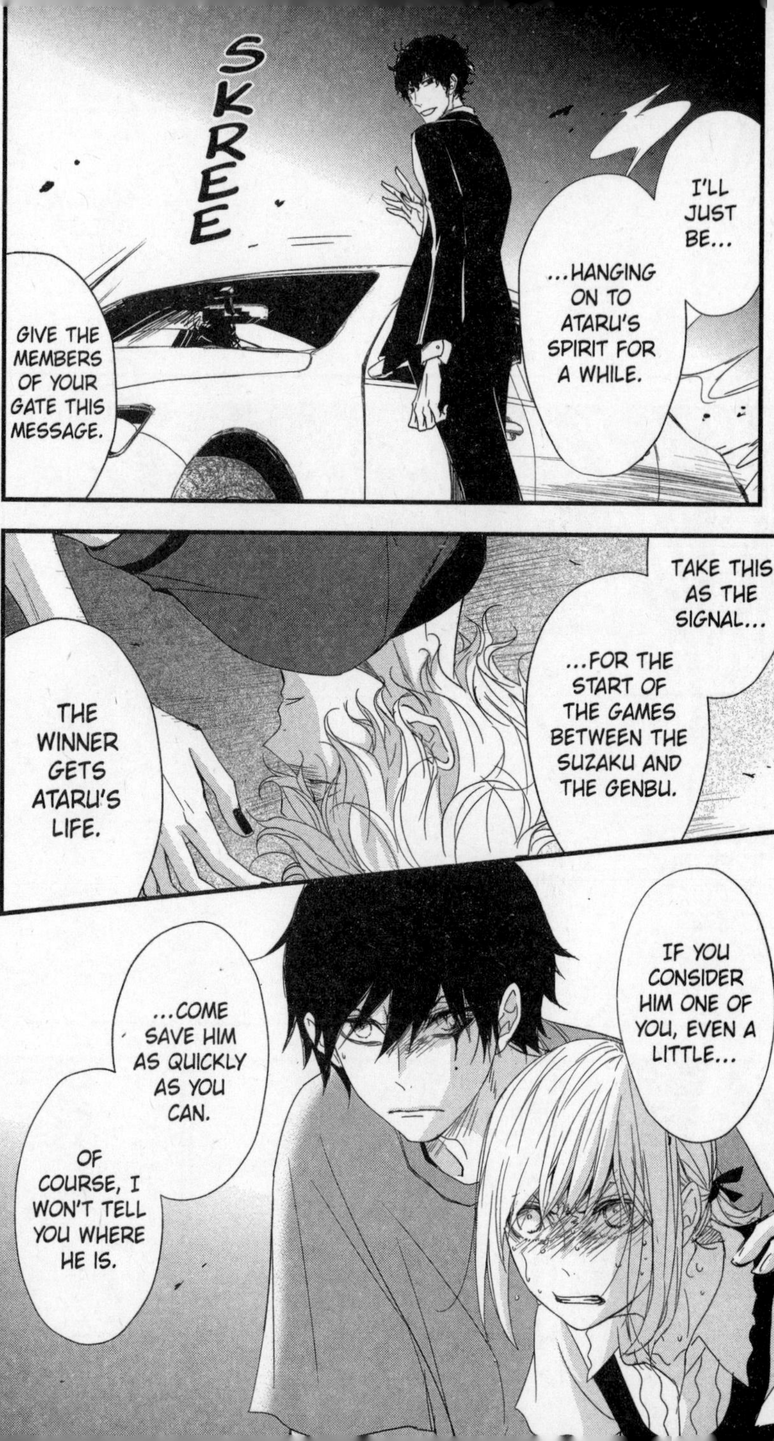
I'LL JUST BE...
...HANGING ON TO ATARU'S SPIRIT FOR A WHILE.
SKREE
GIVE THE MEMBERS OF YOUR GATE THIS MESSAGE.
TAKE THIS AS THE SIGNAL...
...FOR THE START OF THE GAMES BETWEEN THE SUZAKU AND THE GENBU.
THE WINNER GETS ATARU'S LIFE.
IF YOU CONSIDER HIM ONE OF YOU, EVEN A LITTLE...
...COME SAVE HIM AS QUICKLY AS YOU CAN.
OF COURSE, I WON'T TELL YOU WHERE HE IS.

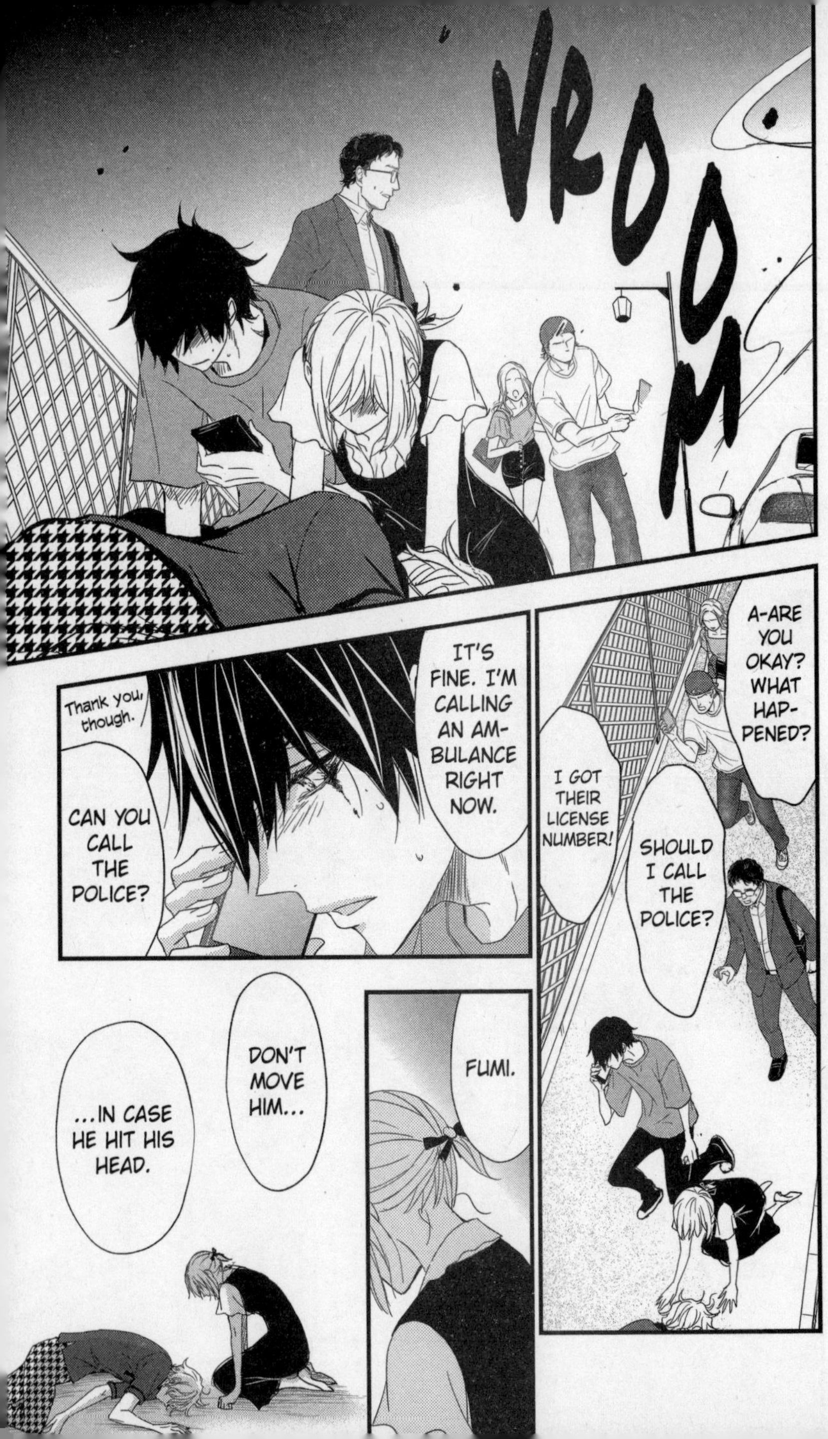
VROOM
A-ARE YOU OKAY? WHAT HAP-PENED?
I GOT THEIR LICENSE NUMBER!
SHOULD I CALL THE POLICE?
IT'S FINE. I'M CALLING AN AM-BULANCE RIGHT NOW.
Thank you, though.
CAN YOU CALL THE POLICE?
FUMI.
DON'T MOVE HIM...
...IN CASE HE HIT HIS HEAD.

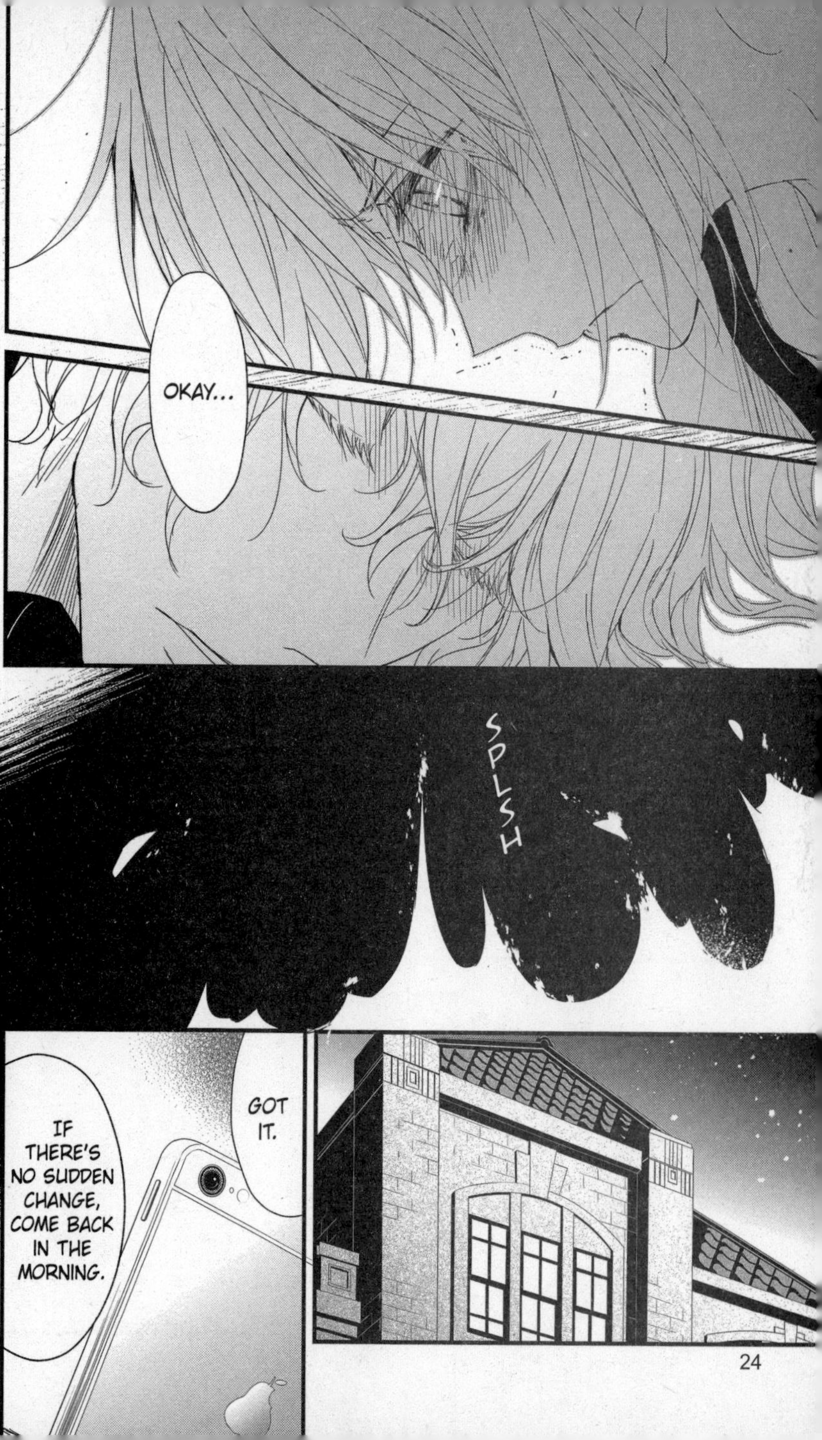
OKAY...
SPLSH
GOT IT.
IF THERE'S NO SUDDEN CHANGE, COME BACK IN THE MORNING.

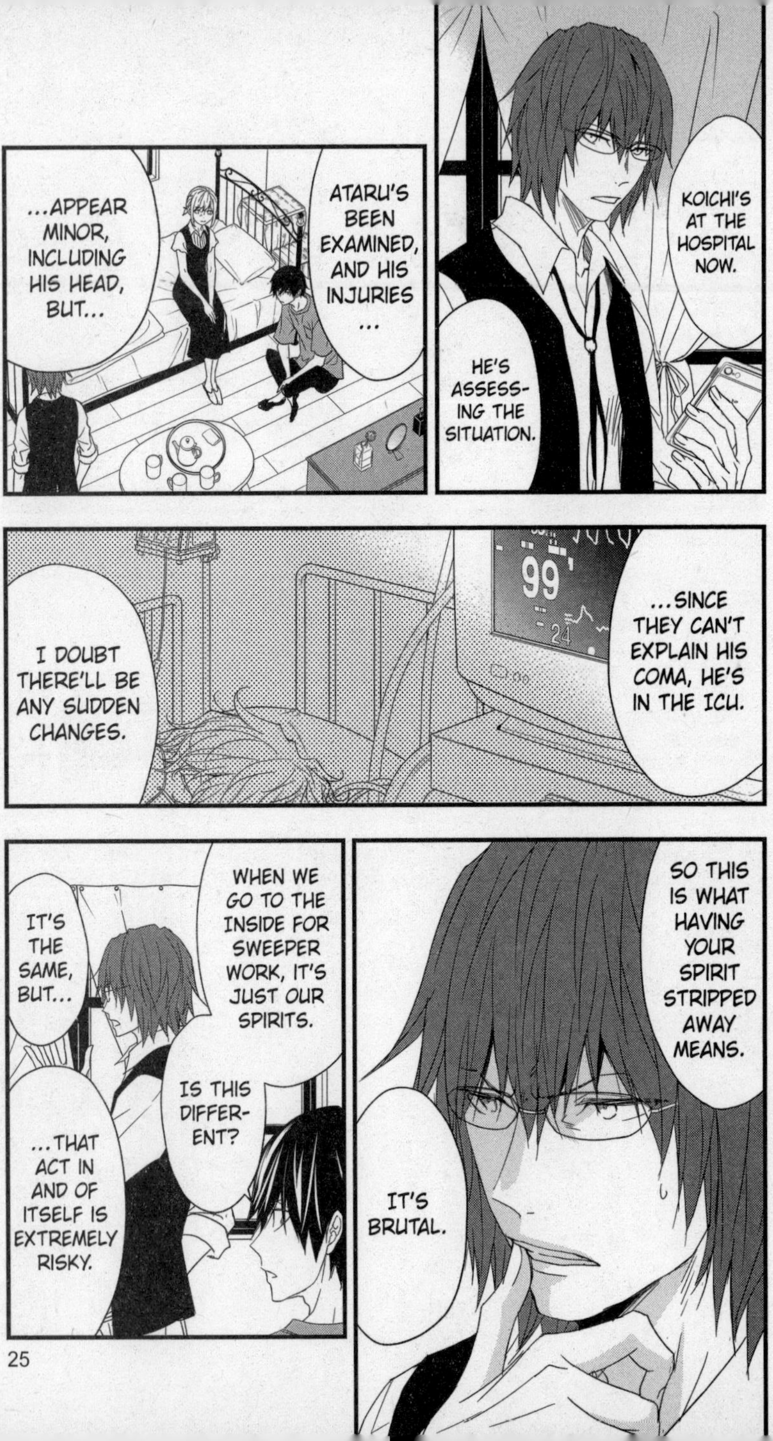
KOICHI'S AT THE HOSPITAL NOW.
HE'S ASSESSING THE SITUATION.
ATARU'S BEEN EXAMINED, AND HIS INJURIES ...
...APPEAR MINOR, INCLUDING HIS HEAD, BUT...
99
24
...SINCE THEY CAN'T EXPLAIN HIS COMA, HE'S IN THE ICU.
I DOUBT THERE'LL BE ANY SUDDEN CHANGES.
SO THIS IS WHAT HAVING YOUR SPIRIT STRIPPED AWAY MEANS.
IT'S BRUTAL.
WHEN WE GO TO THE INSIDE FOR SWEEPER WORK, IT'S JUST OUR SPIRITS.
IT'S THE SAME, BUT...
IS THIS DIFFERENT?
...THAT ACT IN AND OF ITSELF IS EXTREMELY RISKY.

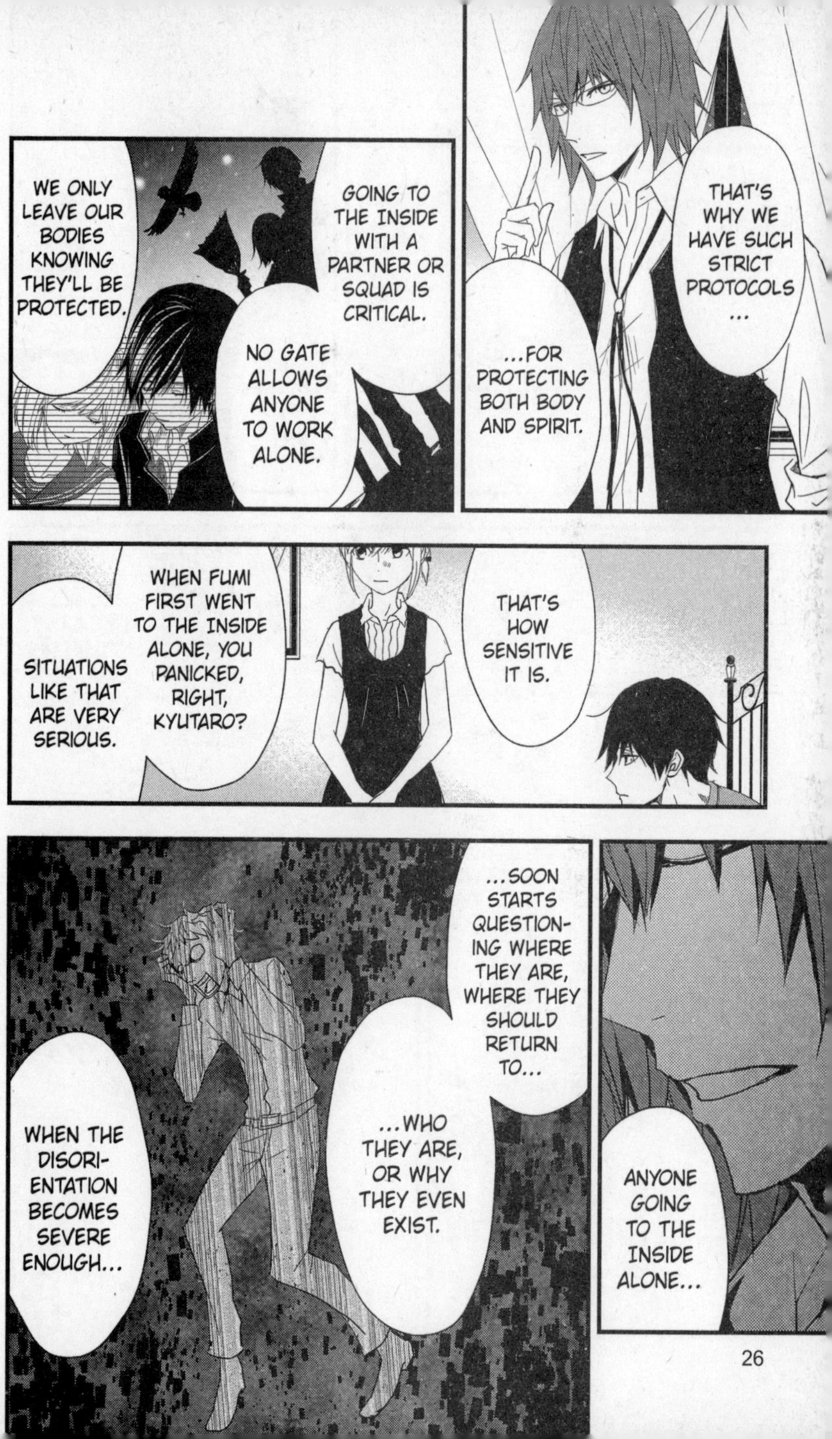
THAT'S WHY WE HAVE SUCH STRICT PROTOCOLS...
...FOR PROTECTING BOTH BODY AND SPIRIT.
GOING TO THE INSIDE WITH A PARTNER OR SQUAD IS CRITICAL.
WE ONLY LEAVE OUR BODIES KNOWING THEY'LL BE PROTECTED.
NO GATE ALLOWS ANYONE TO WORK ALONE.
THAT'S HOW SENSITIVE IT IS.
WHEN FUMI FIRST WENT TO THE INSIDE ALONE, YOU PANICKED, RIGHT, KYUTARO?
SITUATIONS LIKE THAT ARE VERY SERIOUS.
ANYONE GOING TO THE INSIDE ALONE...
...SOON STARTS QUESTION-ING WHERE THEY ARE, WHERE THEY SHOULD RETURN TO...
...WHO THEY ARE, OR WHY THEY EVEN EXIST.
WHEN THE DISORI-ENTATION BECOMES SEVERE ENOUGH...

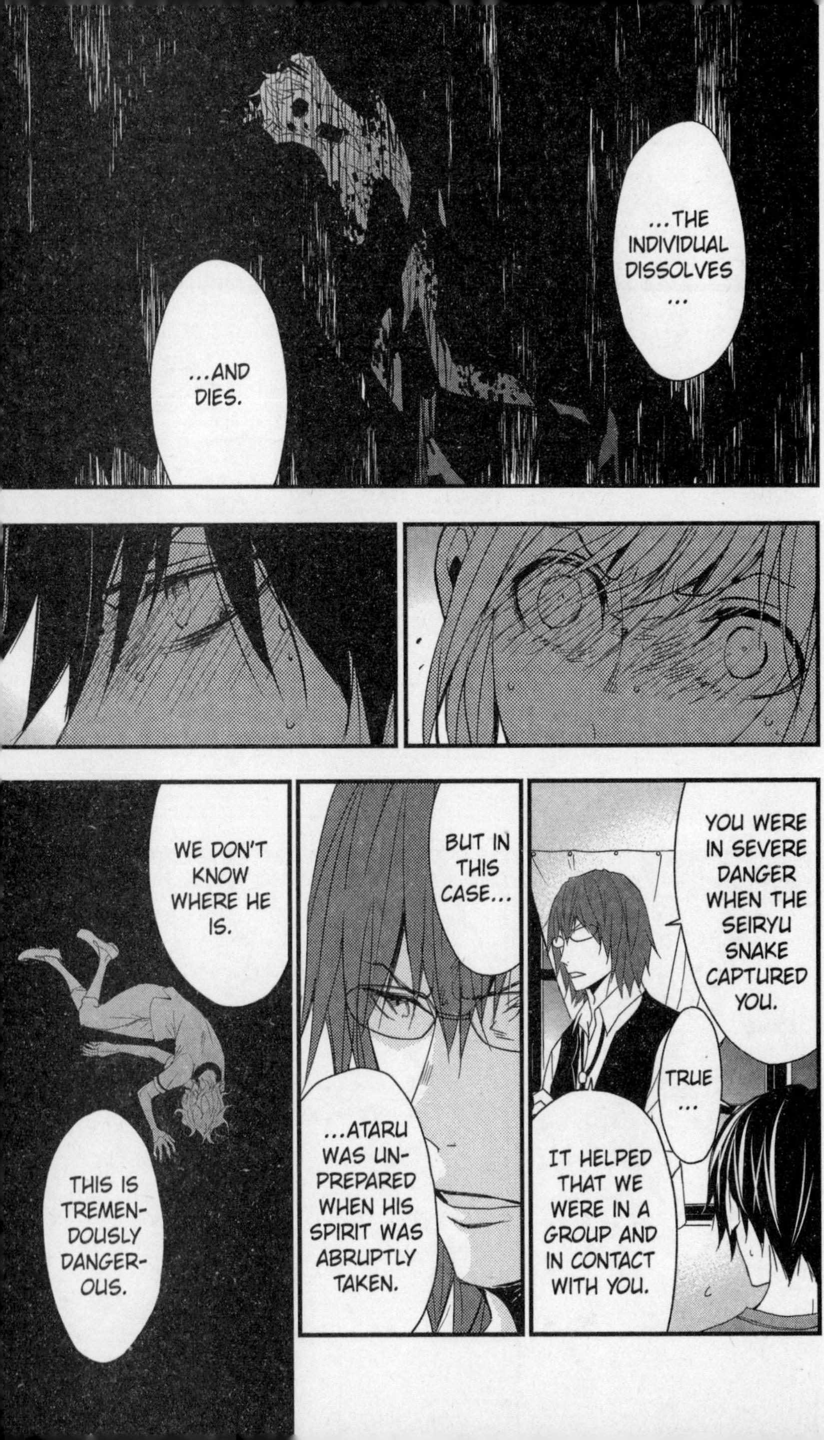
...THE INDIVIDUAL DISSOLVES ...
...AND DIES.
YOU WERE IN SEVERE DANGER WHEN THE SEIRYU SNAKE CAPTURED YOU.
TRUE ...
IT HELPED THAT WE WERE IN A GROUP AND IN CONTACT WITH YOU.
BUT IN THIS CASE...
...ATARU WAS UN-PREPARED WHEN HIS SPIRIT WAS ABRUPTLY TAKEN.
WE DON'T KNOW WHERE HE IS.
THIS IS TREMEN-DOUSLY DANGER-OUS.

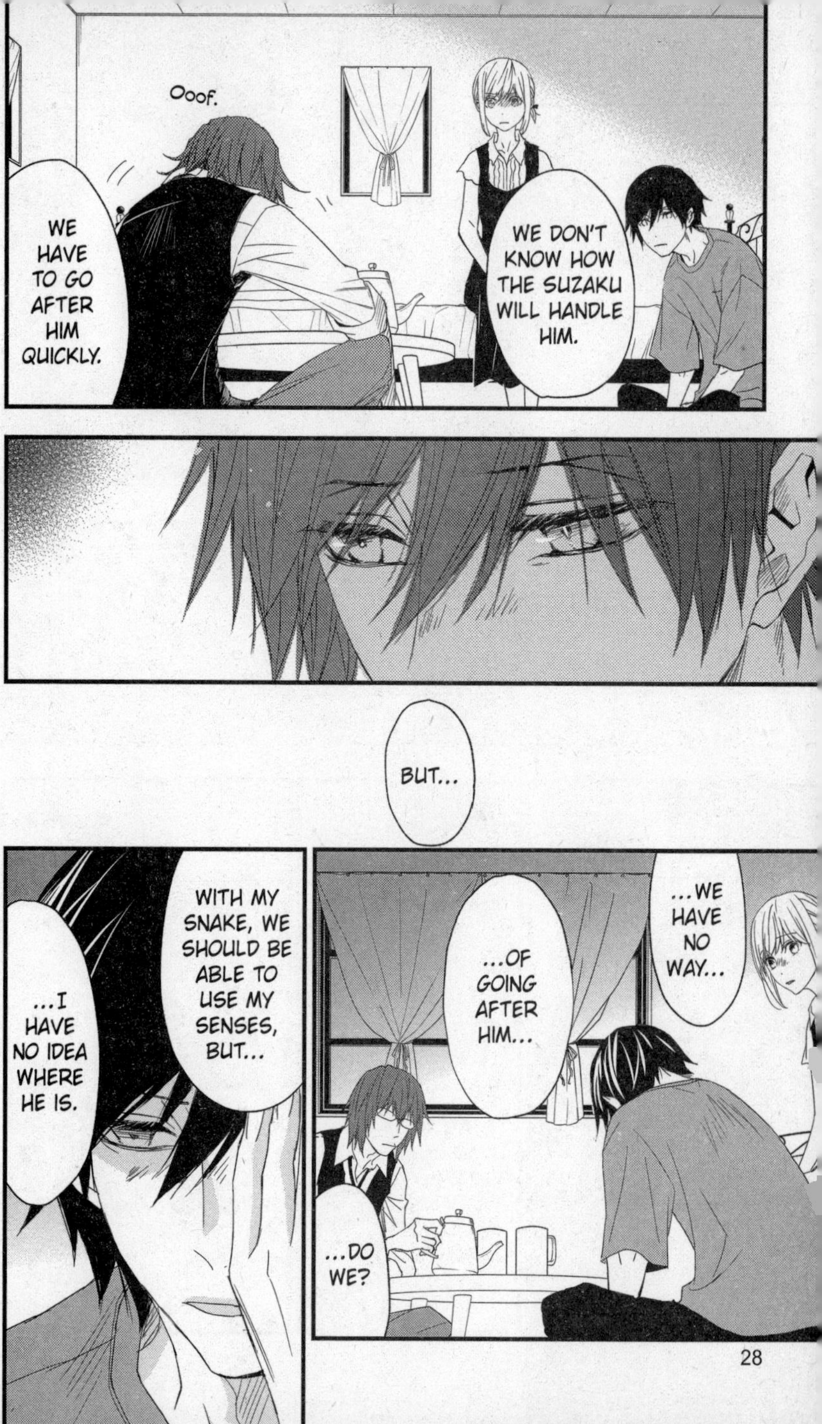

WE DON'T KNOW HOW THE SUZAKU WILL HANDLE HIM.
Ooof.
WE HAVE TO GO AFTER HIM QUICKLY.
BUT...
...WE HAVE NO WAY...
...OF GOING AFTER HIM...
...DO WE?
WITH MY SNAKE, WE SHOULD BE ABLE TO USE MY SENSES, BUT...
...I HAVE NO IDEA WHERE HE IS.

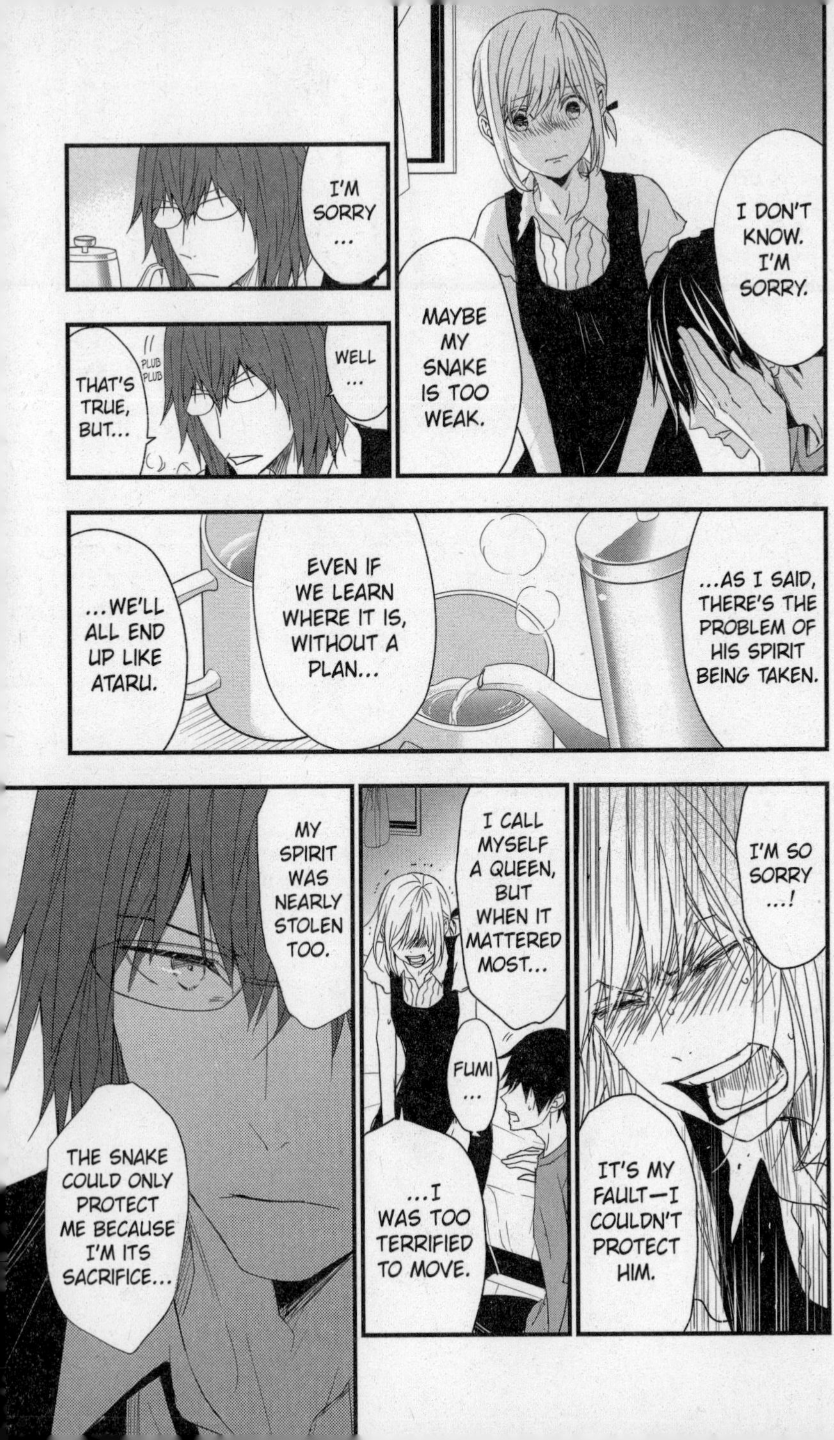
I DON'T KNOW. I'M SORRY.
MAYBE MY SNAKE IS TOO WEAK.
I'M SORRY ...
WELL ...
PLUB PLUB
THAT'S TRUE, BUT...
...AS I SAID, THERE'S THE PROBLEM OF HIS SPIRIT BEING TAKEN.
EVEN IF WE LEARN WHERE IT IS, WITHOUT A PLAN...
...WE'LL ALL END UP LIKE ATARU.
I'M SO SORRY ...!
IT'S MY FAULT—I COULDN'T PROTECT HIM.
I CALL MYSELF A QUEEN, BUT WHEN IT MATTERED MOST...
FUMI ...
...I WAS TOO TERRIFIED TO MOVE.
MY SPIRIT WAS NEARLY STOLEN TOO.
THE SNAKE COULD ONLY PROTECT ME BECAUSE I'M ITS SACRIFICE...

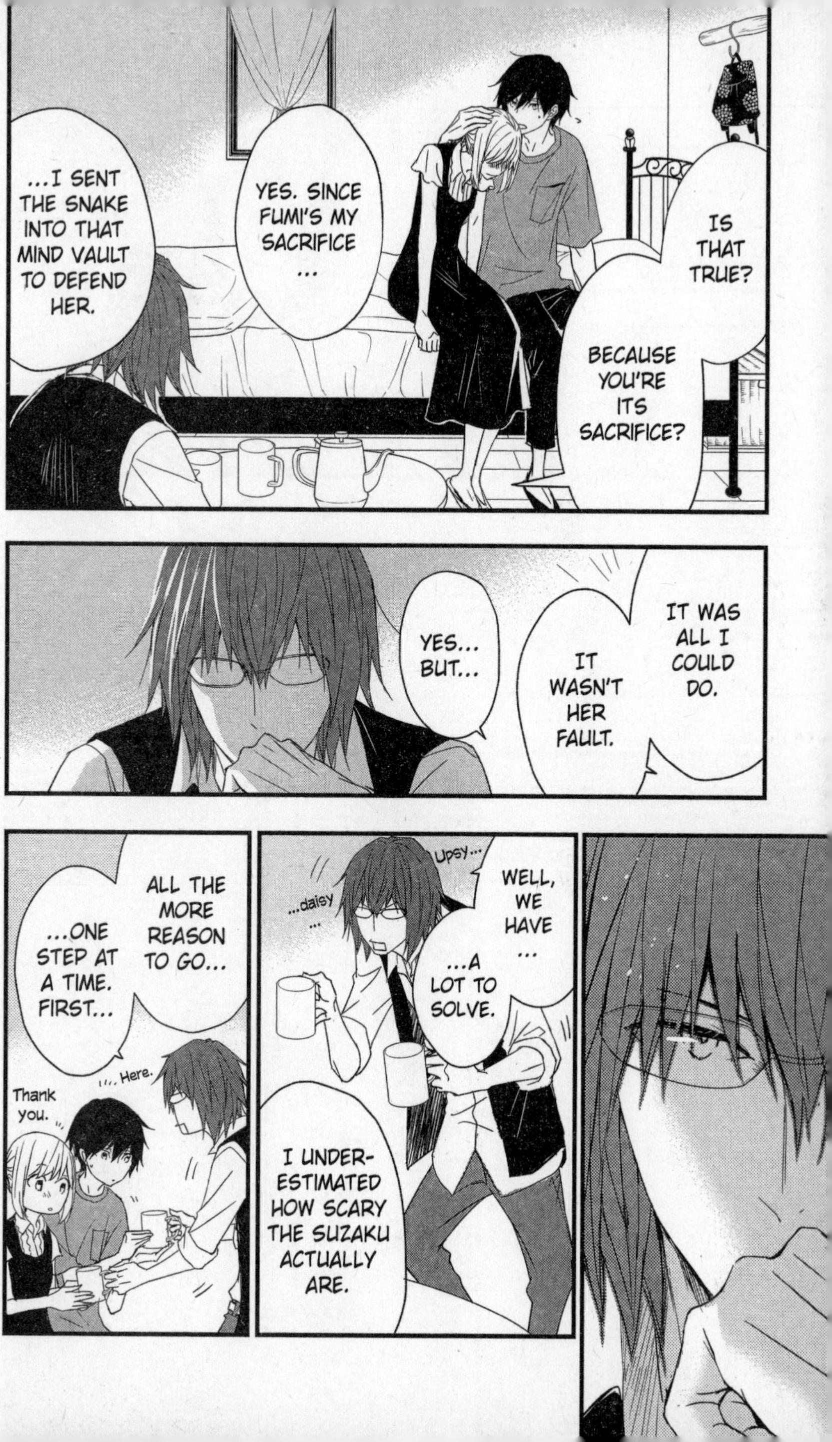
IS THAT TRUE?
BECAUSE YOU'RE ITS SACRIFICE?
YES. SINCE FUMI'S MY SACRIFICE ...
...I SENT THE SNAKE INTO THAT MIND VAULT TO DEFEND HER.
IT WAS ALL I COULD DO.
IT WASN'T HER FAULT.
YES... BUT...
Upsy...
WELL, WE HAVE ...
...daisy ...
...A LOT TO SOLVE.
I UNDER-ESTIMATED HOW SCARY THE SUZAKU ACTUALLY ARE.
ALL THE MORE REASON TO GO...
...ONE STEP AT A TIME. FIRST...
Here.
Thank you.

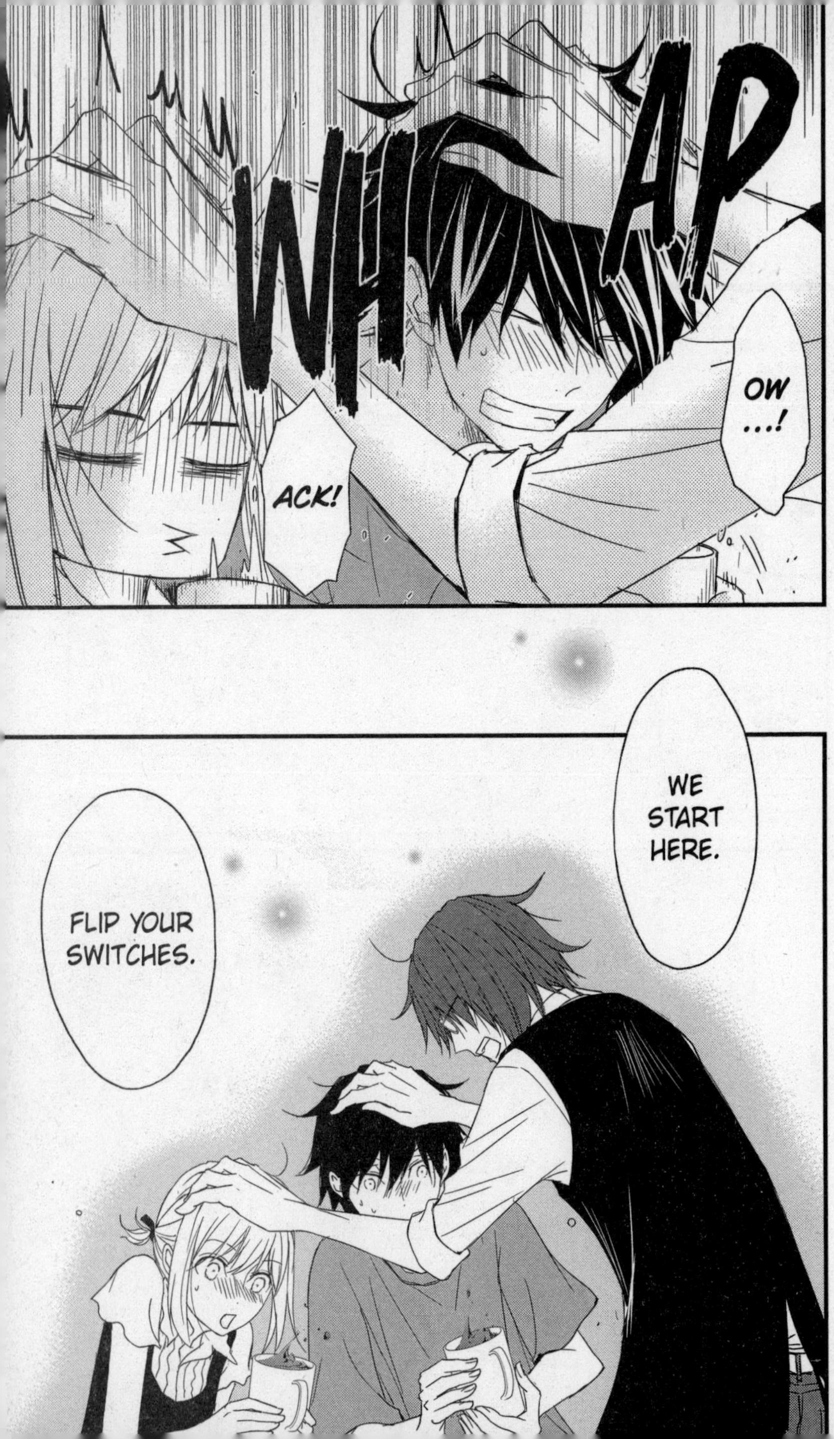
WHAP
OW ...!
ACK!
WE START HERE.
FLIP YOUR SWITCHES.

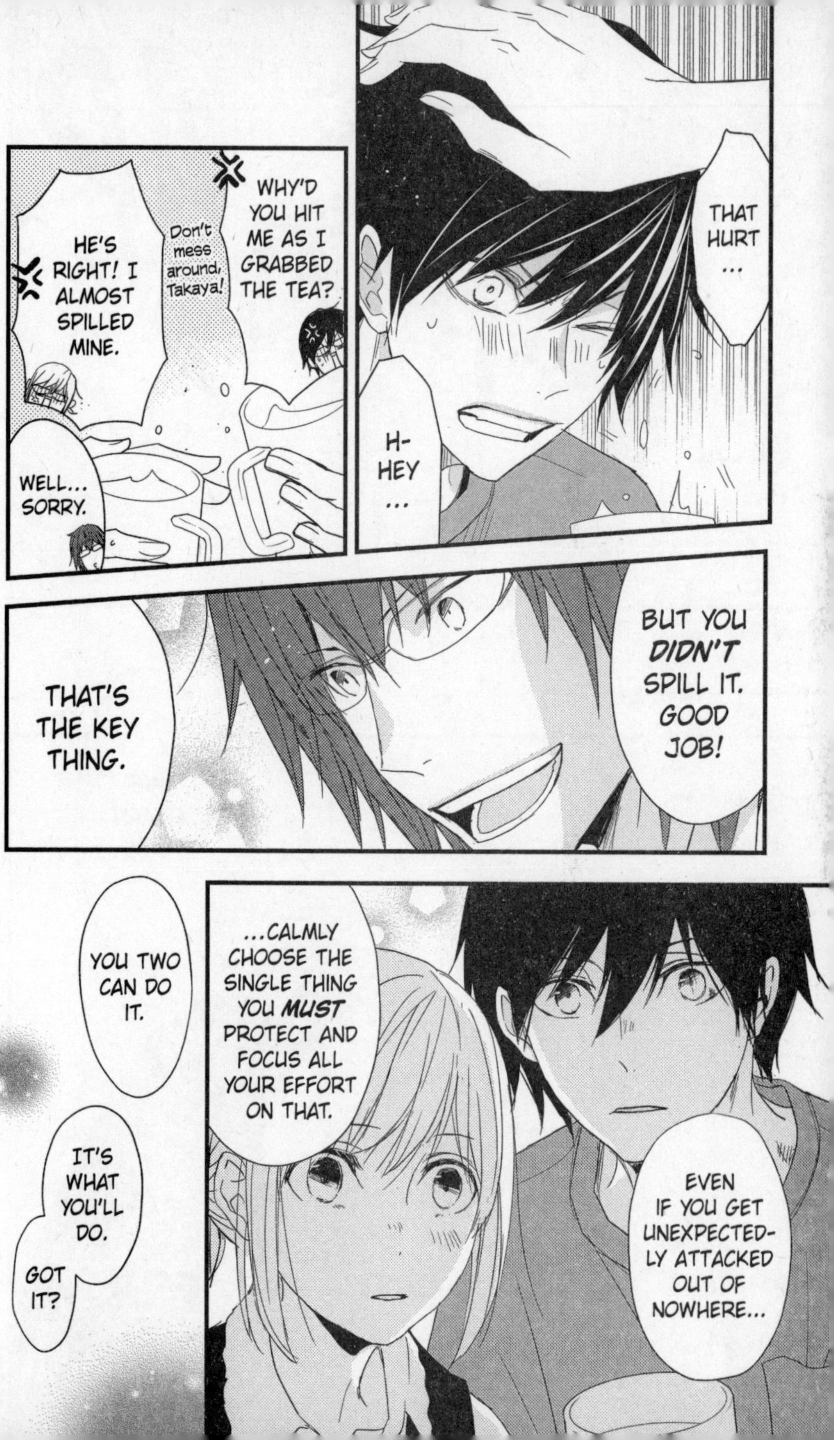
THAT HURT...
H-HEY...
WHY'D YOU HIT ME AS I GRABBED THE TEA?
Don't mess around, Takaya!
HE'S RIGHT! I ALMOST SPILLED MINE.
WELL... SORRY.
BUT YOU *DIDN'T* SPILL IT. GOOD JOB!
THAT'S THE KEY THING.
EVEN IF YOU GET UNEXPECTED-LY ATTACKED OUT OF NOWHERE...
...CALMLY CHOOSE THE SINGLE THING YOU *MUST* PROTECT AND FOCUS ALL YOUR EFFORT ON THAT.
YOU TWO CAN DO IT.
IT'S WHAT YOU'LL DO.
GOT IT?

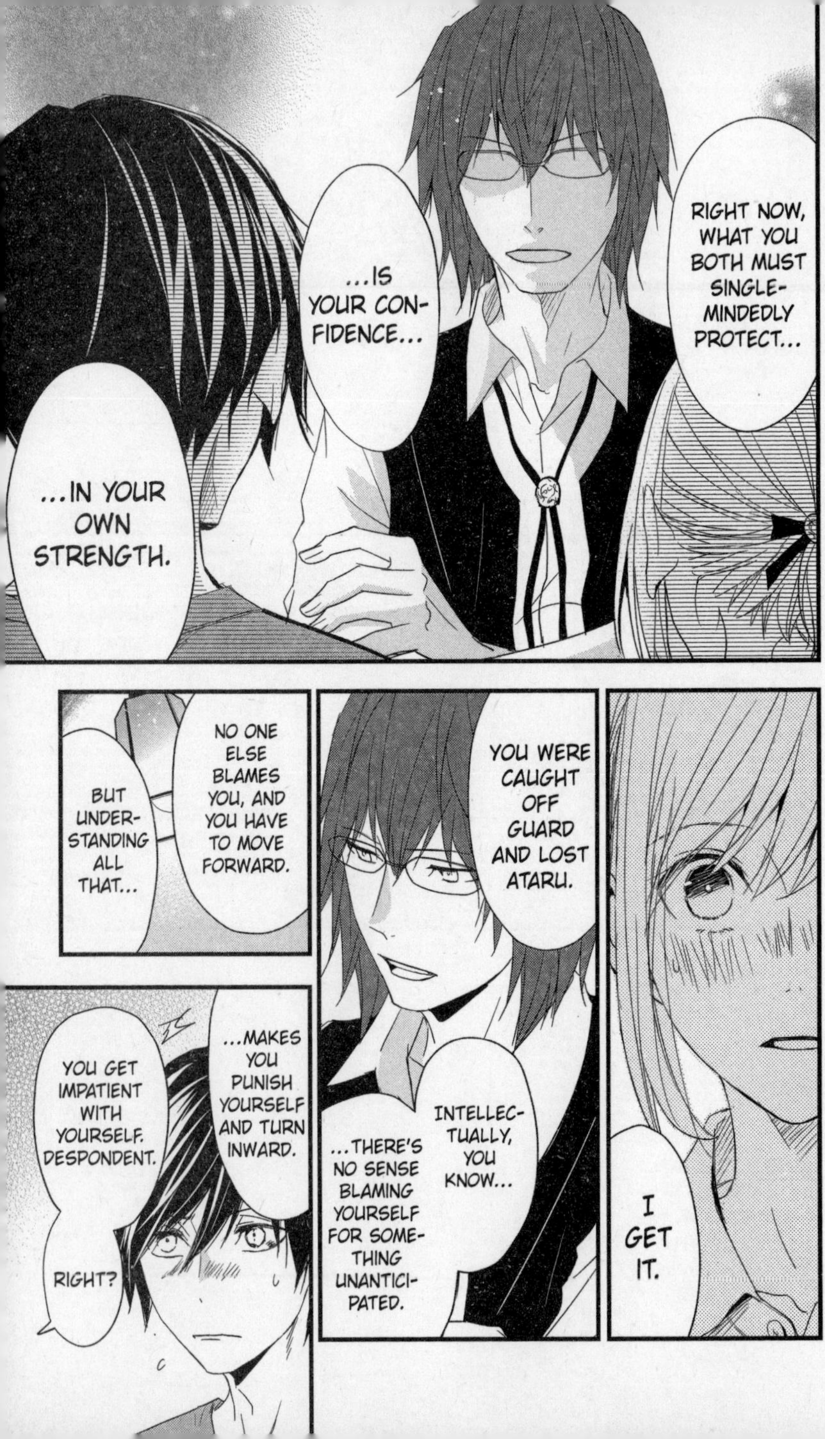
RIGHT NOW, WHAT YOU BOTH MUST SINGLE-MINDEDLY PROTECT...
...IS YOUR CONFIDENCE...
...IN YOUR OWN STRENGTH.
I GET IT.
YOU WERE CAUGHT OFF GUARD AND LOST ATARU.
INTELLECTUALLY, YOU KNOW...
...THERE'S NO SENSE BLAMING YOURSELF FOR SOMETHING UNANTICIPATED.
NO ONE ELSE BLAMES YOU, AND YOU HAVE TO MOVE FORWARD.
BUT UNDERSTANDING ALL THAT...
...MAKES YOU PUNISH YOURSELF AND TURN INWARD.
YOU GET IMPATIENT WITH YOURSELF. DESPONDENT.
RIGHT?

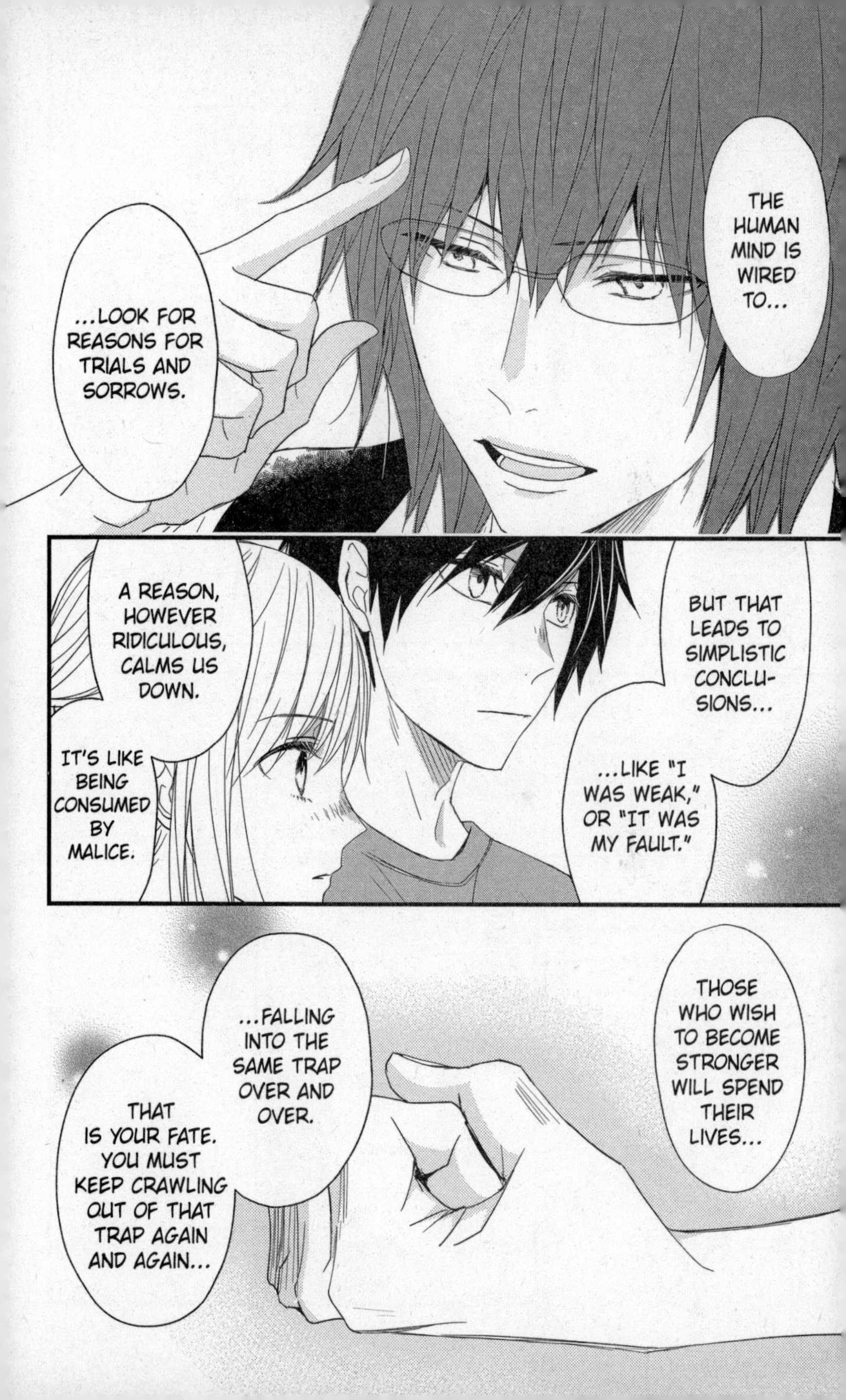
THE HUMAN MIND IS WIRED TO...
...LOOK FOR REASONS FOR TRIALS AND SORROWS.
BUT THAT LEADS TO SIMPLISTIC CONCLU-SIONS...
...LIKE "I WAS WEAK," OR "IT WAS MY FAULT."
A REASON, HOWEVER RIDICULOUS, CALMS US DOWN.
IT'S LIKE BEING CONSUMED BY MALICE.
THOSE WHO WISH TO BECOME STRONGER WILL SPEND THEIR LIVES...
...FALLING INTO THE SAME TRAP OVER AND OVER.
THAT IS YOUR FATE. YOU MUST KEEP CRAWLING OUT OF THAT TRAP AGAIN AND AGAIN...

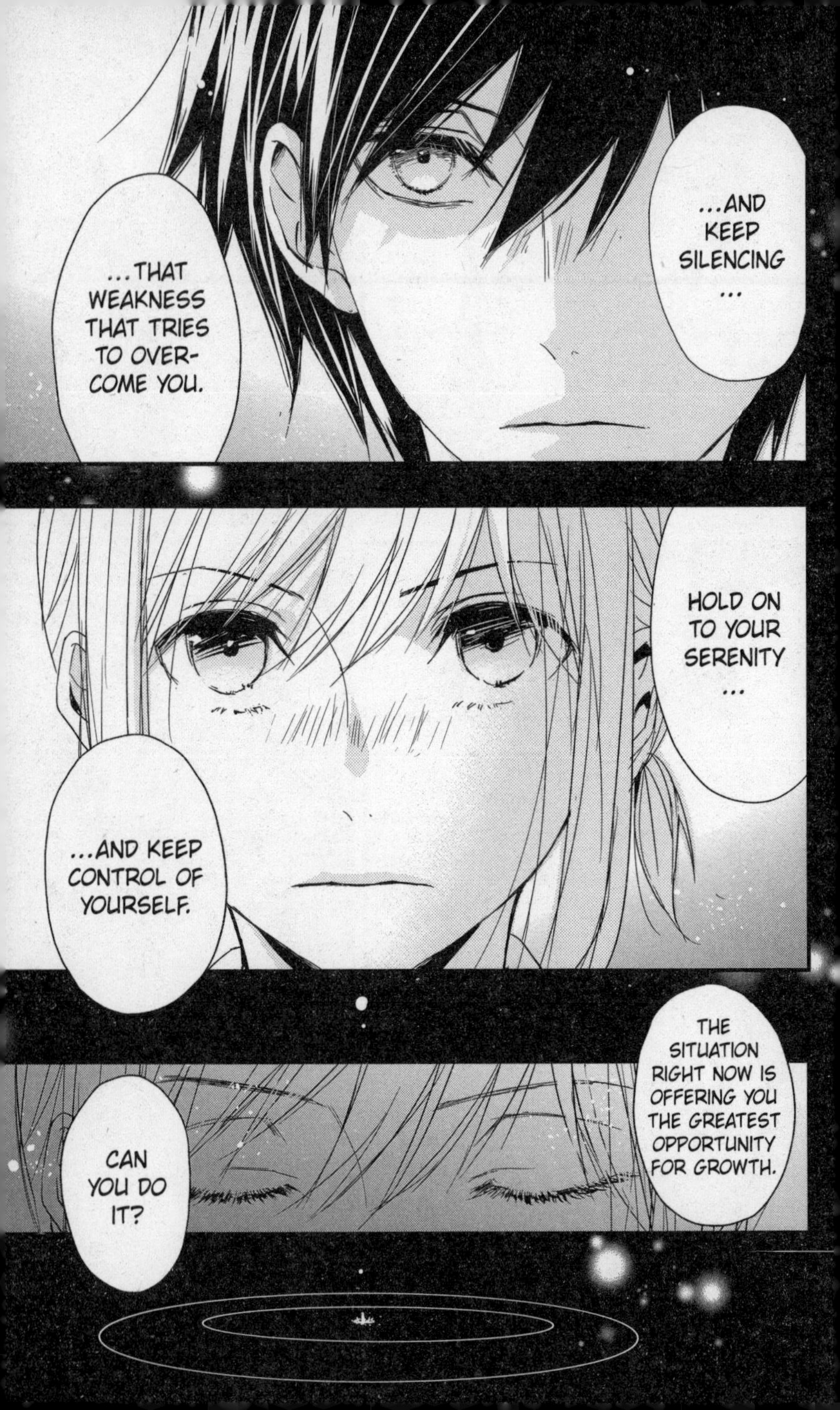

...AND KEEP SILENCING ...
...THAT WEAKNESS THAT TRIES TO OVER-COME YOU.
HOLD ON TO YOUR SERENITY ...
...AND KEEP CONTROL OF YOURSELF.
THE SITUATION RIGHT NOW IS OFFERING YOU THE GREATEST OPPORTUNITY FOR GROWTH.
CAN YOU DO IT?

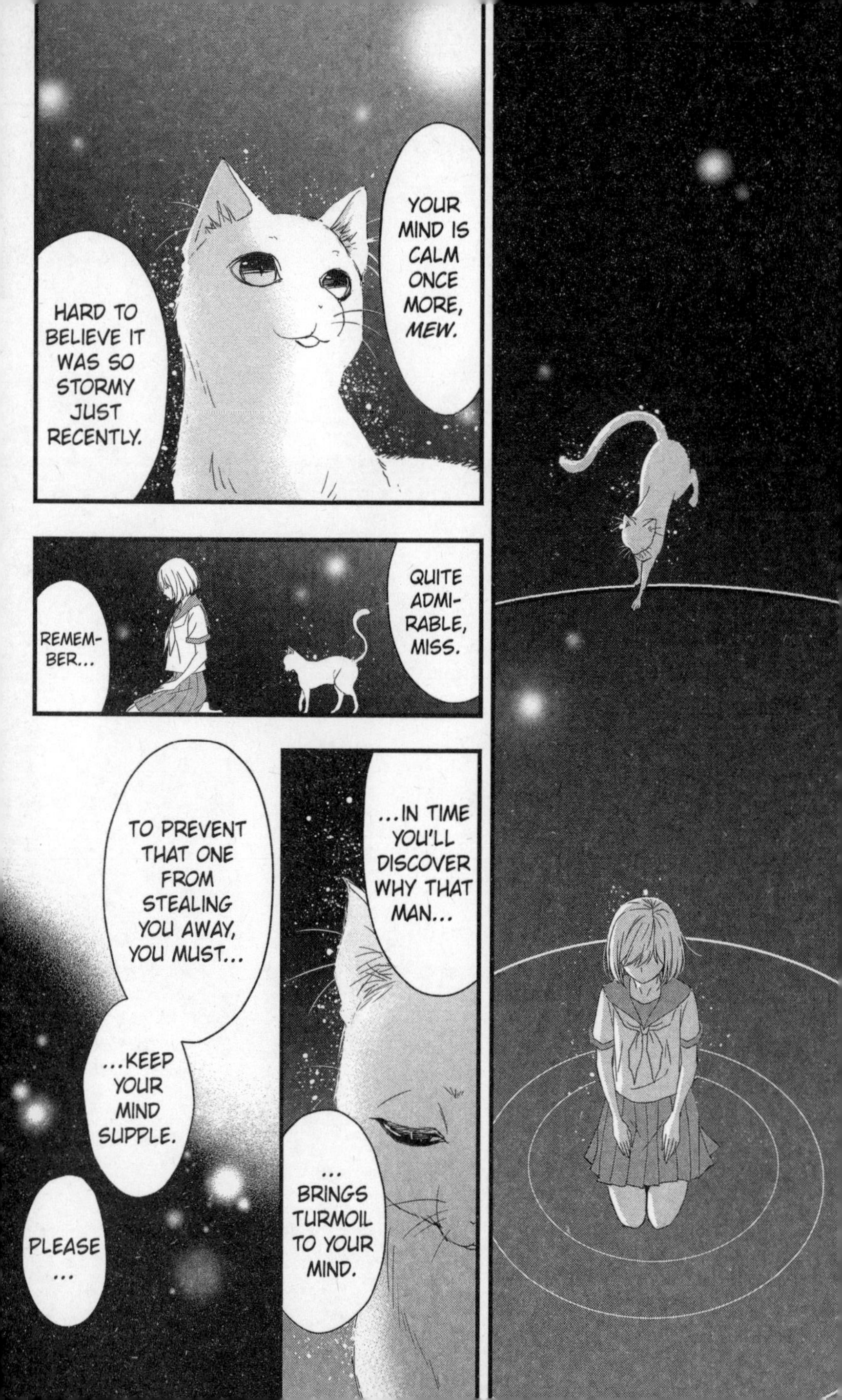
YOUR MIND IS CALM ONCE MORE, *MEW.*
HARD TO BELIEVE IT WAS SO STORMY JUST RECENTLY.
QUITE ADMIRABLE, MISS.
REMEMBER...
...IN TIME YOU'LL DISCOVER WHY THAT MAN...
...BRINGS TURMOIL TO YOUR MIND.
TO PREVENT THAT ONE FROM STEALING YOU AWAY, YOU MUST...
...KEEP YOUR MIND SUPPLE.
PLEASE...

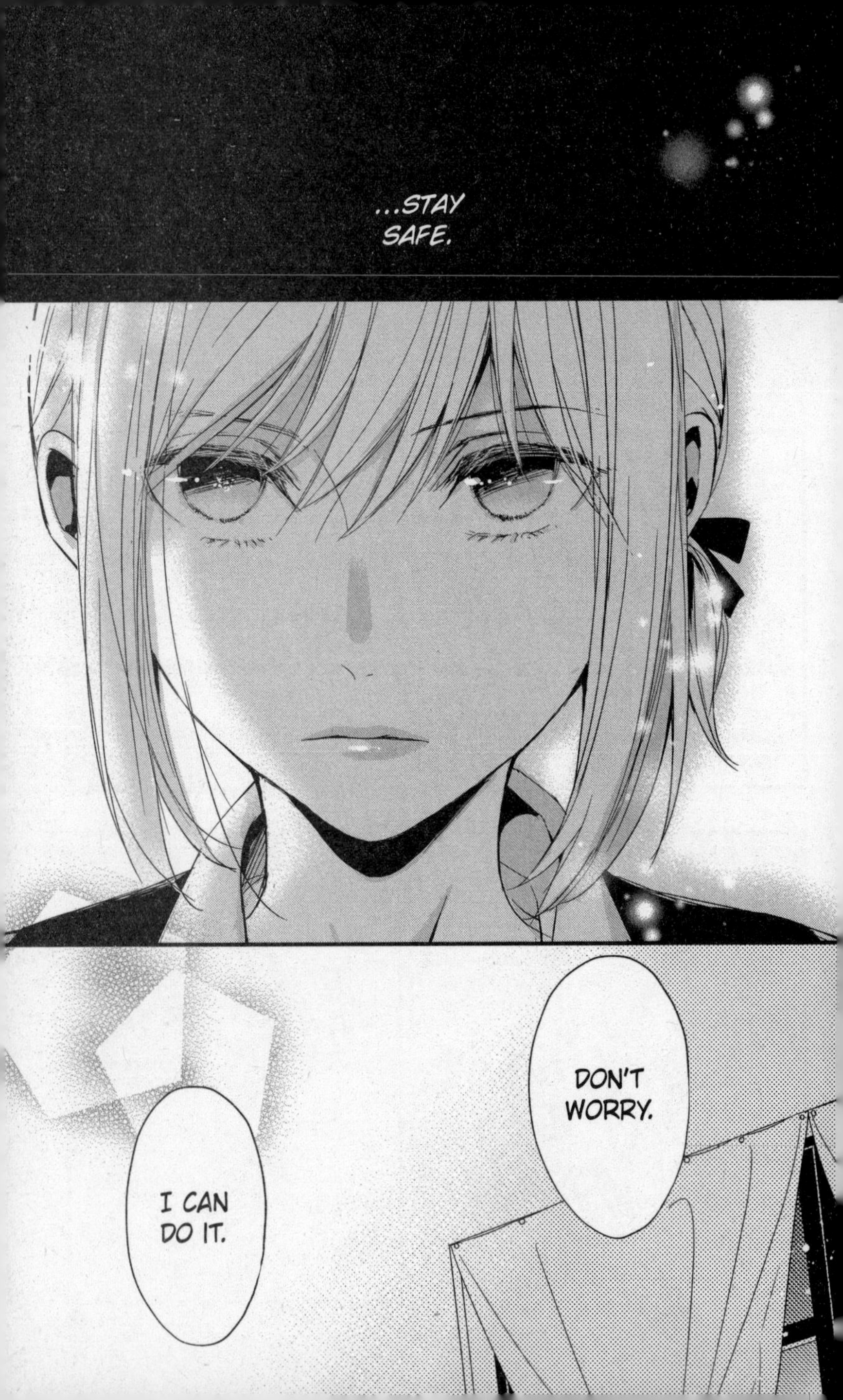
...STAY SAFE.
DON'T WORRY.
I CAN DO IT.

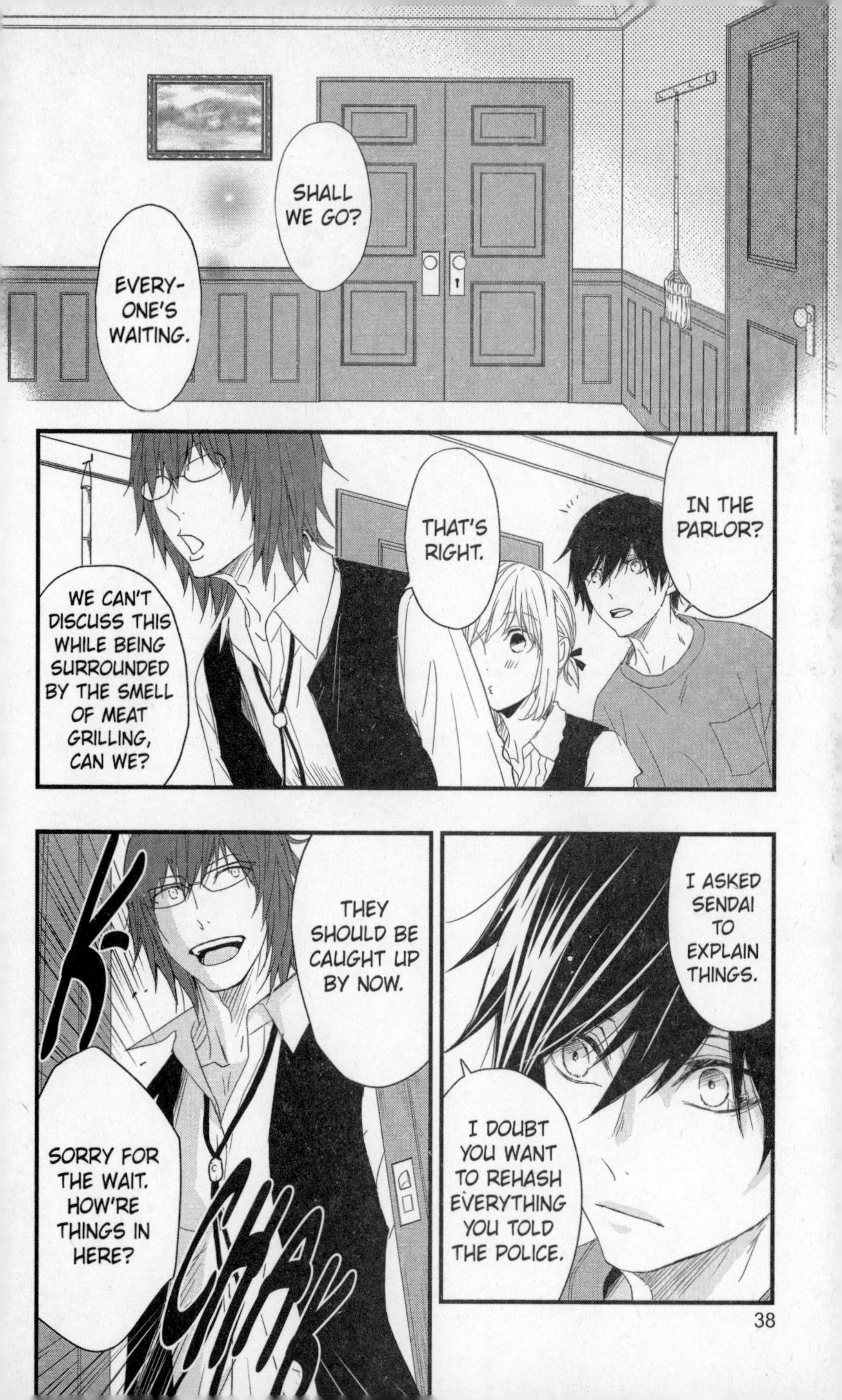
SHALL WE GO?
EVERY-ONE'S WAITING.
IN THE PARLOR?
THAT'S RIGHT.
WE CAN'T DISCUSS THIS WHILE BEING SURROUNDED BY THE SMELL OF MEAT GRILLING, CAN WE?
I ASKED SENDAI TO EXPLAIN THINGS.
I DOUBT YOU WANT TO REHASH EVERYTHING YOU TOLD THE POLICE.
THEY SHOULD BE CAUGHT UP BY NOW.
K-CHAK
SORRY FOR THE WAIT. HOW'RE THINGS IN HERE?

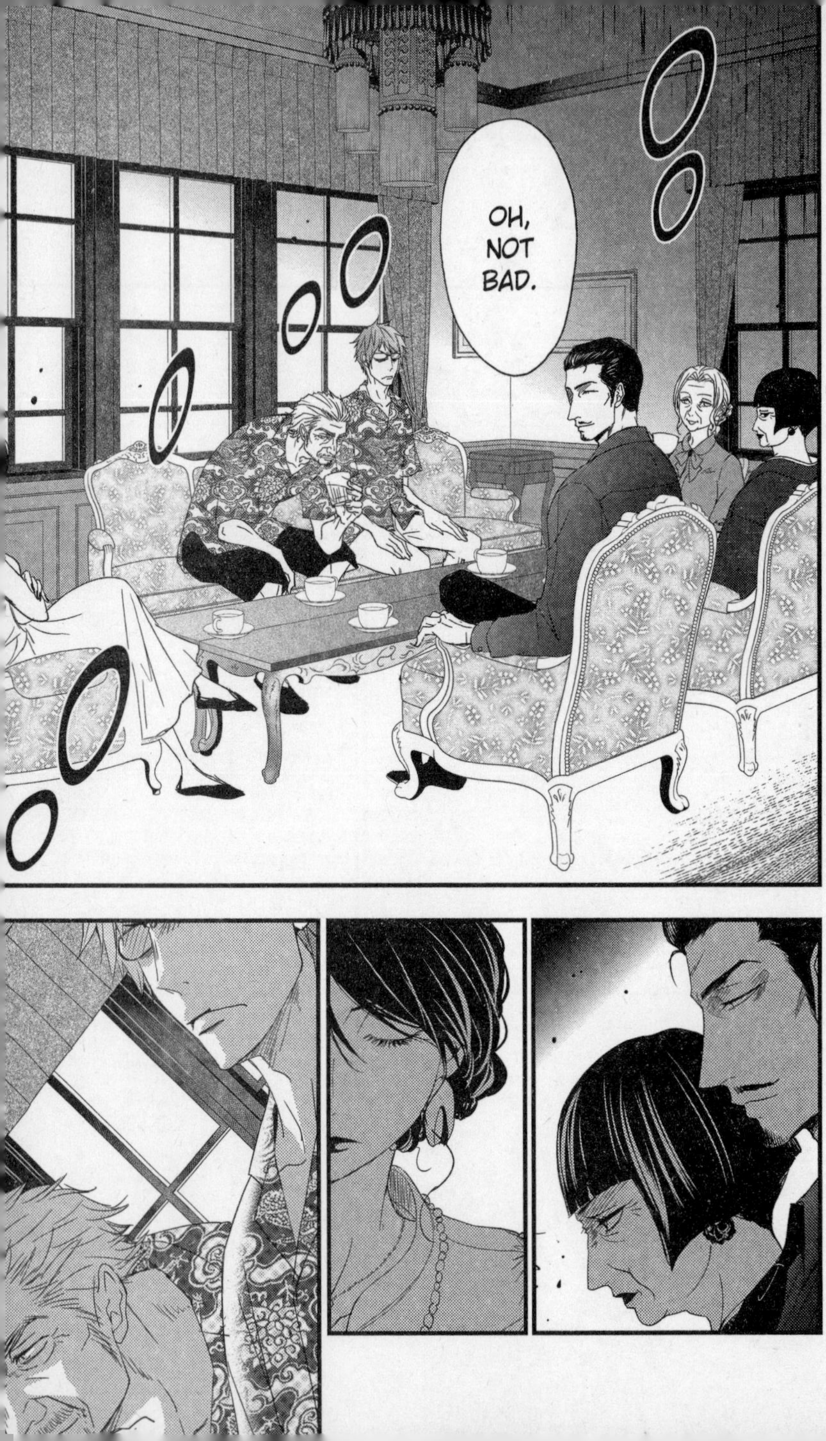
OH, NOT BAD.

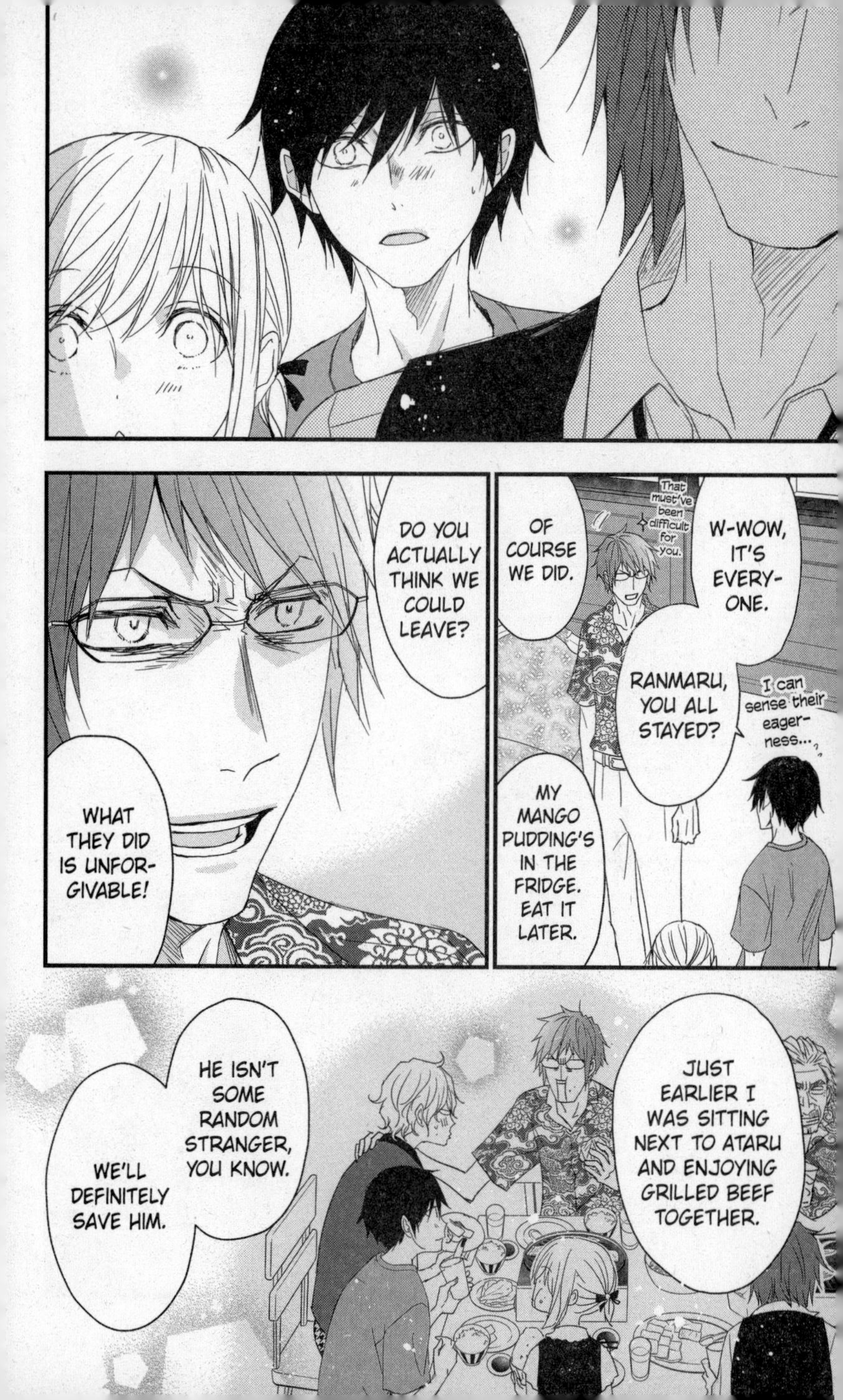
W-WOW, IT'S EVERY-ONE.
RANMARU, YOU ALL STAYED?
That must've been difficult for you.
OF COURSE WE DID.
I can sense their eager-ness...
MY MANGO PUDDING'S IN THE FRIDGE. EAT IT LATER.
DO YOU ACTUALLY THINK WE COULD LEAVE?
WHAT THEY DID IS UNFOR-GIVABLE!
JUST EARLIER I WAS SITTING NEXT TO ATARU AND ENJOYING GRILLED BEEF TOGETHER.
HE ISN'T SOME RANDOM STRANGER, YOU KNOW.
WE'LL DEFINITELY SAVE HIM.

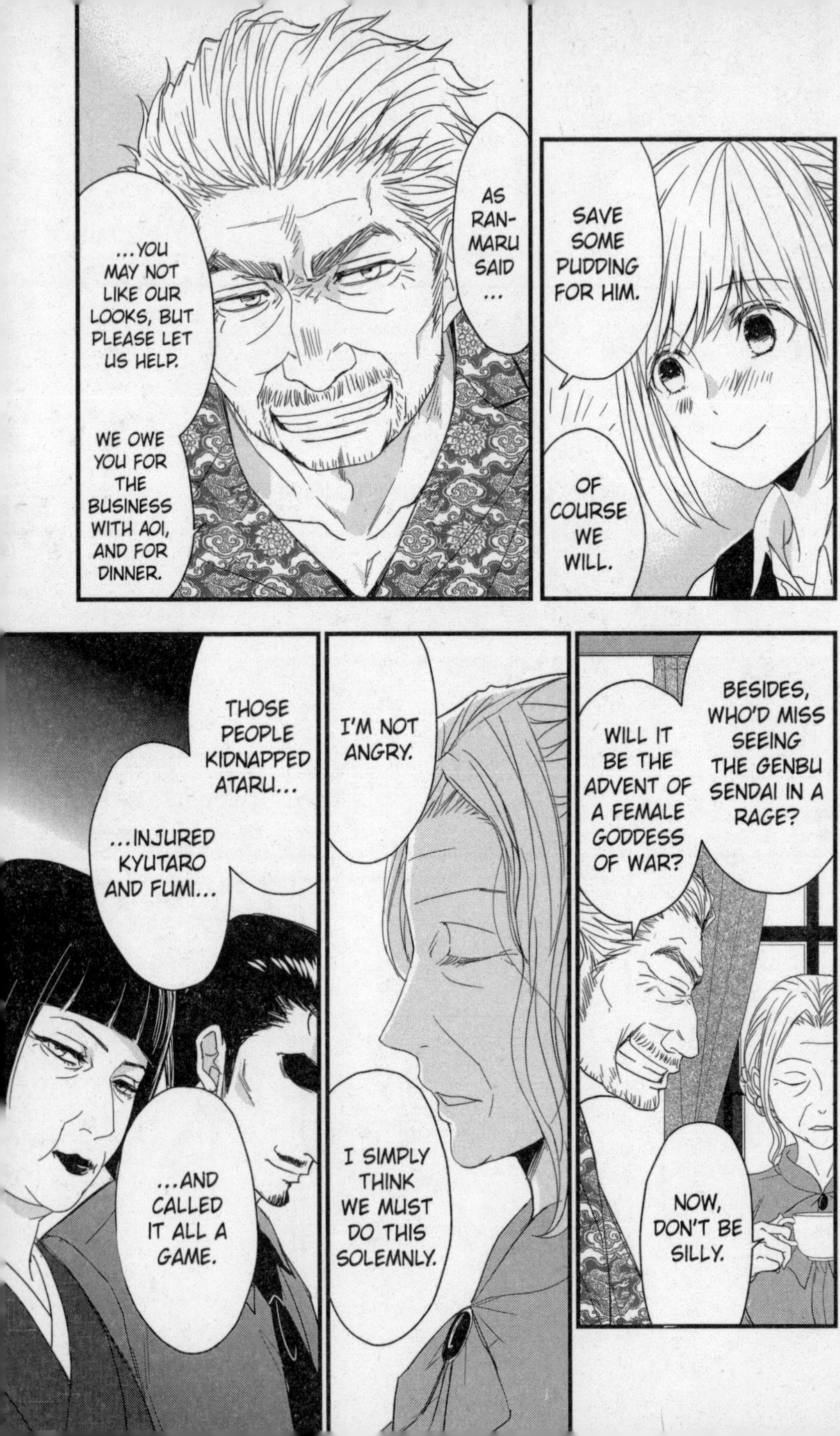
SAVE SOME PUDDING FOR HIM.
OF COURSE WE WILL.
AS RANMARU SAID...
...YOU MAY NOT LIKE OUR LOOKS, BUT PLEASE LET US HELP.
WE OWE YOU FOR THE BUSINESS WITH AOI, AND FOR DINNER.
BESIDES, WHO'D MISS SEEING THE GENBU SENDAI IN A RAGE?
WILL IT BE THE ADVENT OF A FEMALE GODDESS OF WAR?
NOW, DON'T BE SILLY.
I'M NOT ANGRY.
I SIMPLY THINK WE MUST DO THIS SOLEMNLY.
THOSE PEOPLE KIDNAPPED ATARU...
...INJURED KYUTARO AND FUMI...
...AND CALLED IT ALL A GAME.

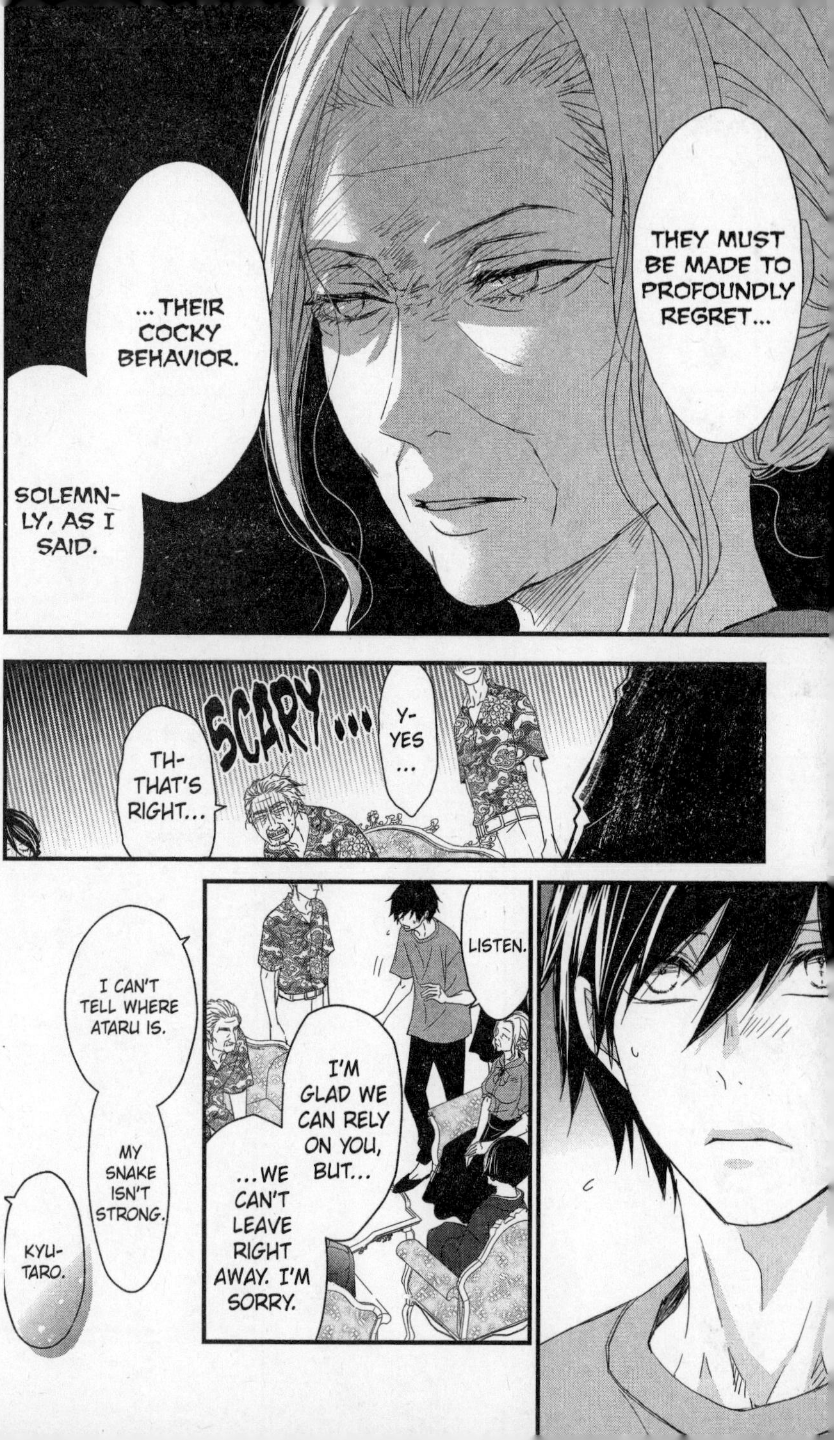
THEY MUST BE MADE TO PROFOUNDLY REGRET...
...THEIR COCKY BEHAVIOR.
SOLEMN-LY, AS I SAID.
Y-YES...
SCARY...
TH-THAT'S RIGHT...
LISTEN.
I'M GLAD WE CAN RELY ON YOU, BUT...
...WE CAN'T LEAVE RIGHT AWAY. I'M SORRY.
I CAN'T TELL WHERE ATARU IS.
MY SNAKE ISN'T STRONG.
KYU-TARO.

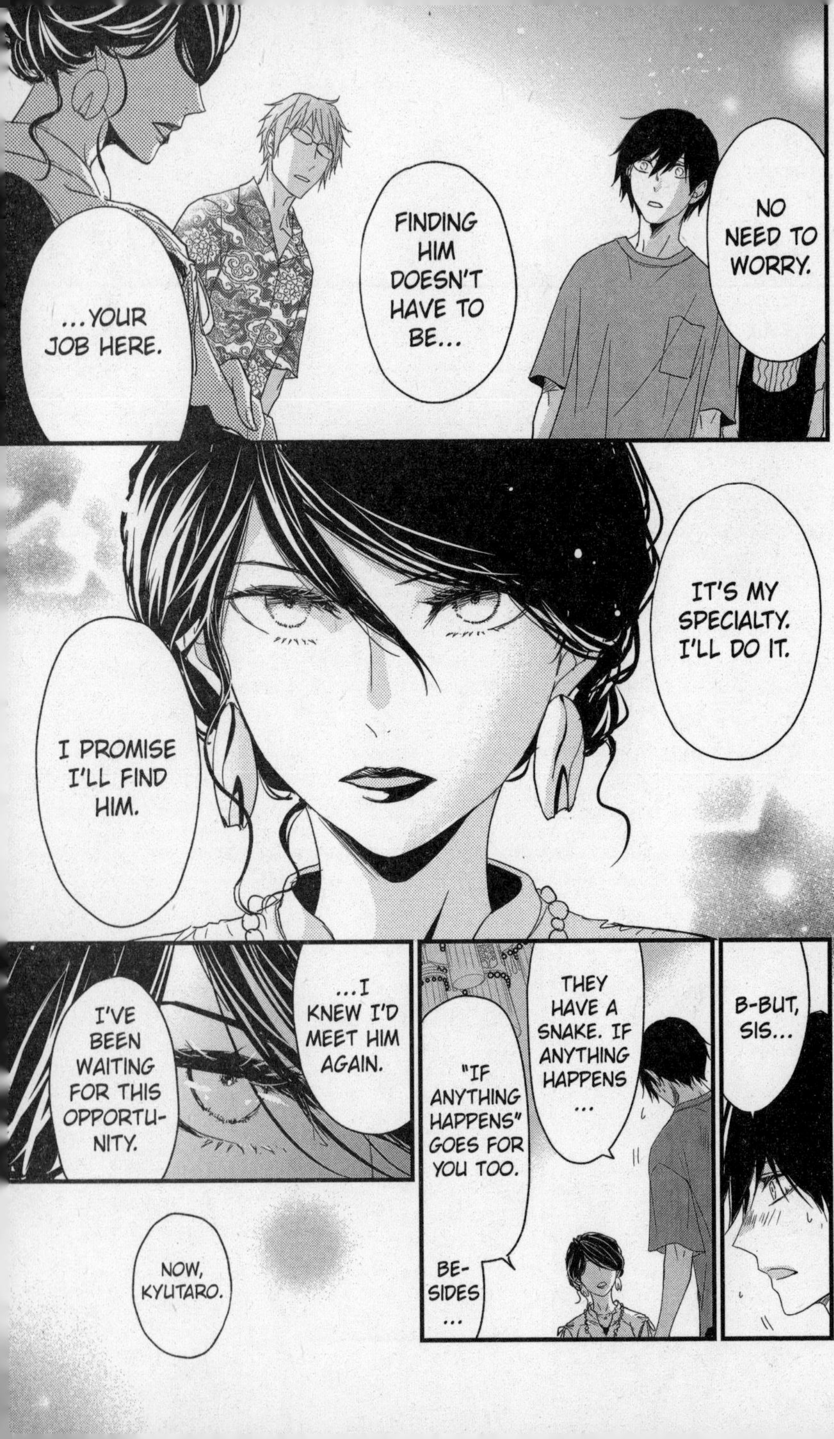
NO NEED TO WORRY.
FINDING HIM DOESN'T HAVE TO BE...
...YOUR JOB HERE.
IT'S MY SPECIALTY. I'LL DO IT.
I PROMISE I'LL FIND HIM.
B-BUT, SIS...
THEY HAVE A SNAKE. IF ANYTHING HAPPENS ...
"IF ANYTHING HAPPENS" GOES FOR YOU TOO.
BESIDES ...
...I KNEW I'D MEET HIM AGAIN.
I'VE BEEN WAITING FOR THIS OPPORTUNITY.
NOW, KYUTARO.

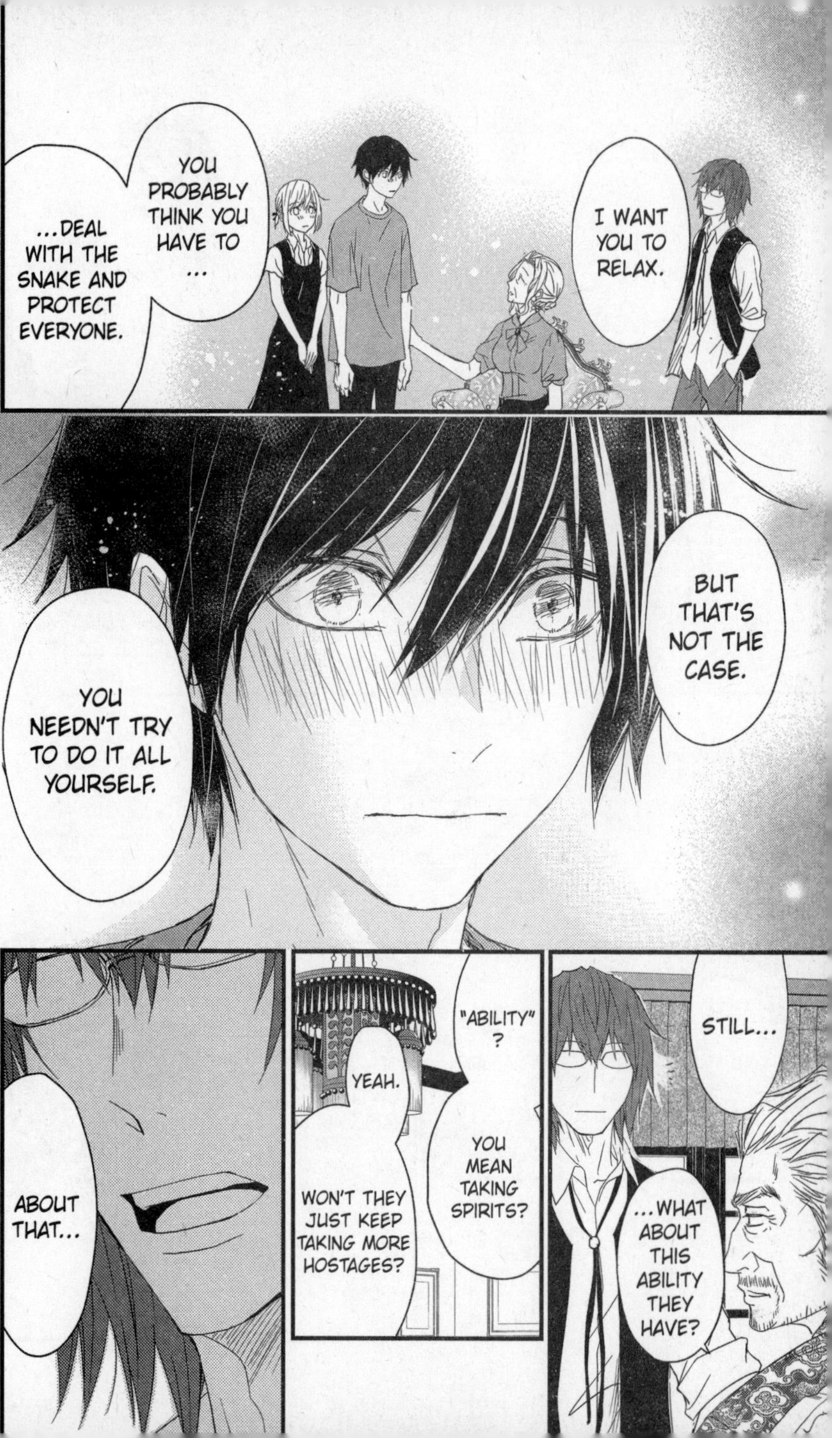
I WANT YOU TO RELAX.
YOU PROBABLY THINK YOU HAVE TO ...
...DEAL WITH THE SNAKE AND PROTECT EVERYONE.
BUT THAT'S NOT THE CASE.
YOU NEEDN'T TRY TO DO IT ALL YOURSELF.
STILL...
...WHAT ABOUT THIS ABILITY THEY HAVE?
"ABILITY"?
YOU MEAN TAKING SPIRITS?
YEAH.
WON'T THEY JUST KEEP TAKING MORE HOSTAGES?
ABOUT THAT...

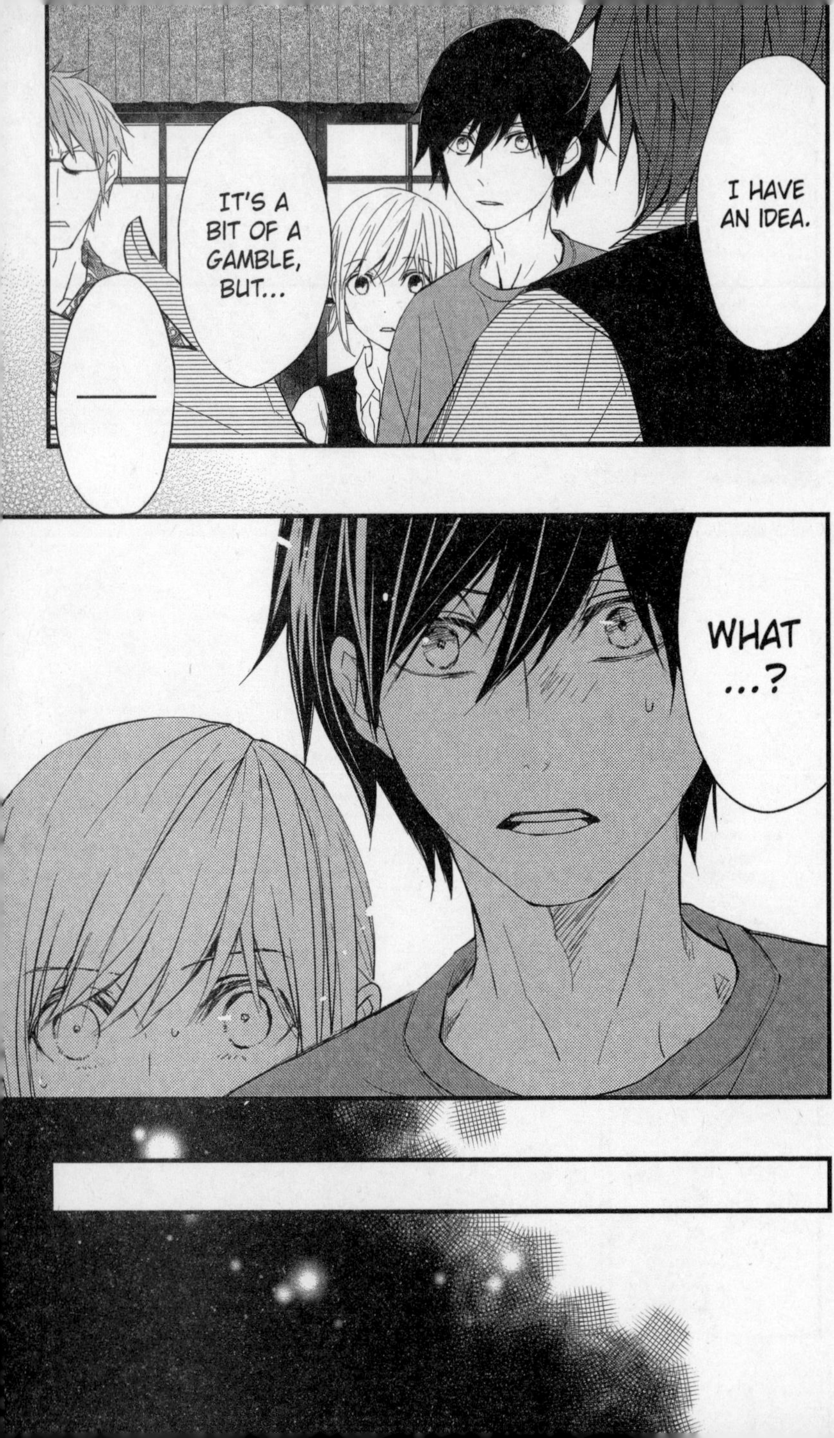
I HAVE AN IDEA.
IT'S A BIT OF A GAMBLE, BUT...
——
WHAT ...?

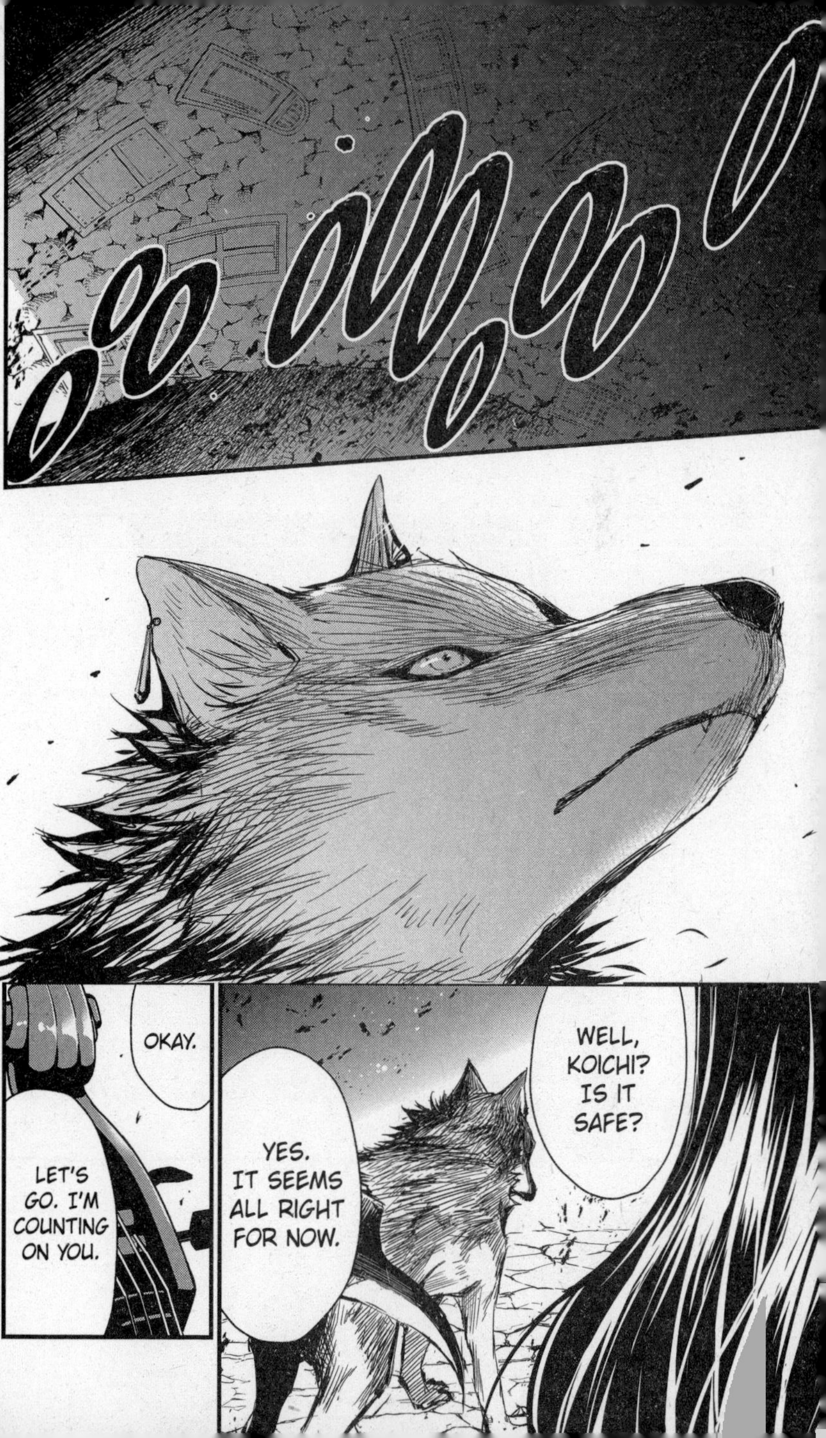
WELL, KOICHI? IS IT SAFE?
YES. IT SEEMS ALL RIGHT FOR NOW.
OKAY.
LET'S GO. I'M COUNTING ON YOU.

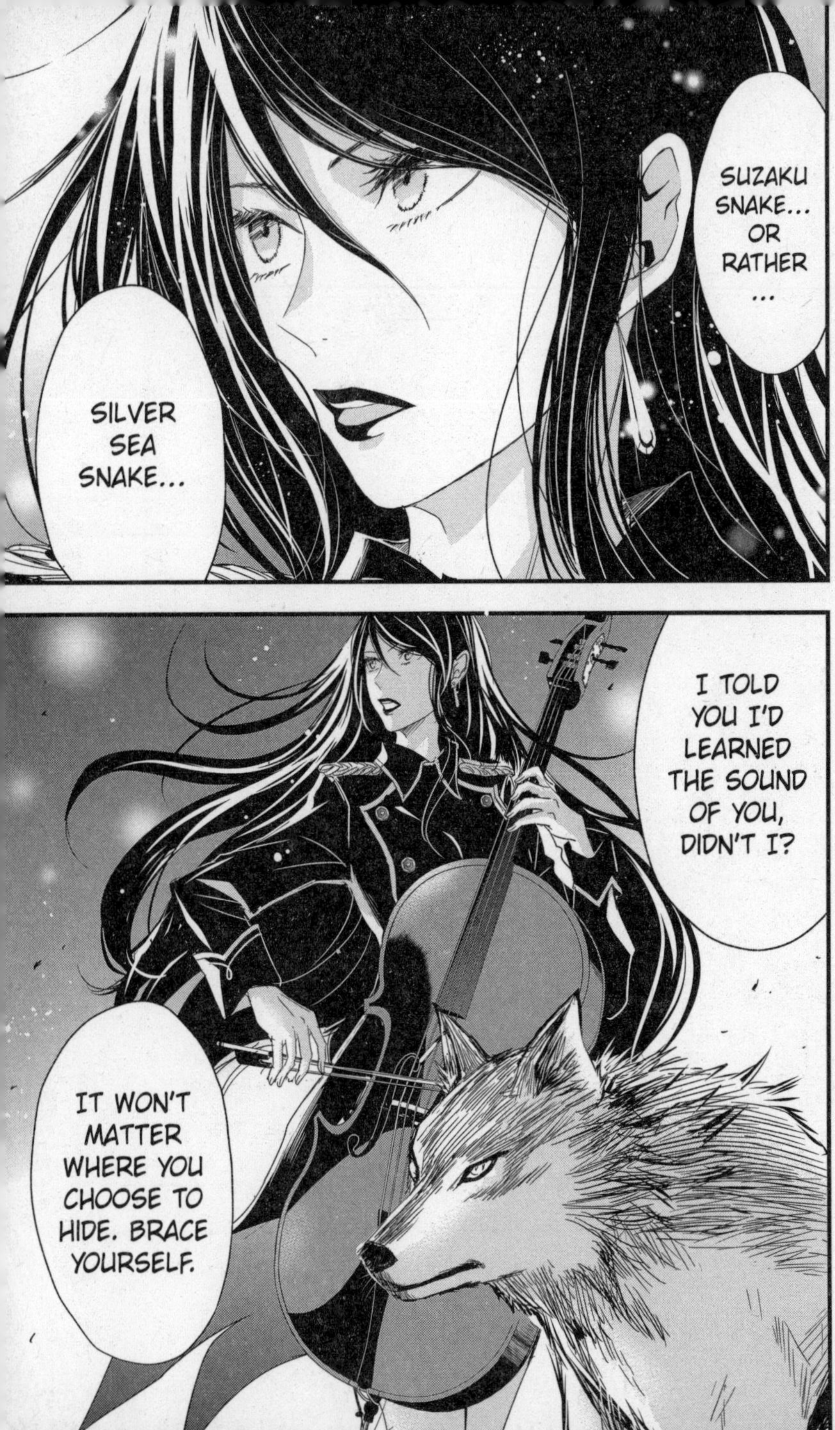
SUZAKU SNAKE... OR RATHER...
SILVER SEA SNAKE...
I TOLD YOU I'D LEARNED THE SOUND OF YOU, DIDN'T I?
IT WON'T MATTER WHERE YOU CHOOSE TO HIDE. BRACE YOURSELF.

CHAPTER 63

MONTHLY BETSUCOMI SALE DATE NOTICE ON TWITTER

ISN'T THIS A NICE BALL? SO MUCH MYSTERY AND VITALITY IN IT. I LOVE BALLS.
I WONDER IF THE BALLS LOOK DIFFERENT FROM PERSON TO PERSON. ISN'T IT MARVELOUS?
PLEASE SHOW ME YOUR BALL AGAIN, KYUTARO. IT'S PROBABLY VERY CUTE.
It's so smooth, I just want to touch it all day.
FUMI.
CAN WE STOP TALKING ABOUT BALLS?

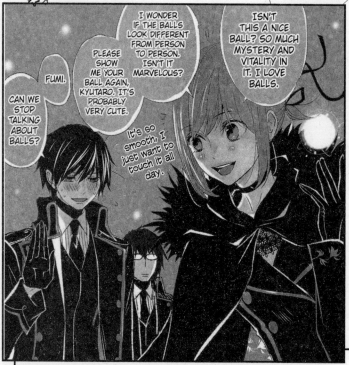

LET'S SEE... WHAT'S UP IN *QUEEN'S QUALITY* THIS MONTH?
1) THE SEIRYU LEADER AND KOICHI THE WOLF... AREN'T THEY HUGE?
2) IN A SITUATION LIKE THIS, THERE'S NO WAY HE CAN TURN INTO HIS FEMALE FORM.
3) THIS MONTH, SO MANY PEOPLE SPONTANEOUSLY CHANGE THE WAY THEIR HAIR PARTS. I DO APOLOGIZE.

ATARU'S IN A PINCH. CONVENIENT "BALLS" PLAY AN ACTIVE ROLE IN CHAPTER 63.

THE SUBJECT MATTER HERE IS QUITE JUVENILE, BUT THE SUBJECT OF BALLS WAS PRETTY POPULAR AMONG SOME OF THE EDITORIAL STAFF. THERE ARE SOME CHILDISH PEOPLE EVERYWHERE.

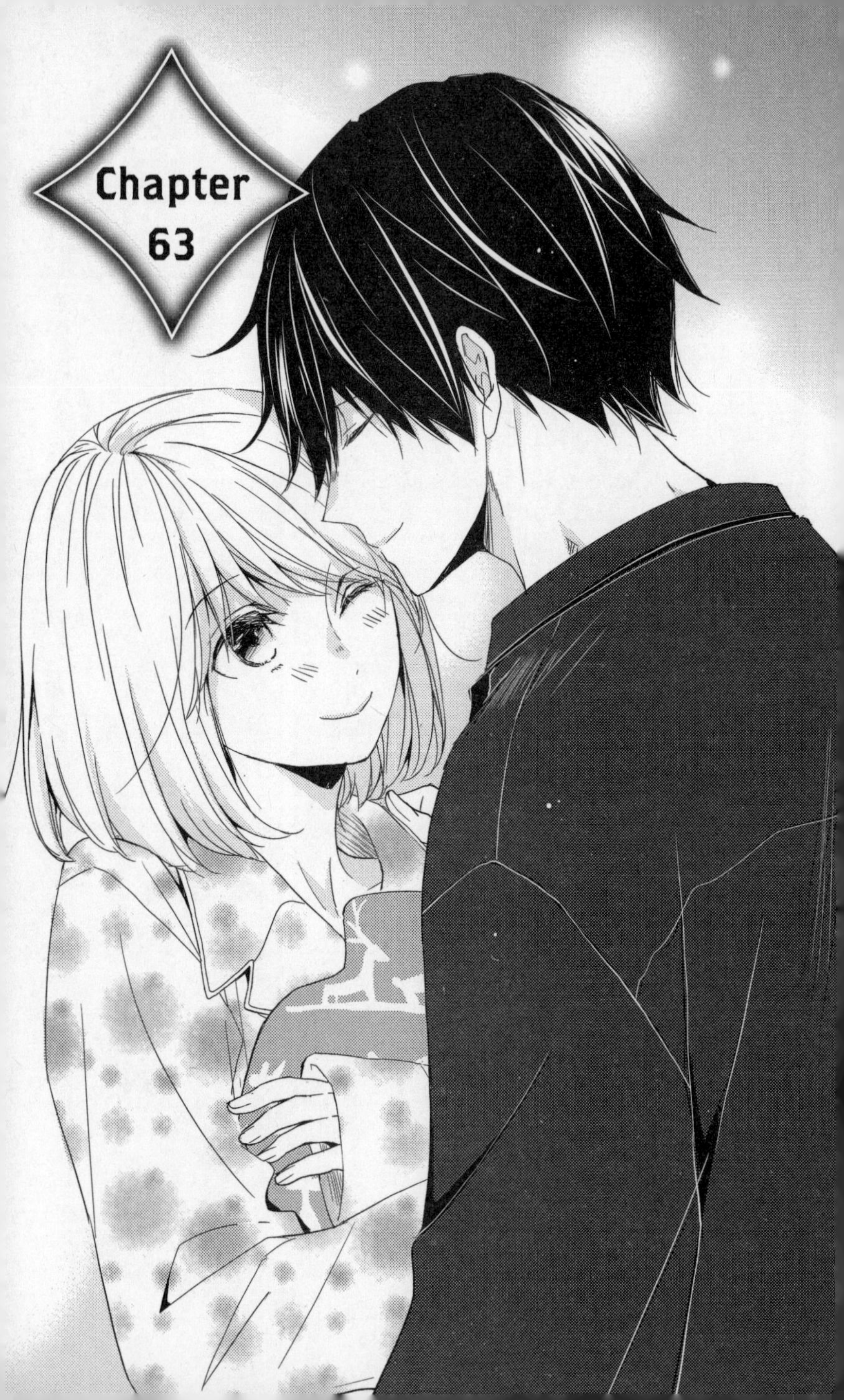
Chapter
63

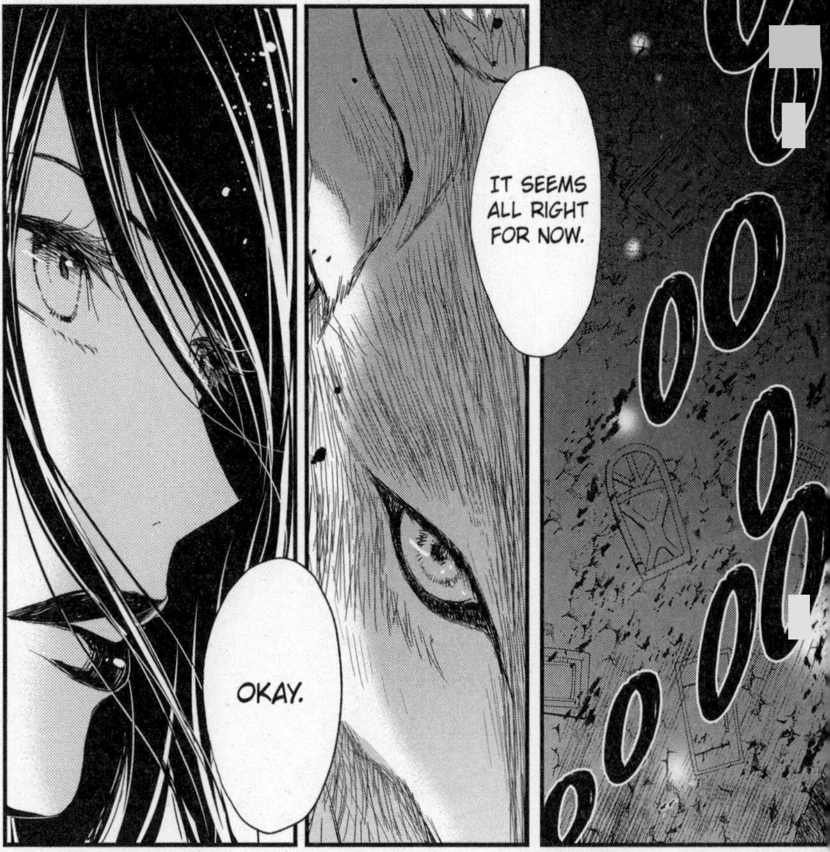
IT SEEMS ALL RIGHT FOR NOW.
OKAY.

I got myself *Ring Fit Adventure*. To my own surprise, I've been exercising nearly every day. Games are amazing. The thought of "defeating the enemy" has me exercising without thinking about the effort involved.

I haven't lost any weight, but I've seen improvements in my mental and physical condition. I don't get headaches anymore, and I no longer think, "I'm dying because I'm no good at this." This is great exercise. I recommend it.

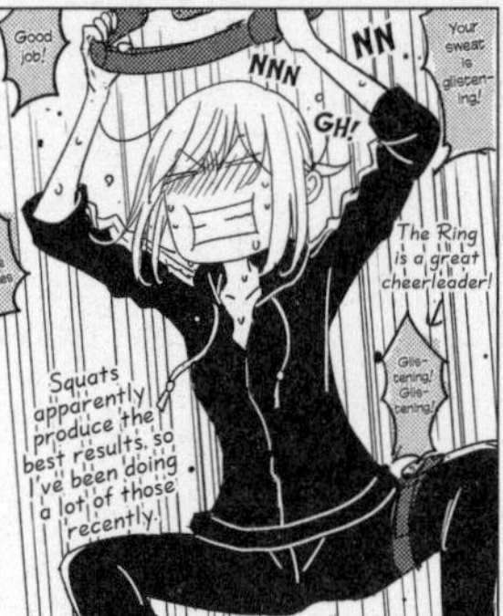
Your sweat is glisten-ing!
NN
NNN
GH!
Good job!
The Ring is a great cheerleader!
Glis-tening! Glis-tening!
Look at those muscles!
Squats apparently produce the best results, so I've been doing a lot of those recently.

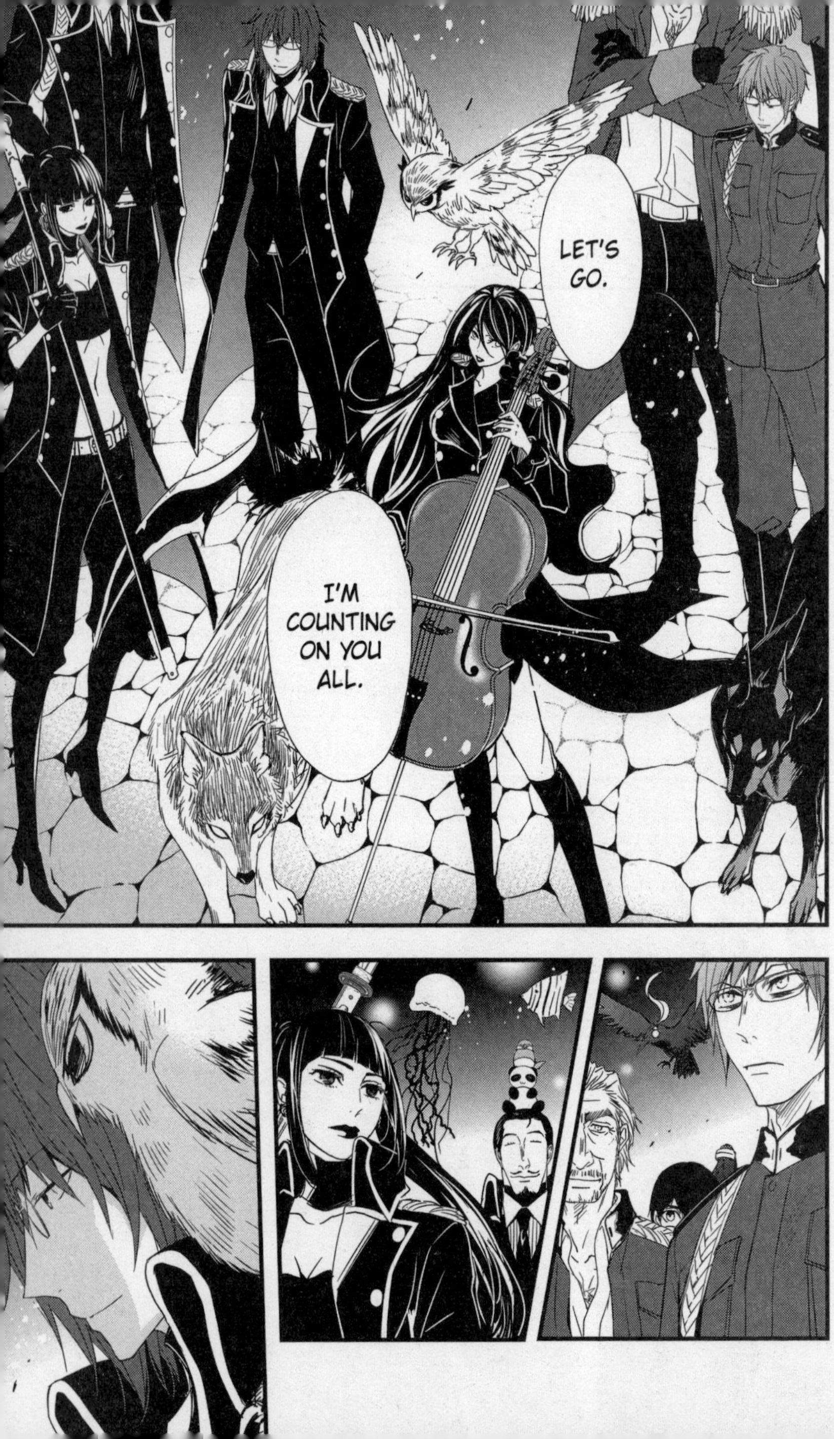
LET'S GO.
I'M COUNTING ON YOU ALL.

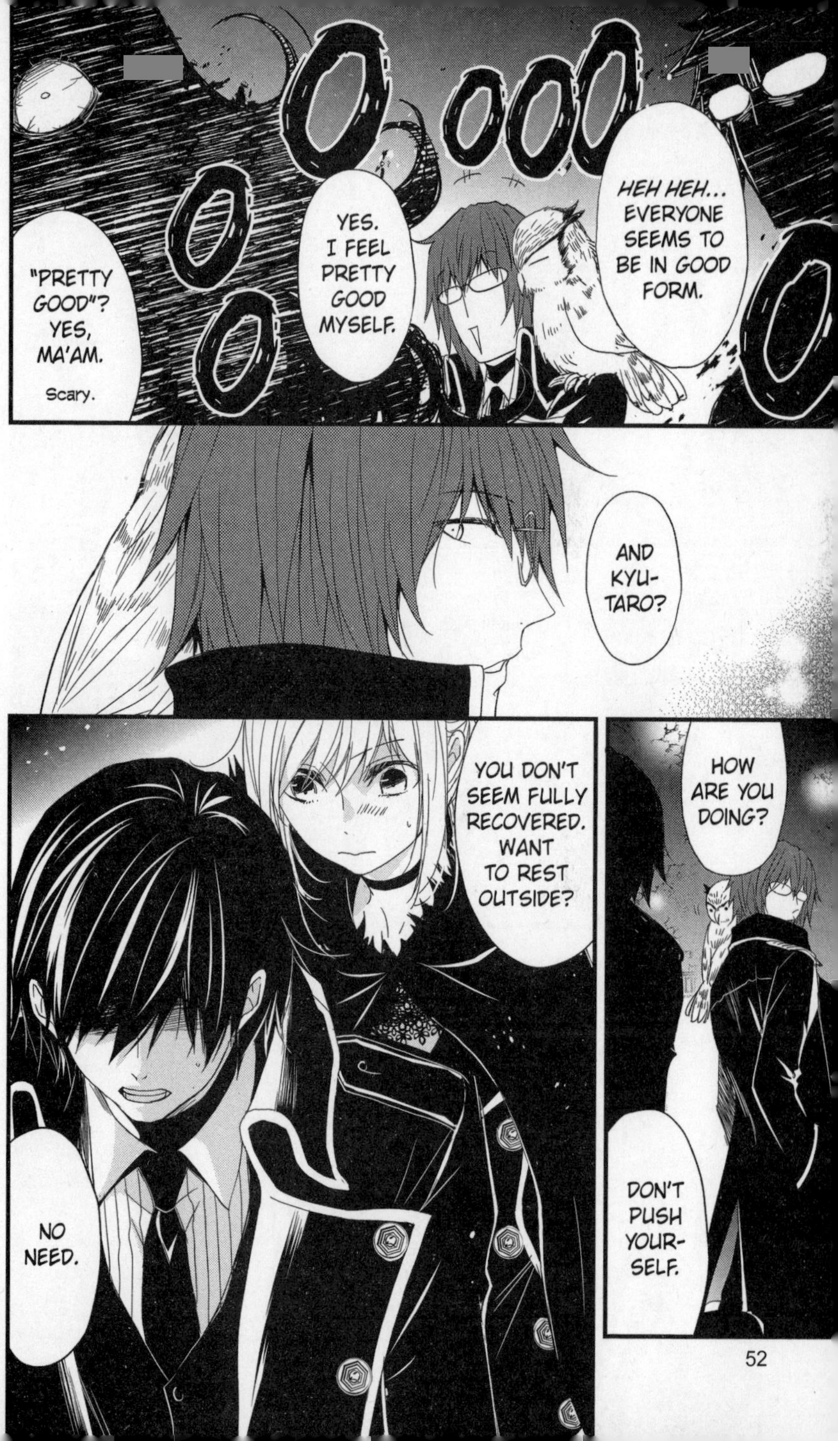
HEH HEH... EVERYONE SEEMS TO BE IN GOOD FORM.
YES. I FEEL PRETTY GOOD MYSELF.
"PRETTY GOOD"? YES, MA'AM.
Scary.
AND KYU-TARO?
HOW ARE YOU DOING?
DON'T PUSH YOUR-SELF.
YOU DON'T SEEM FULLY RECOVERED. WANT TO REST OUTSIDE?
NO NEED.

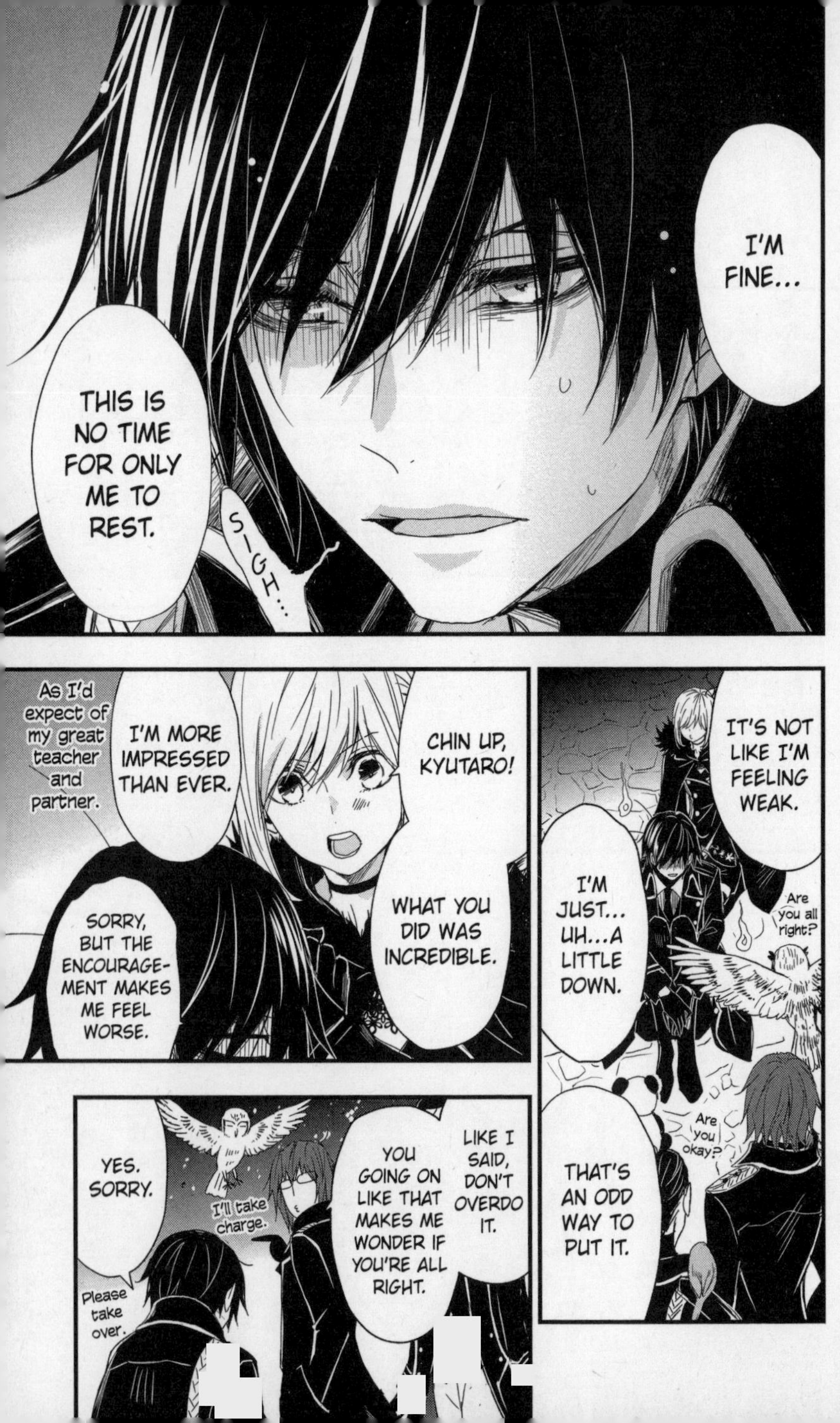
I'M FINE...
THIS IS NO TIME FOR ONLY ME TO REST.
SIGH...
IT'S NOT LIKE I'M FEELING WEAK.
Are you all right?
I'M JUST... UH...A LITTLE DOWN.
Are you okay?
THAT'S AN ODD WAY TO PUT IT.
CHIN UP, KYUTARO!
WHAT YOU DID WAS INCREDIBLE.
I'M MORE IMPRESSED THAN EVER.
As I'd expect of my great teacher and partner.
SORRY, BUT THE ENCOURAGE-MENT MAKES ME FEEL WORSE.
LIKE I SAID, DON'T OVERDO IT.
YOU GOING ON LIKE THAT MAKES ME WONDER IF YOU'RE ALL RIGHT.
I'll take charge.
YES. SORRY.
Please take over.

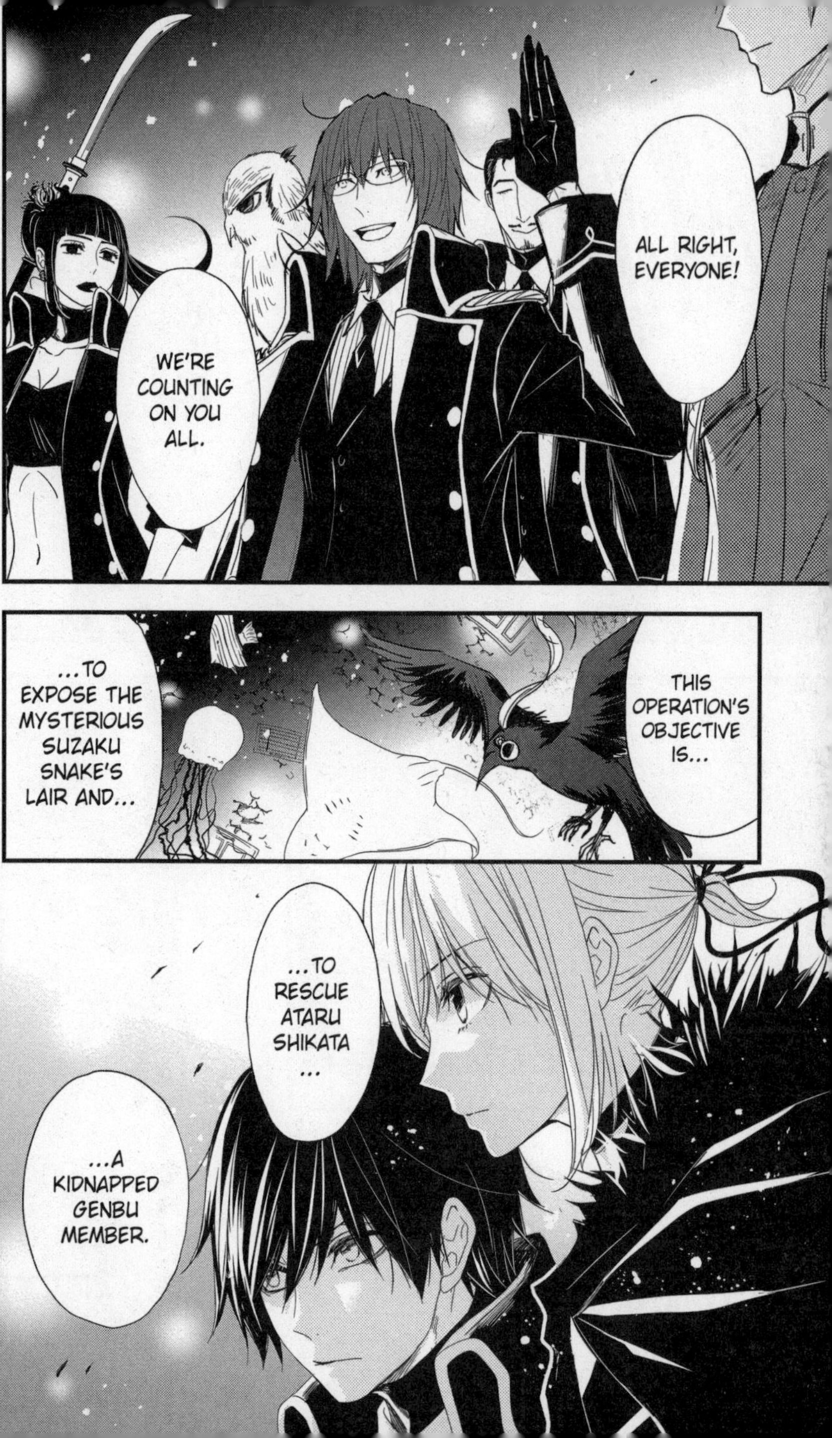
ALL RIGHT, EVERYONE!
WE'RE COUNTING ON YOU ALL.
THIS OPERATION'S OBJECTIVE IS...
...TO EXPOSE THE MYSTERIOUS SUZAKU SNAKE'S LAIR AND...
...TO RESCUE ATARU SHIKATA...
...A KIDNAPPED GENBU MEMBER.

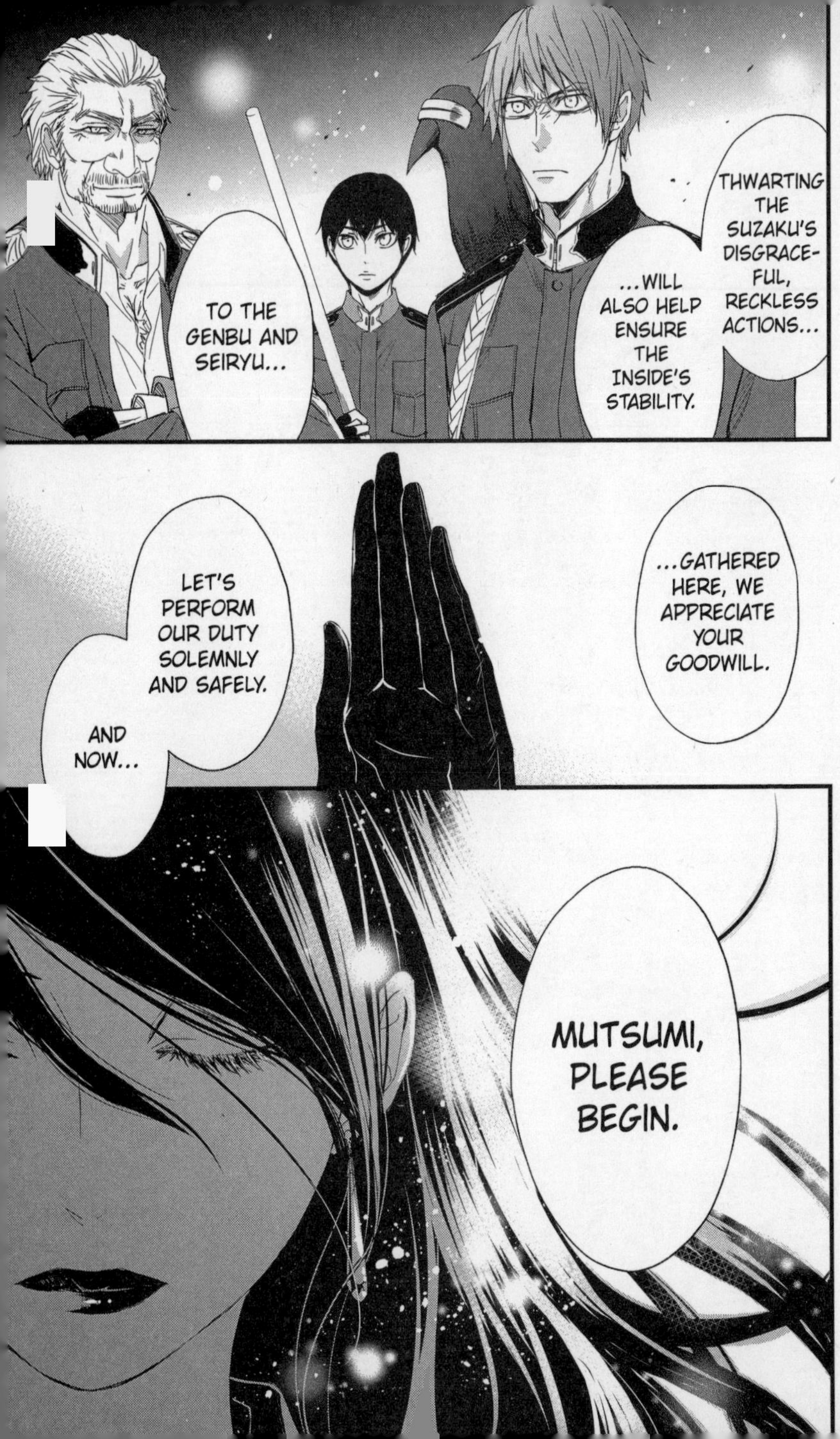
THWARTING THE SUZAKU'S DISGRACE-FUL, RECKLESS ACTIONS...
...WILL ALSO HELP ENSURE THE INSIDE'S STABILITY.
TO THE GENBU AND SEIRYU...
...GATHERED HERE, WE APPRECIATE YOUR GOODWILL.
LET'S PERFORM OUR DUTY SOLEMNLY AND SAFELY.
AND NOW...
MUTSUMI, PLEASE BEGIN.

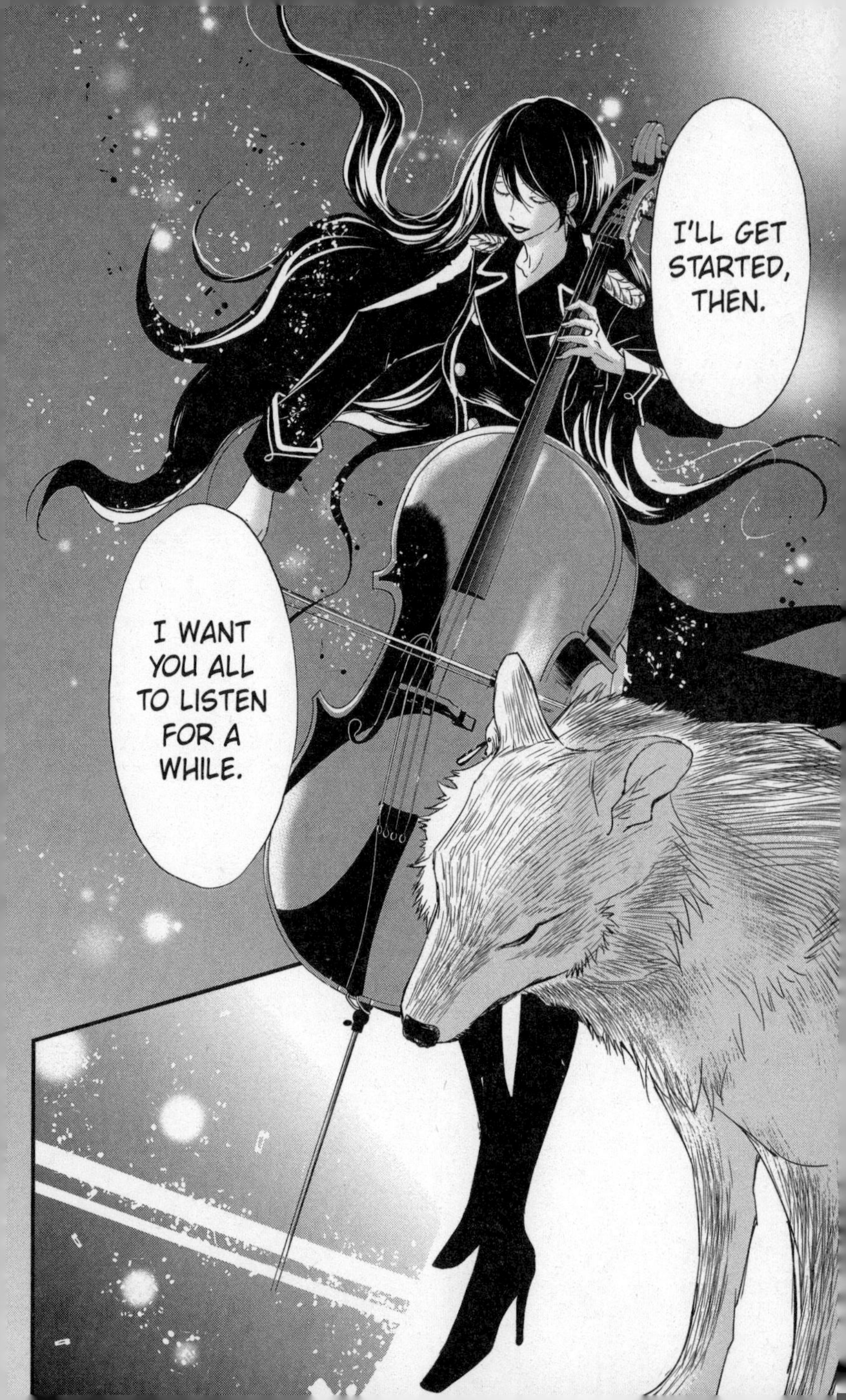
I'LL GET STARTED, THEN.
I WANT YOU ALL TO LISTEN FOR A WHILE.

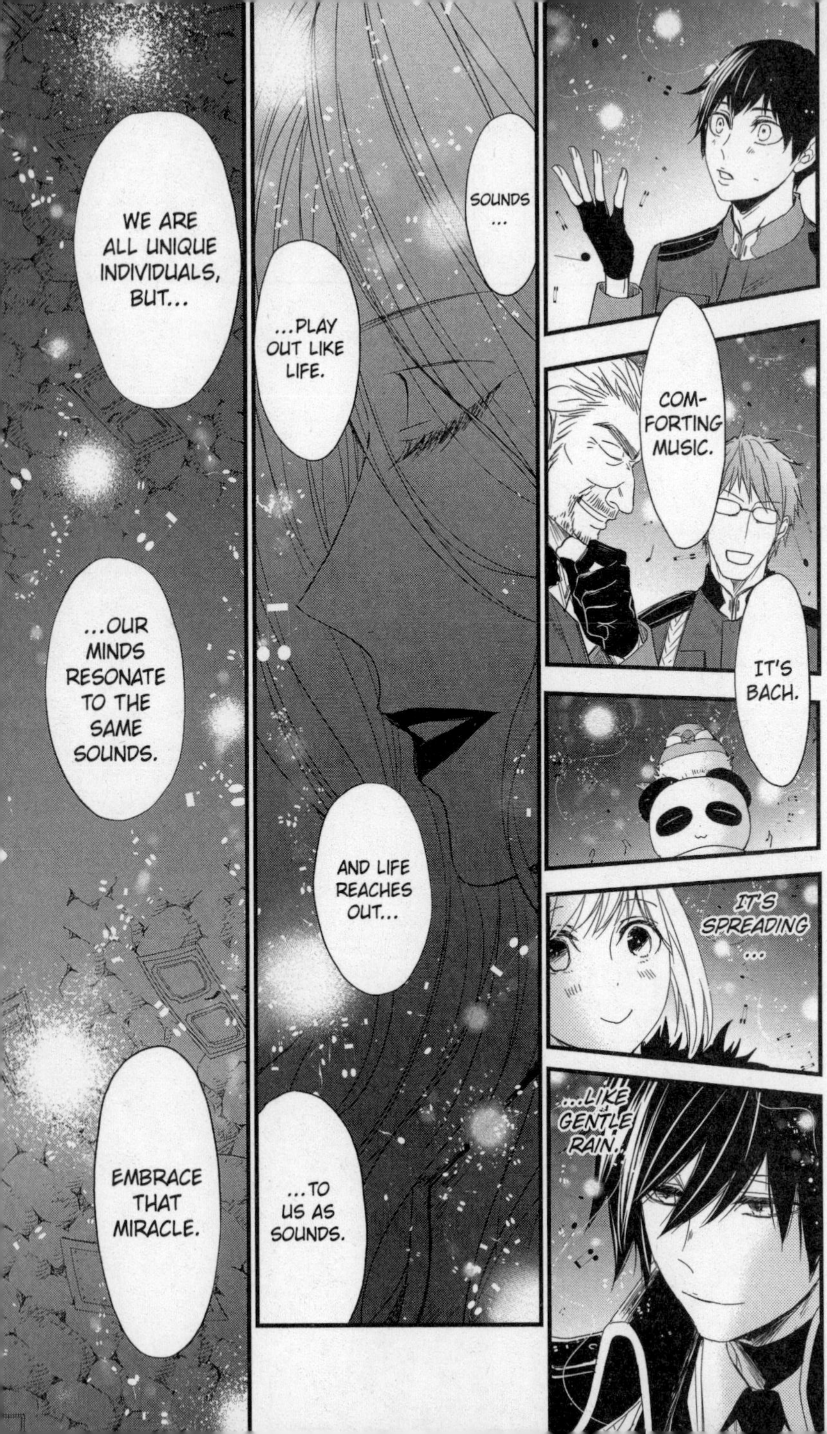
COM-FORTING MUSIC.
IT'S BACH.
IT'S SPREADING...
...LIKE GENTLE RAIN...
SOUNDS...
...PLAY OUT LIKE LIFE.
AND LIFE REACHES OUT...
...TO US AS SOUNDS.
WE ARE ALL UNIQUE INDIVIDUALS, BUT...
...OUR MINDS RESONATE TO THE SAME SOUNDS.
EMBRACE THAT MIRACLE.

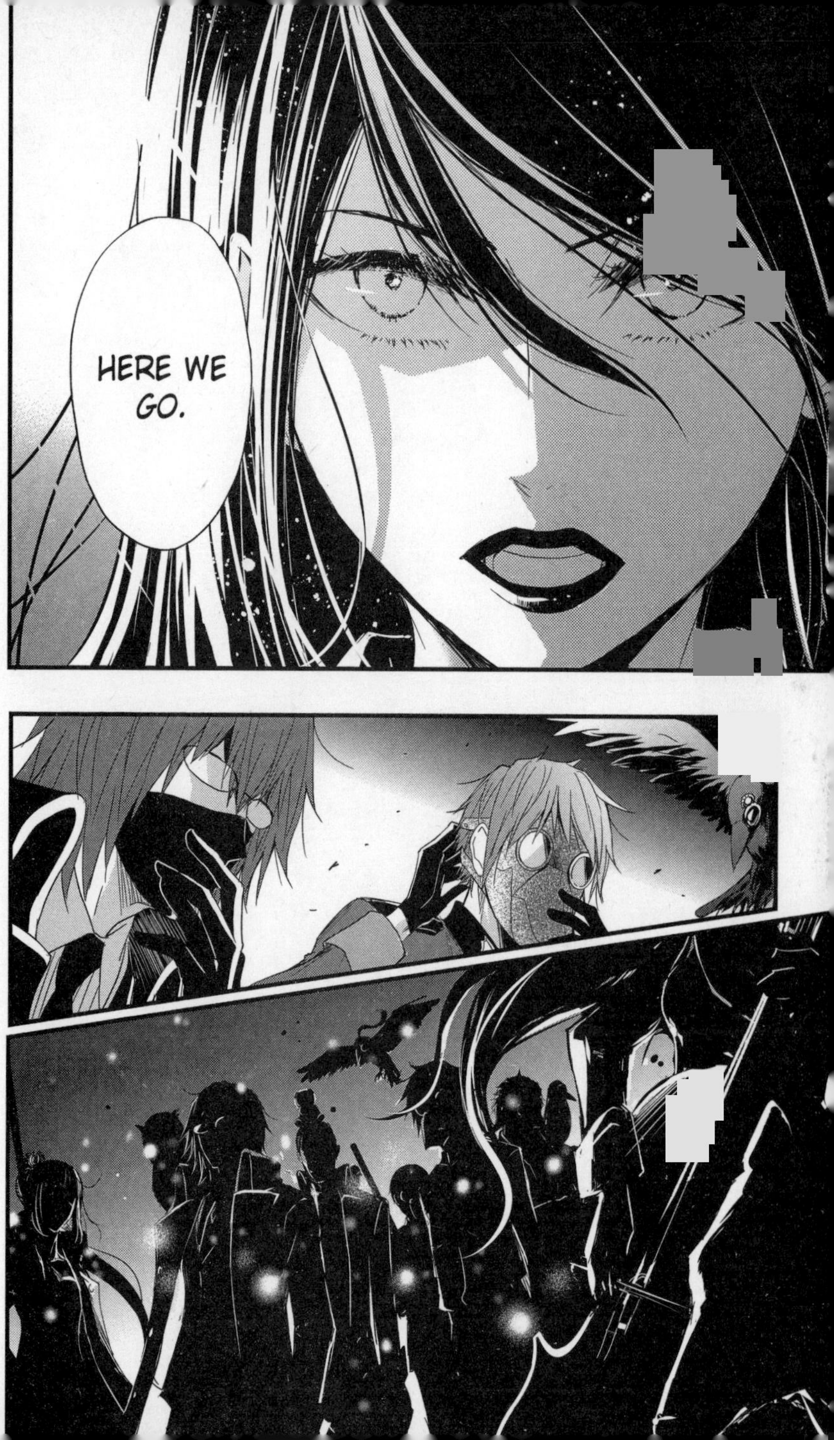
HERE WE GO.

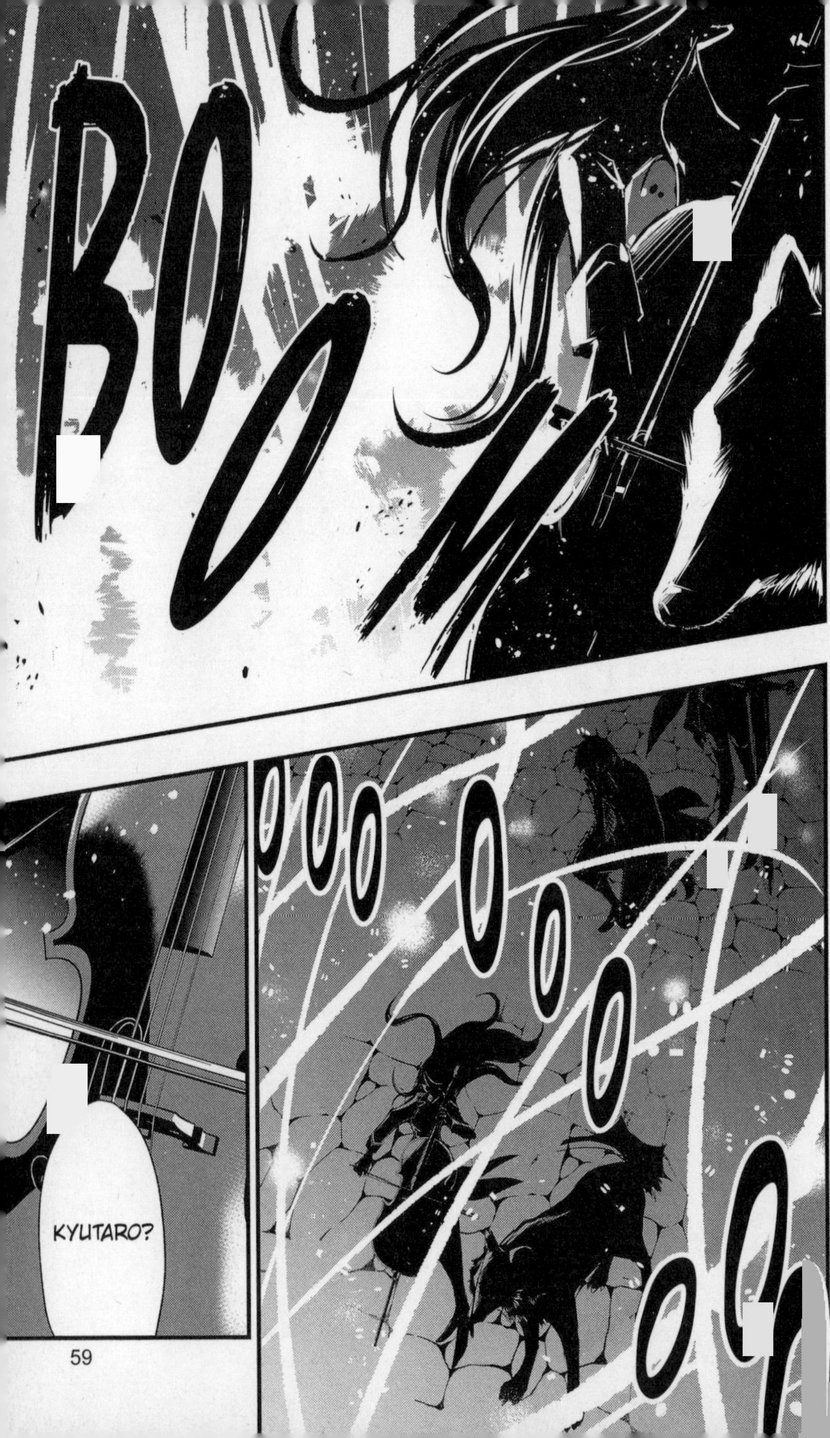
BOOM
KYUTARO?

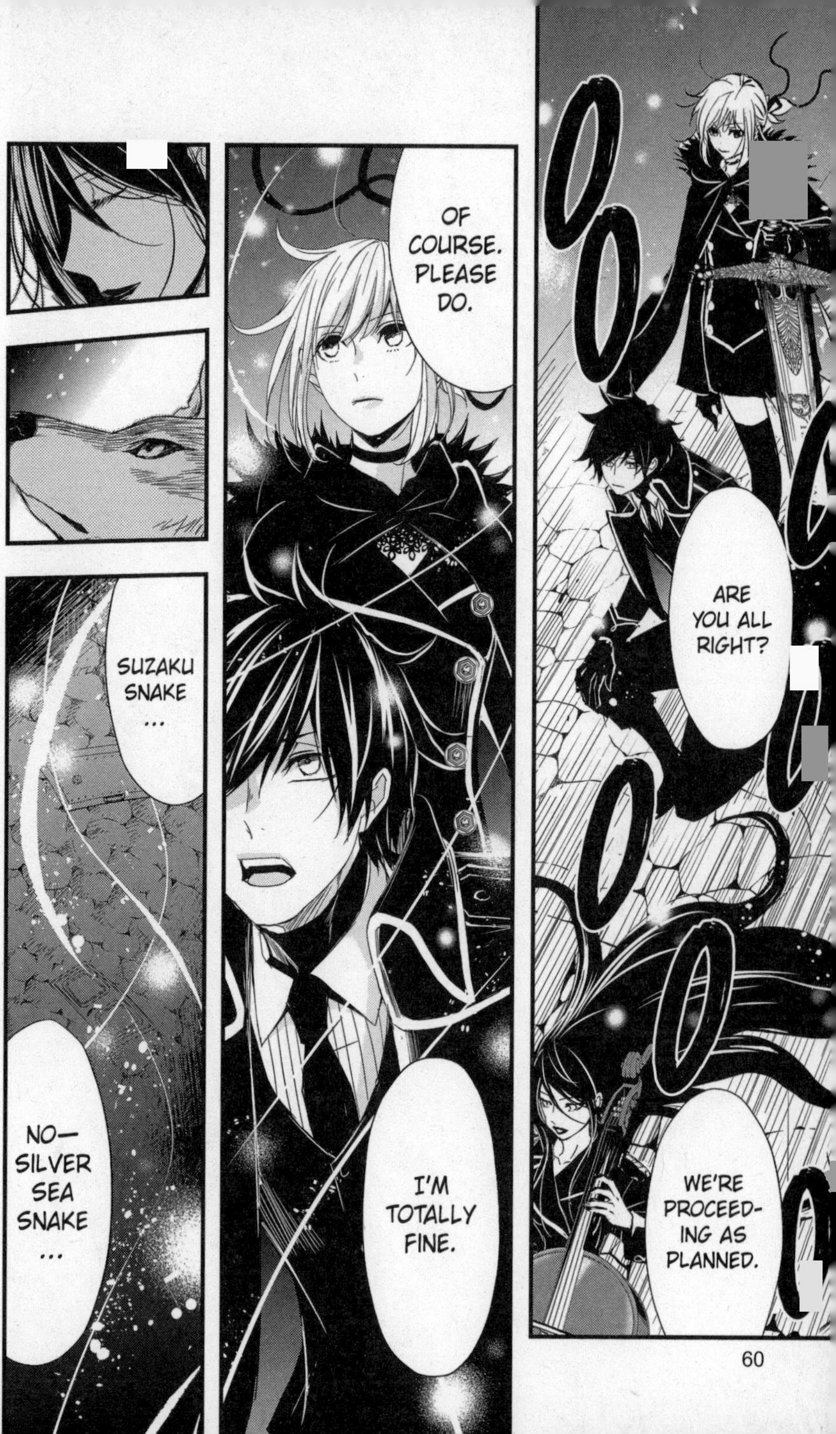
ARE YOU ALL RIGHT?
WE'RE PROCEED-ING AS PLANNED.
OF COURSE. PLEASE DO.
I'M TOTALLY FINE.
SUZAKU SNAKE...
NO— SILVER SEA SNAKE...

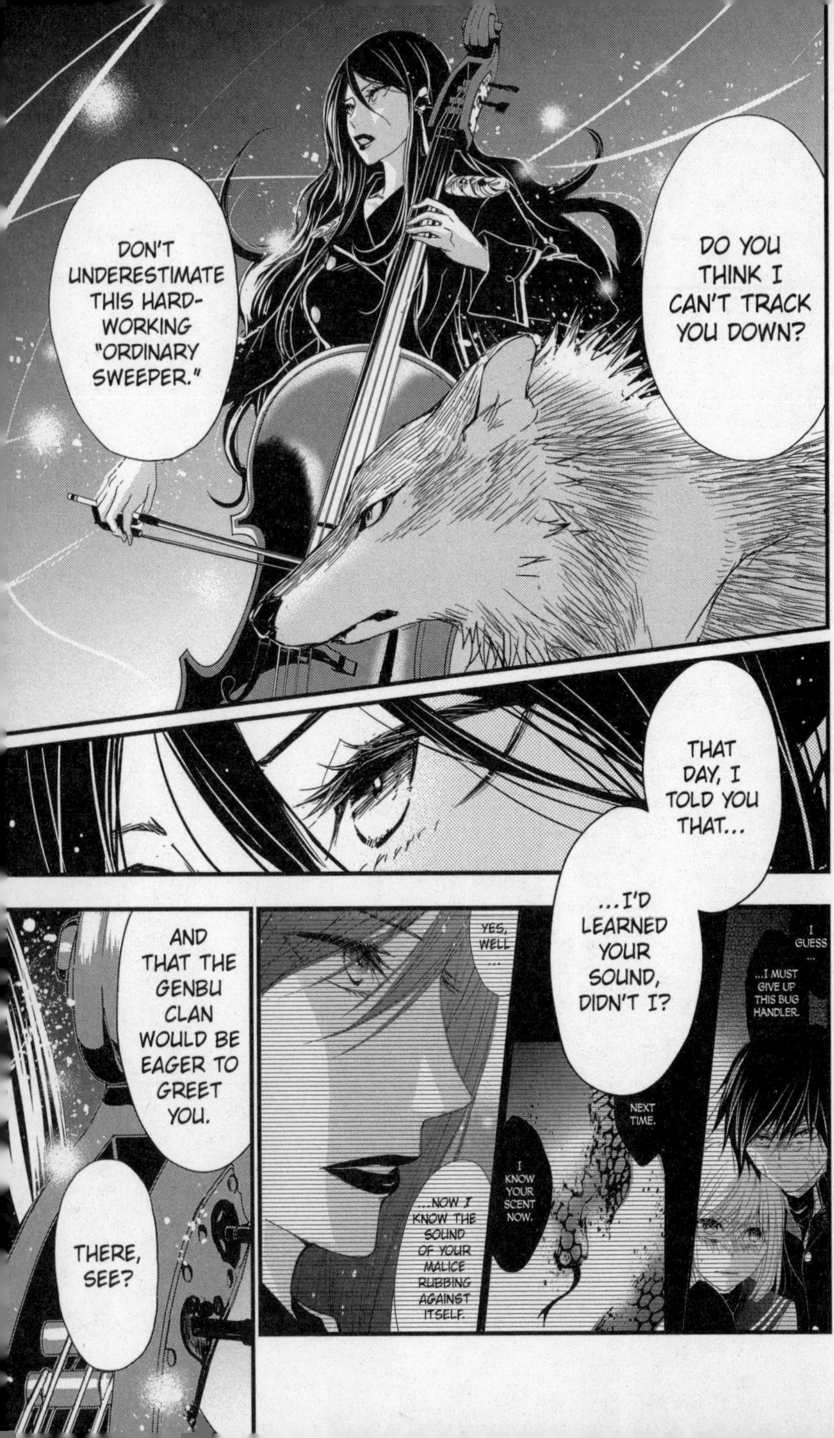
DO YOU THINK I CAN'T TRACK YOU DOWN?
DON'T UNDERESTIMATE THIS HARD-WORKING "ORDINARY SWEEPER."
THAT DAY, I TOLD YOU THAT...
...I'D LEARNED YOUR SOUND, DIDN'T I?
I GUESS...
...I MUST GIVE UP THIS BUG HANDLER.
NEXT TIME.
I KNOW YOUR SCENT NOW.
YES, WELL...
...NOW I KNOW THE SOUND OF YOUR MALICE RUBBING AGAINST ITSELF.
AND THAT THE GENBU CLAN WOULD BE EAGER TO GREET YOU.
THERE, SEE?

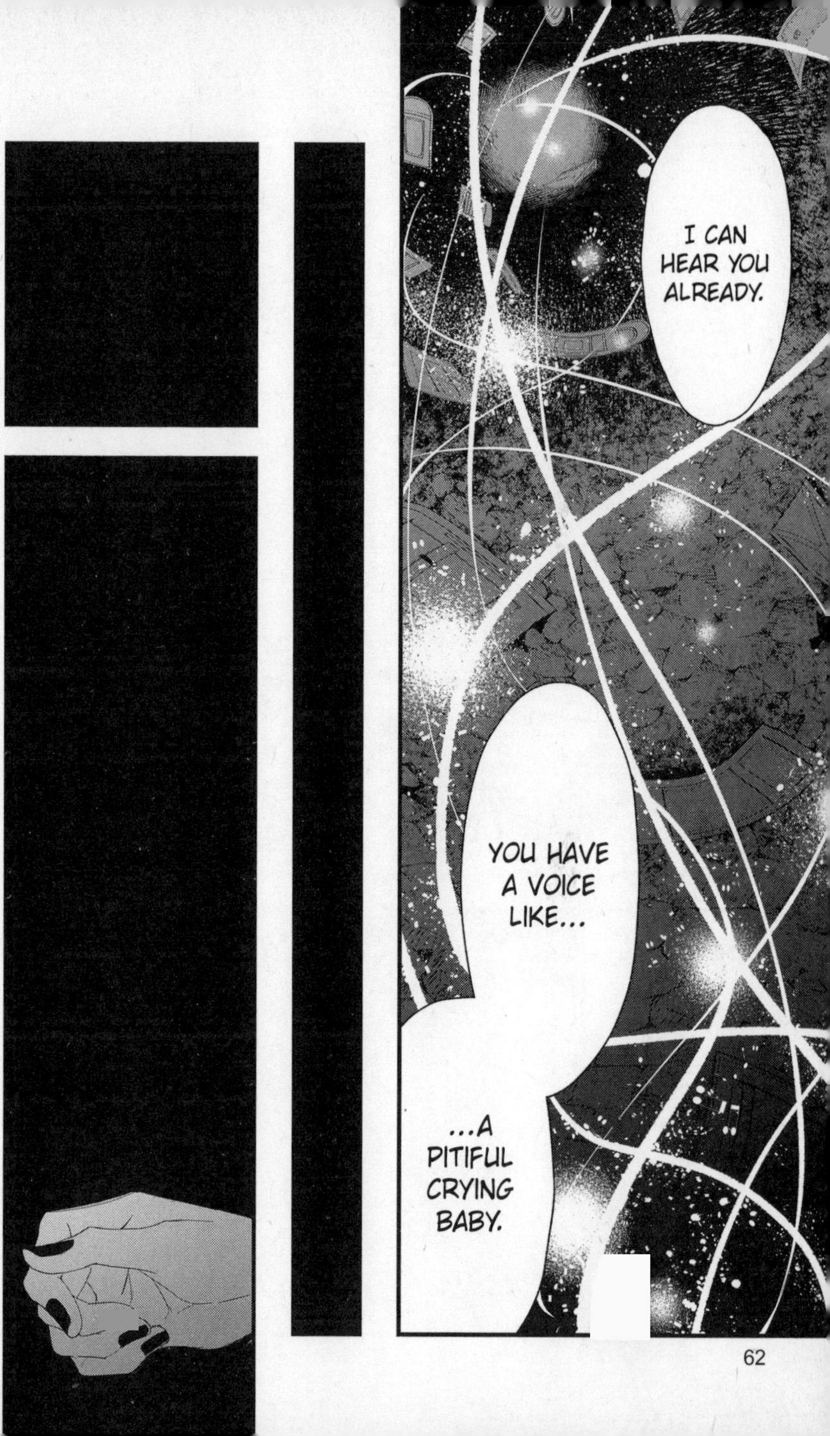
I CAN HEAR YOU ALREADY.
YOU HAVE A VOICE LIKE...
...A PITIFUL CRYING BABY.

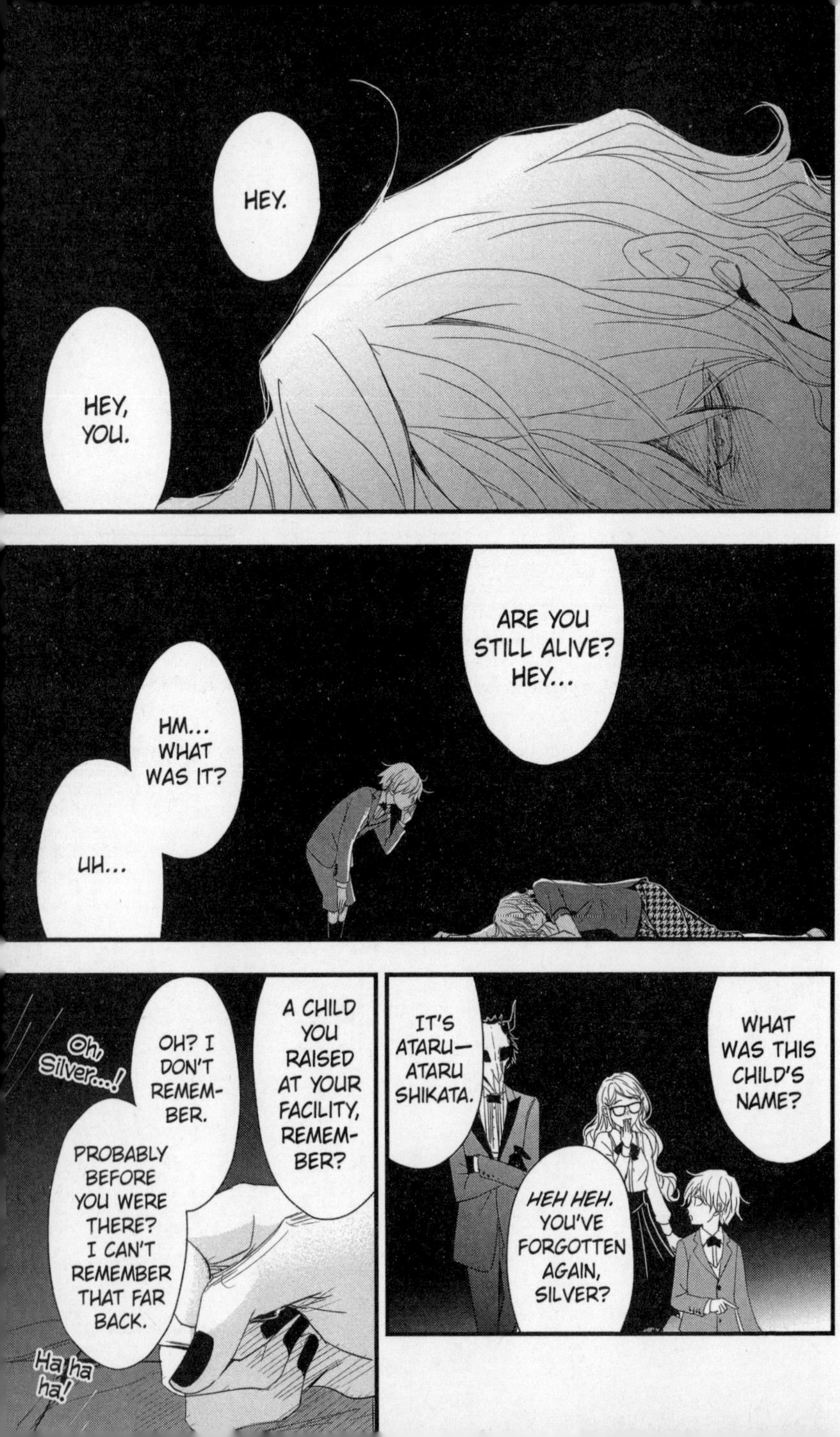
HEY.
HEY, YOU.
ARE YOU STILL ALIVE? HEY...
HM... WHAT WAS IT?
UH...
WHAT WAS THIS CHILD'S NAME?
IT'S ATARU—ATARU SHIKATA.
HEH HEH. YOU'VE FORGOTTEN AGAIN, SILVER?
A CHILD YOU RAISED AT YOUR FACILITY, REMEMBER?
OH? I DON'T REMEMBER.
Oh, Silver...!
PROBABLY BEFORE YOU WERE THERE? I CAN'T REMEMBER THAT FAR BACK.
Ha ha ha!

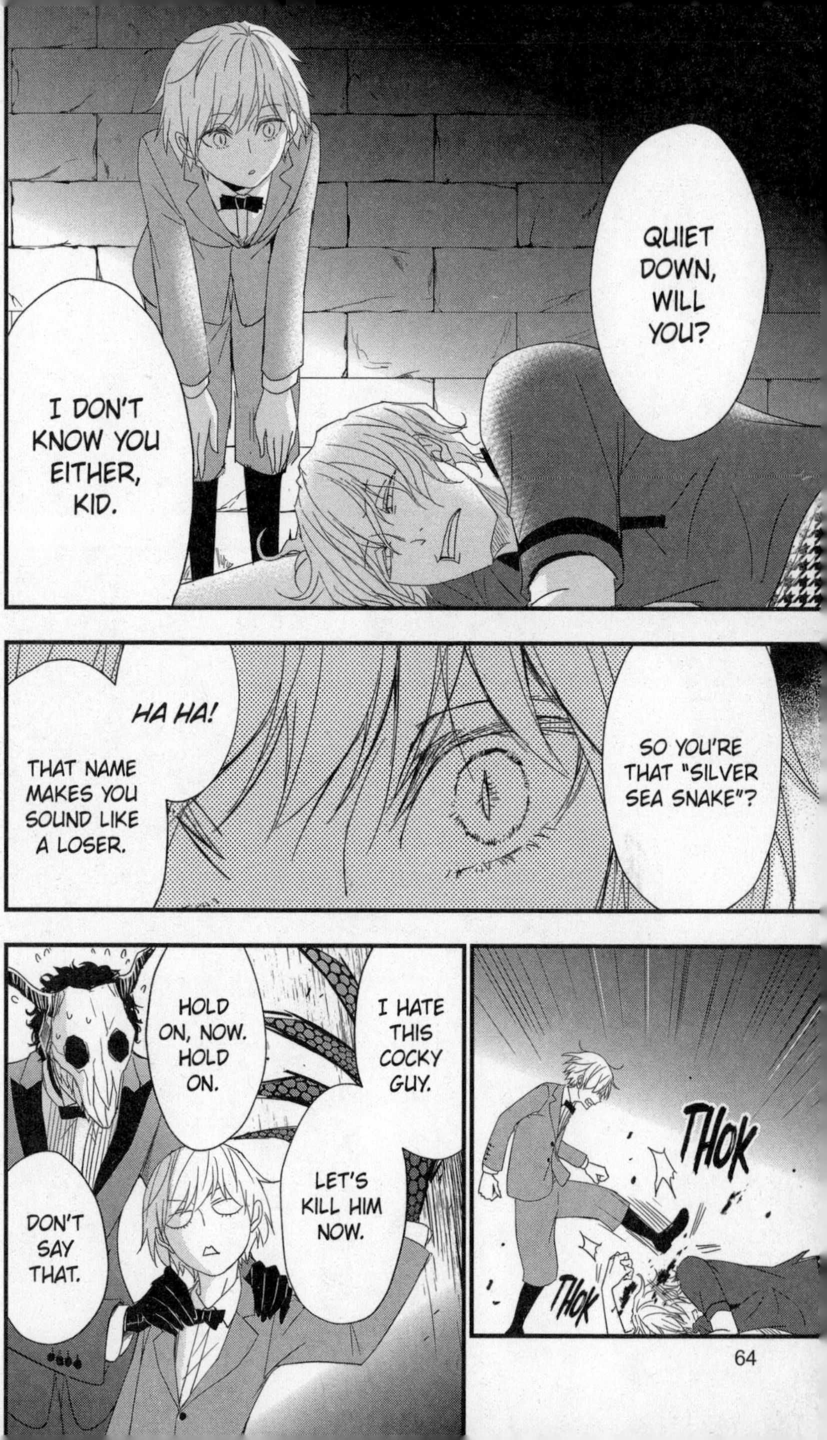
QUIET DOWN, WILL YOU?
I DON'T KNOW YOU EITHER, KID.
SO YOU'RE THAT "SILVER SEA SNAKE"?
HA HA!
THAT NAME MAKES YOU SOUND LIKE A LOSER.
THOK
THOK
I HATE THIS COCKY GUY.
HOLD ON, NOW. HOLD ON.
LET'S KILL HIM NOW.
DON'T SAY THAT.

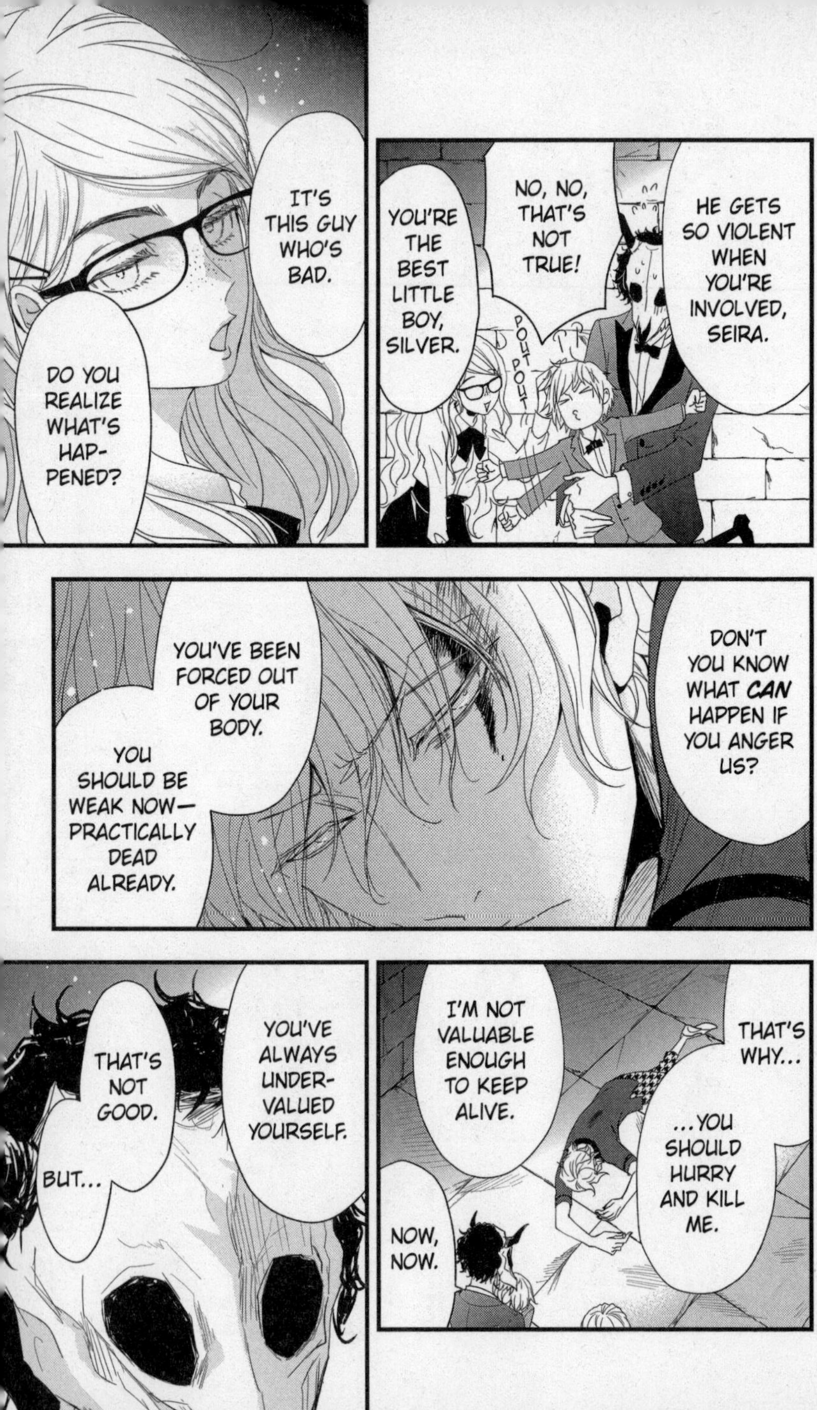
HE GETS SO VIOLENT WHEN YOU'RE INVOLVED, SEIRA.
NO, NO, THAT'S NOT TRUE!
YOU'RE THE BEST LITTLE BOY, SILVER.
POUT POUT
IT'S THIS GUY WHO'S BAD.
DO YOU REALIZE WHAT'S HAP-PENED?
DON'T YOU KNOW WHAT *CAN* HAPPEN IF YOU ANGER US?
YOU'VE BEEN FORCED OUT OF YOUR BODY.
YOU SHOULD BE WEAK NOW—PRACTICALLY DEAD ALREADY.
I'M NOT VALUABLE ENOUGH TO KEEP ALIVE.
THAT'S WHY...
...YOU SHOULD HURRY AND KILL ME.
NOW, NOW.
YOU'VE ALWAYS UNDER-VALUED YOURSELF.
THAT'S NOT GOOD.
BUT...

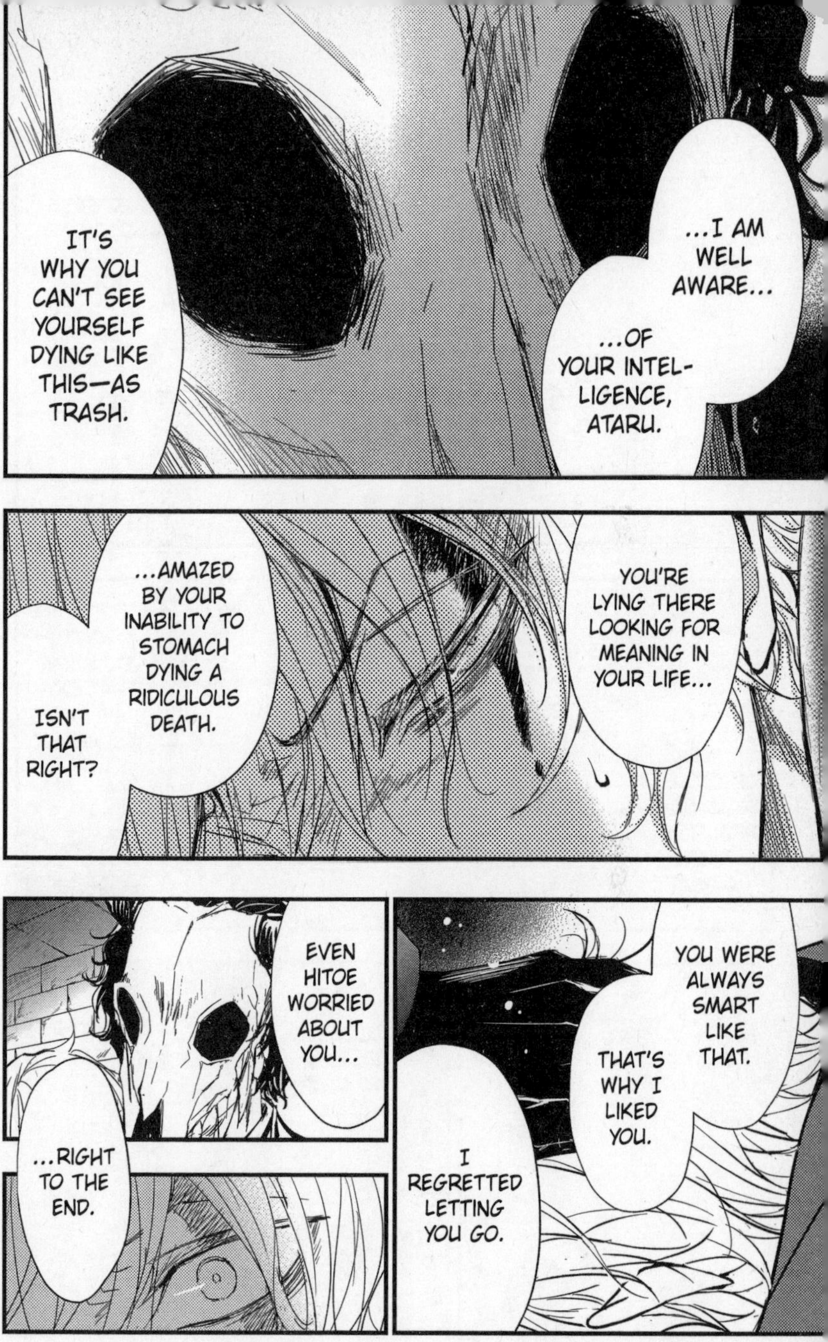
...I AM WELL AWARE...
...OF YOUR INTEL-LIGENCE, ATARU.
IT'S WHY YOU CAN'T SEE YOURSELF DYING LIKE THIS—AS TRASH.
YOU'RE LYING THERE LOOKING FOR MEANING IN YOUR LIFE...
...AMAZED BY YOUR INABILITY TO STOMACH DYING A RIDICULOUS DEATH.
ISN'T THAT RIGHT?
YOU WERE ALWAYS SMART LIKE THAT.
THAT'S WHY I LIKED YOU.
I REGRETTED LETTING YOU GO.
EVEN HITOE WORRIED ABOUT YOU...
...RIGHT TO THE END.

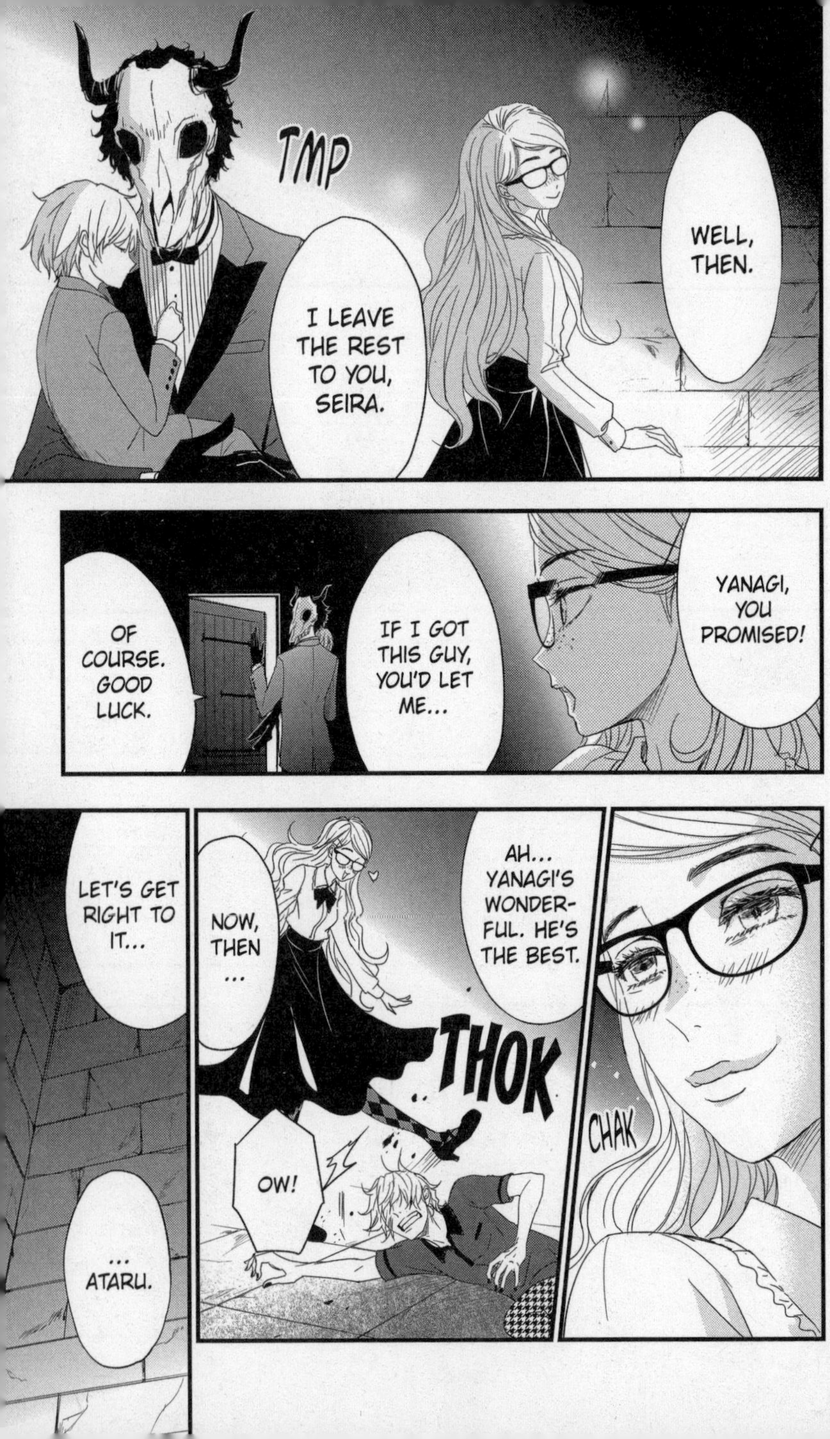
WELL, THEN.
TMP
I LEAVE THE REST TO YOU, SEIRA.
YANAGI, YOU PROMISED!
IF I GOT THIS GUY, YOU'D LET ME...
OF COURSE. GOOD LUCK.
CHAK
AH... YANAGI'S WONDERFUL. HE'S THE BEST.
NOW, THEN ...
THOK
OW!
LET'S GET RIGHT TO IT...
... ATARU.

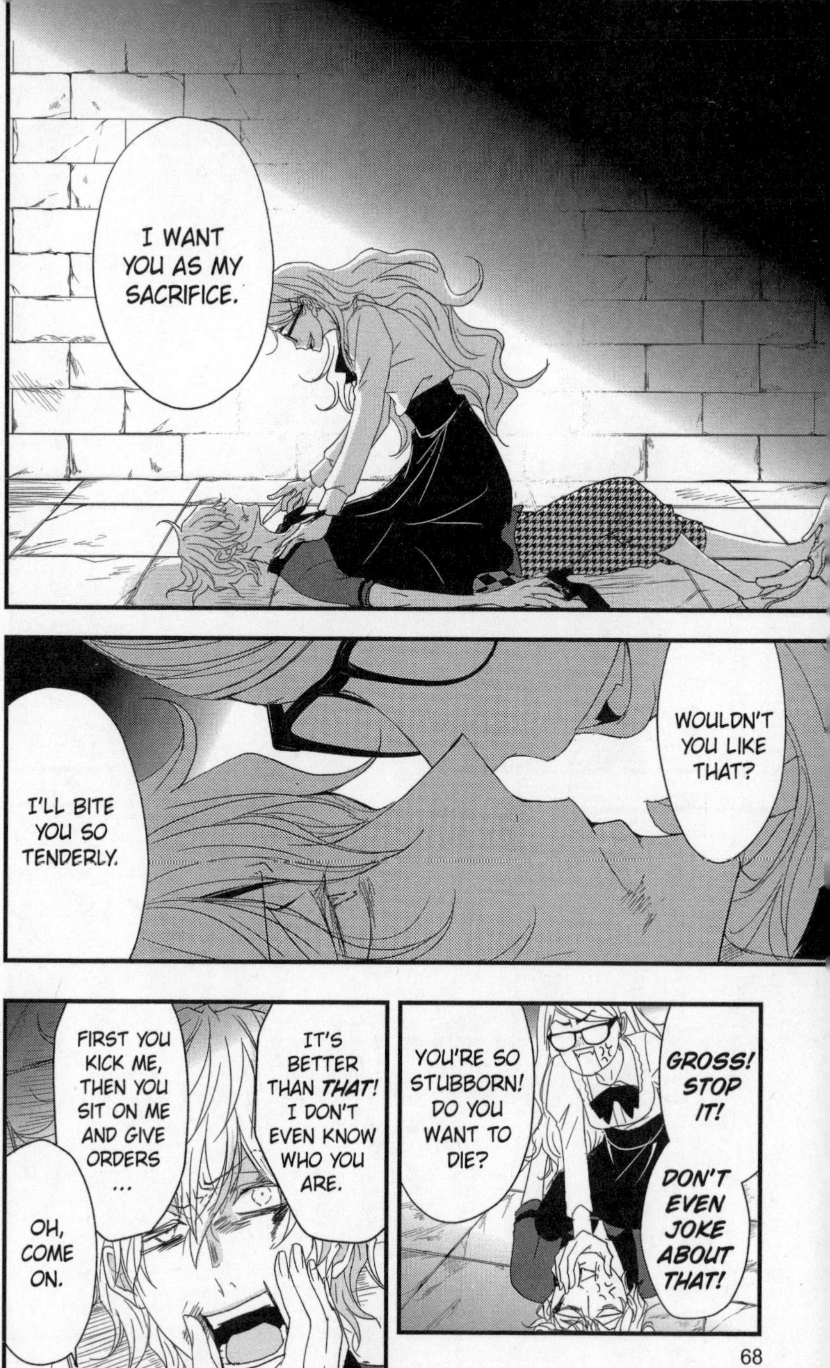

I WANT YOU AS MY SACRIFICE.
WOULDN'T YOU LIKE THAT?
I'LL BITE YOU SO TENDERLY.
GROSS! STOP IT!
YOU'RE SO STUBBORN! DO YOU WANT TO DIE?
DON'T EVEN JOKE ABOUT THAT!
IT'S BETTER THAN *THAT*! I DON'T EVEN KNOW WHO YOU ARE.
FIRST YOU KICK ME, THEN YOU SIT ON ME AND GIVE ORDERS ...
OH, COME ON.

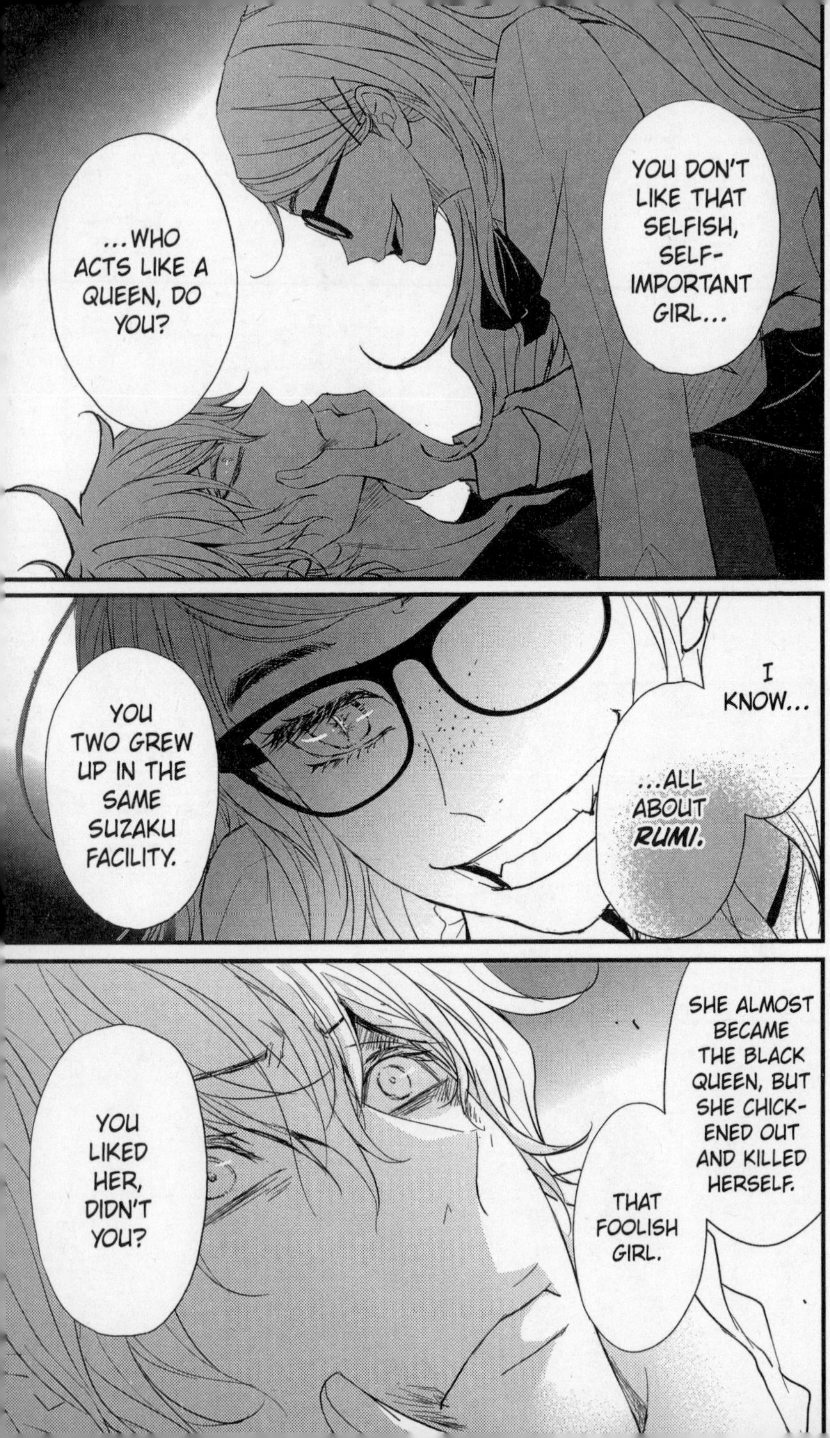
YOU DON'T LIKE THAT SELFISH, SELF-IMPORTANT GIRL...
...WHO ACTS LIKE A QUEEN, DO YOU?
I KNOW...
...ALL ABOUT RUMI.
YOU TWO GREW UP IN THE SAME SUZAKU FACILITY.
SHE ALMOST BECAME THE BLACK QUEEN, BUT SHE CHICK-ENED OUT AND KILLED HERSELF.
THAT FOOLISH GIRL.
YOU LIKED HER, DIDN'T YOU?

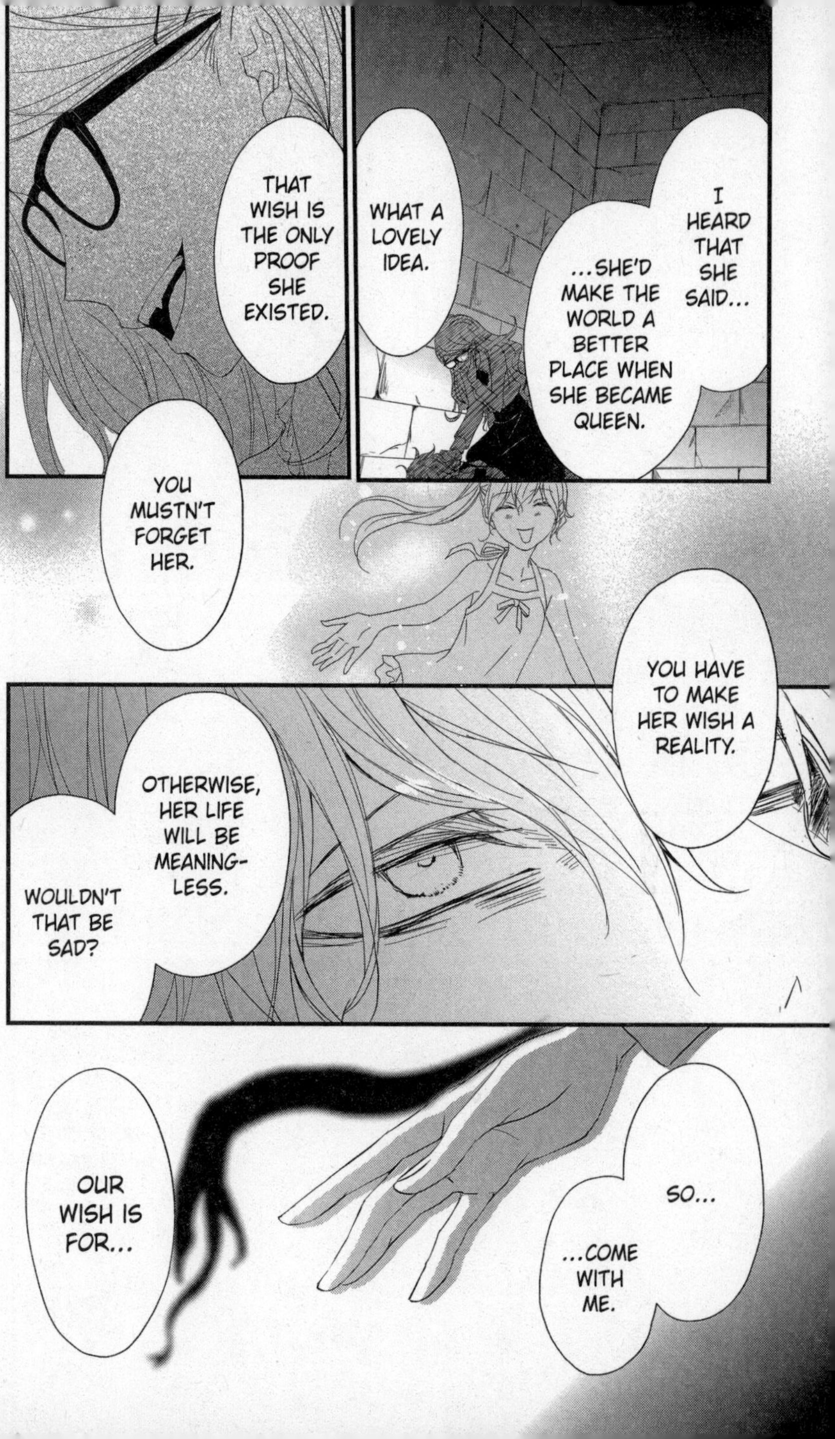
I HEARD THAT SHE SAID...
...SHE'D MAKE THE WORLD A BETTER PLACE WHEN SHE BECAME QUEEN.
WHAT A LOVELY IDEA.
THAT WISH IS THE ONLY PROOF SHE EXISTED.
YOU MUSTN'T FORGET HER.
YOU HAVE TO MAKE HER WISH A REALITY.
OTHERWISE, HER LIFE WILL BE MEANING-LESS.
WOULDN'T THAT BE SAD?
SO...
...COME WITH ME.
OUR WISH IS FOR...

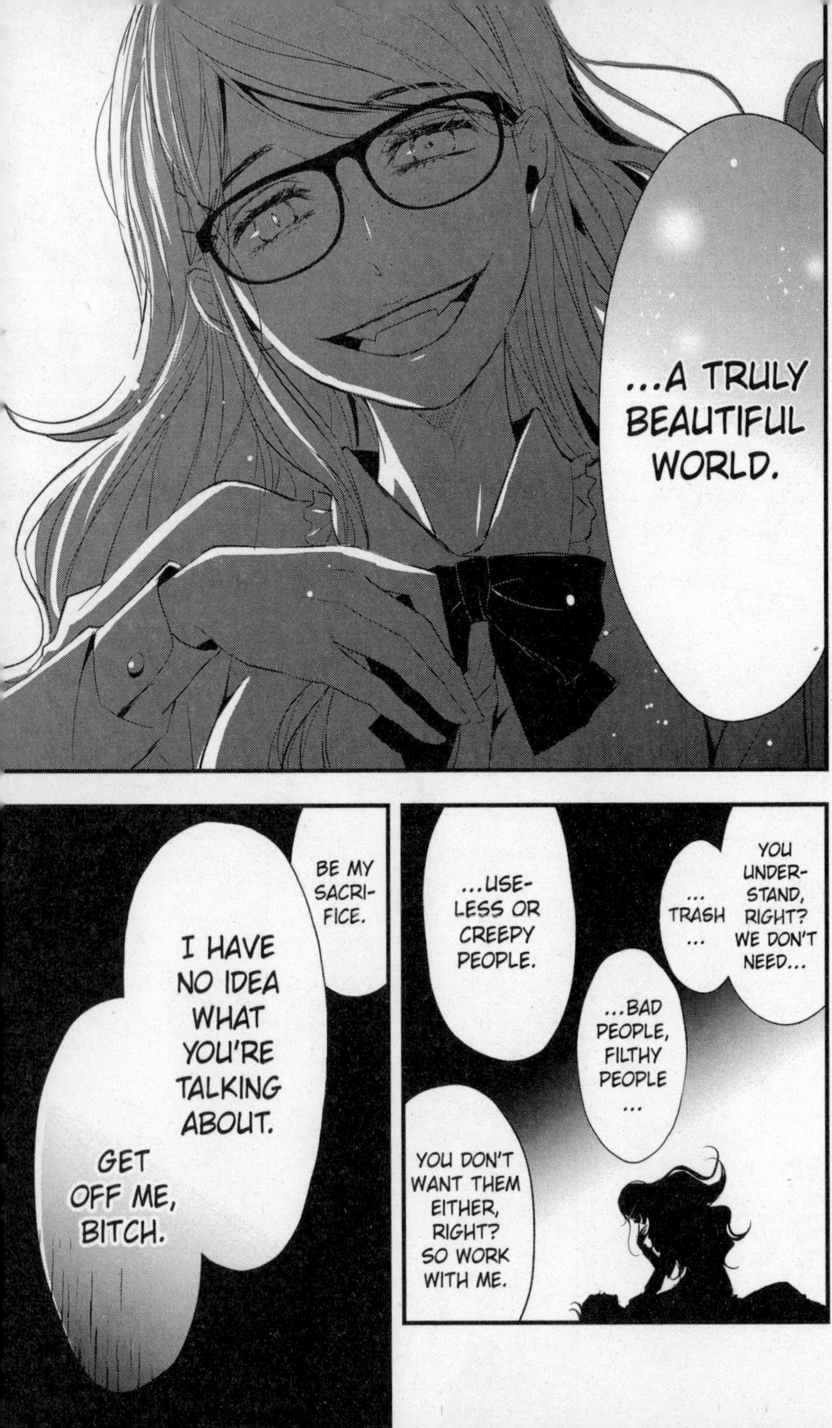
...A TRULY BEAUTIFUL WORLD.
YOU UNDERSTAND, RIGHT? WE DON'T NEED...
...TRASH...
...USELESS OR CREEPY PEOPLE.
...BAD PEOPLE, FILTHY PEOPLE...
YOU DON'T WANT THEM EITHER, RIGHT? SO WORK WITH ME.
BE MY SACRIFICE.
I HAVE NO IDEA WHAT YOU'RE TALKING ABOUT.
GET OFF ME, BITCH.

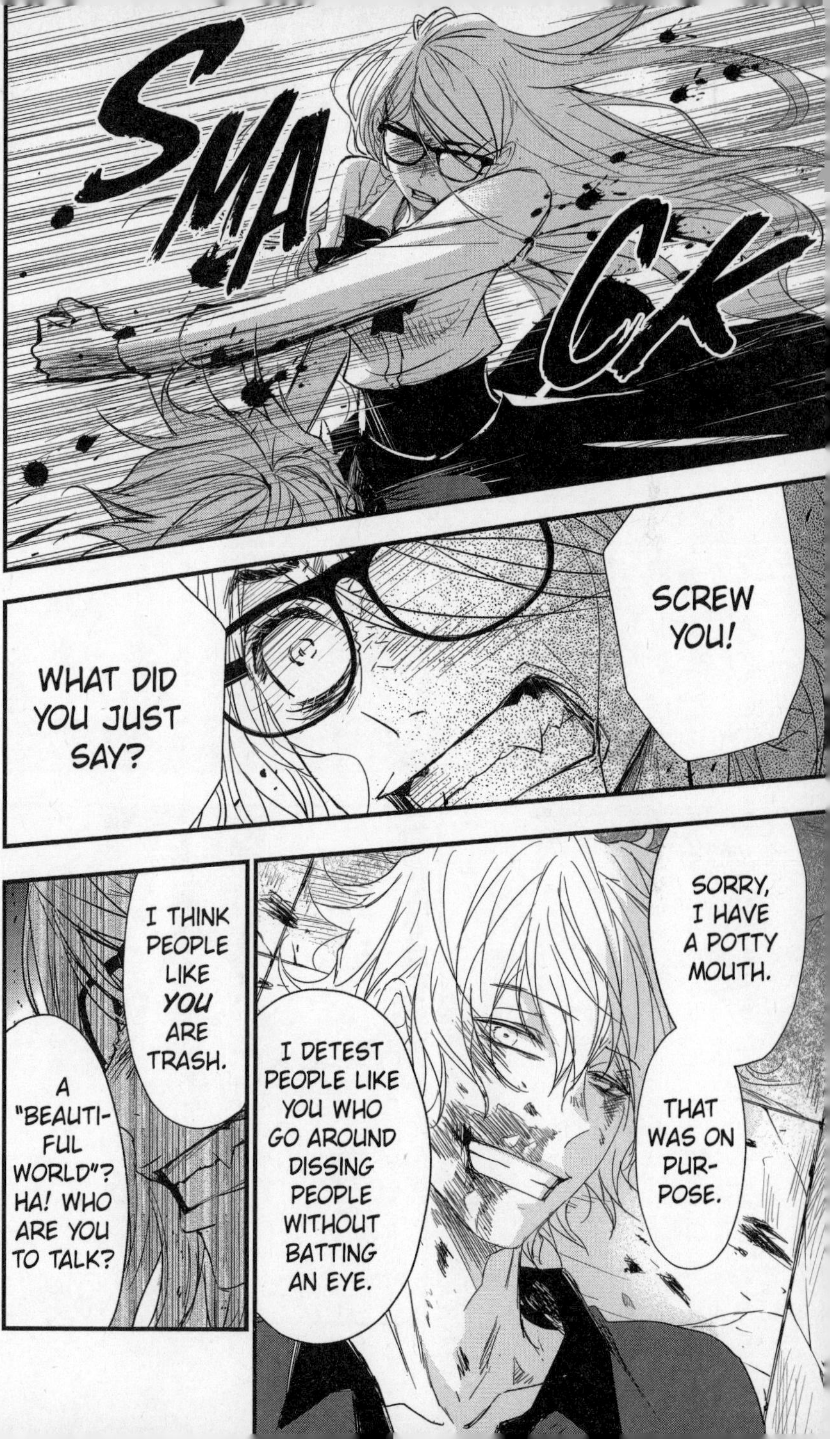
SMACK
SCREW YOU!
WHAT DID YOU JUST SAY?
SORRY, I HAVE A POTTY MOUTH.
THAT WAS ON PUR-POSE.
I DETEST PEOPLE LIKE YOU WHO GO AROUND DISSING PEOPLE WITHOUT BATTING AN EYE.
I THINK PEOPLE LIKE *YOU* ARE TRASH.
A "BEAUTI-FUL WORLD"? HA! WHO ARE YOU TO TALK?

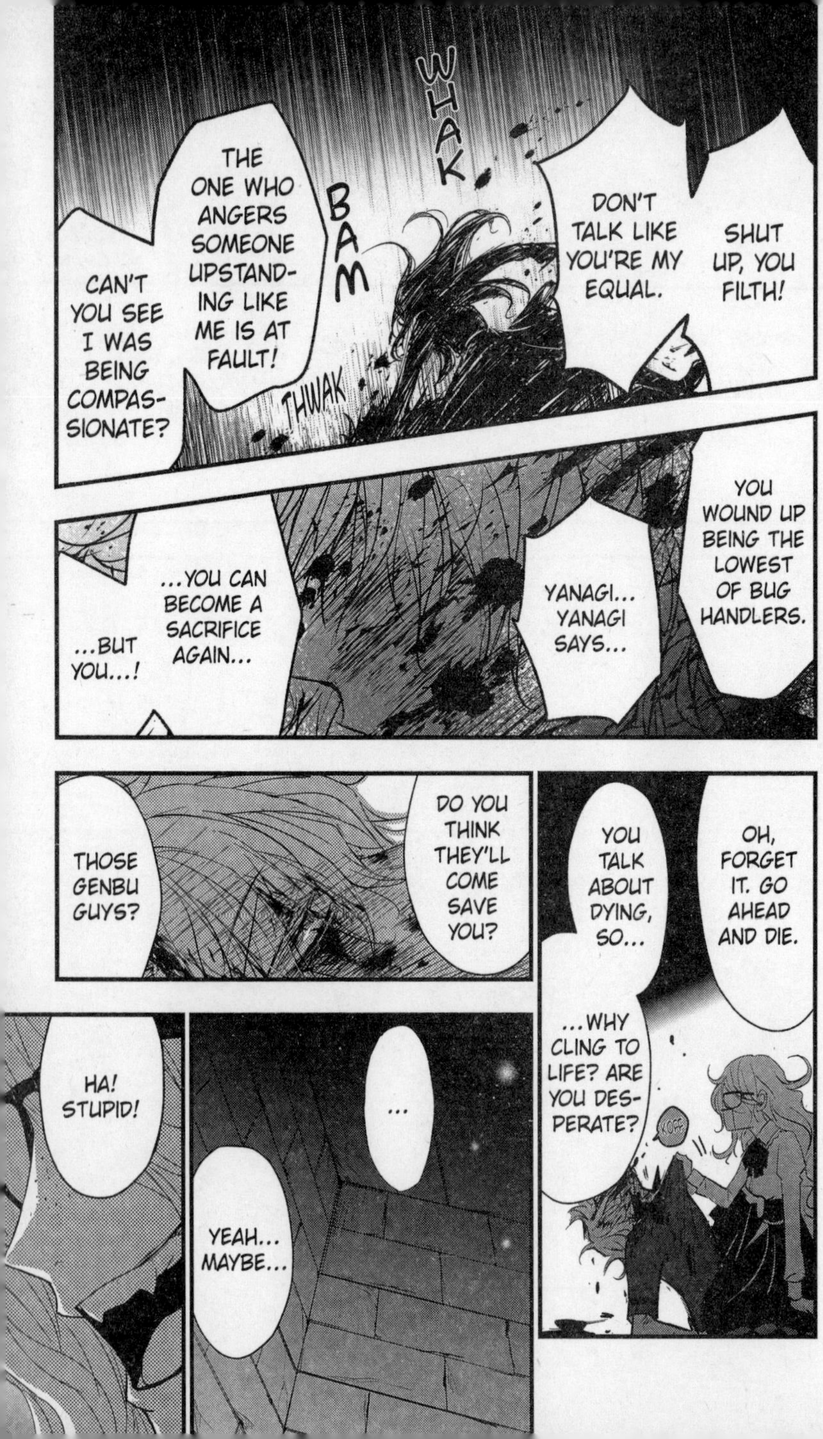
SHUT UP, YOU FILTH!
DON'T TALK LIKE YOU'RE MY EQUAL.
WHAK
BAM
THE ONE WHO ANGERS SOMEONE UPSTANDING LIKE ME IS AT FAULT!
CAN'T YOU SEE I WAS BEING COMPASSIONATE?
THWAK
YOU WOUND UP BEING THE LOWEST OF BUG HANDLERS.
YANAGI... YANAGI SAYS...
...YOU CAN BECOME A SACRIFICE AGAIN...
...BUT YOU...!
OH, FORGET IT. GO AHEAD AND DIE.
YOU TALK ABOUT DYING, SO...
...WHY CLING TO LIFE? ARE YOU DESPERATE?
KOFF
DO YOU THINK THEY'LL COME SAVE YOU?
THOSE GENBU GUYS?
...
YEAH... MAYBE...
HA! STUPID!

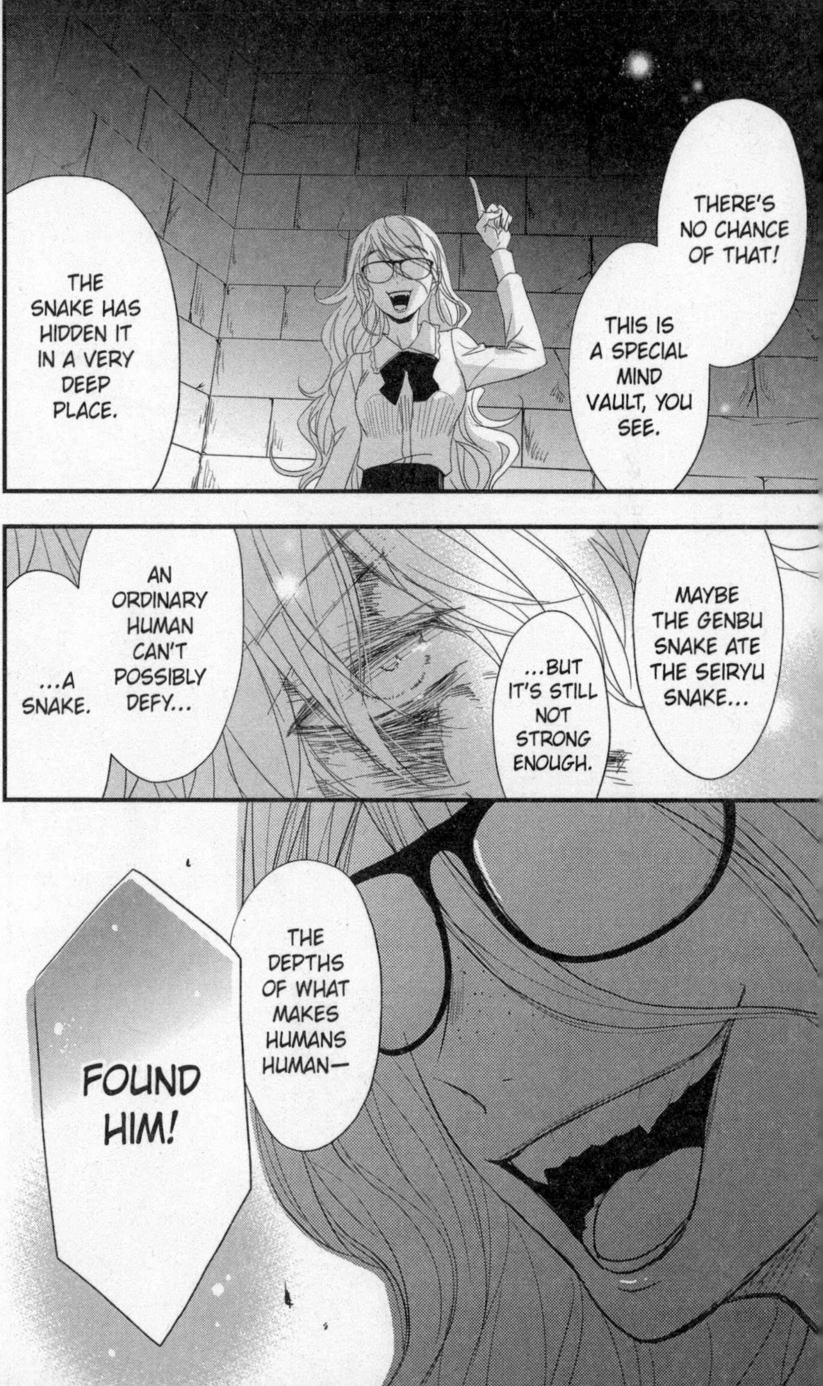
THERE'S NO CHANCE OF THAT!
THIS IS A SPECIAL MIND VAULT, YOU SEE.
THE SNAKE HAS HIDDEN IT IN A VERY DEEP PLACE.
MAYBE THE GENBU SNAKE ATE THE SEIRYU SNAKE...
...BUT IT'S STILL NOT STRONG ENOUGH.
AN ORDINARY HUMAN CAN'T POSSIBLY DEFY...
...A SNAKE.
THE DEPTHS OF WHAT MAKES HUMANS HUMAN—
FOUND HIM!

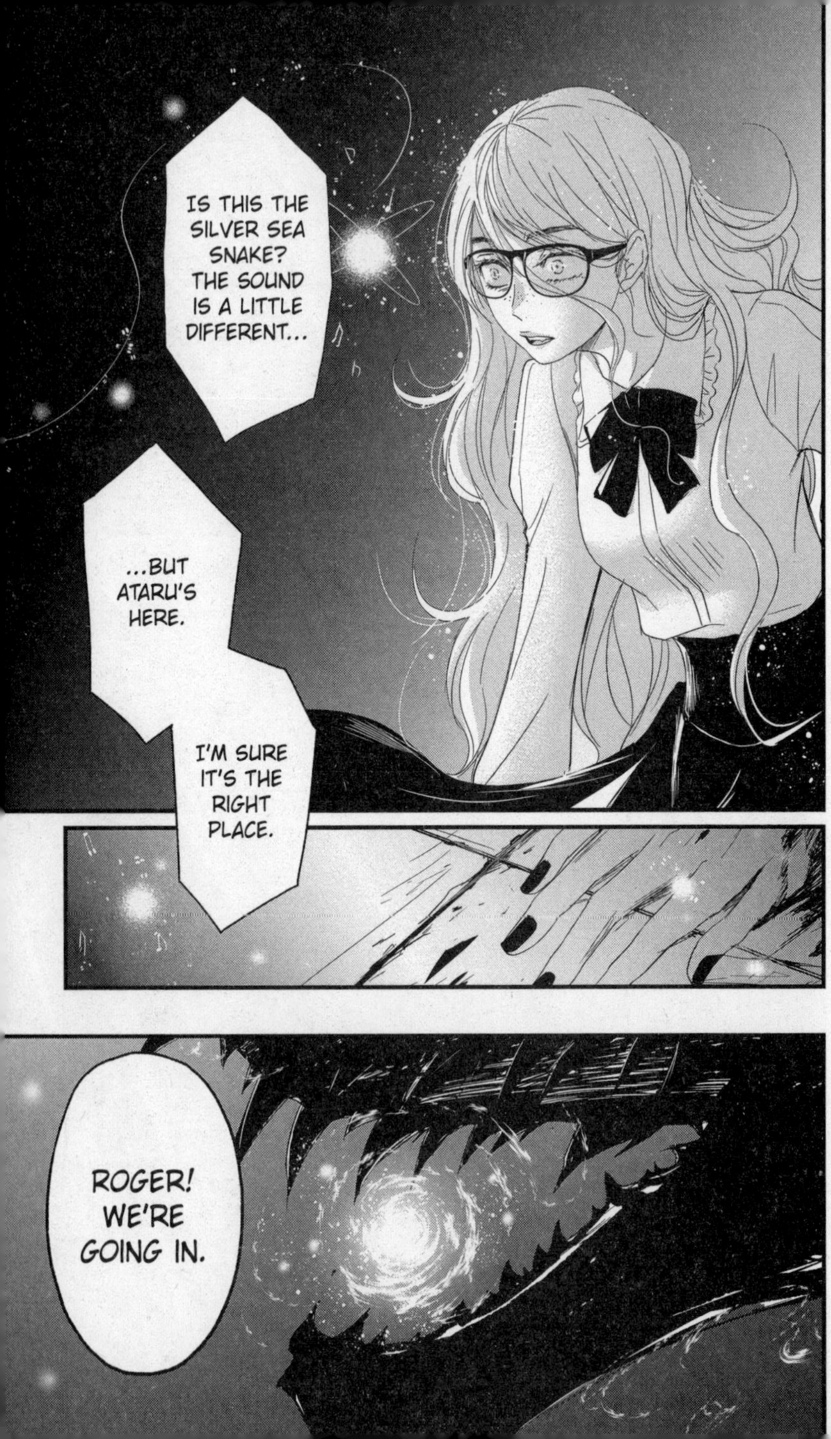
IS THIS THE SILVER SEA SNAKE? THE SOUND IS A LITTLE DIFFERENT...
...BUT ATARU'S HERE.
I'M SURE IT'S THE RIGHT PLACE.
ROGER! WE'RE GOING IN.

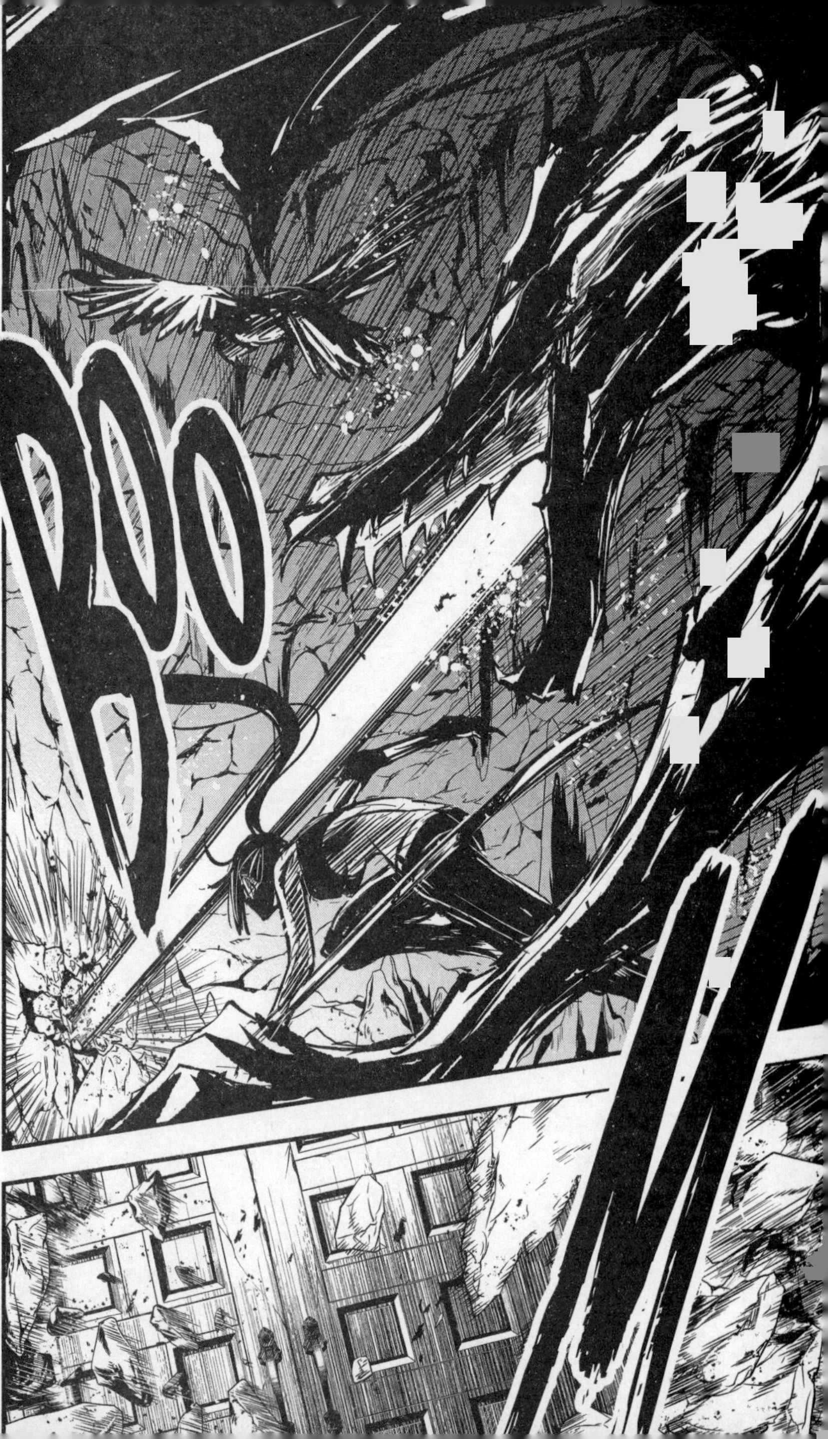

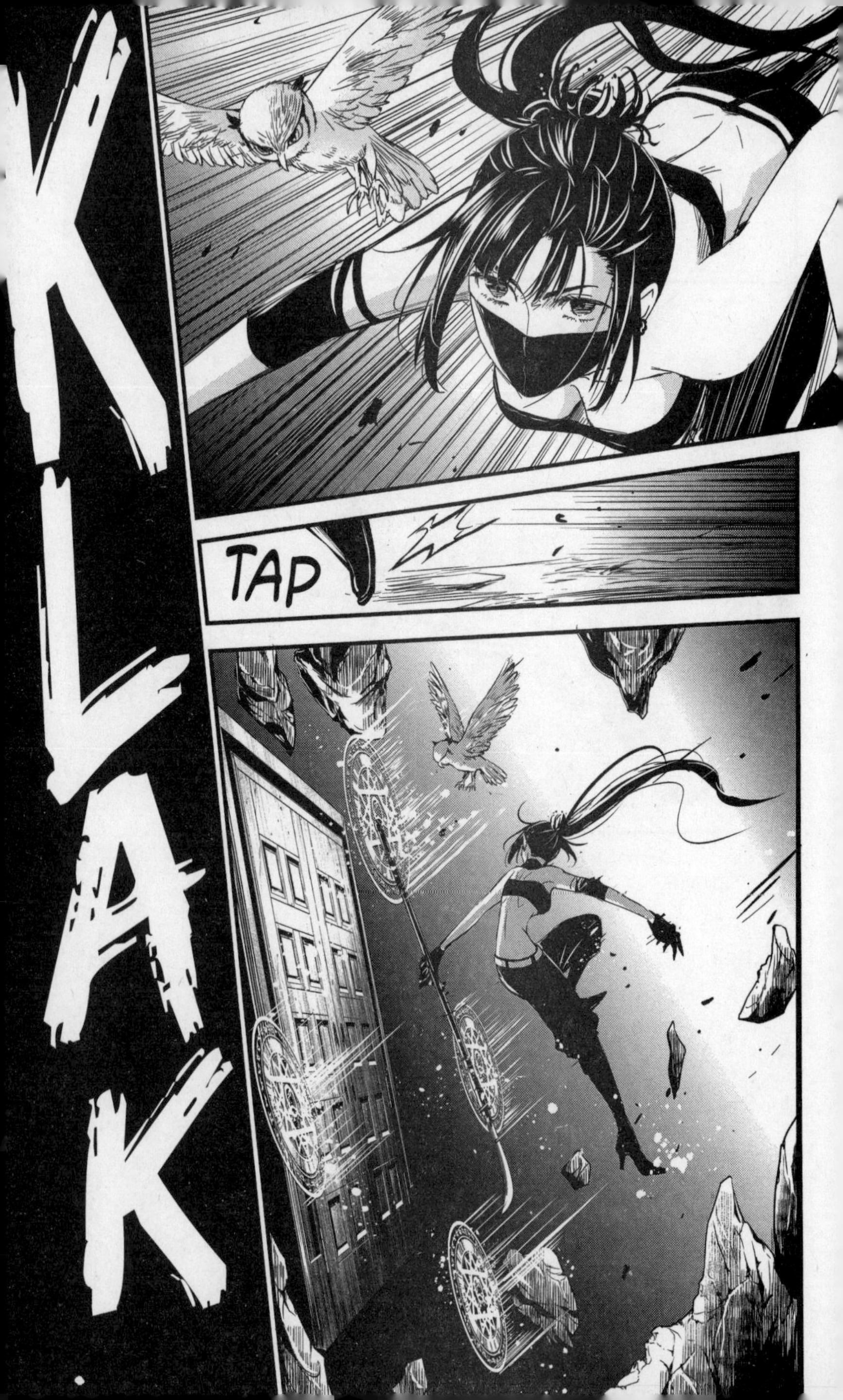
TAP
KLAK

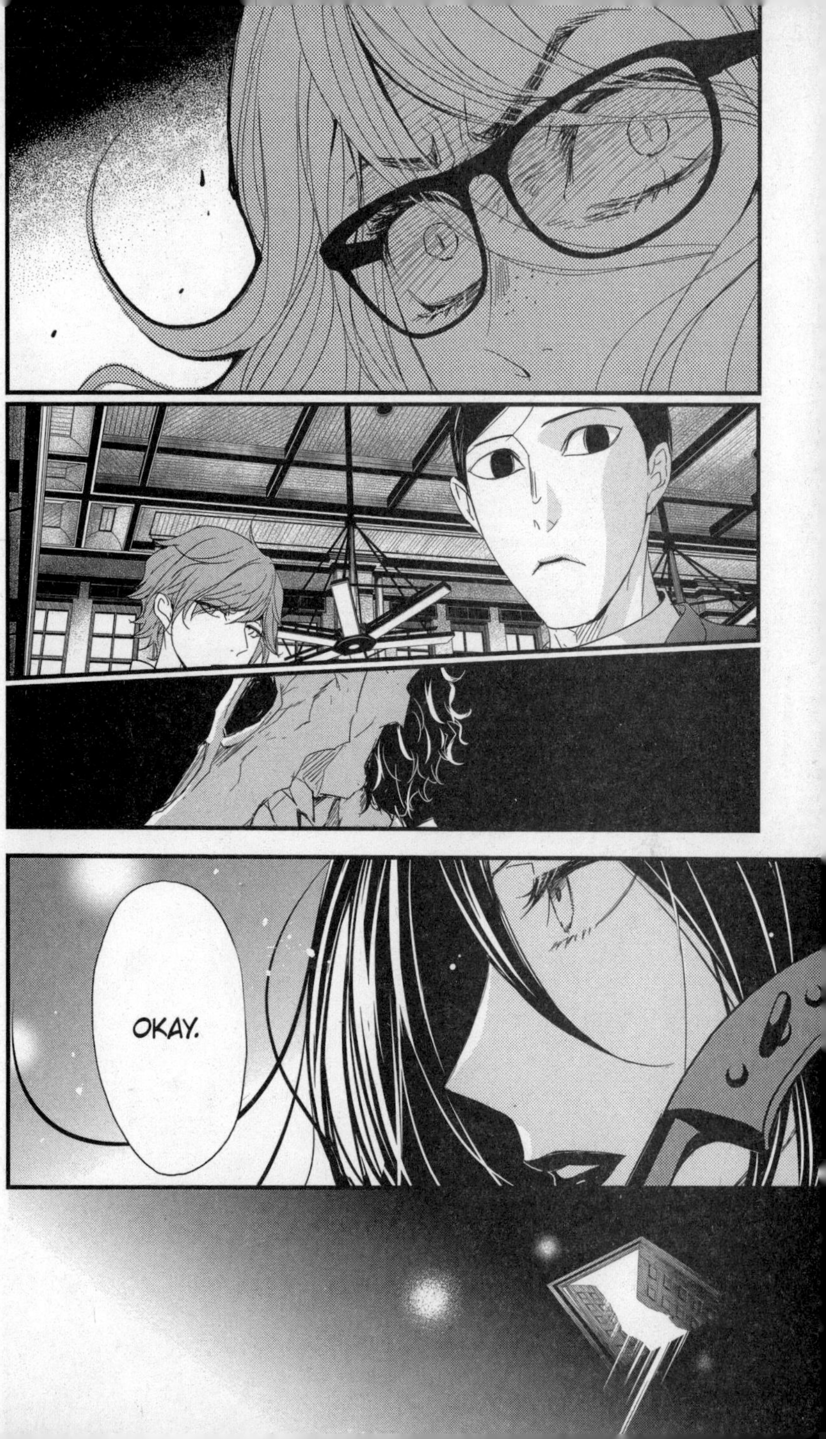
OKAY.

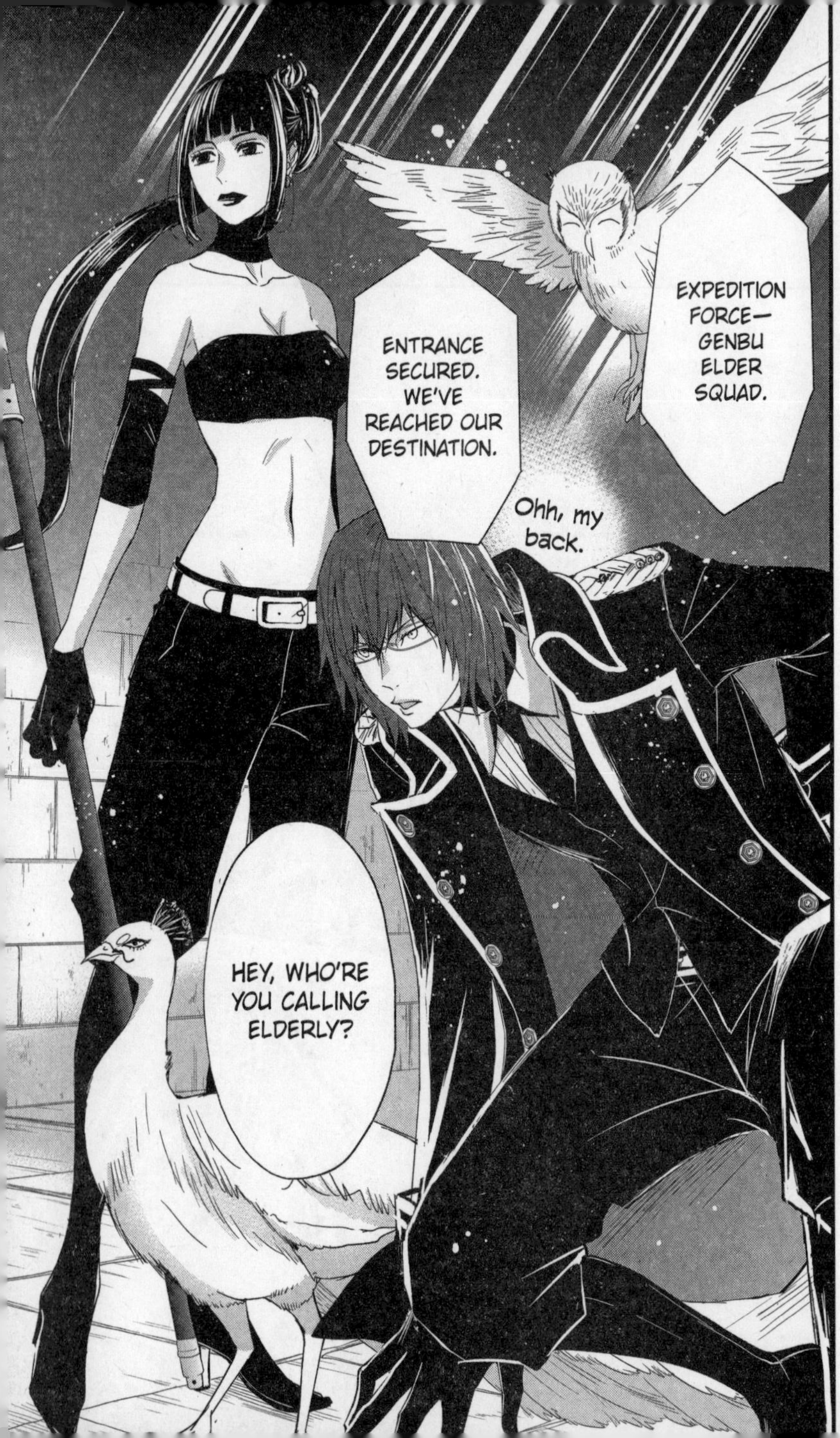
EXPEDITION FORCE—GENBU ELDER SQUAD.
ENTRANCE SECURED. WE'VE REACHED OUR DESTINATION.
Ohh, my back.
HEY, WHO'RE YOU CALLING ELDERLY?

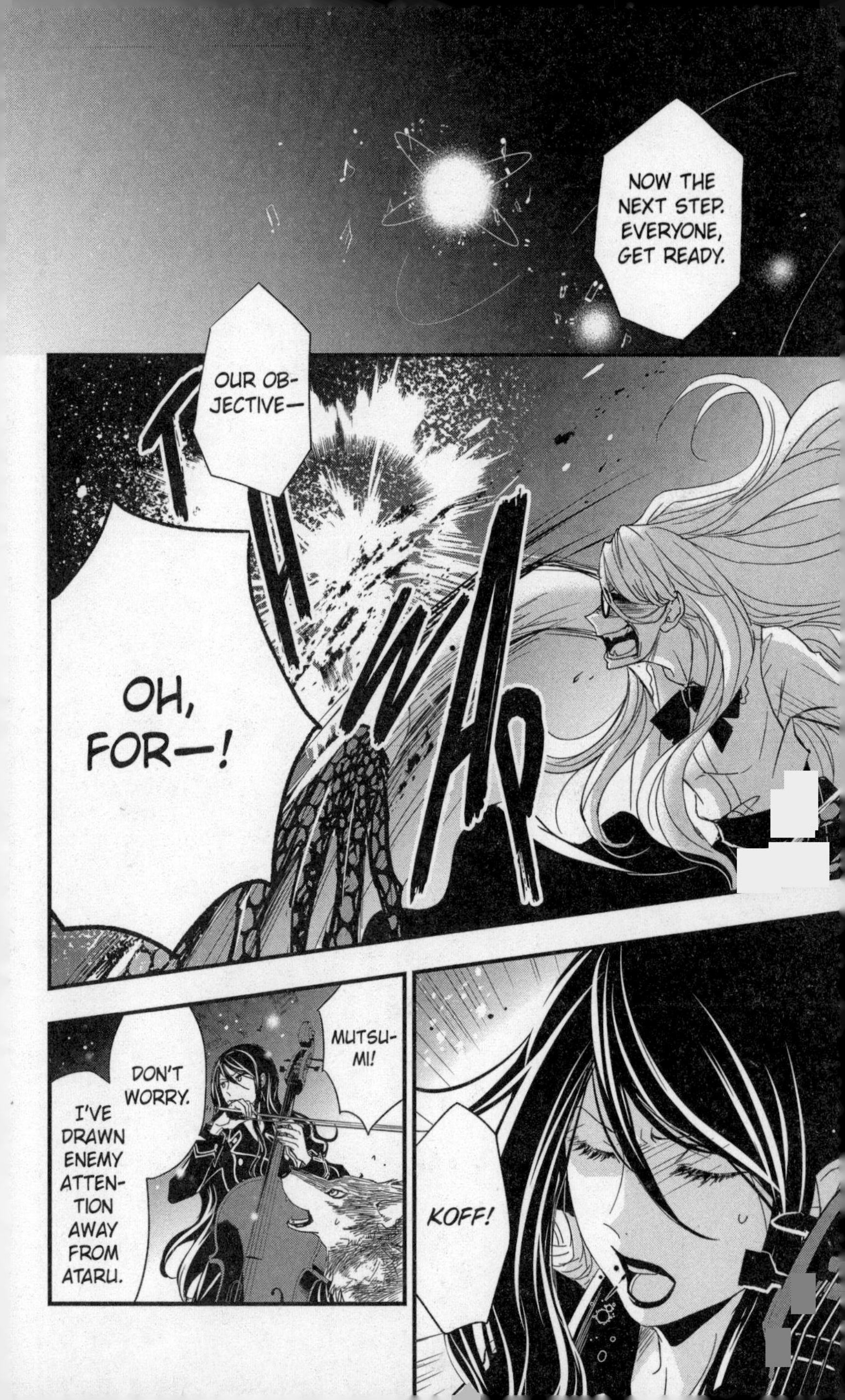
NOW THE NEXT STEP. EVERYONE, GET READY.
OUR OB-JECTIVE—
THWAP
OH, FOR—!
KOFF!
MUTSU-MI!
DON'T WORRY.
I'VE DRAWN ENEMY ATTEN-TION AWAY FROM ATARU.

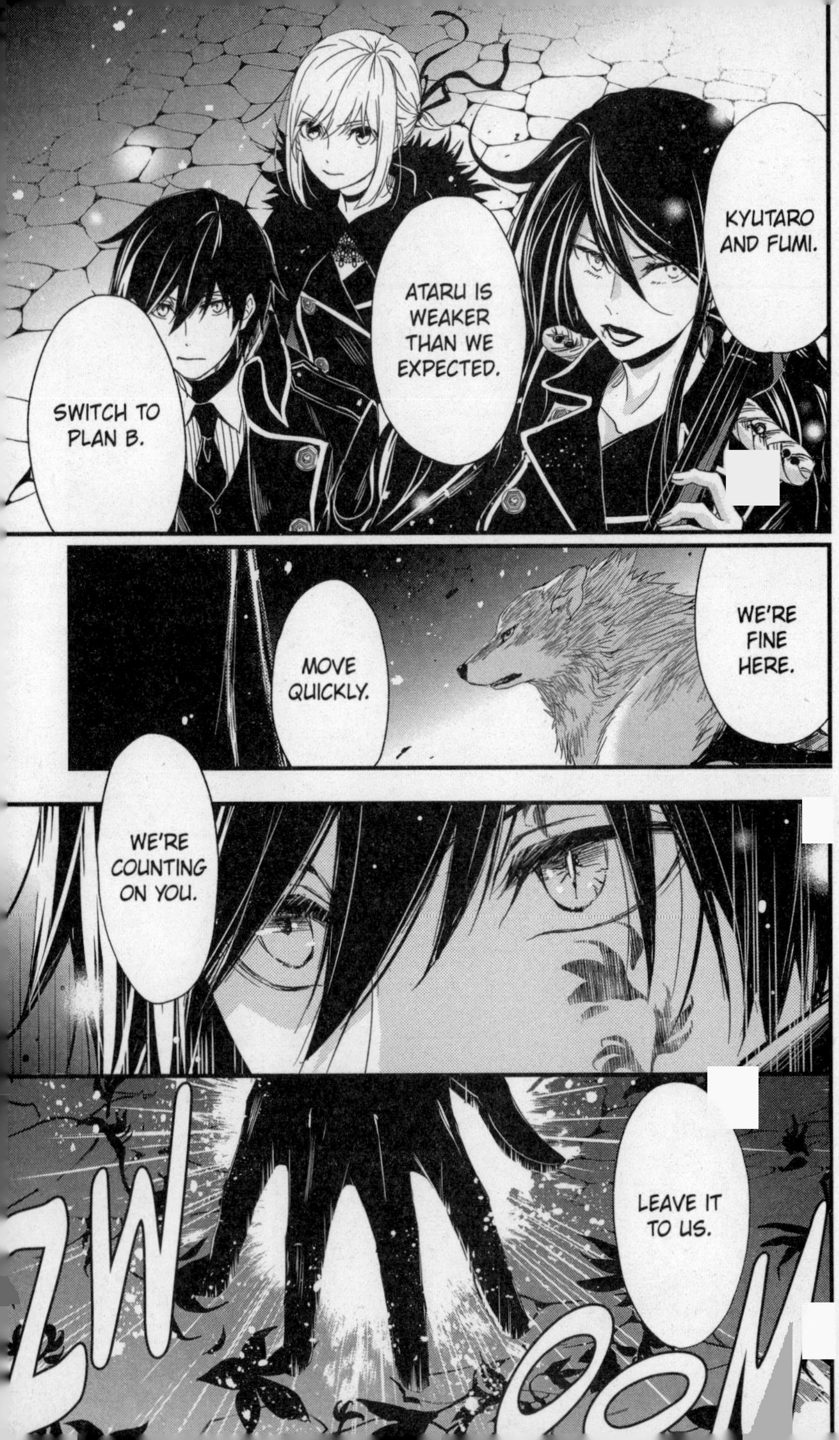
KYUTARO AND FUMI.
ATARU IS WEAKER THAN WE EXPECTED.
SWITCH TO PLAN B.
WE'RE FINE HERE.
MOVE QUICKLY.
WE'RE COUNTING ON YOU.
LEAVE IT TO US.
ZWOOM

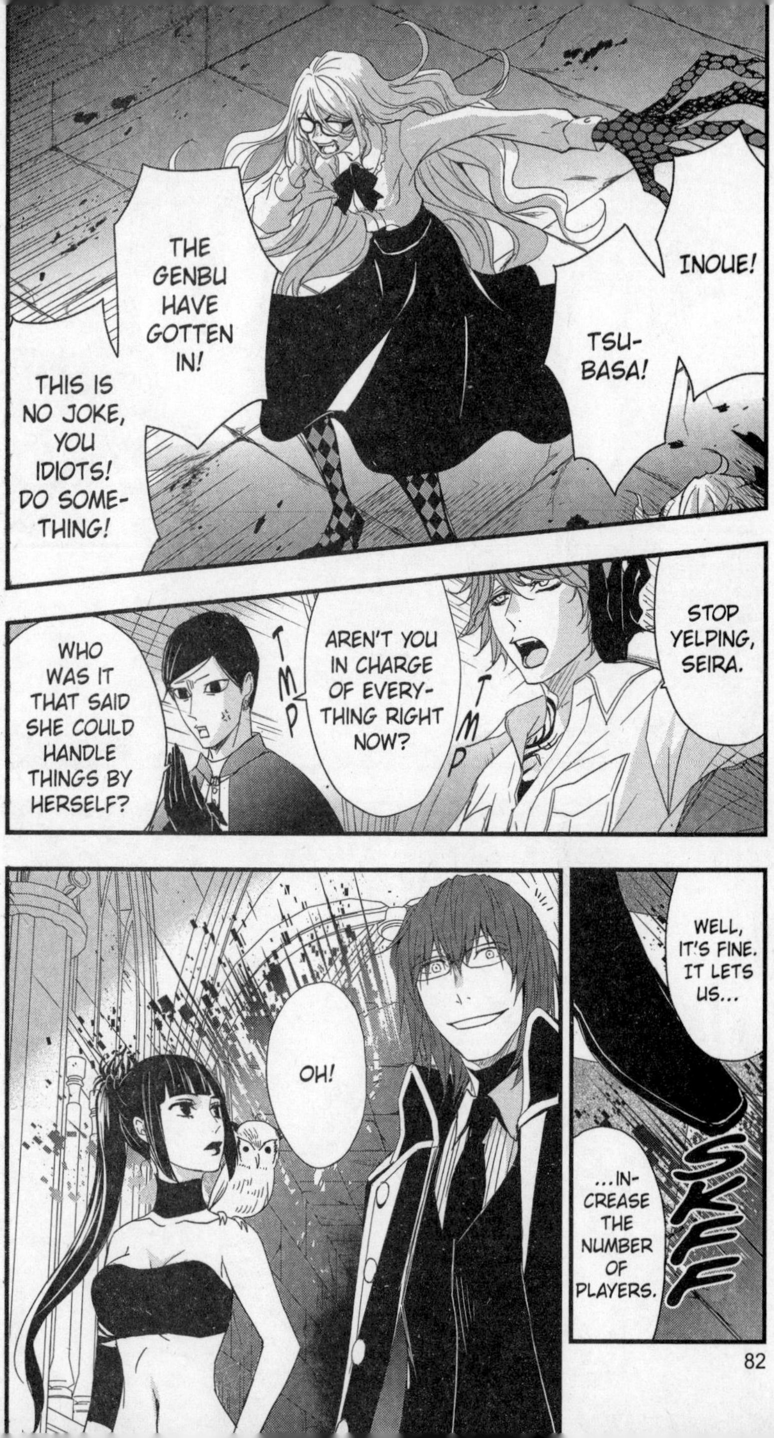
INOUE!
TSU-
BASA!
THE GENBU HAVE GOTTEN IN!
THIS IS NO JOKE, YOU IDIOTS! DO SOME-
THING!
STOP YELPING, SEIRA.
TMP
AREN'T YOU IN CHARGE OF EVERY-
THING RIGHT NOW?
TMP
WHO WAS IT THAT SAID SHE COULD HANDLE THINGS BY HERSELF?
WELL, IT'S FINE. IT LETS US...
...IN-
CREASE THE NUMBER OF PLAYERS.
SKFF
OH!

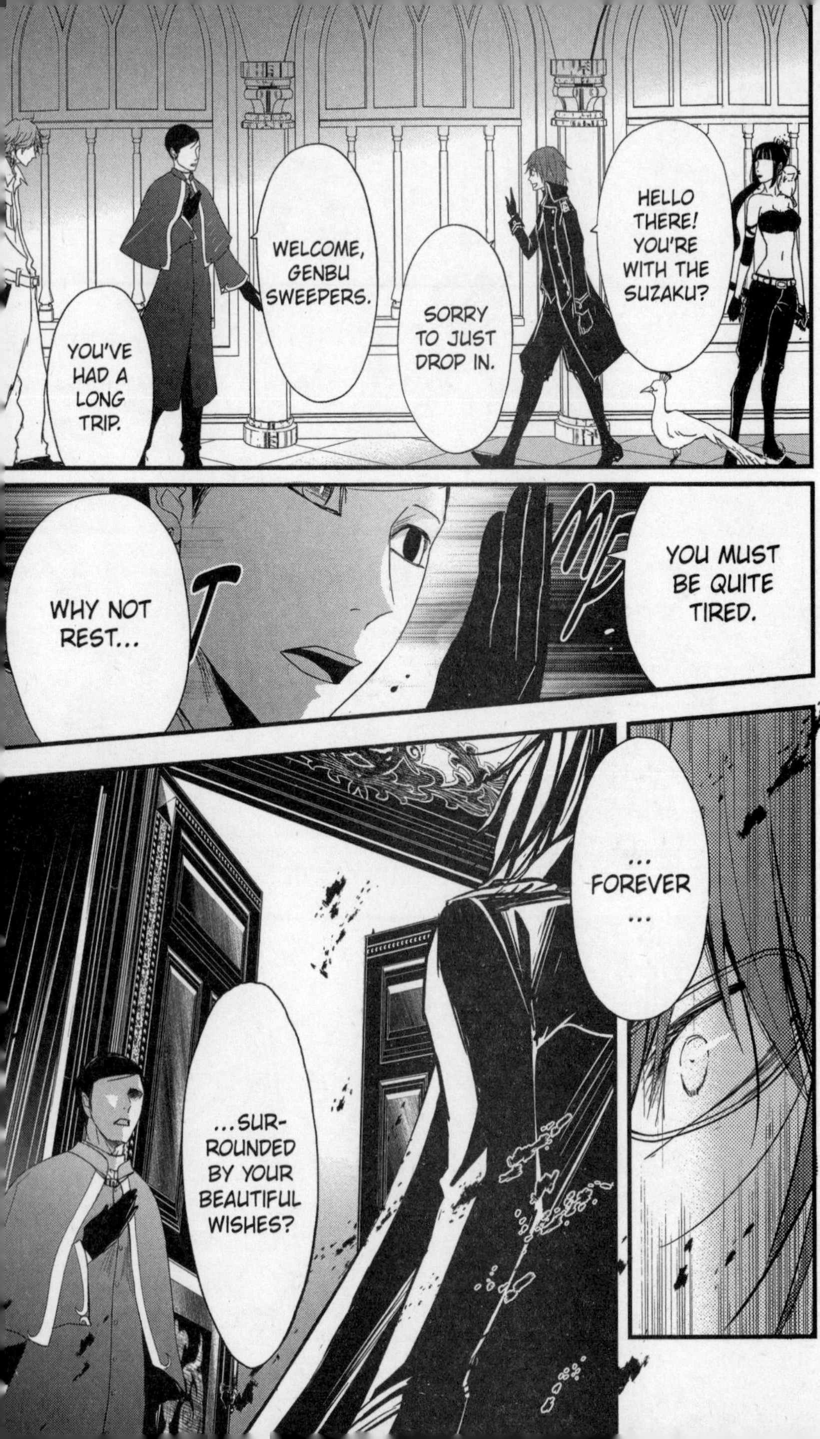
HELLO THERE! YOU'RE WITH THE SUZAKU?
SORRY TO JUST DROP IN.
WELCOME, GENBU SWEEPERS.
YOU'VE HAD A LONG TRIP.
YOU MUST BE QUITE TIRED.
WHY NOT REST...
...FOREVER...
...SUR-ROUNDED BY YOUR BEAUTIFUL WISHES?

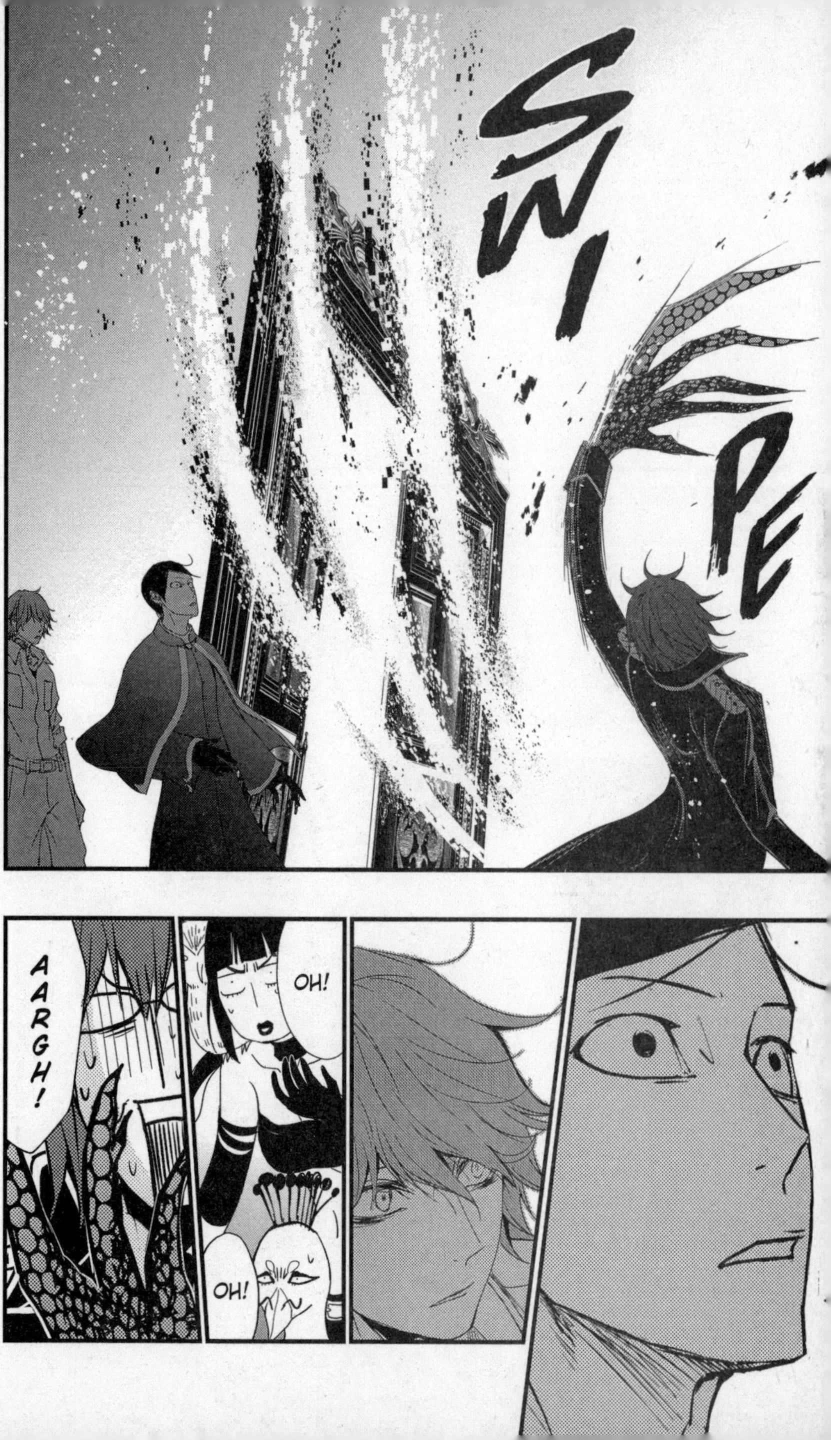
SWIPE
OH!
OH!
AARGH!

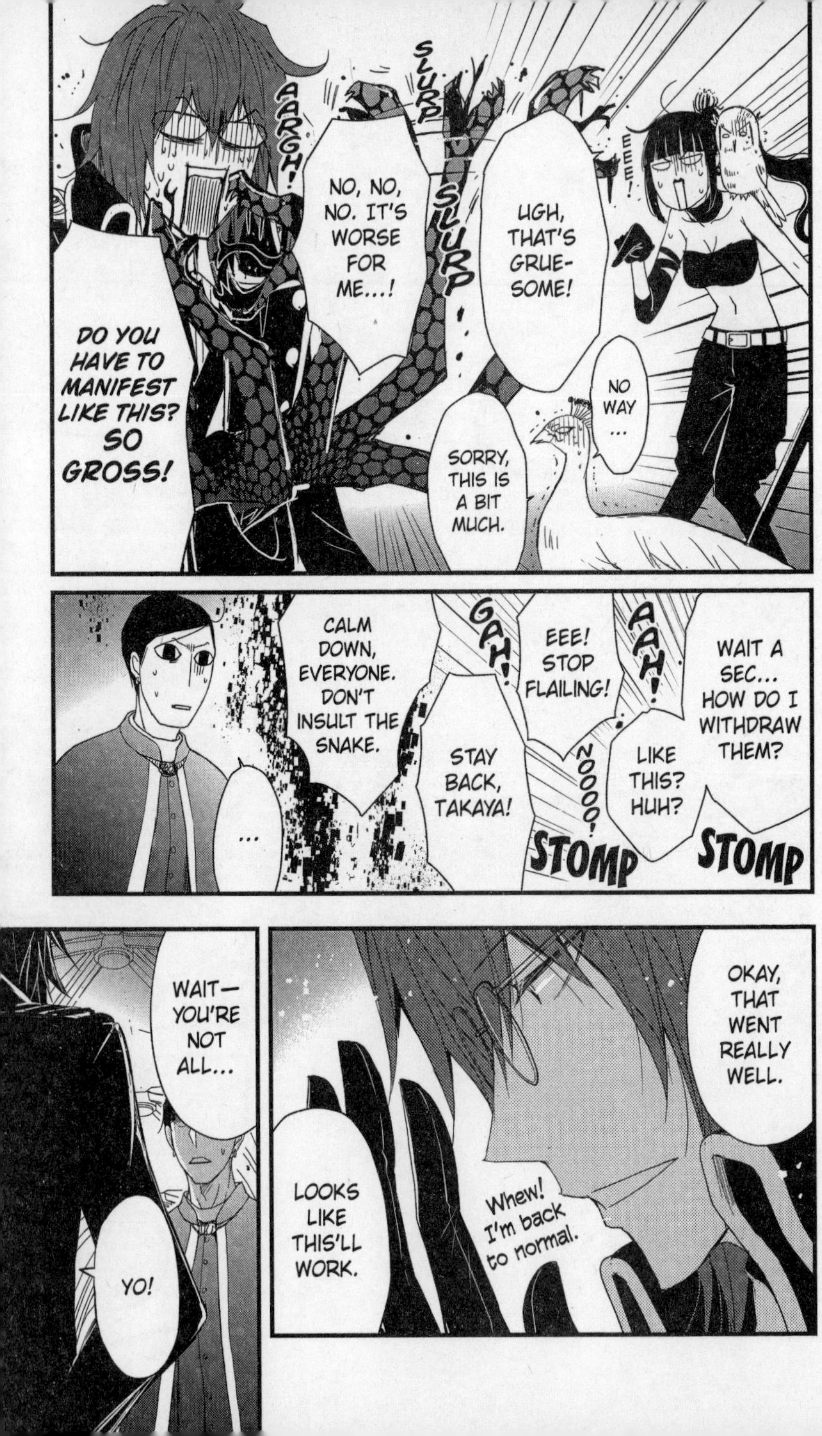
EEE!
UGH, THAT'S GRUE-SOME!
NO WAY ...
SLURP
SLURP
NO, NO, NO. IT'S WORSE FOR ME...!
AARGH!
SORRY, THIS IS A BIT MUCH.
DO YOU HAVE TO MANIFEST LIKE THIS? SO GROSS!
WAIT A SEC... HOW DO I WITHDRAW THEM?
AAH!
LIKE THIS? HUH?
STOMP
EEE! STOP FLAILING!
GAH!
NOOOO!
STOMP
STAY BACK, TAKAYA!
CALM DOWN, EVERYONE. DON'T INSULT THE SNAKE.
...
OKAY, THAT WENT REALLY WELL.
Whew! I'm back to normal.
LOOKS LIKE THIS'LL WORK.
WAIT—YOU'RE NOT ALL...
YO!

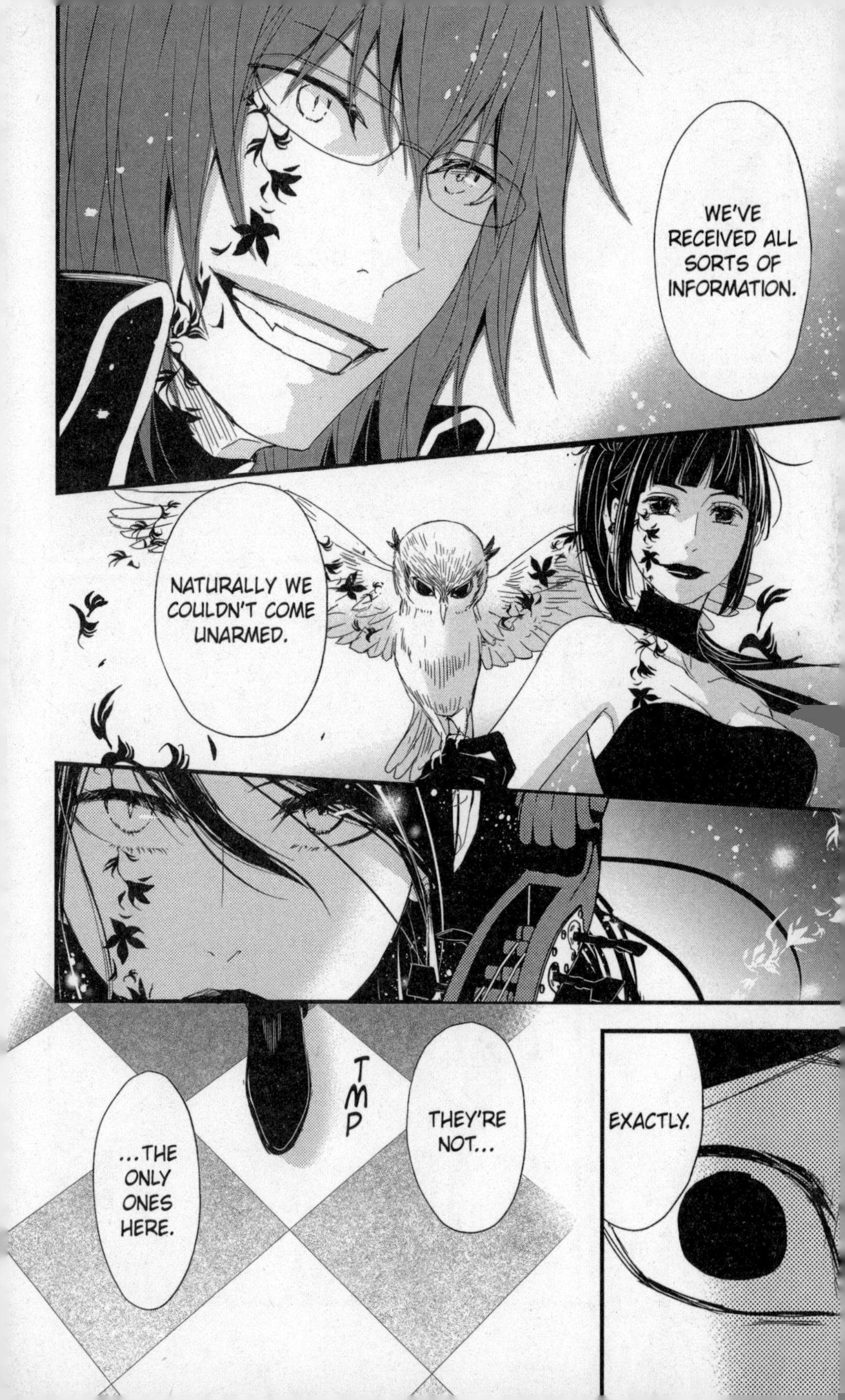
WE'VE RECEIVED ALL SORTS OF INFORMATION.
NATURALLY WE COULDN'T COME UNARMED.
EXACTLY.
THEY'RE NOT...
TMP
...THE ONLY ONES HERE.

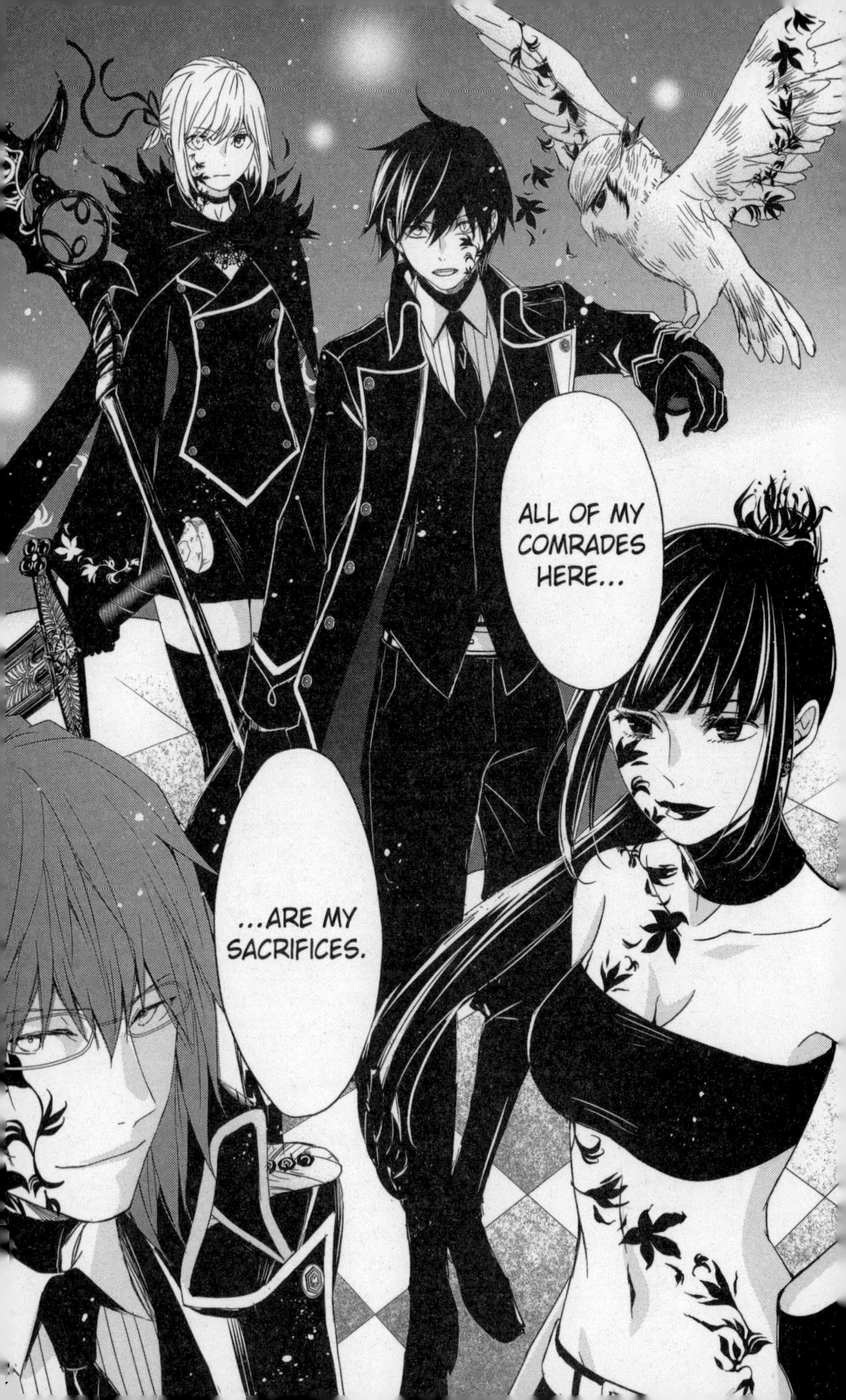
ALL OF MY COMRADES HERE...
...ARE MY SACRIFICES.

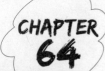

MONTHLY BETSUCOMI SALE DATE NOTICE ON TWITTER

CHAPTER 64

HEH! THE SUZAKU UNDERESTI-MATED US. THE GENBU HAVE MUTSUMI ON OUR SIDE.
WITH HER "SCARY SAUCER-EYED CHALLENGE," VICTORY IS OURS!
I DON'T REMEMBER A CHALLENGE LIKE THAT...
But we'll take whatever win we can get.

LET'S SEE... WHAT'S UP IN *QUEEN'S QUALITY* THIS MONTH?
1) I DIDN'T SPELL IT OUT, BUT THE PEACOCK IS MIZUHO.
2) CAN A WOMAN'S CLEAVAGE HOLD SO MUCH? ISN'T THAT SO CONVENIENT?
3) GENBU PEOPLE, YOUR FACIAL EXPRESSIONS ARE NO MATCH FOR THOSE OF THE SUZAKU.

WHILE DRAWING THE SUZAKU CHARACTERS IN CHAPTER 64, I FOUND I KEPT OPENING MY EYES TOO WIDE, WORSENING MY DRY EYE PROBLEM.

FUMI'S FACE WAS PRETTY BAD IN THIS CHAPTER, BUT I FOUND KYUTARO'S SUBTLE FACIAL EXPRESSIONS HARDER TO DRAW.

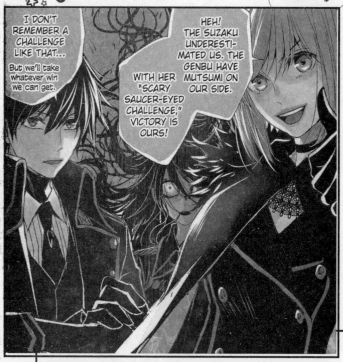

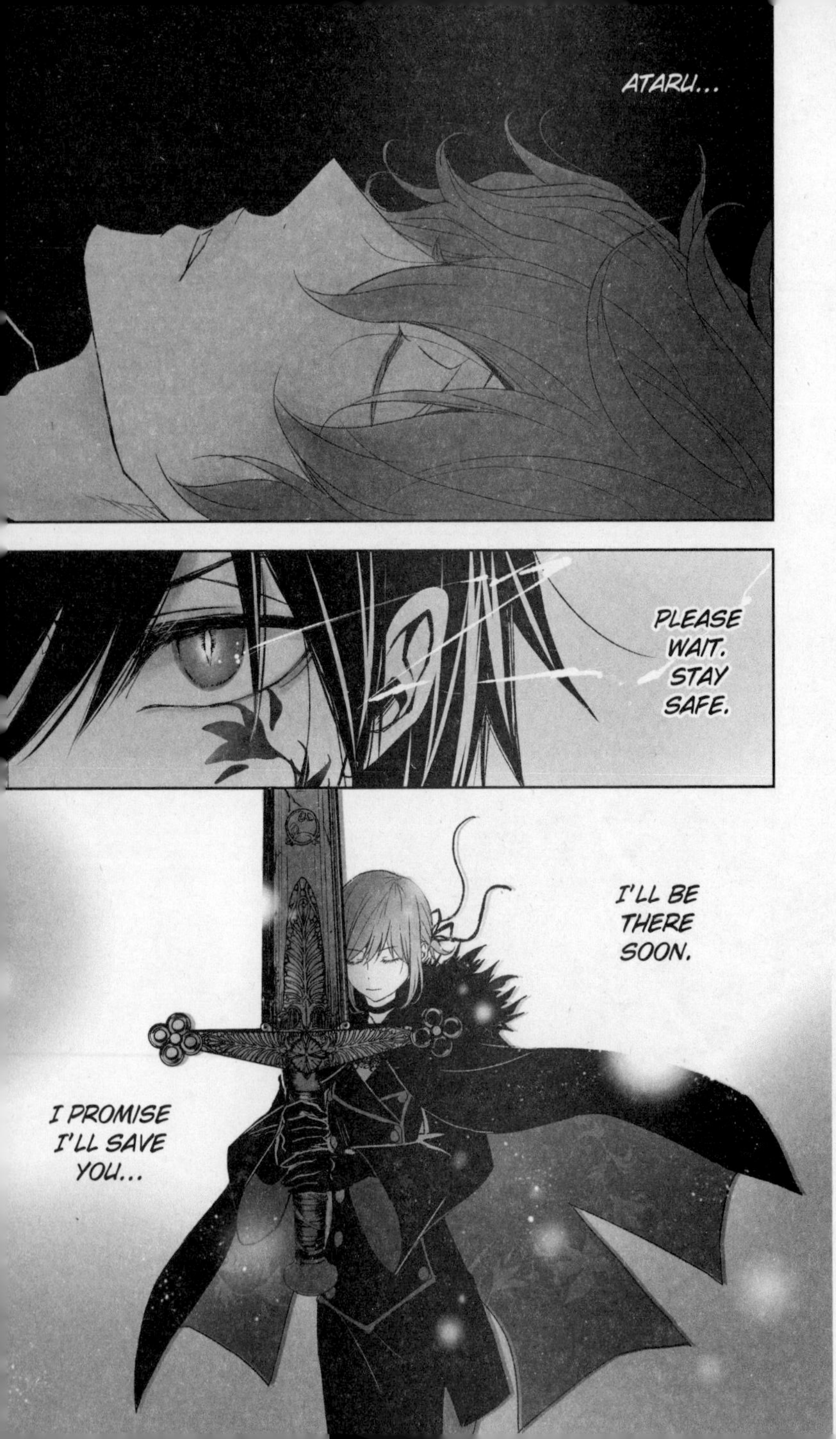
ATARU...
PLEASE WAIT. STAY SAFE.
I'LL BE THERE SOON.
I PROMISE I'LL SAVE YOU...

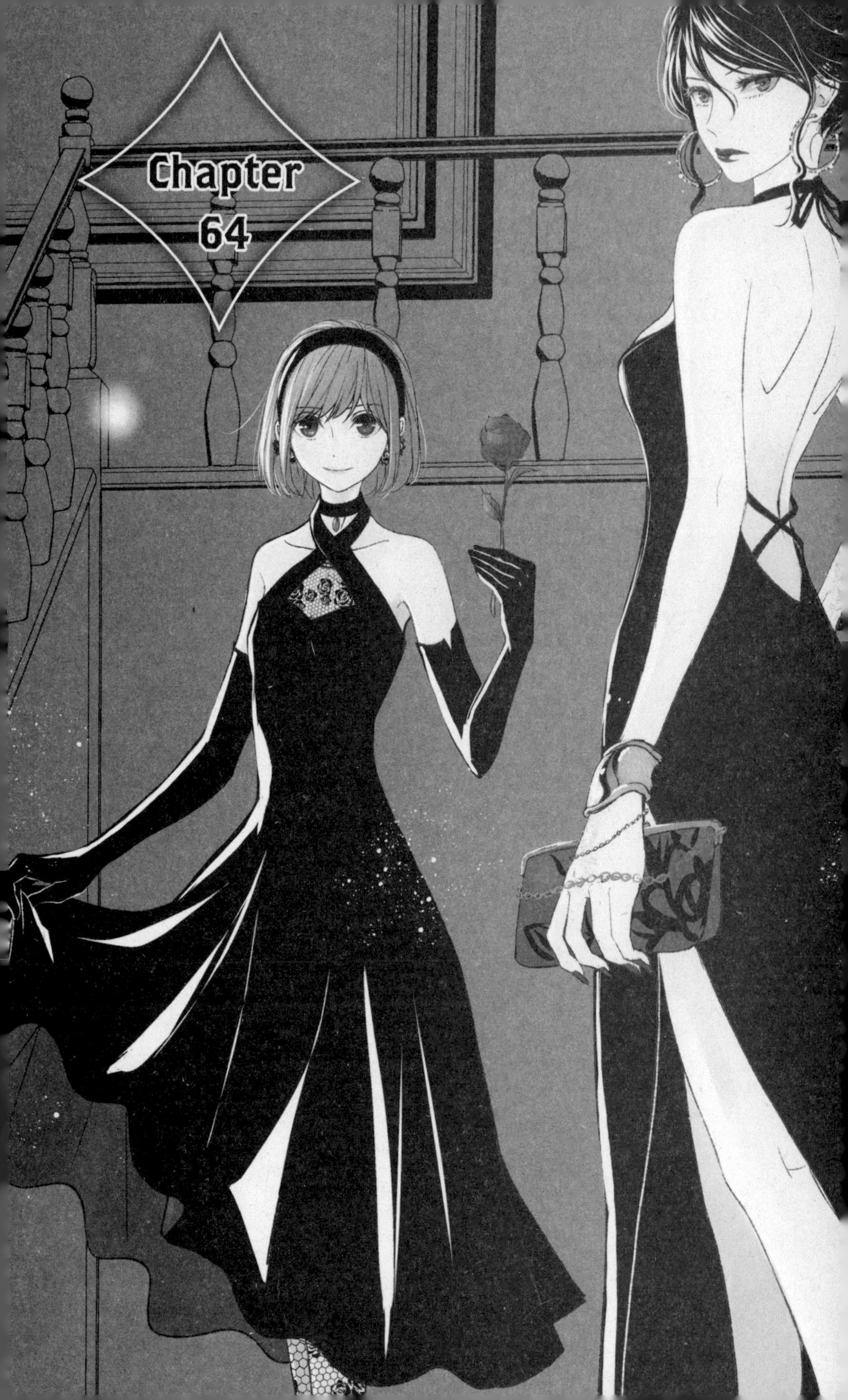
Chapter
64

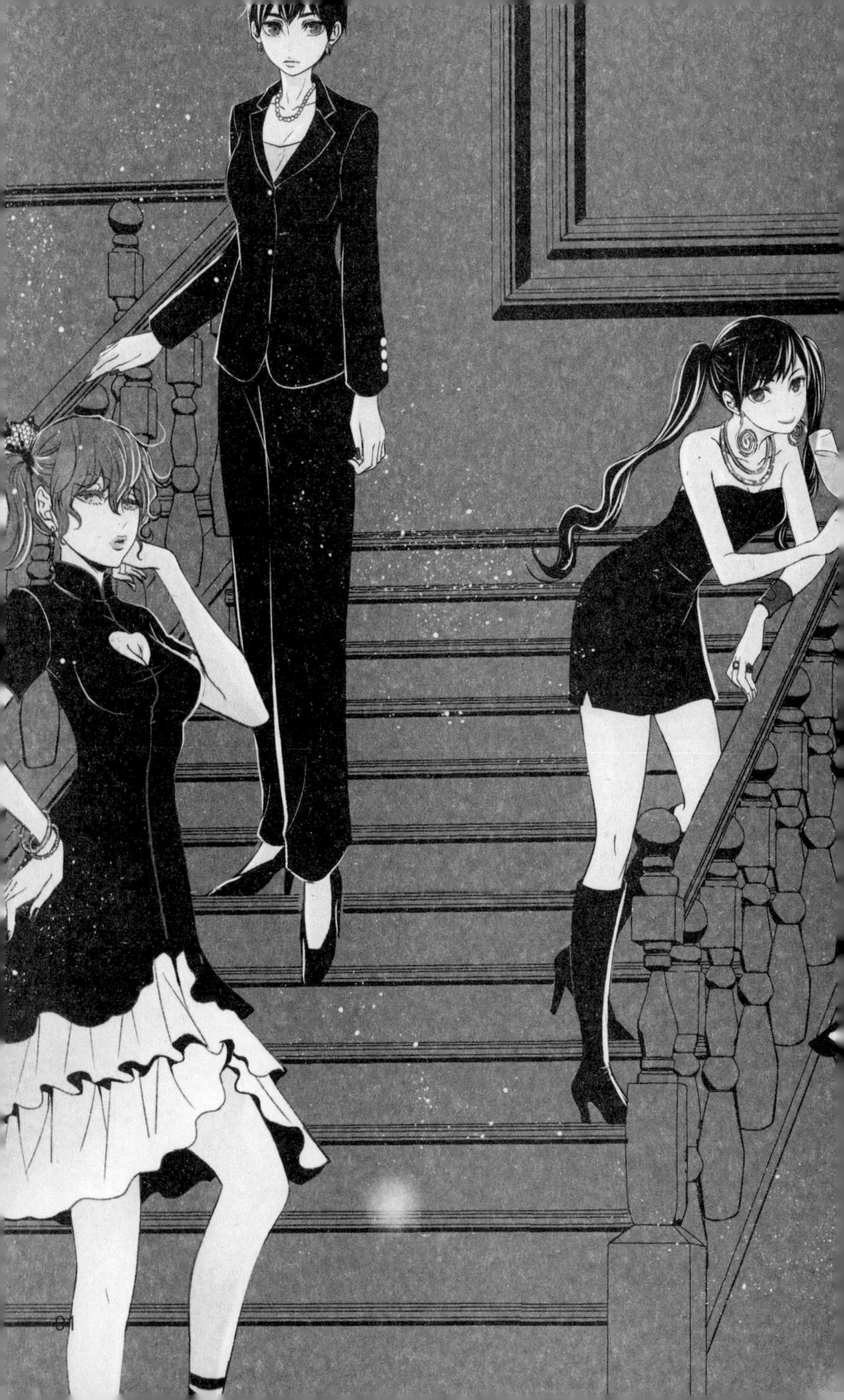

KYOUSUKE MOTOMI
C/O QUEEN'S QUALITY EDITOR
VIZ MEDIA
P.O. BOX 77010
SAN FRANCISCO, CA 94107

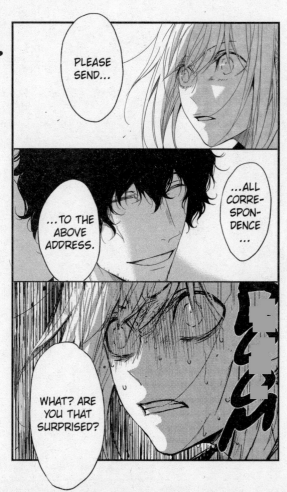

PLEASE SEND...

...ALL CORRE- SPON- DENCE ...

...TO THE ABOVE ADDRESS.

WHAT? ARE YOU THAT SURPRISED?

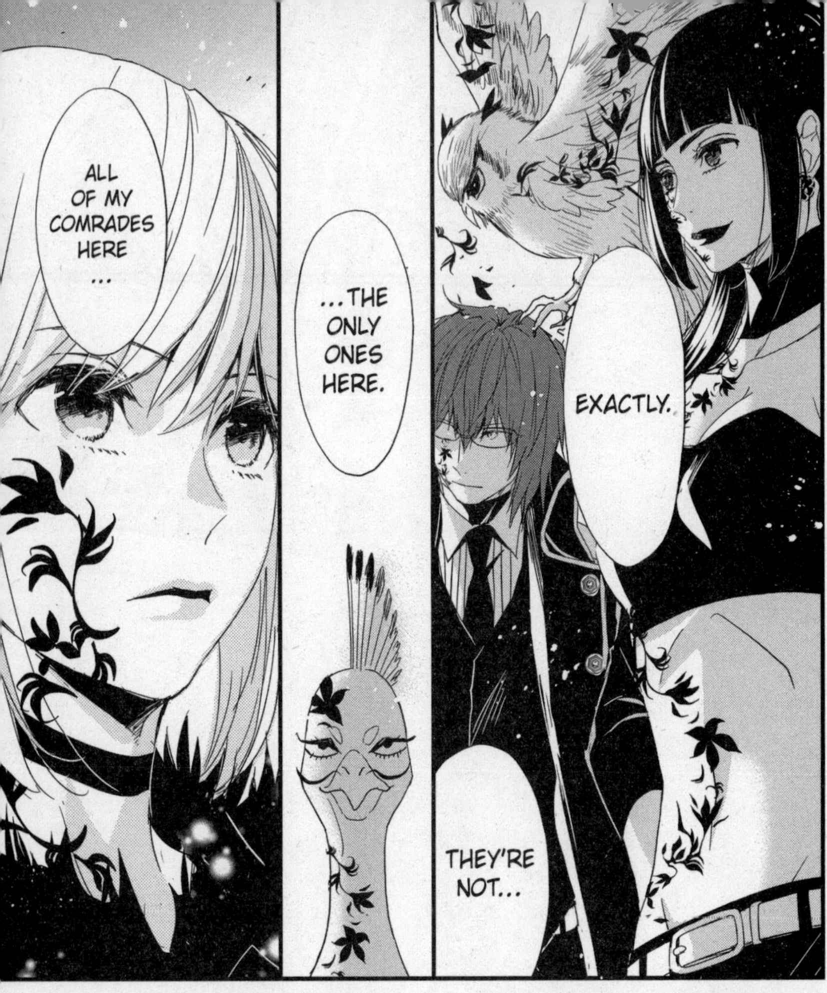
ALL OF MY COMRADES HERE ...
...THE ONLY ONES HERE.
THEY'RE NOT...
EXACTLY.

When I got *Ring Fit*, I also got my long-awaited Nintendo Switch. (There was a shortage.) I purchased *Fit Boxing 2* and have been alternating between it and *Ring Fit*. I studied Shorinji Kempo (Shaolin Temple Boxing) years ago, so I thought it would be easy, but I couldn't win any points in the beginning. And it was really tough—great for masochists! It loosened muscles around my shoulder blades, made me incredibly sweaty, and cleared my head, so it was perfect for a masochist like me who tends to hit roadblocks in my work.

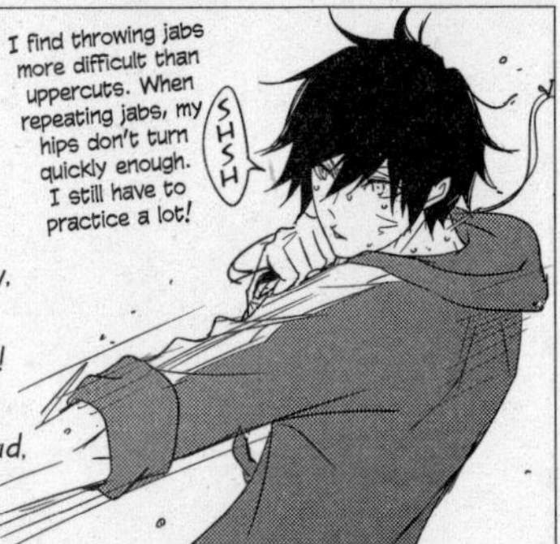
I find throwing jabs more difficult than uppercuts. When repeating jabs, my hips don't turn quickly enough. I still have to practice a lot!
SHSH

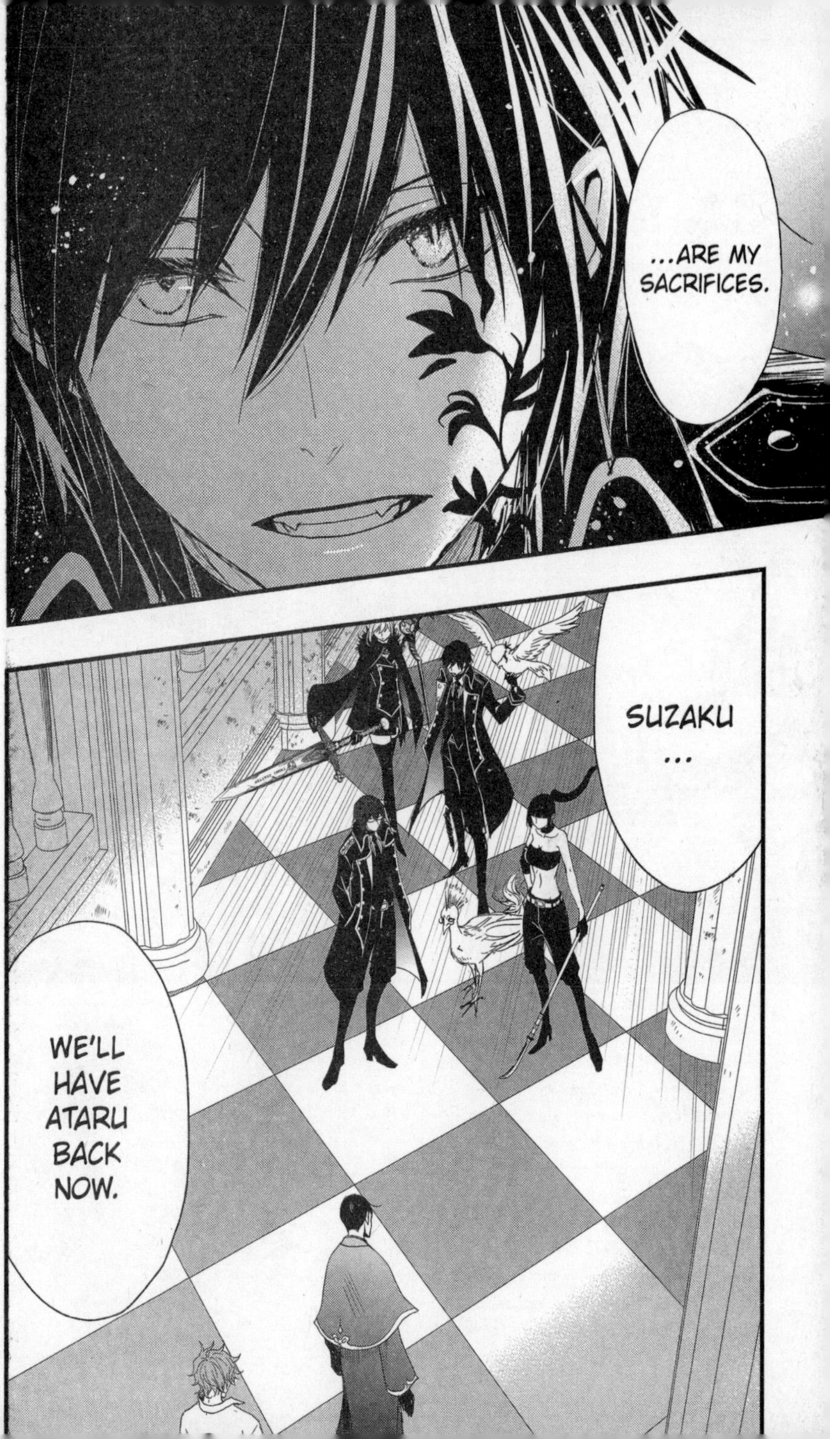
...ARE MY SACRIFICES.
SUZAKU ...
WE'LL HAVE ATARU BACK NOW.

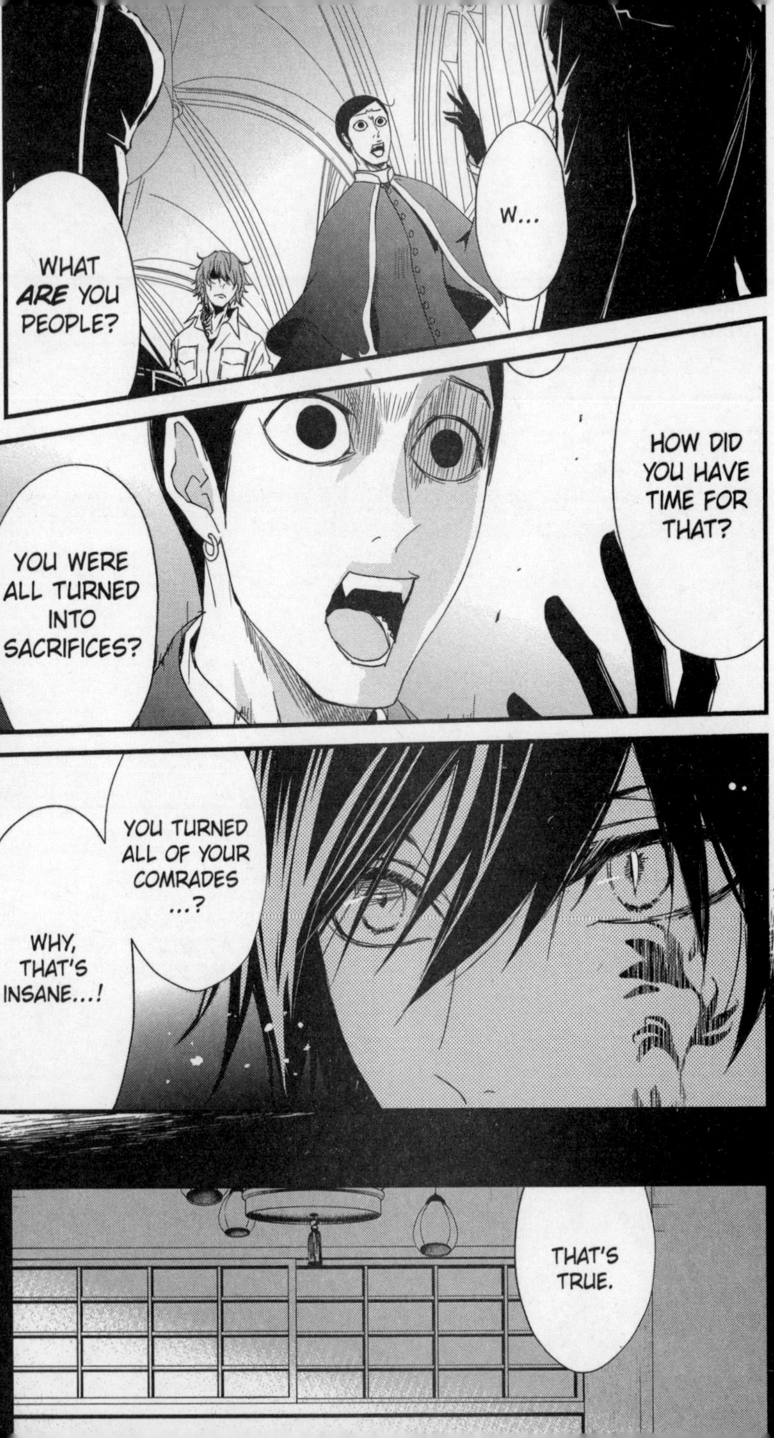
W...
WHAT *ARE* YOU PEOPLE?
HOW DID YOU HAVE TIME FOR THAT?
YOU WERE ALL TURNED INTO SACRIFICES?
YOU TURNED ALL OF YOUR COMRADES ...?
WHY, THAT'S INSANE...!
THAT'S TRUE.

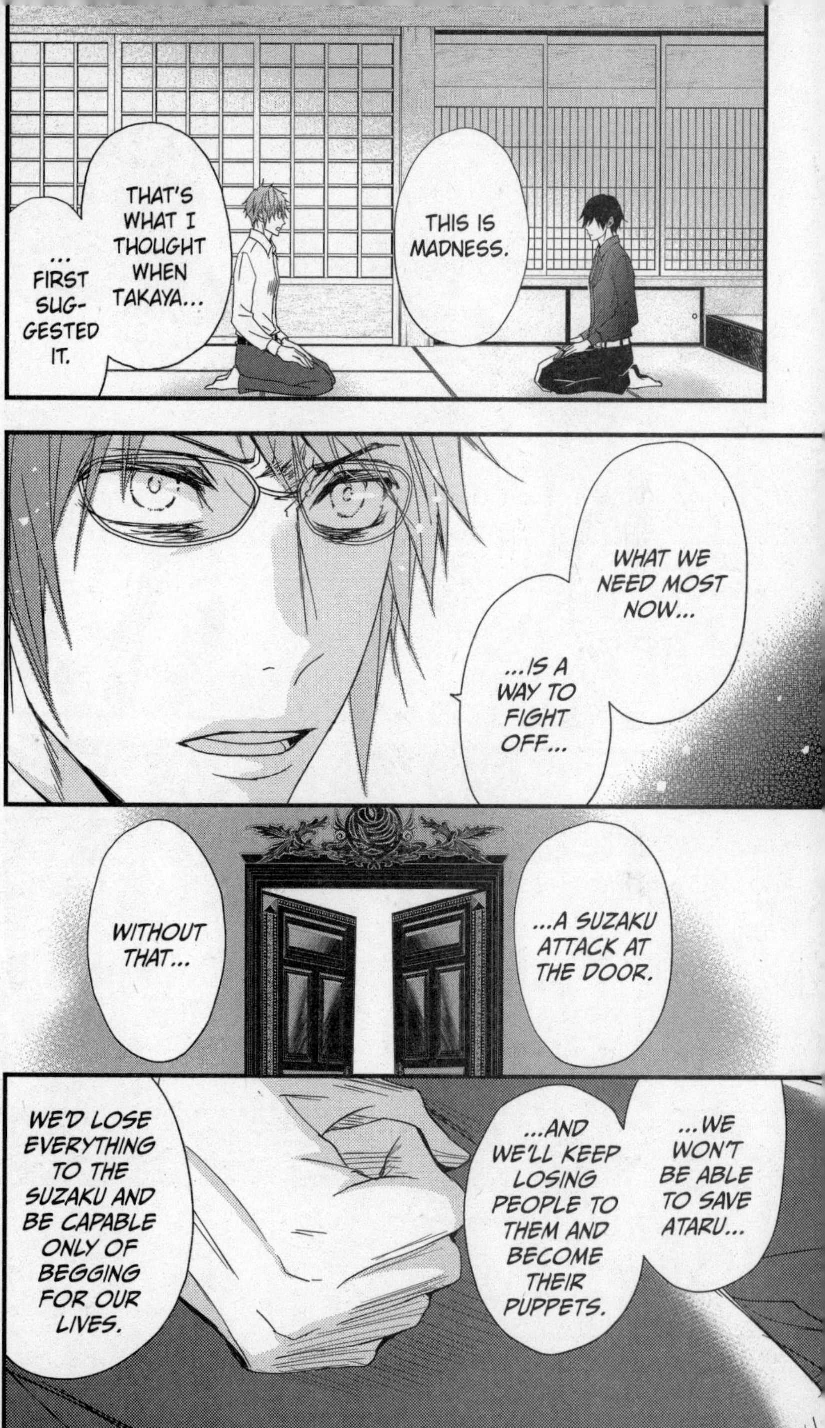
THIS IS MADNESS.
THAT'S WHAT I THOUGHT WHEN TAKAYA...
...FIRST SUG-GESTED IT.
WHAT WE NEED MOST NOW...
...IS A WAY TO FIGHT OFF...
...A SUZAKU ATTACK AT THE DOOR.
WITHOUT THAT...
...WE WON'T BE ABLE TO SAVE ATARU...
...AND WE'LL KEEP LOSING PEOPLE TO THEM AND BECOME THEIR PUPPETS.
WE'D LOSE EVERYTHING TO THE SUZAKU AND BE CAPABLE ONLY OF BEGGING FOR OUR LIVES.

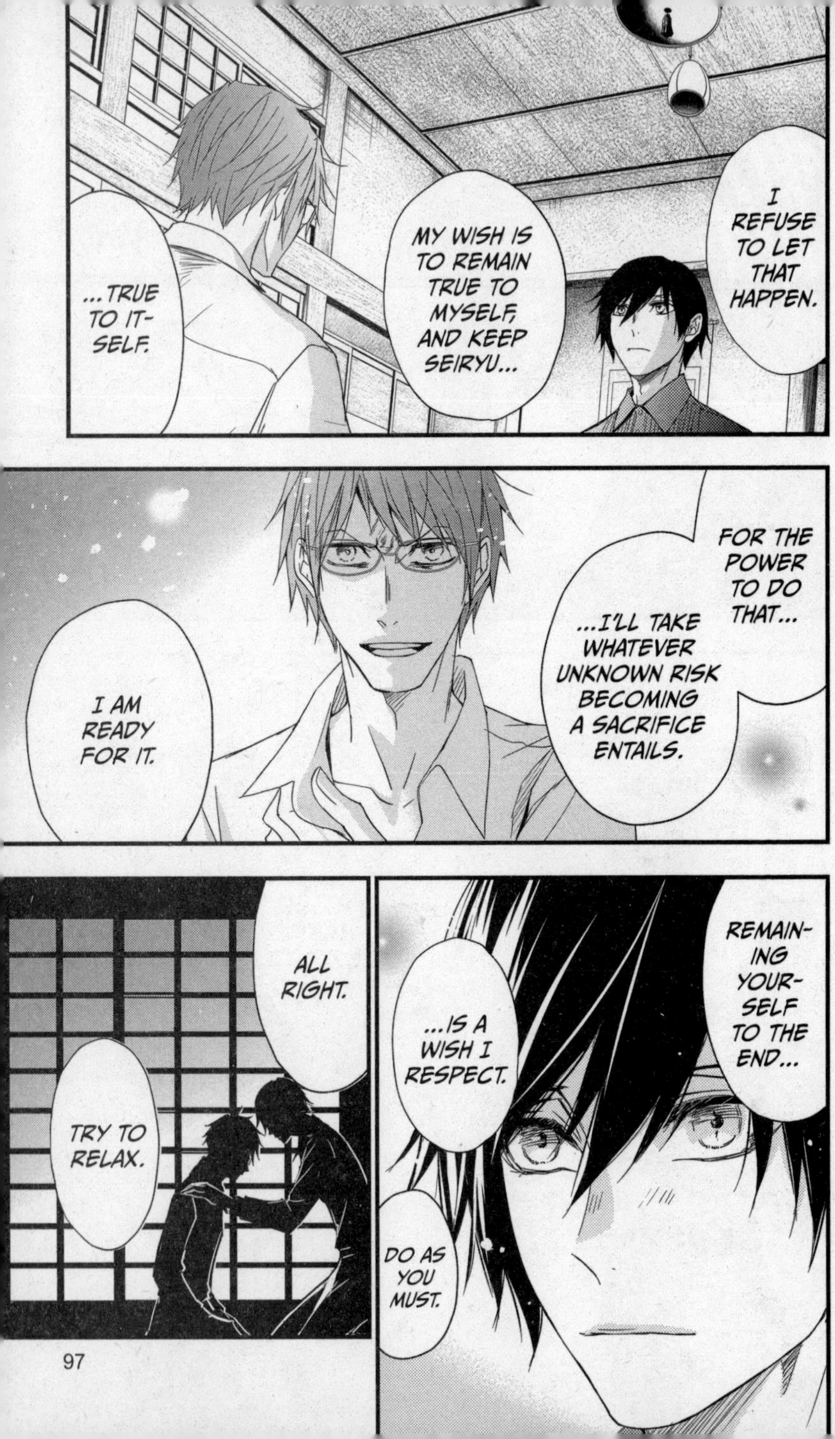
I REFUSE TO LET THAT HAPPEN.
MY WISH IS TO REMAIN TRUE TO MYSELF, AND KEEP SEIRYU...
...TRUE TO IT-SELF.
FOR THE POWER TO DO THAT...
...I'LL TAKE WHATEVER UNKNOWN RISK BECOMING A SACRIFICE ENTAILS.
I AM READY FOR IT.
REMAIN-ING YOUR-SELF TO THE END...
...IS A WISH I RESPECT.
DO AS YOU MUST.
ALL RIGHT.
TRY TO RELAX.

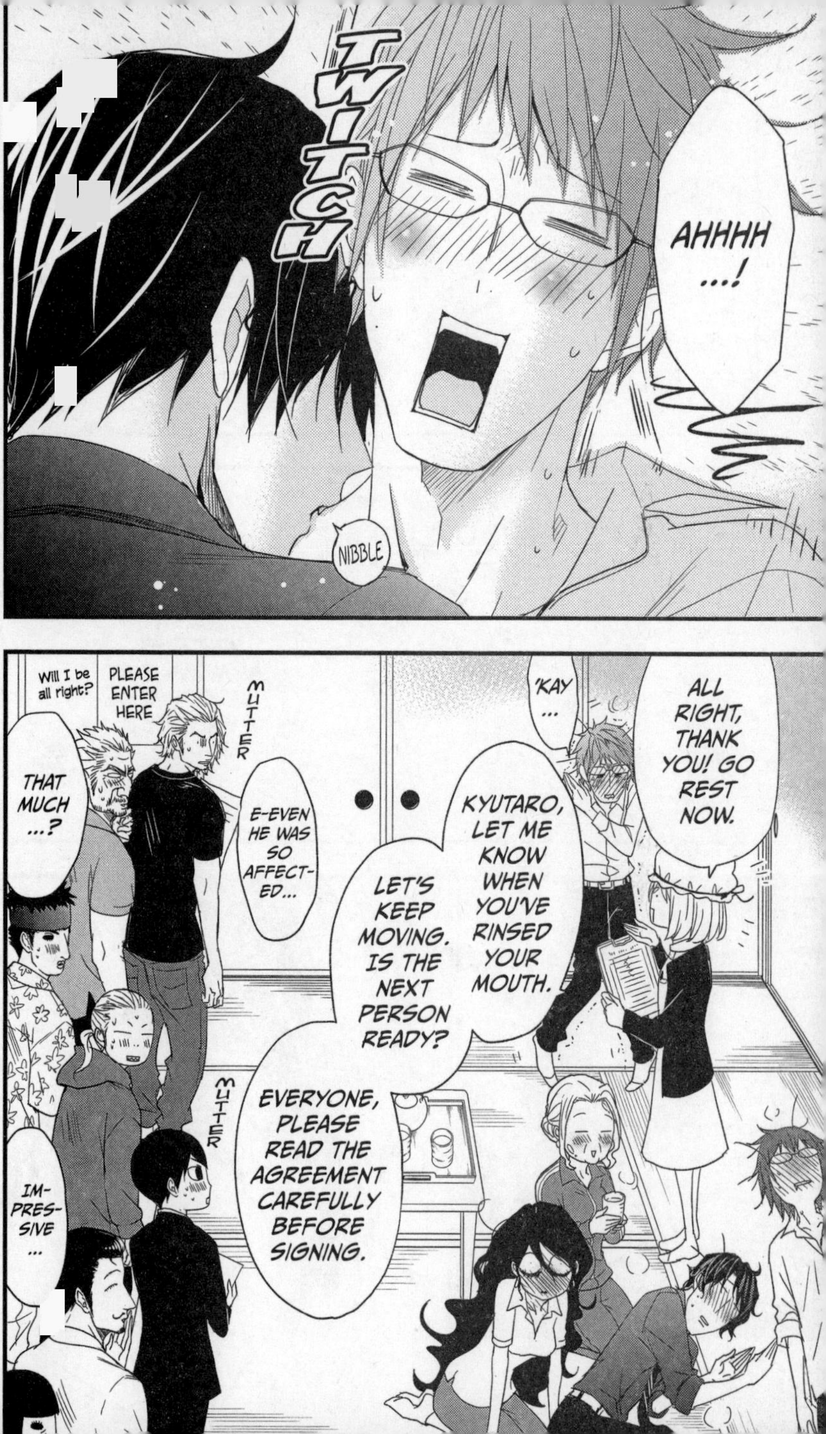
AHHHH ...!
TWITCH
NIBBLE
ALL RIGHT, THANK YOU! GO REST NOW.
'KAY ...
KYUTARO, LET ME KNOW WHEN YOU'VE RINSED YOUR MOUTH.
LET'S KEEP MOVING. IS THE NEXT PERSON READY?
EVERYONE, PLEASE READ THE AGREEMENT CAREFULLY BEFORE SIGNING.
MUTTER
E-EVEN HE WAS SO AFFECT-ED...
MUTTER
PLEASE ENTER HERE
Will I be all right?
THAT MUCH ...?
IM-PRES-SIVE ...

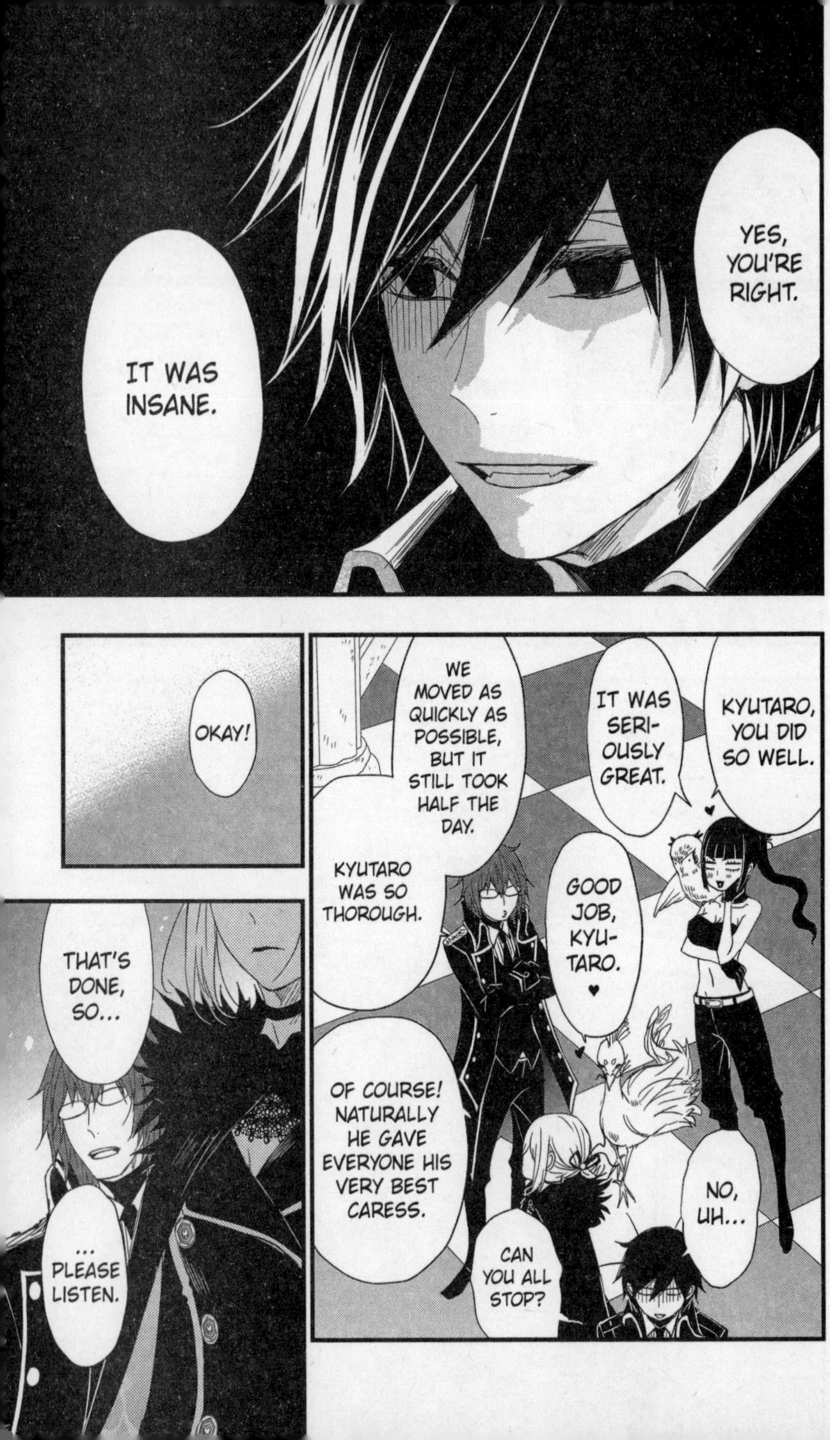
YES, YOU'RE RIGHT.
IT WAS INSANE.
KYUTARO, YOU DID SO WELL.
IT WAS SERI-OUSLY GREAT.
WE MOVED AS QUICKLY AS POSSIBLE, BUT IT STILL TOOK HALF THE DAY.
GOOD JOB, KYU-TARO.
KYUTARO WAS SO THOROUGH.
NO, UH...
OF COURSE! NATURALLY HE GAVE EVERYONE HIS VERY BEST CARESS.
CAN YOU ALL STOP?
OKAY!
THAT'S DONE, SO...
...PLEASE LISTEN.

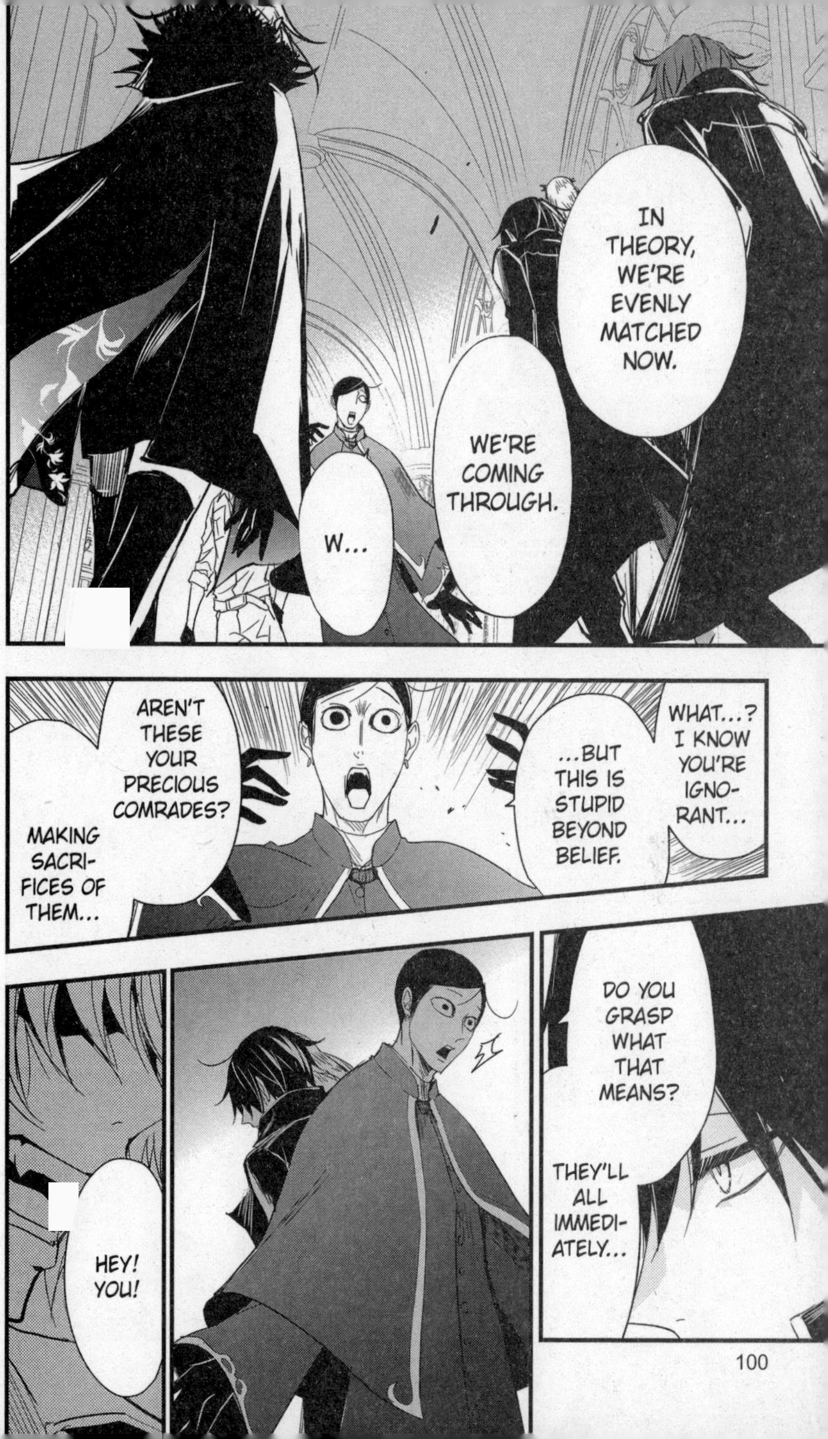
IN THEORY, WE'RE EVENLY MATCHED NOW.
WE'RE COMING THROUGH.
W...
WHAT...? I KNOW YOU'RE IGNO-RANT...
...BUT THIS IS STUPID BEYOND BELIEF.
AREN'T THESE YOUR PRECIOUS COMRADES?
MAKING SACRI-FICES OF THEM...
DO YOU GRASP WHAT THAT MEANS?
THEY'LL ALL IMMEDI-ATELY...
HEY! YOU!

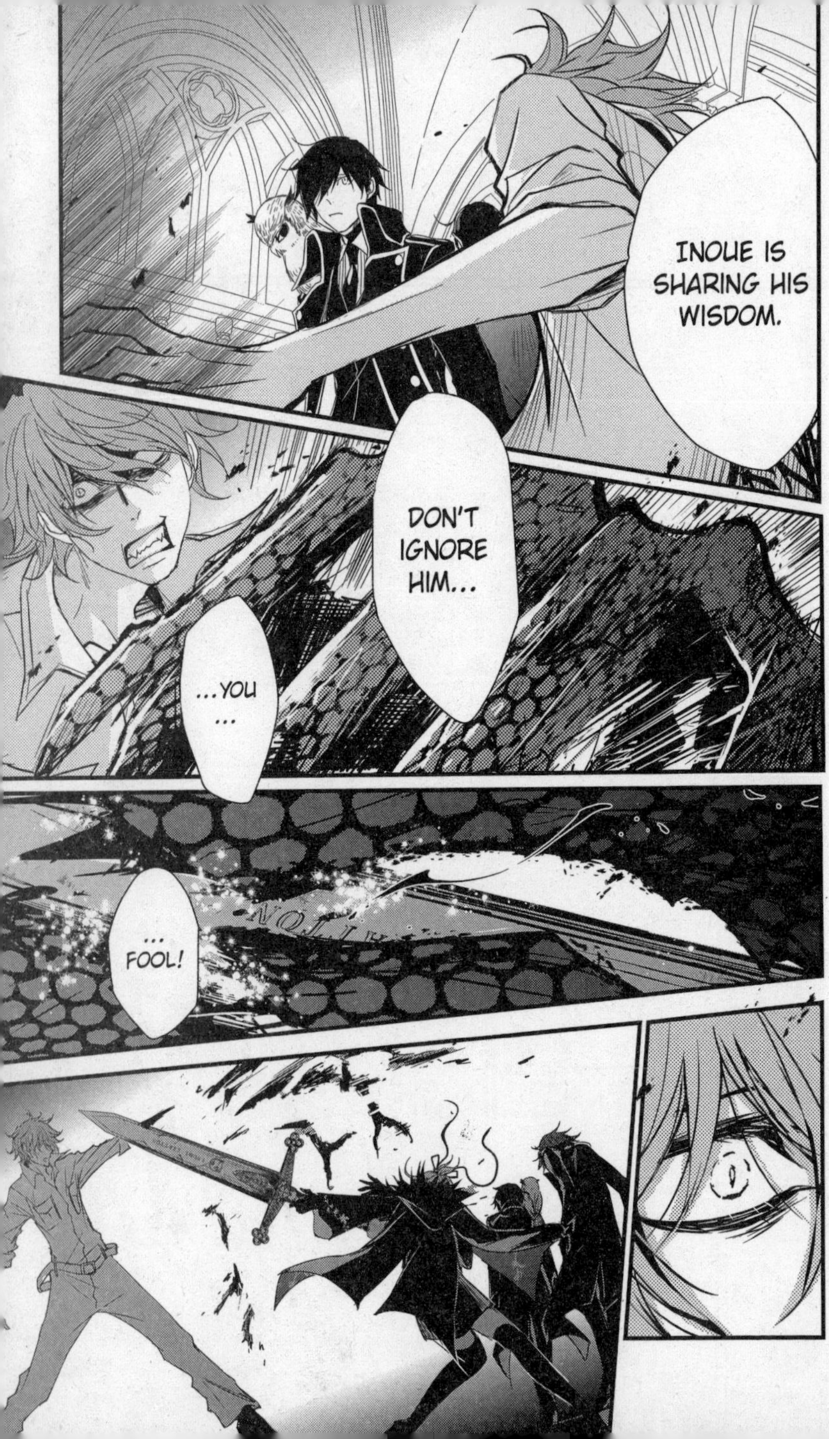
INOUE IS SHARING HIS WISDOM.
DON'T IGNORE HIM...
...YOU ...
... FOOL!

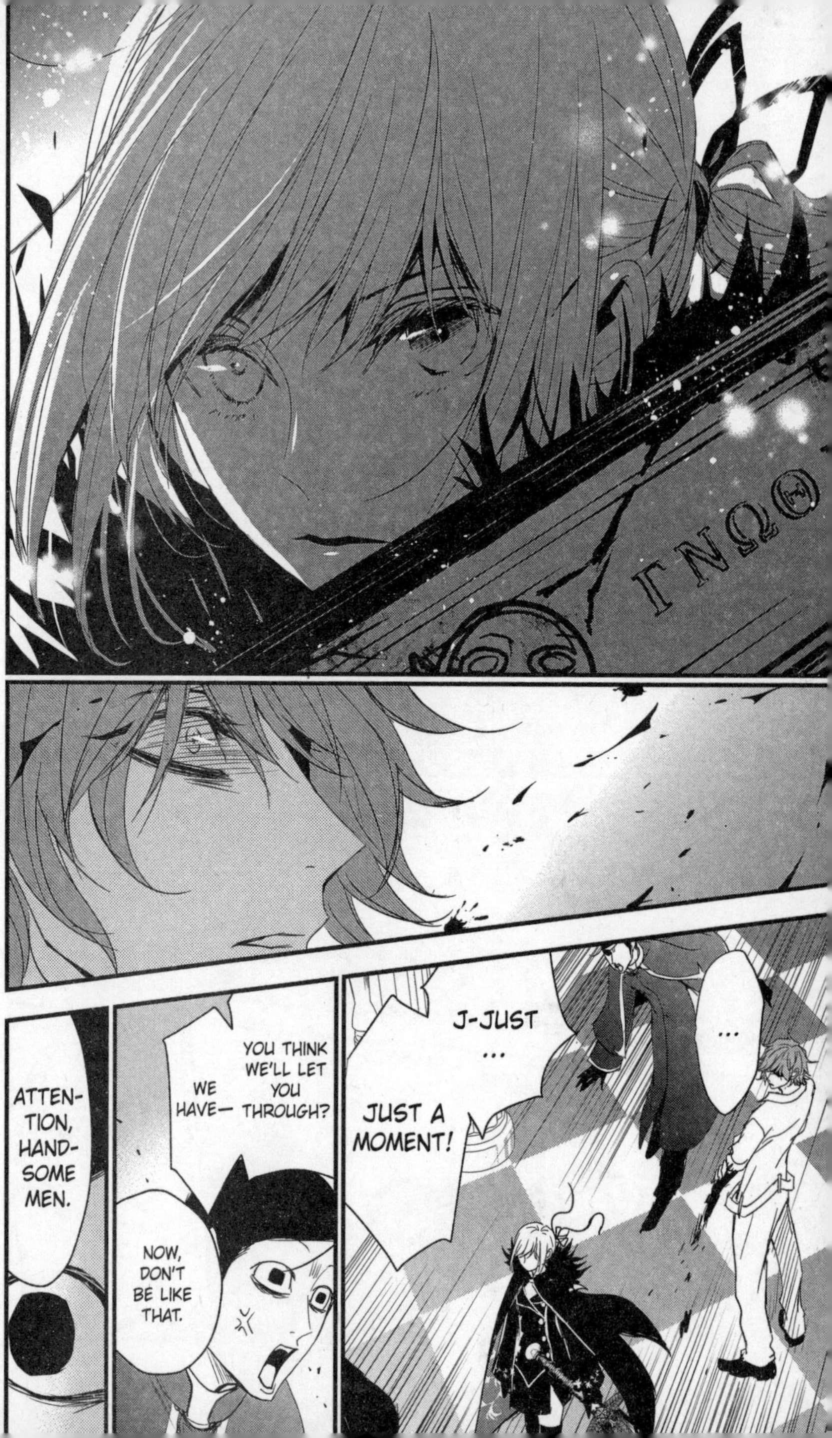
...
J-JUST ...
JUST A MOMENT!
YOU THINK WE'LL LET YOU THROUGH?
WE HAVE—
NOW, DON'T BE LIKE THAT.
ATTEN-TION, HAND-SOME MEN.

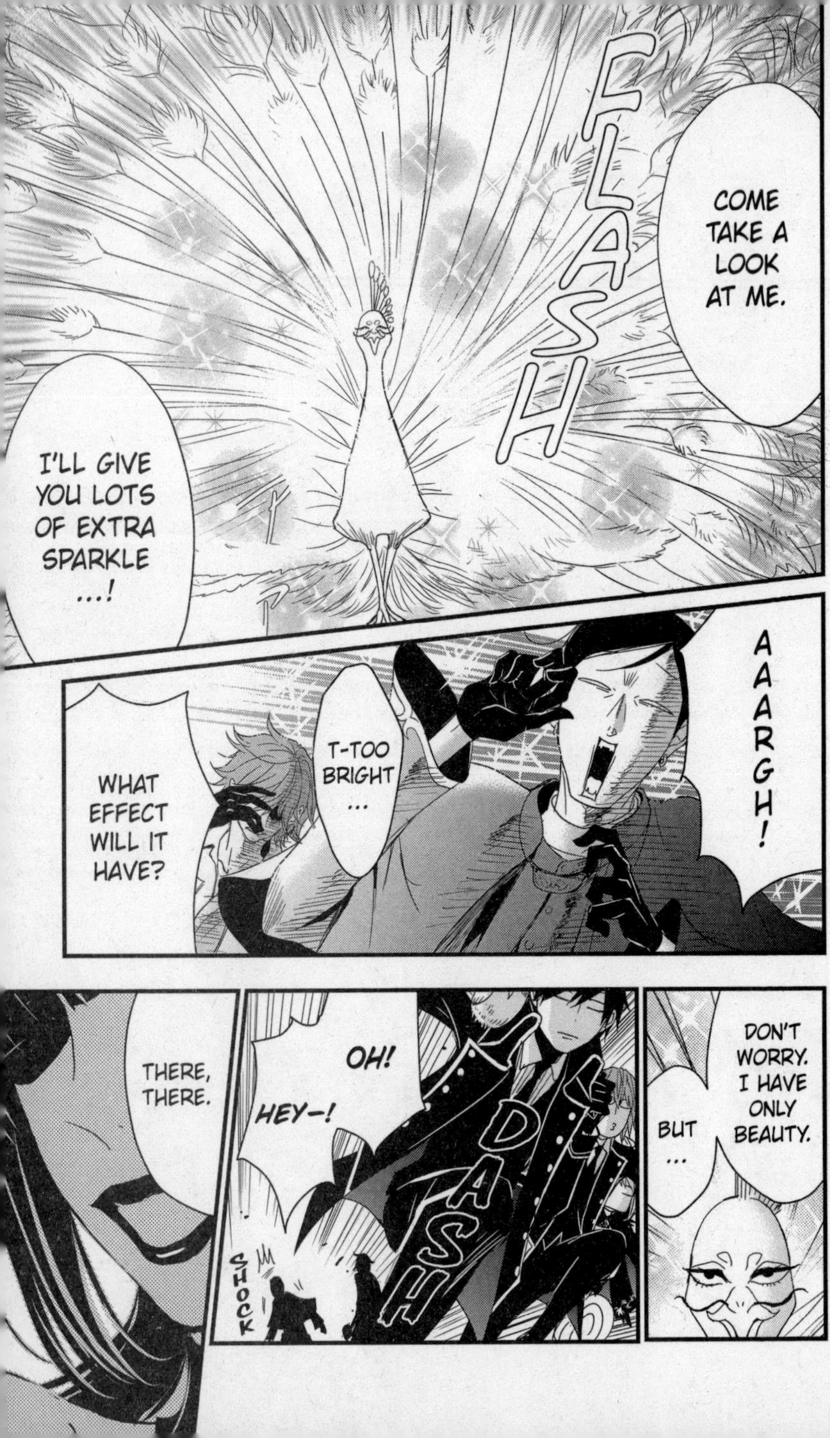
COME TAKE A LOOK AT ME.
FLASH
I'LL GIVE YOU LOTS OF EXTRA SPARKLE ...!
AAAARGH!
T-TOO BRIGHT ...
WHAT EFFECT WILL IT HAVE?
DON'T WORRY. I HAVE ONLY BEAUTY.
BUT ...
OH!
HEY-!
DASH
SHOCK
THERE, THERE.

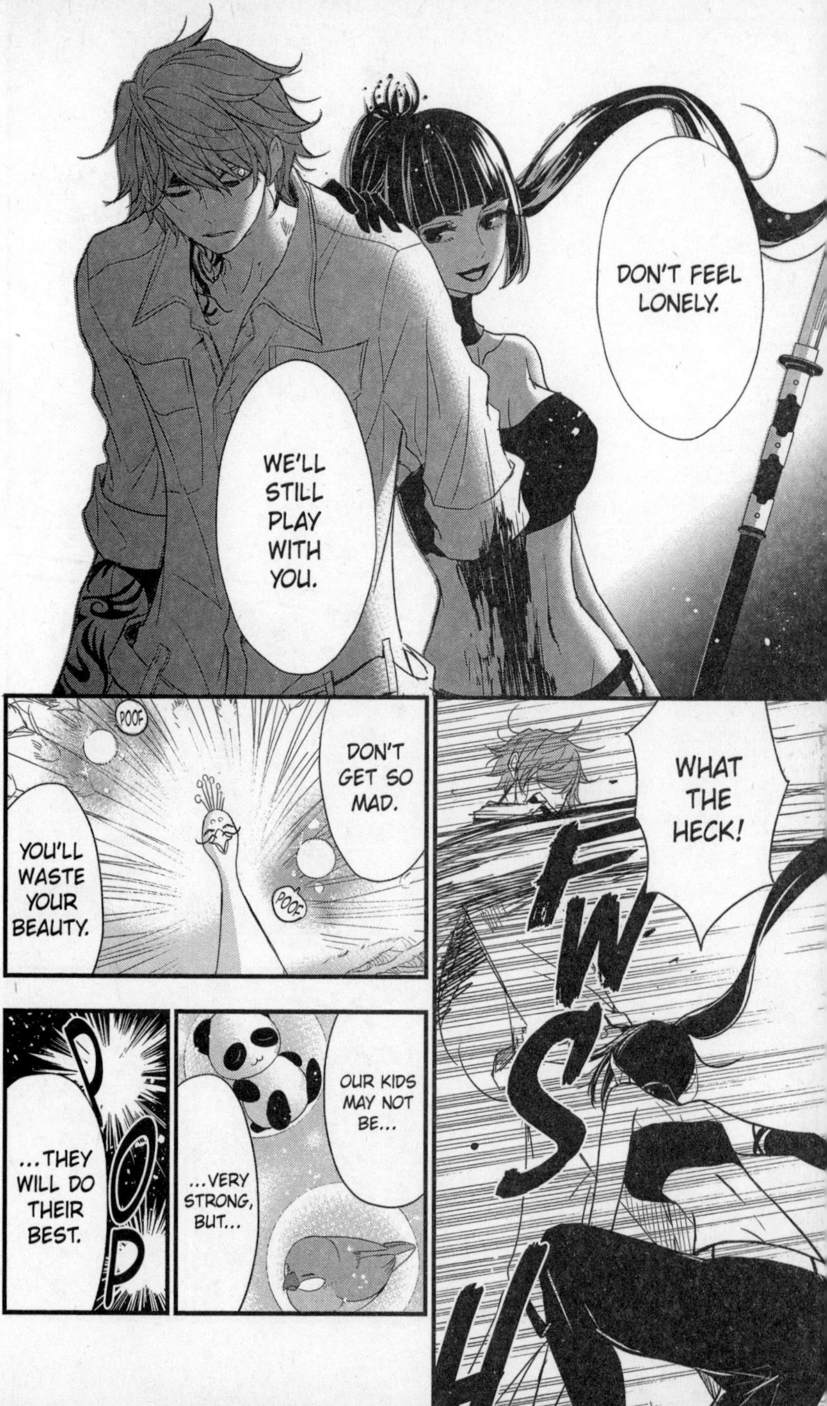
DON'T FEEL LONELY.
WE'LL STILL PLAY WITH YOU.
WHAT THE HECK!
FWSH
DON'T GET SO MAD.
POOF
POOF
YOU'LL WASTE YOUR BEAUTY.
OUR KIDS MAY NOT BE...
...VERY STRONG, BUT...
POOP
...THEY WILL DO THEIR BEST.

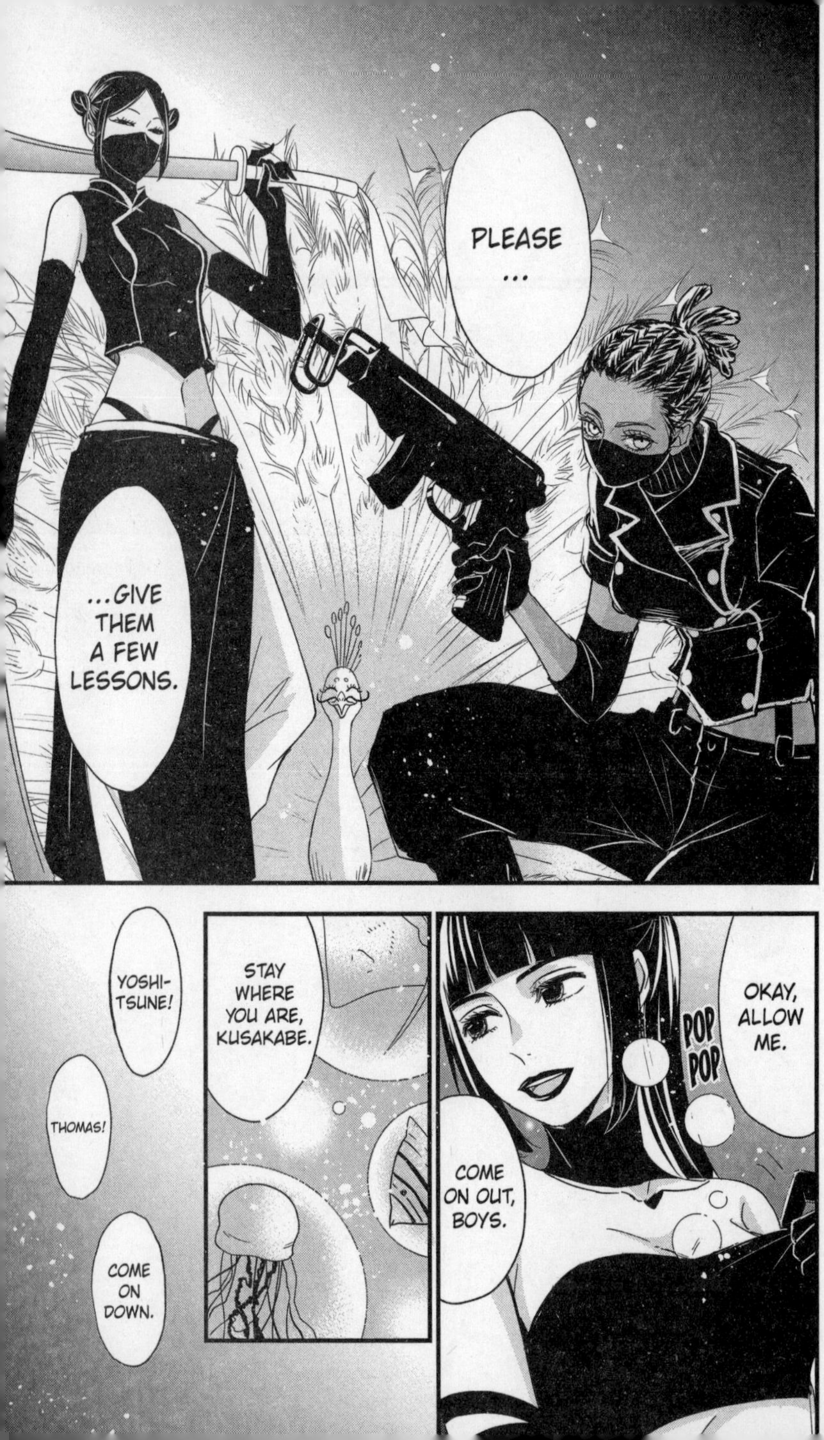
PLEASE ...
...GIVE THEM A FEW LESSONS.
OKAY, ALLOW ME.
POP POP
COME ON OUT, BOYS.
STAY WHERE YOU ARE, KUSAKABE.
YOSHI-TSUNE!
THOMAS!
COME ON DOWN.

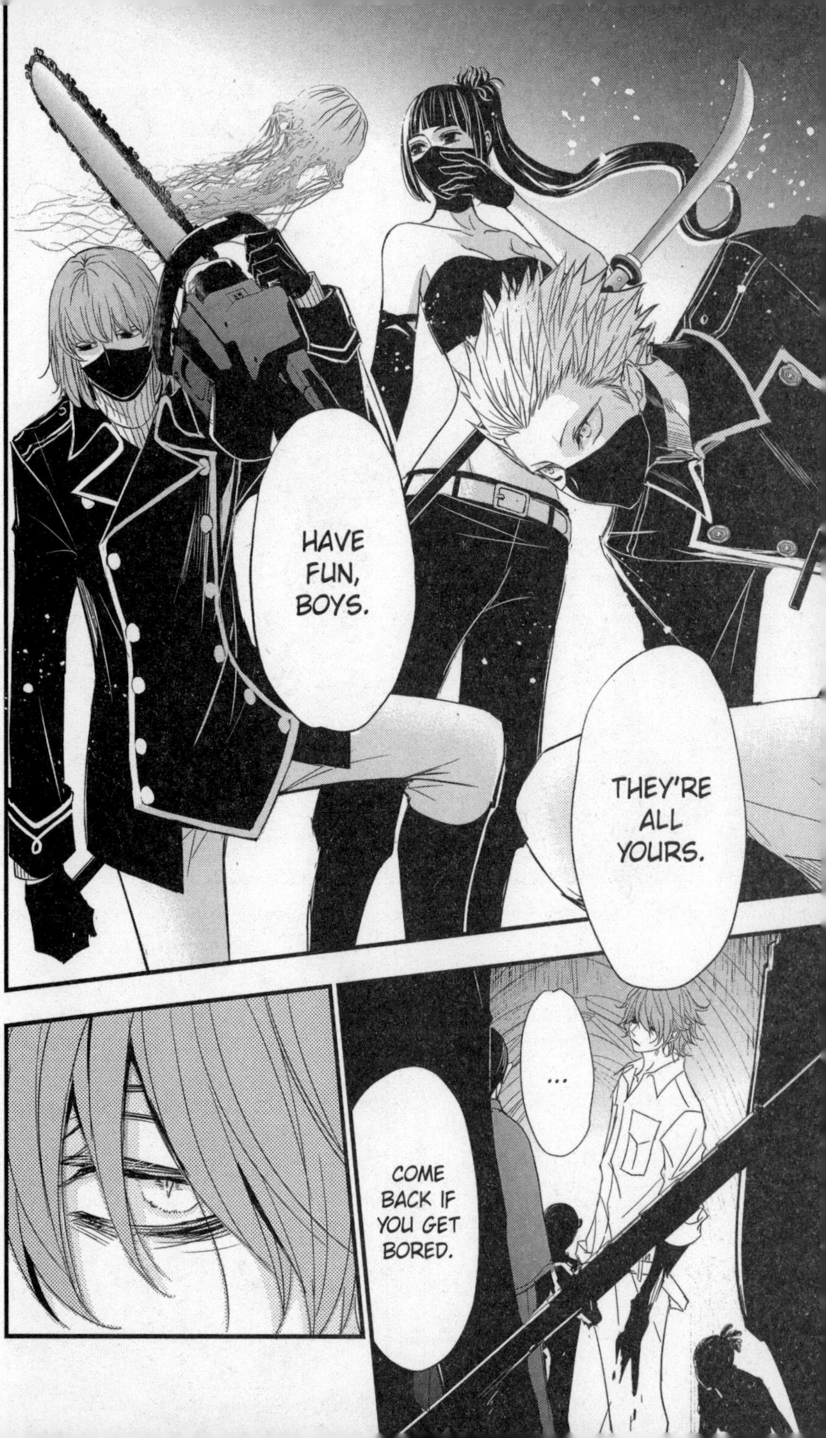
THEY'RE ALL YOURS.
HAVE FUN, BOYS.
...
COME BACK IF YOU GET BORED.

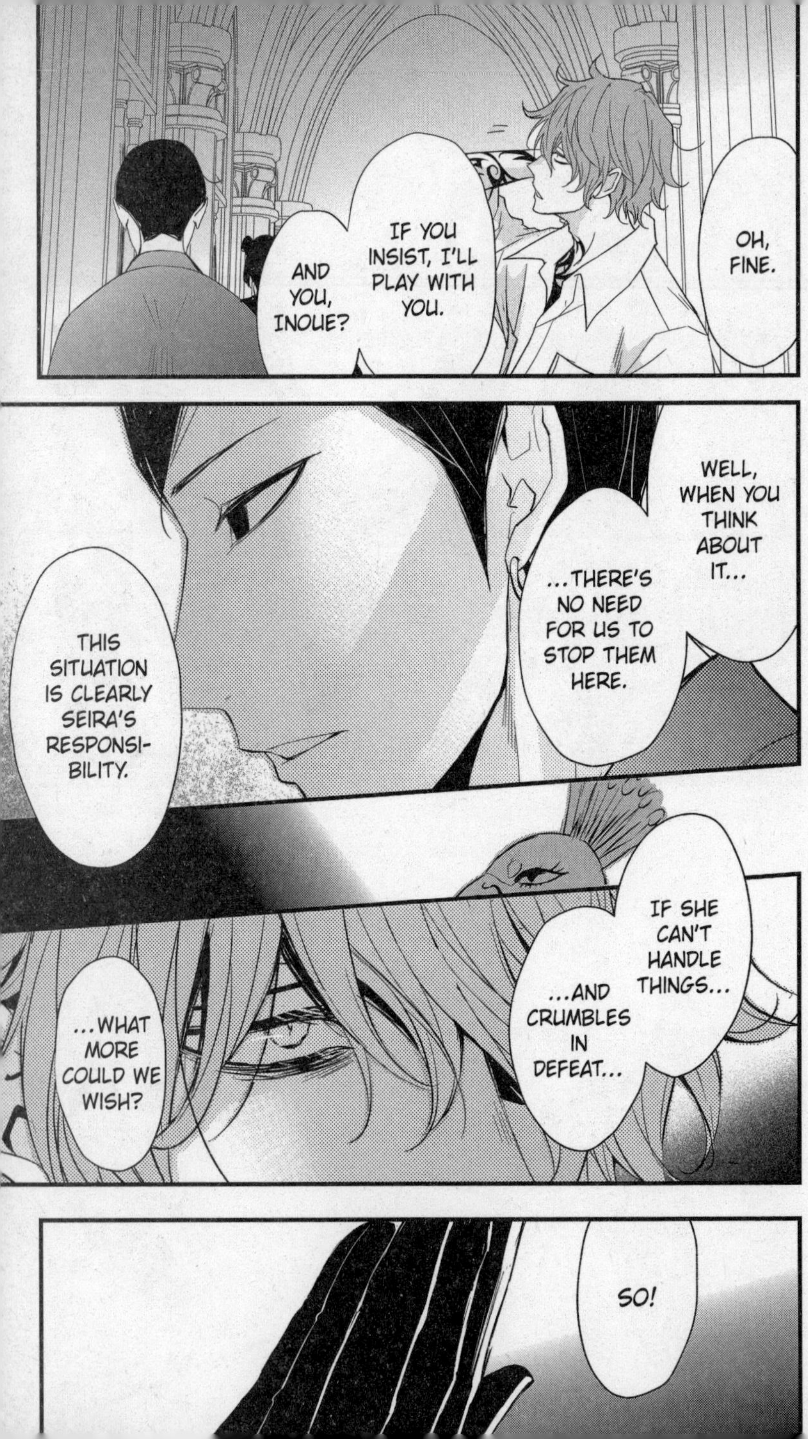
OH, FINE.
IF YOU INSIST, I'LL PLAY WITH YOU.
AND YOU, INOUE?
WELL, WHEN YOU THINK ABOUT IT...
...THERE'S NO NEED FOR US TO STOP THEM HERE.
THIS SITUATION IS CLEARLY SEIRA'S RESPONSI-BILITY.
IF SHE CAN'T HANDLE THINGS...
...AND CRUMBLES IN DEFEAT...
...WHAT MORE COULD WE WISH?
SO!

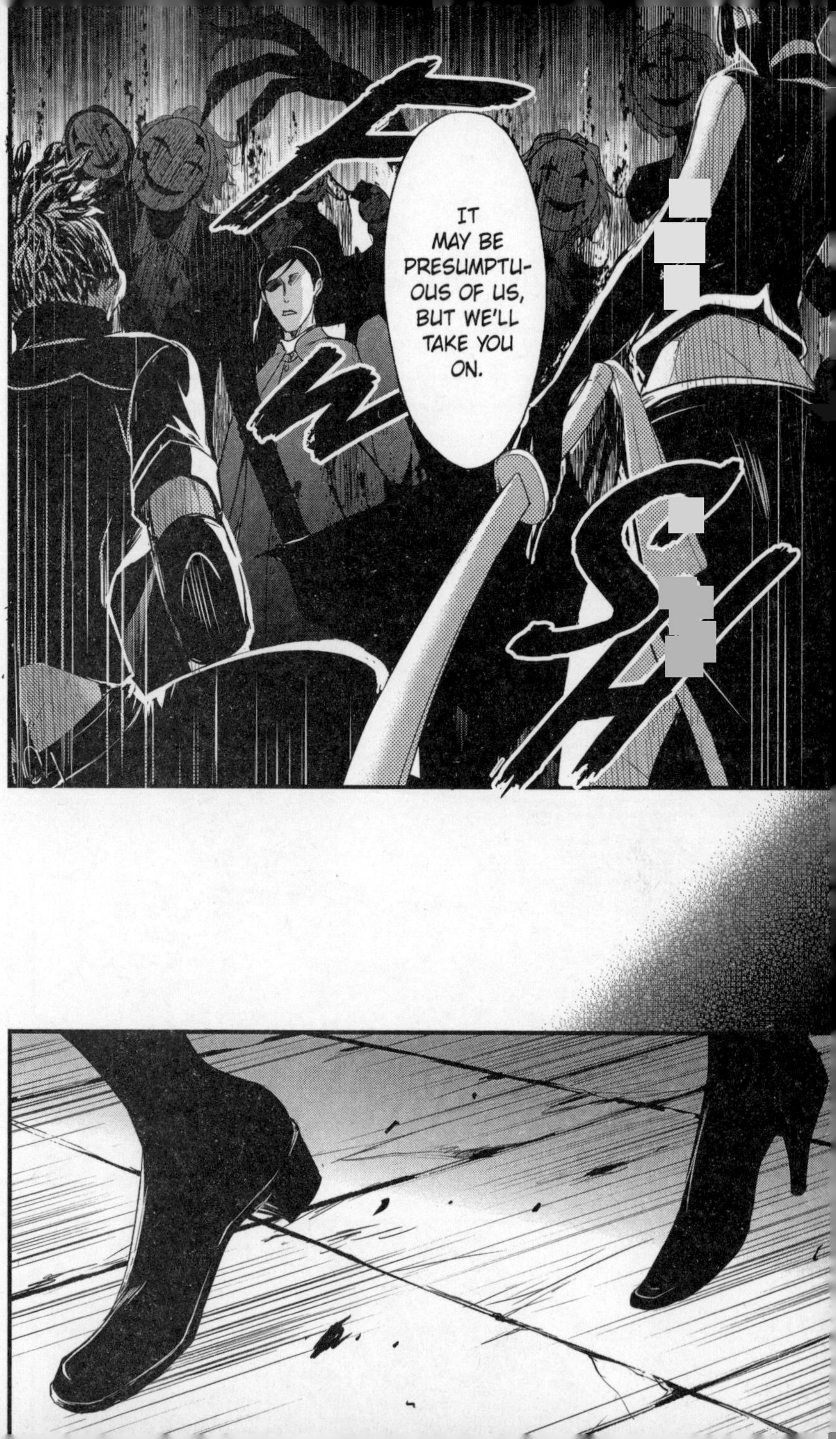
IT MAY BE PRESUMPTUOUS OF US, BUT WE'LL TAKE YOU ON.

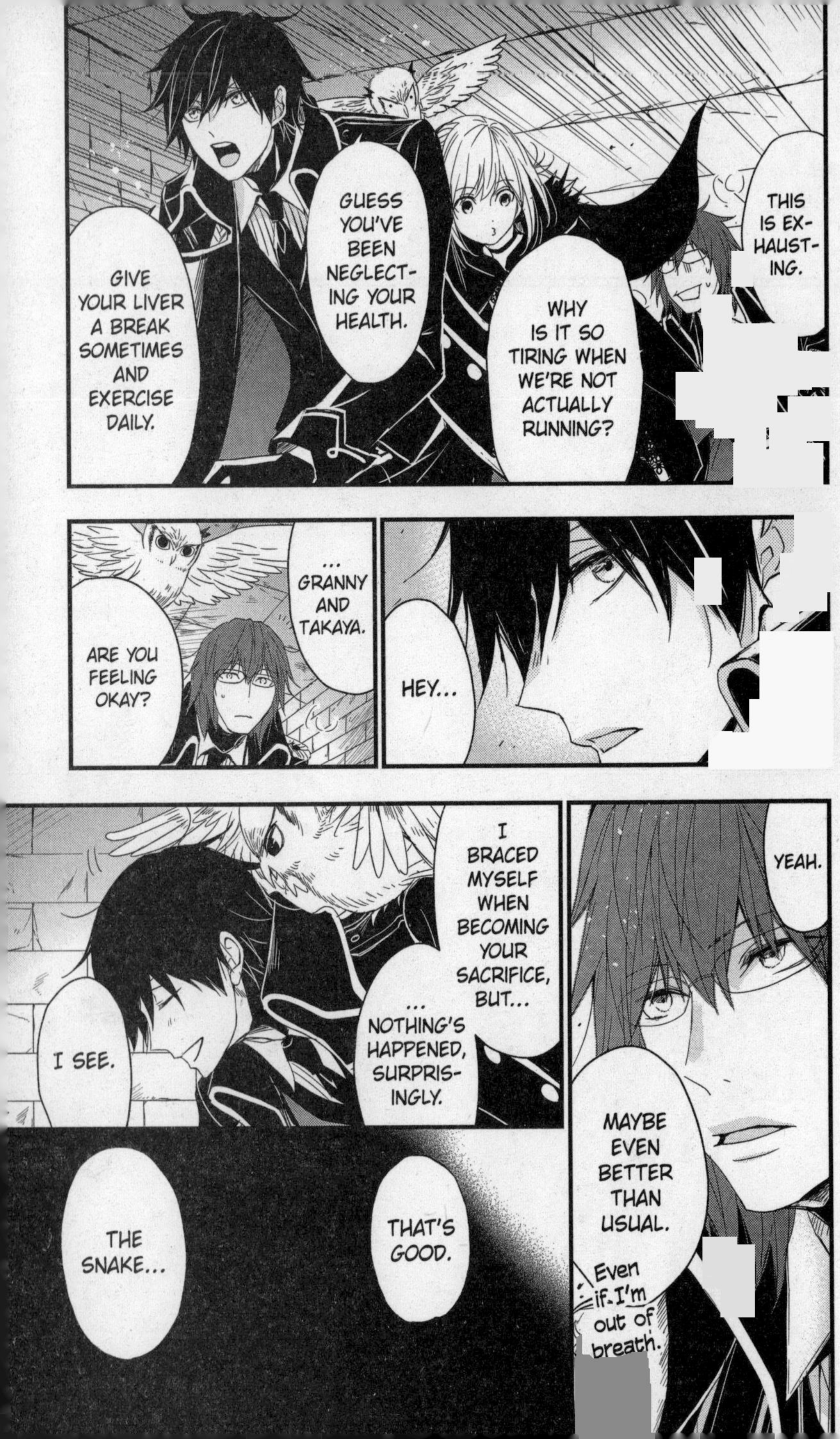
THIS IS EX-HAUSTING.
WHY IS IT SO TIRING WHEN WE'RE NOT ACTUALLY RUNNING?
GUESS YOU'VE BEEN NEGLECTING YOUR HEALTH.
GIVE YOUR LIVER A BREAK SOMETIMES AND EXERCISE DAILY.
HEY...
...GRANNY AND TAKAYA.
ARE YOU FEELING OKAY?
YEAH.
MAYBE EVEN BETTER THAN USUAL.
Even if I'm out of breath.
I BRACED MYSELF WHEN BECOMING YOUR SACRIFICE, BUT...
...NOTHING'S HAPPENED, SURPRISINGLY.
I SEE.
THAT'S GOOD.
THE SNAKE...

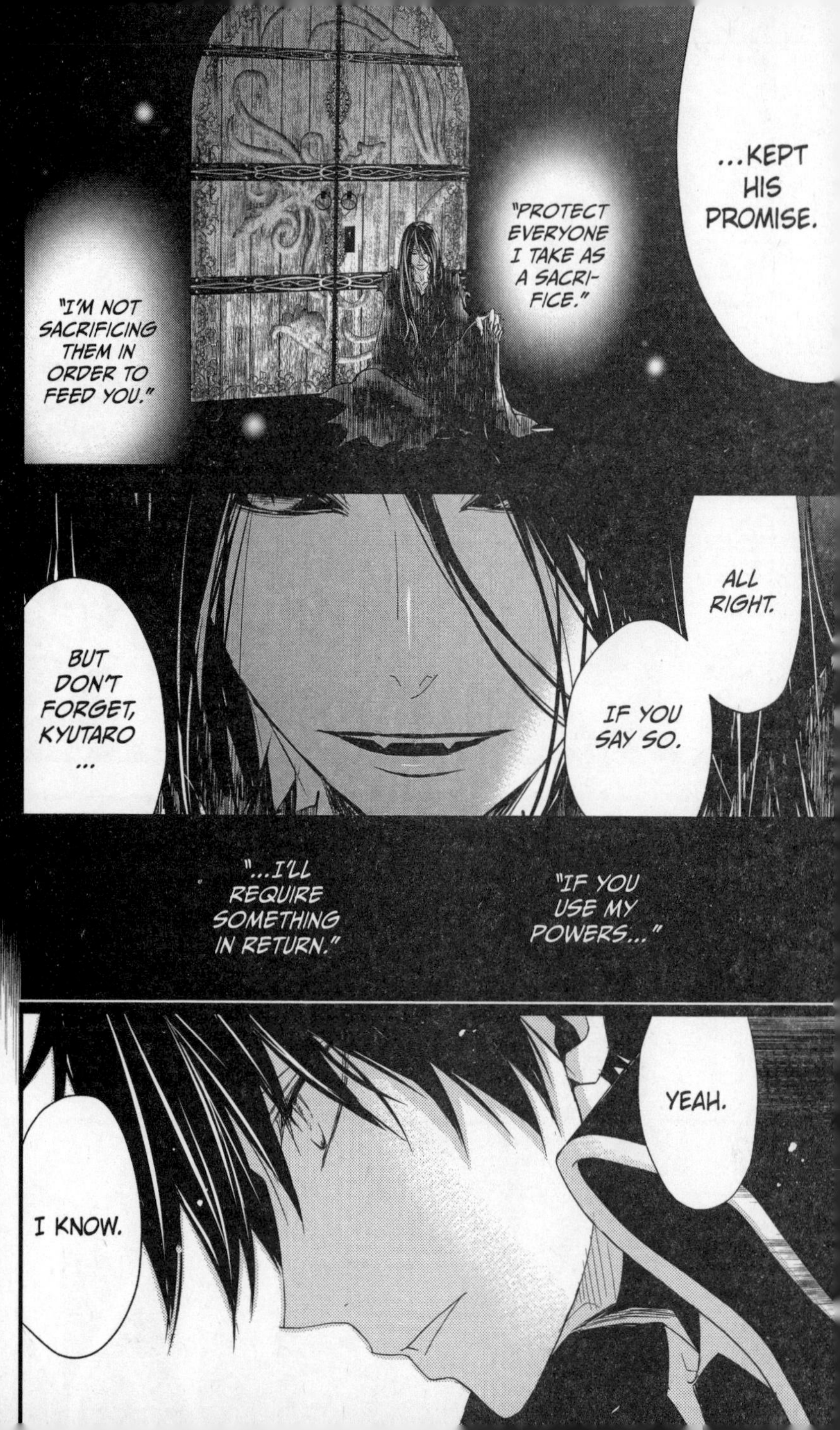
...KEPT HIS PROMISE.
"PROTECT EVERYONE I TAKE AS A SACRIFICE."
"I'M NOT SACRIFICING THEM IN ORDER TO FEED YOU."
ALL RIGHT.
IF YOU SAY SO.
BUT DON'T FORGET, KYUTARO ...
"IF YOU USE MY POWERS..."
"...I'LL REQUIRE SOMETHING IN RETURN."
YEAH.
I KNOW.

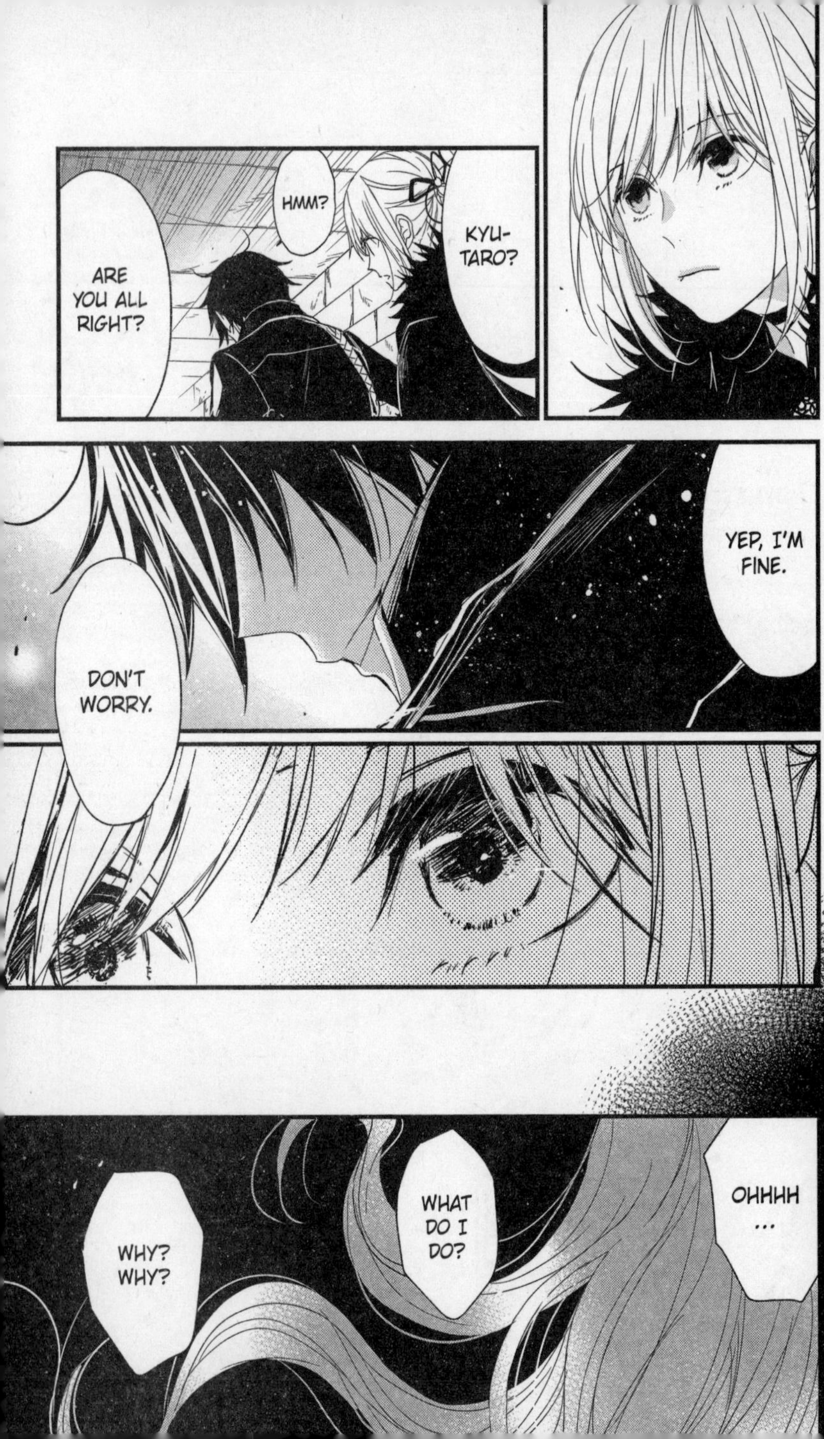
KYU-TARO?
HMM?
ARE YOU ALL RIGHT?
YEP, I'M FINE.
DON'T WORRY.
OHHHH ...
WHAT DO I DO?
WHY? WHY?

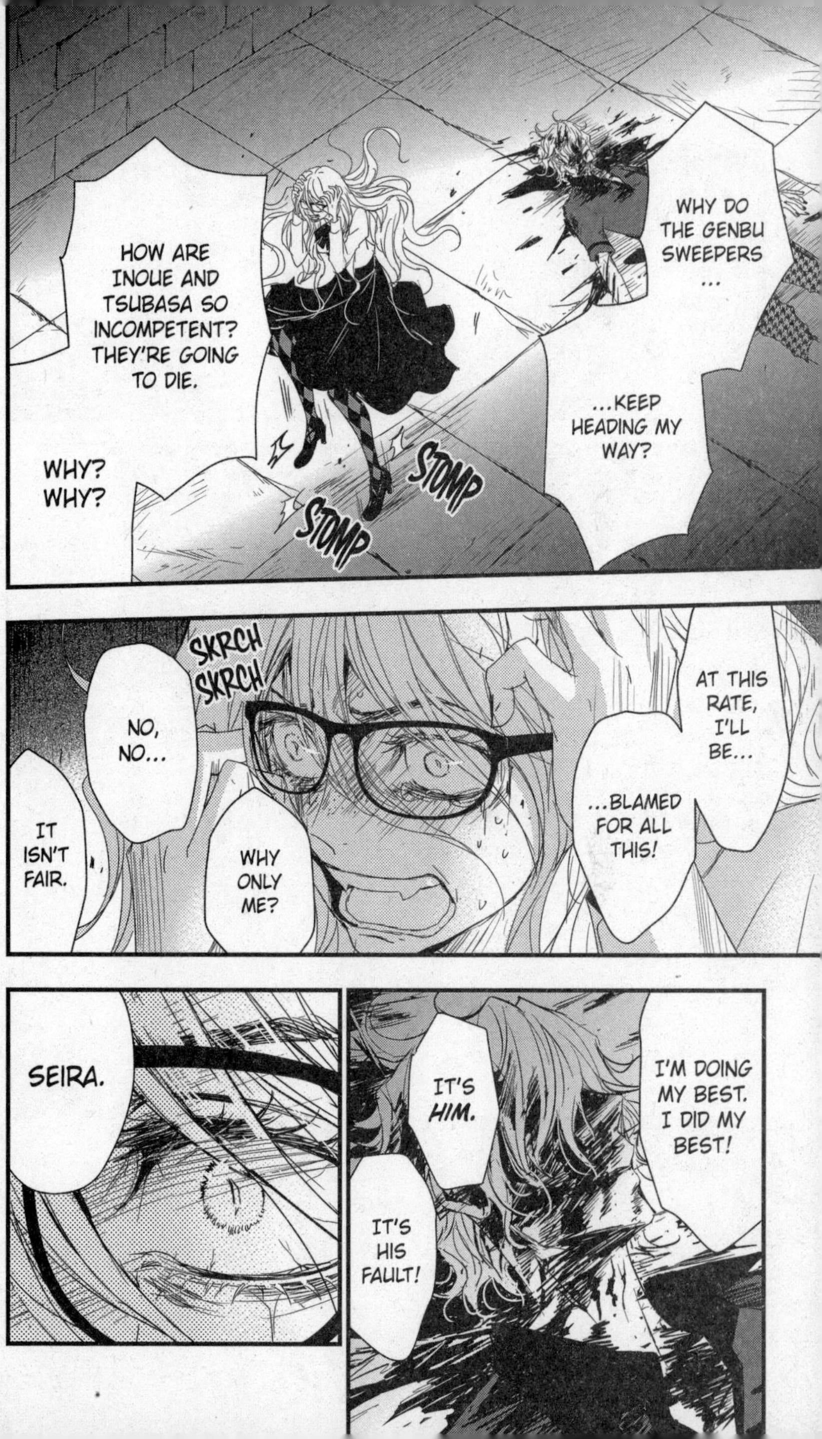
WHY DO THE GENBU SWEEPERS...
...KEEP HEADING MY WAY?
HOW ARE INOUE AND TSUBASA SO INCOMPETENT? THEY'RE GOING TO DIE.
STOMP
STOMP
WHY? WHY?
AT THIS RATE, I'LL BE...
...BLAMED FOR ALL THIS!
SKRCH SKRCH
NO, NO...
WHY ONLY ME?
IT ISN'T FAIR.
I'M DOING MY BEST. I DID MY BEST!
IT'S *HIM*.
IT'S HIS FAULT!
SEIRA.

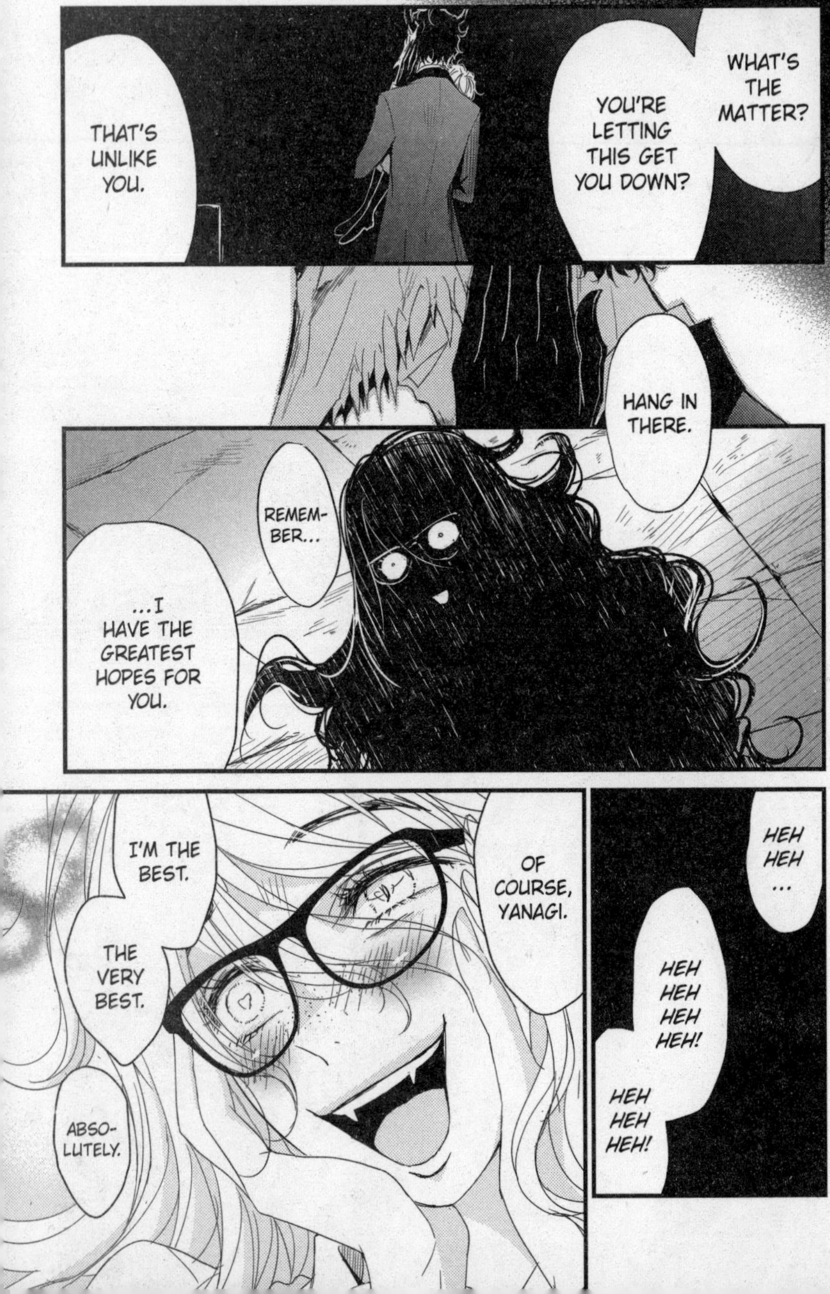
WHAT'S THE MATTER?
YOU'RE LETTING THIS GET YOU DOWN?
THAT'S UNLIKE YOU.
HANG IN THERE.
REMEMBER...
...I HAVE THE GREATEST HOPES FOR YOU.
HEH HEH...
HEH HEH HEH HEH!
HEH HEH HEH!
OF COURSE, YANAGI.
I'M THE BEST.
THE VERY BEST.
ABSOLUTELY.

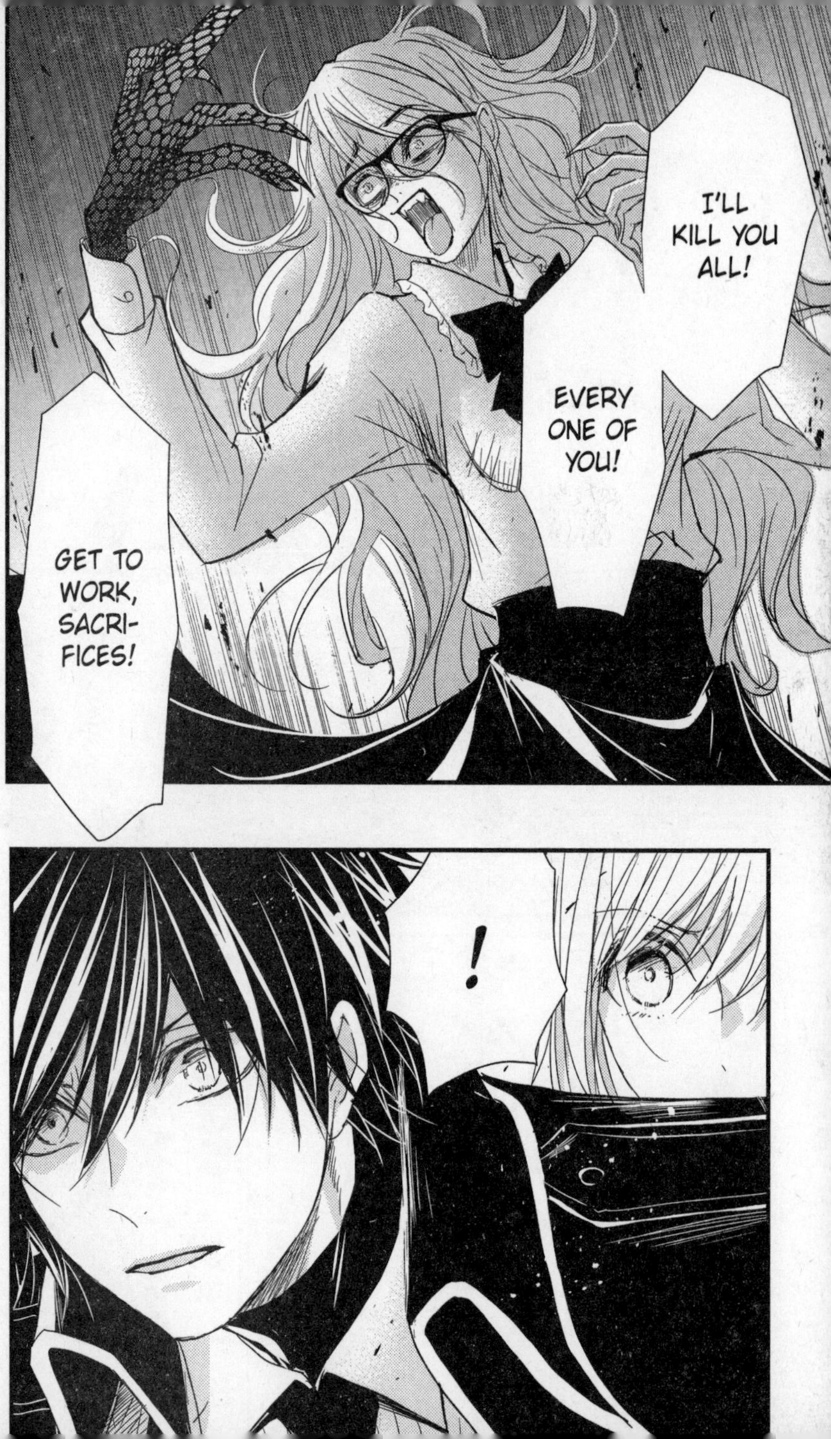
I'LL KILL YOU ALL!
EVERY ONE OF YOU!
GET TO WORK, SACRI-FICES!
!

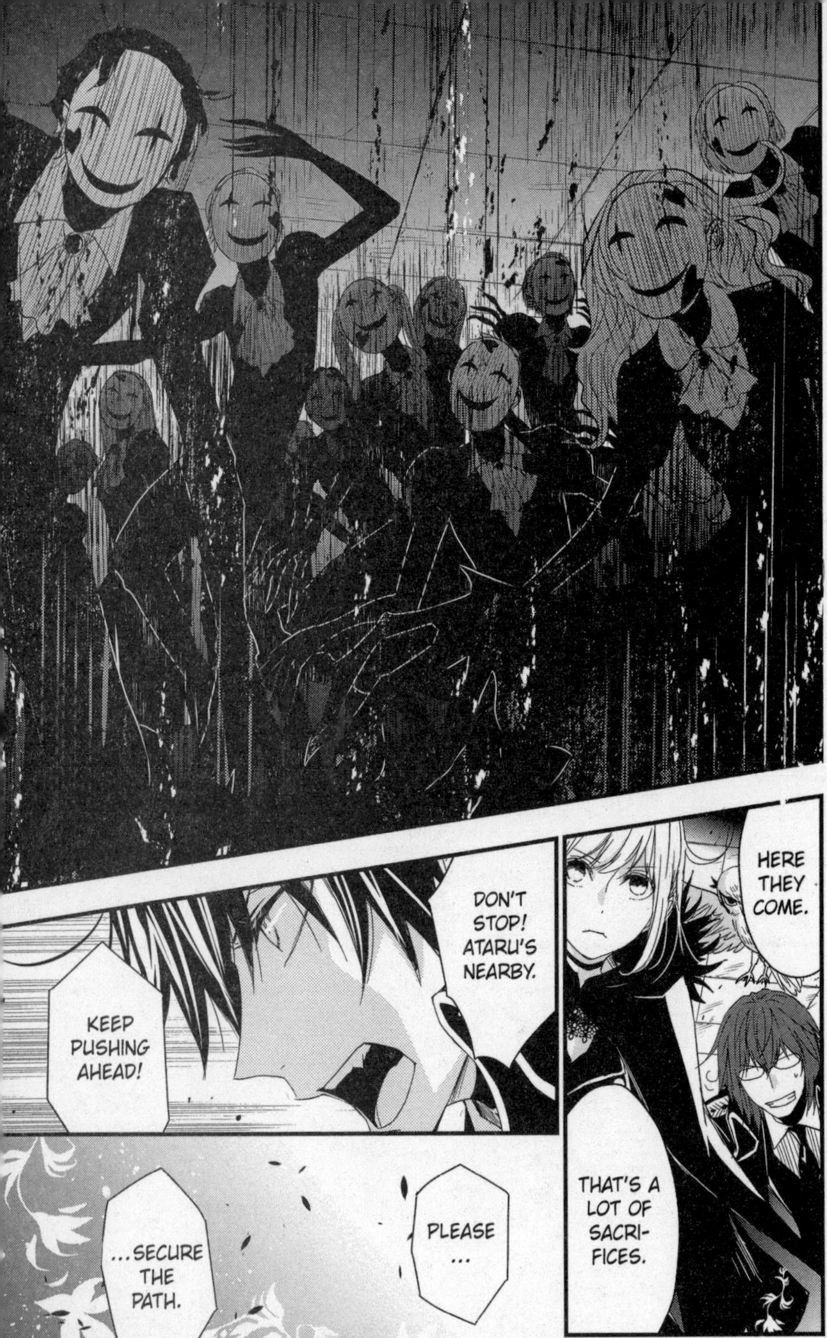
HERE THEY COME.
THAT'S A LOT OF SACRIFICES.
DON'T STOP! ATARU'S NEARBY.
KEEP PUSHING AHEAD!
PLEASE...
...SECURE THE PATH.

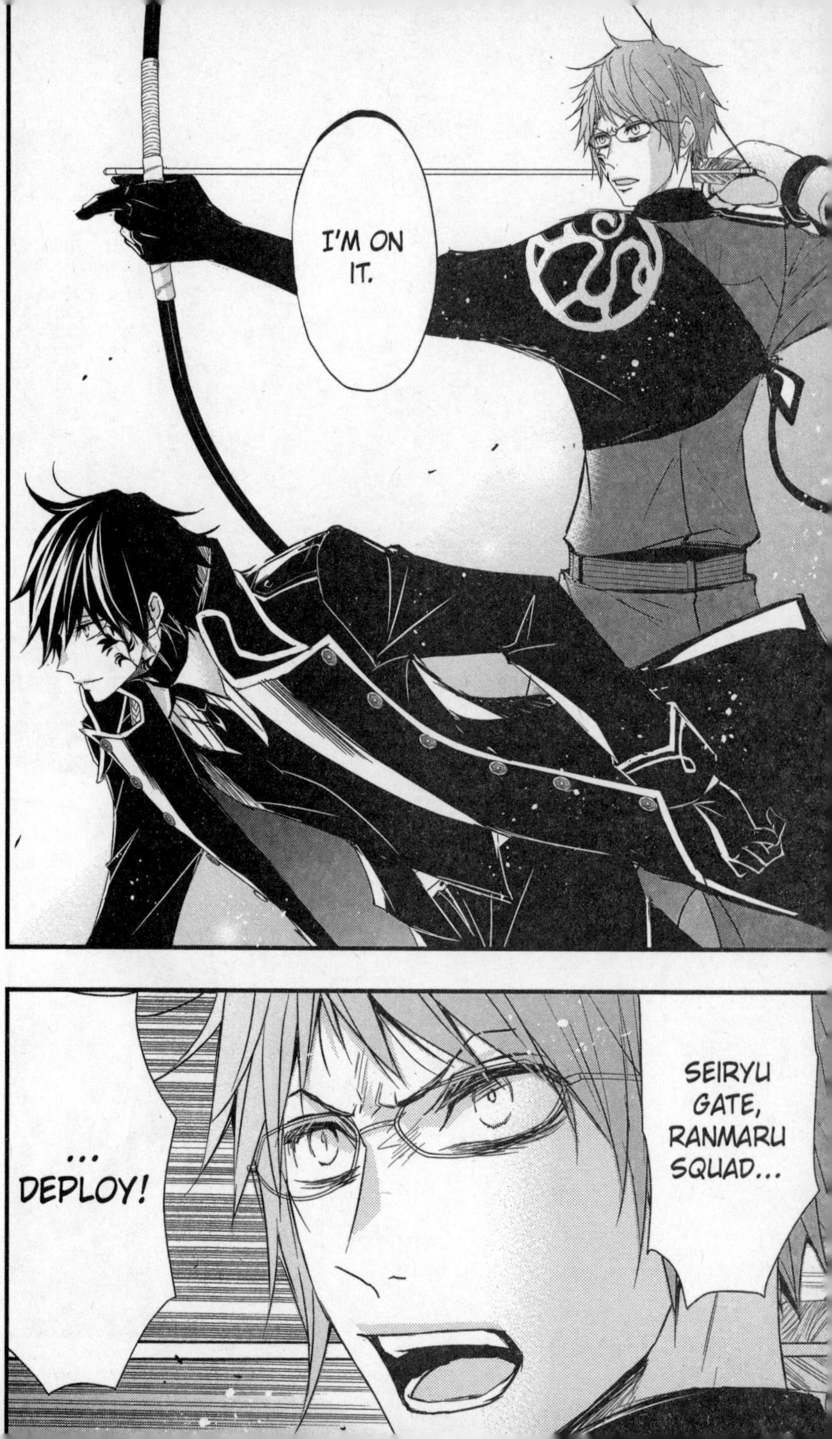
I'M ON IT.
SEIRYU GATE, RANMARU SQUAD...
...DEPLOY!

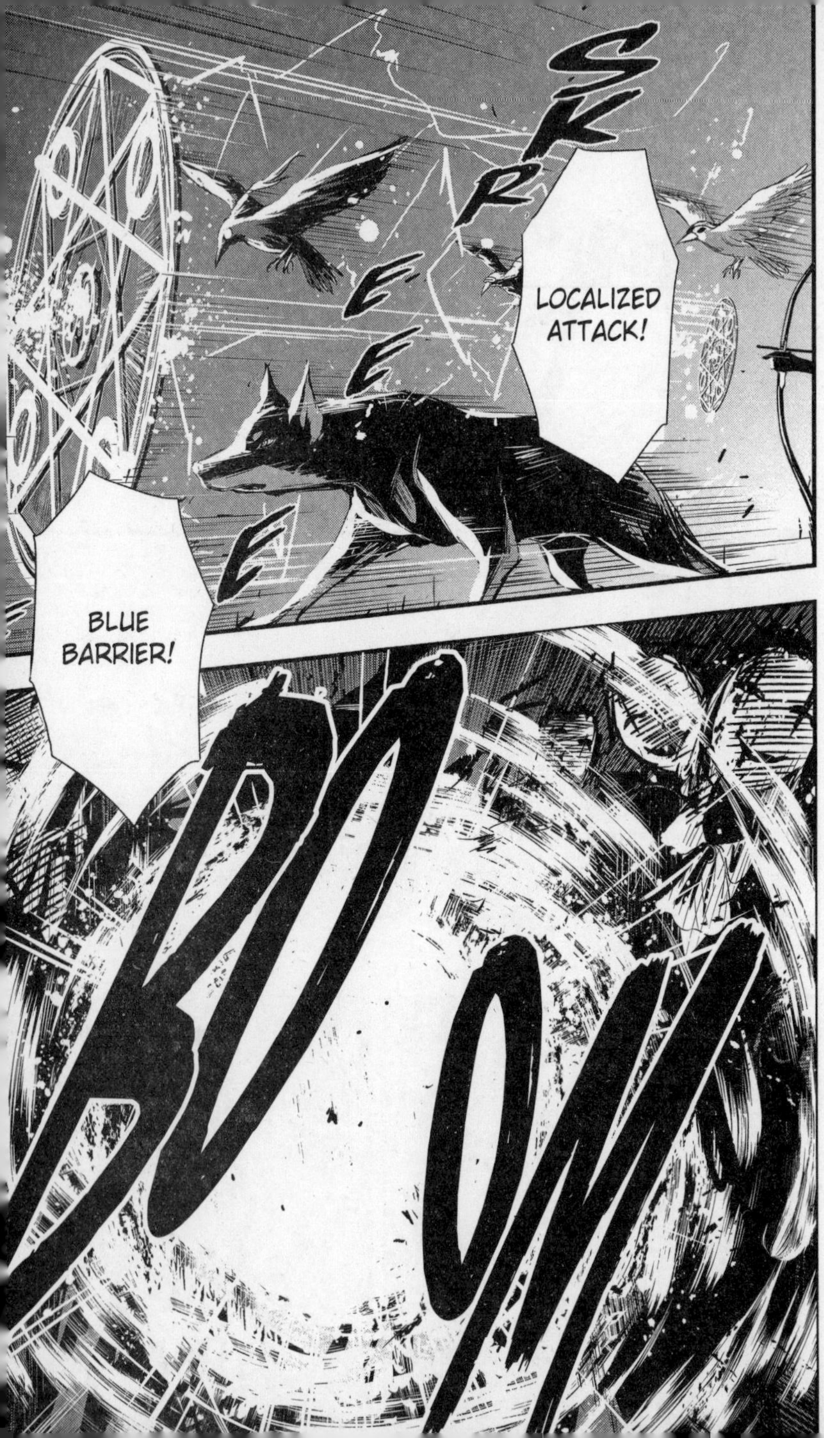
LOCALIZED ATTACK!
SKREEEE
BLUE BARRIER!

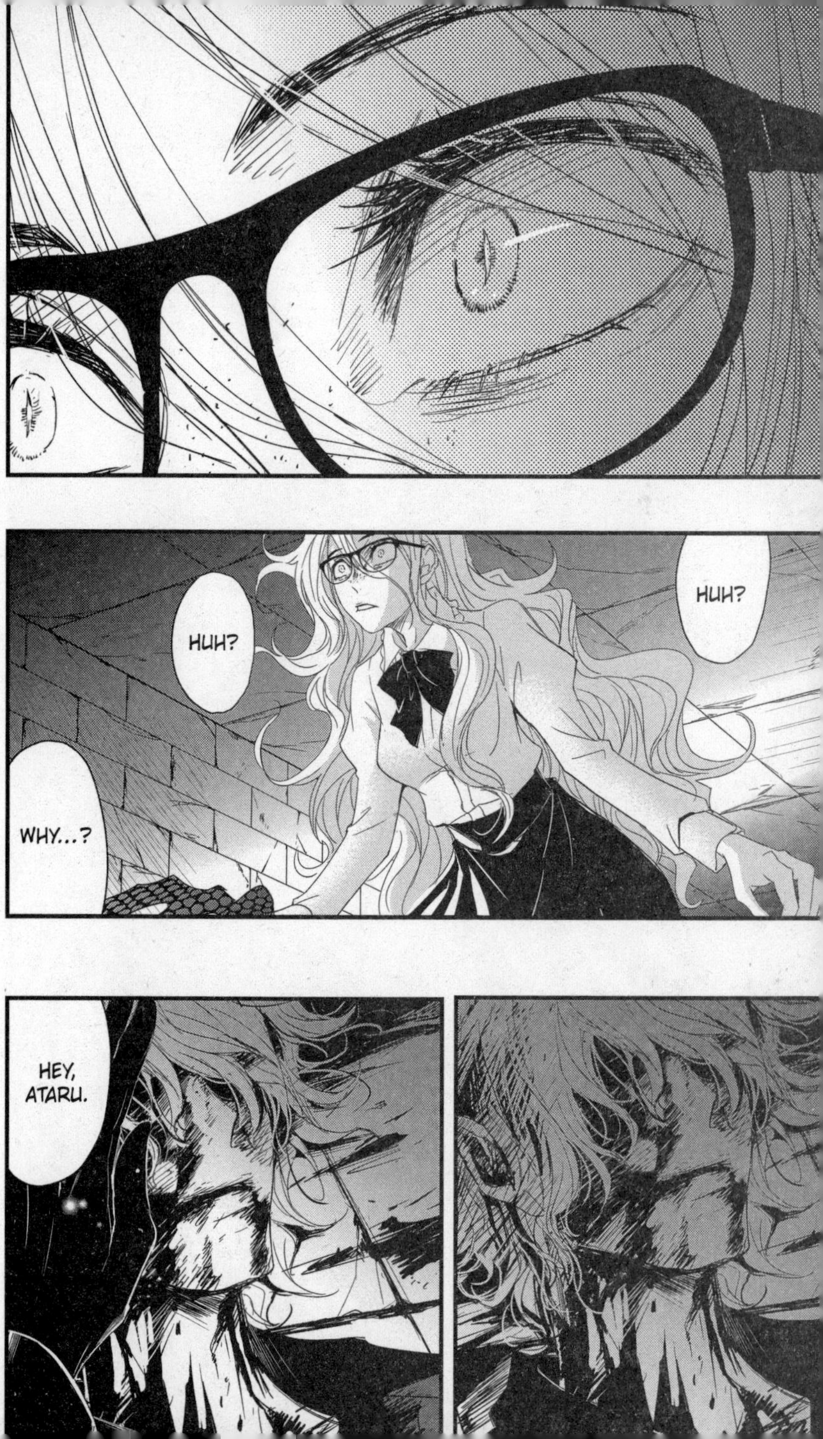
HUH?
HUH?
WHY...?
HEY, ATARU.

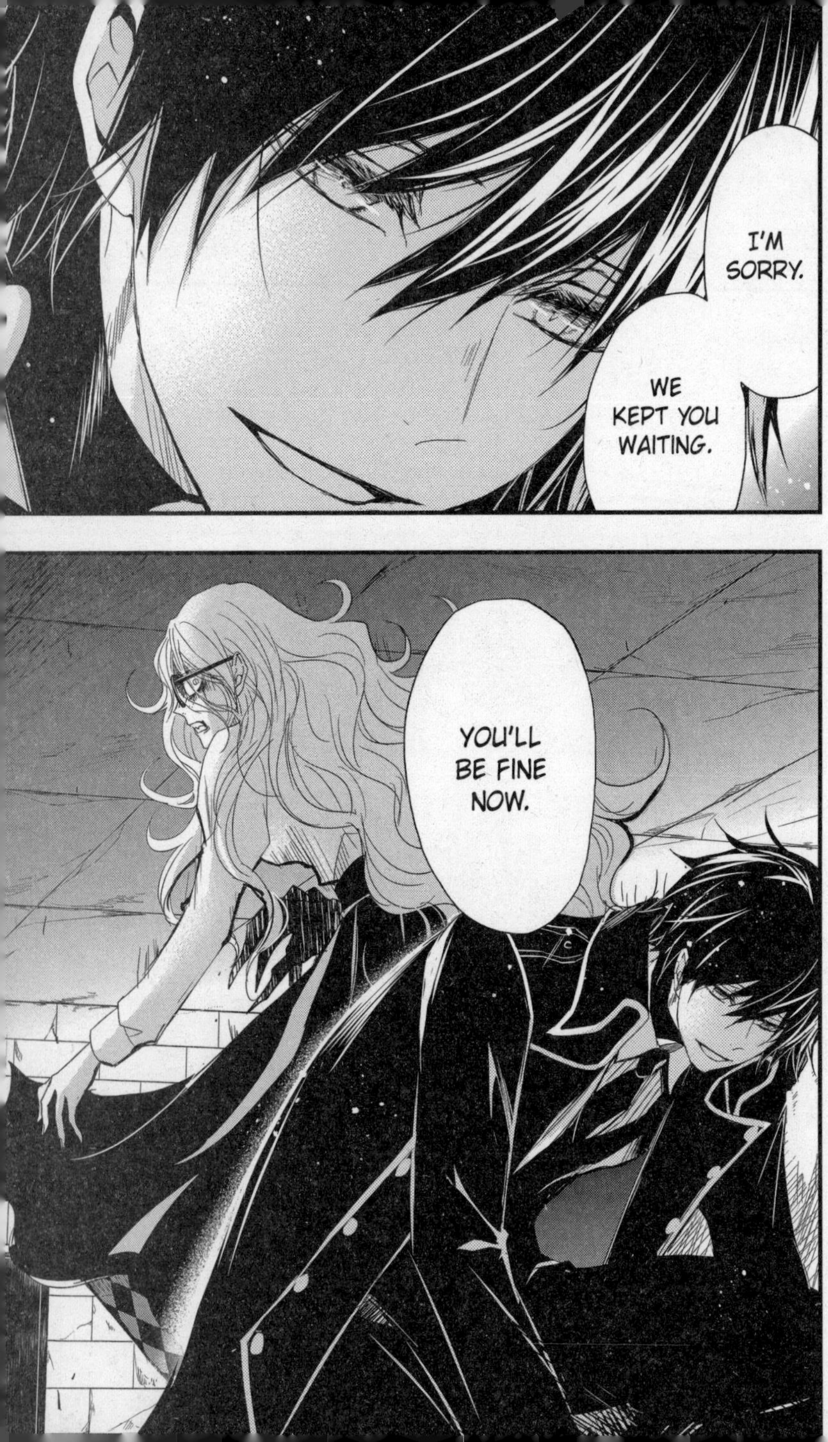
I'M SORRY.
WE KEPT YOU WAITING.
YOU'LL BE FINE NOW.

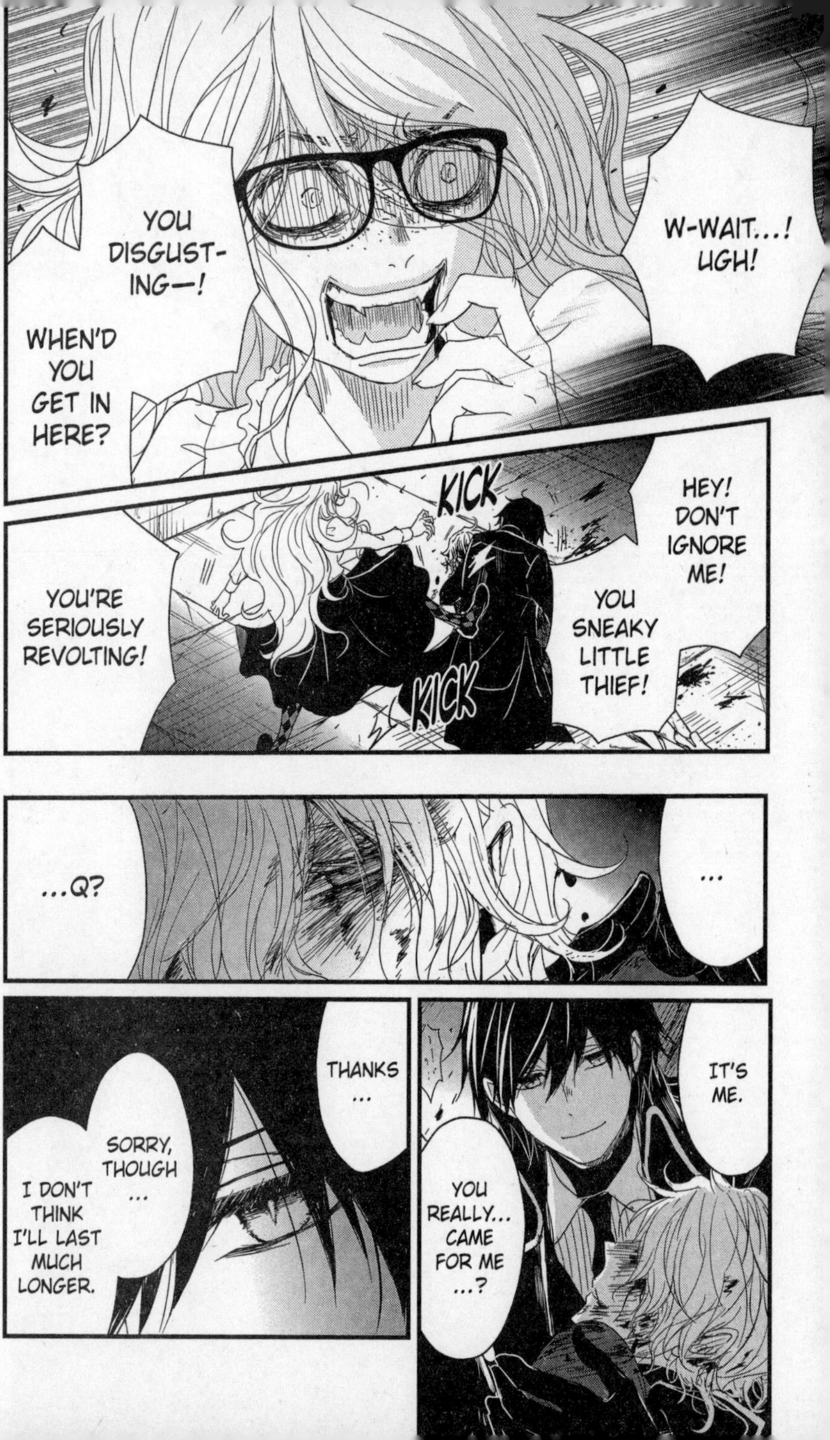
W-WAIT...! UGH!
YOU DISGUST-ING—!
WHEN'D YOU GET IN HERE?
HEY! DON'T IGNORE ME!
YOU SNEAKY LITTLE THIEF!
KICK
KICK
YOU'RE SERIOUSLY REVOLTING!
...
...Q?
IT'S ME.
YOU REALLY... CAME FOR ME ...?
THANKS ...
SORRY, THOUGH ...
I DON'T THINK I'LL LAST MUCH LONGER.

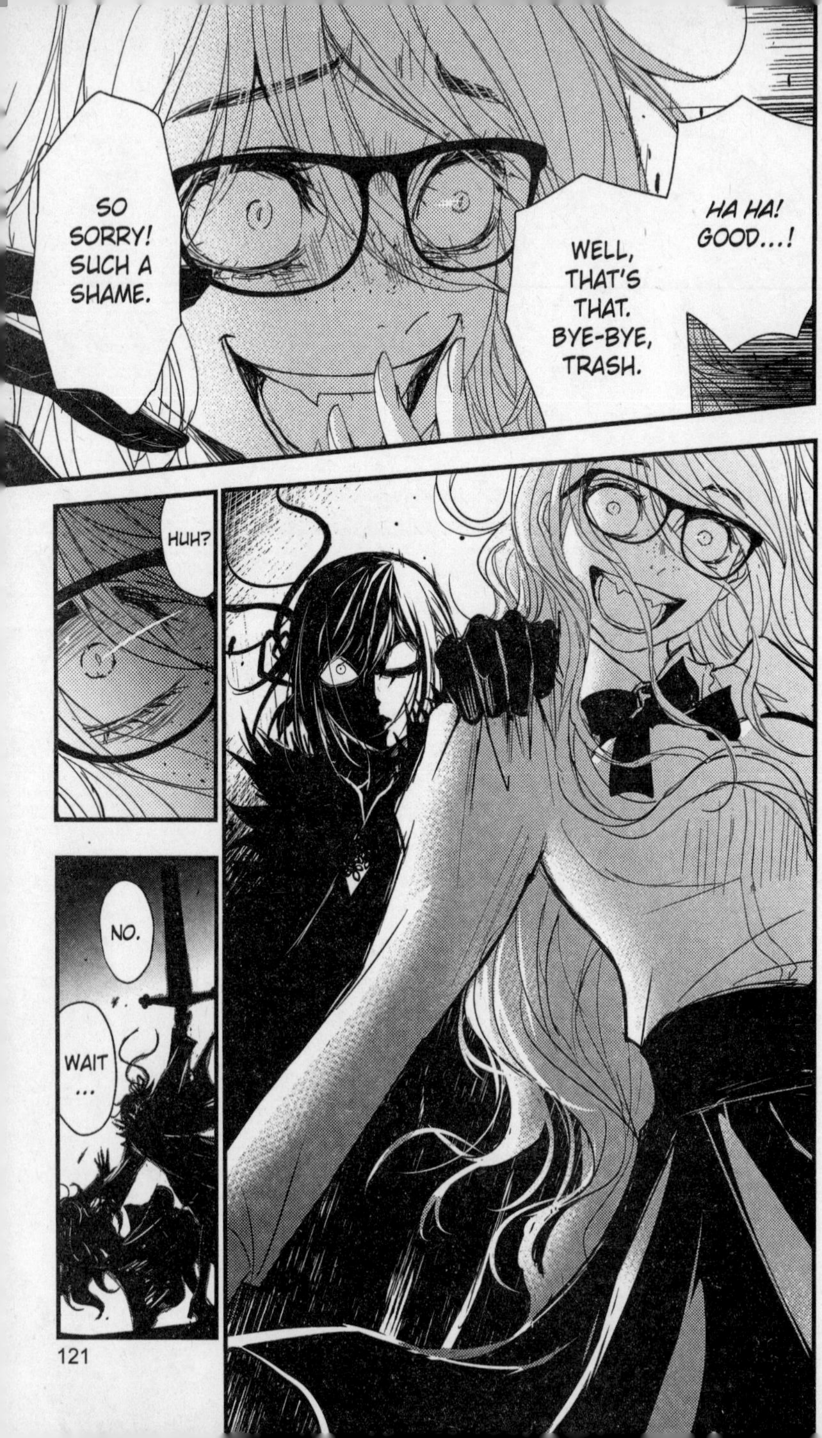
HA HA! GOOD...!
WELL, THAT'S THAT. BYE-BYE, TRASH.
SO SORRY! SUCH A SHAME.
HUH?
NO.
WAIT ...

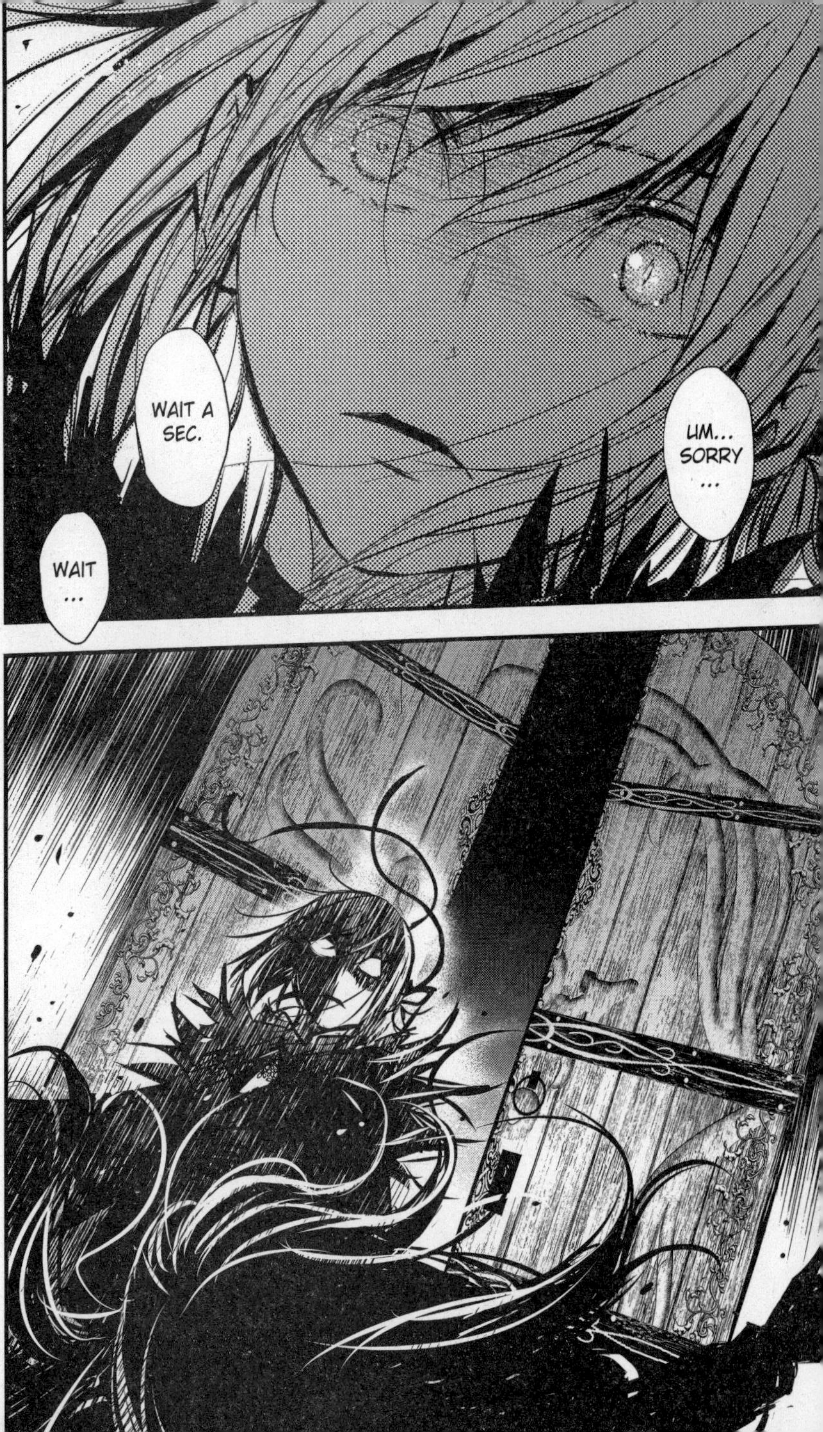
UM... SORRY ...
WAIT A SEC.
WAIT ...

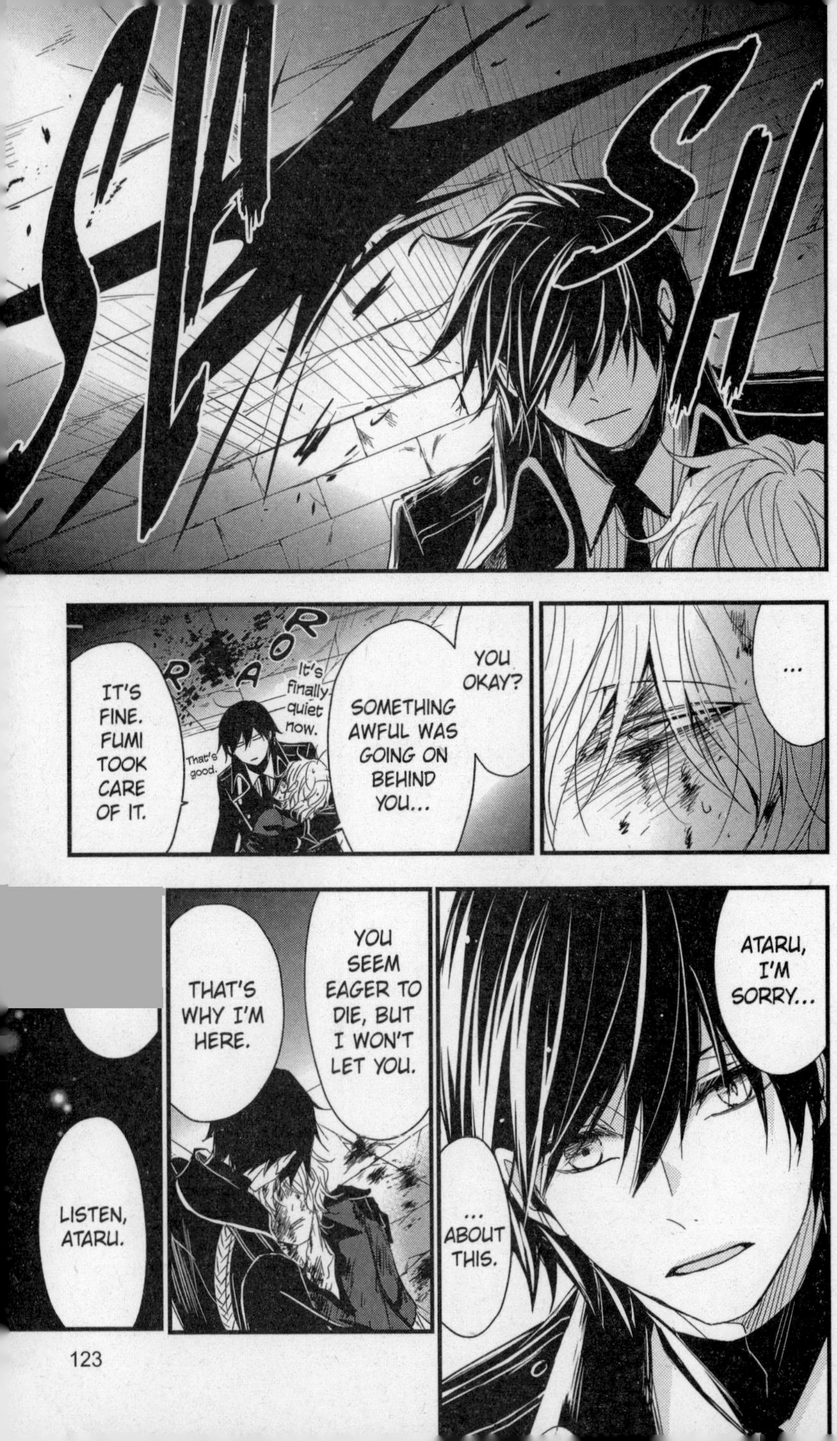
SHASH
...
YOU OKAY?
SOMETHING AWFUL WAS GOING ON BEHIND YOU...
It's finally quiet now.
ROAR
IT'S FINE. FUMI TOOK CARE OF IT.
That's good.
ATARU, I'M SORRY...
...ABOUT THIS.
YOU SEEM EAGER TO DIE, BUT I WON'T LET YOU.
THAT'S WHY I'M HERE.
LISTEN, ATARU.

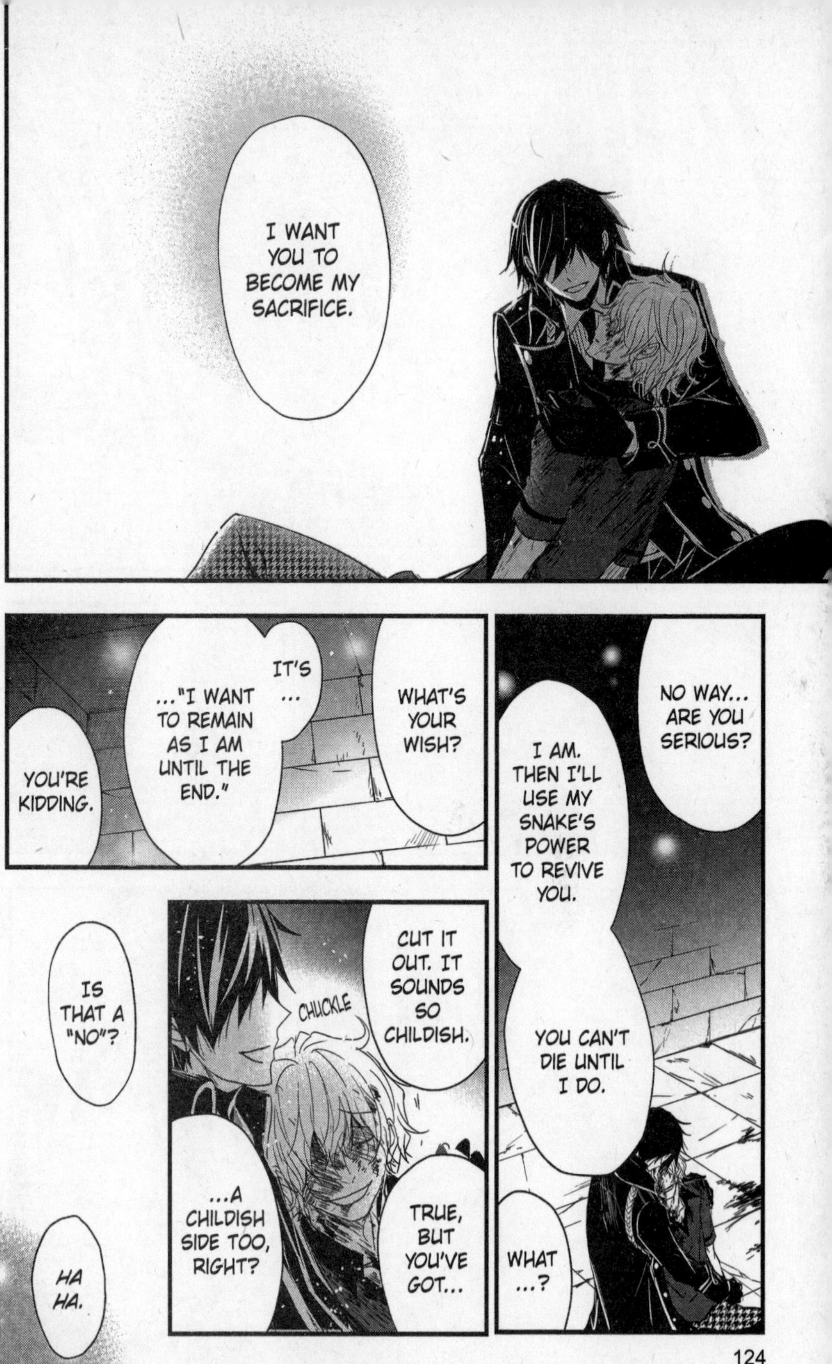
I WANT YOU TO BECOME MY SACRIFICE.
NO WAY... ARE YOU SERIOUS?
I AM. THEN I'LL USE MY SNAKE'S POWER TO REVIVE YOU.
YOU CAN'T DIE UNTIL I DO.
WHAT ...?
WHAT'S YOUR WISH?
IT'S ...
..."I WANT TO REMAIN AS I AM UNTIL THE END."
YOU'RE KIDDING.
CUT IT OUT. IT SOUNDS SO CHILDISH.
CHUCKLE
IS THAT A "NO"?
TRUE, BUT YOU'VE GOT...
...A CHILDISH SIDE TOO, RIGHT?
HA HA.

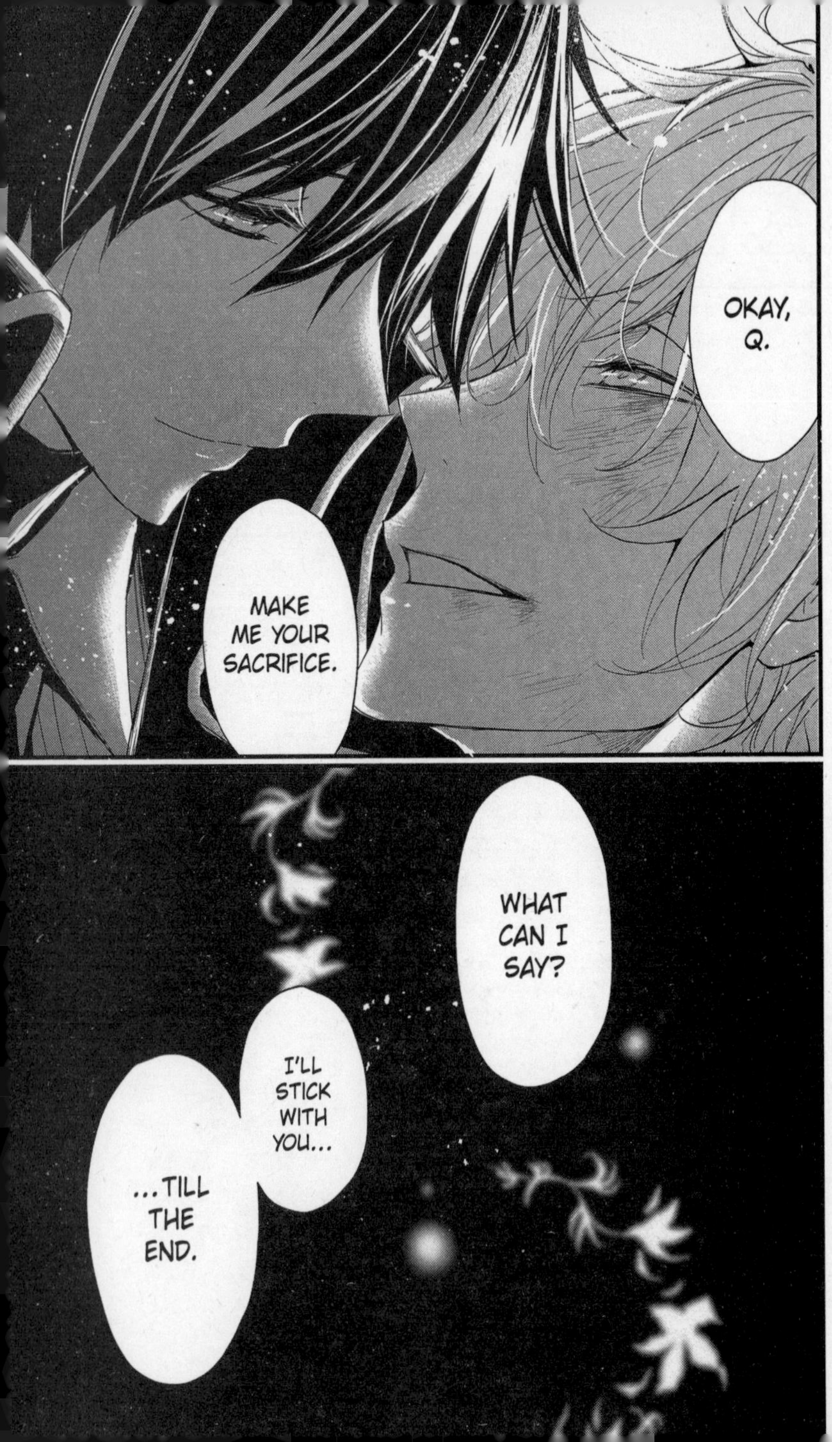
OKAY, Q.
MAKE ME YOUR SACRIFICE.
WHAT CAN I SAY?
I'LL STICK WITH YOU...
...TILL THE END.

MONTHLY BETSUCOMI SALE DATE NOTICE ON TWITTER AND INSTAGRAM

CHAPTER 65

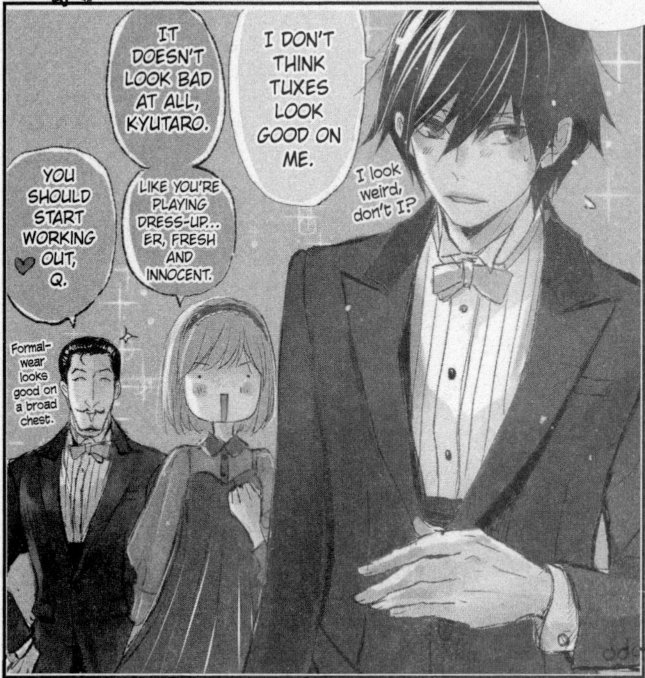
I DON'T THINK TUXES LOOK GOOD ON ME.
I look weird, don't I?
IT DOESN'T LOOK BAD AT ALL, KYUTARO.
LIKE YOU'RE PLAYING DRESS-UP... ER, FRESH AND INNOCENT.
YOU SHOULD START WORKING OUT, Q.
Formal-wear looks good on a broad chest.

LET'S SEE... WHAT'S UP IN *QUEEN'S QUALITY* THIS MONTH?
1) I HAVEN'T SAID SO, BUT THE BEAR IS THE SEIRYU LEADER.
2) ATARU OFTEN ENDS UP BEING CUDDLED.
3) WITHOUT HIS BONY SKULL, YANAGI LOOKS SO OUT OF PLACE IN HIS TUX THAT I HAD TO LAUGH OUT LOUD.

IN THIS SERIOUS CHAPTER, YANAGI IN HIS TUX IS PRETTY AWFUL.

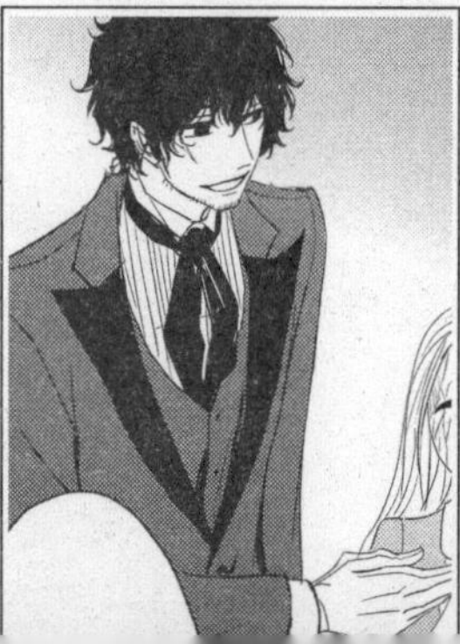

I ADMIT I FIDDLED WITH YANAGI'S TUX A LOT, BUT DOES ANYONE REALLY LOOK SO AWKWARD IN ONE? HE LOOKED TOO MUCH LIKE SOMEONE WHO JUST SWITCHED CAREERS TO BECOME A MAGICIAN, SO I MADE SOME CORRECTIONS FOR THE GRAPHIC NOVEL VERSION. HE HAD TO CHANGE HIS CLOTHES BECAUSE HIS RENTAL DEADLINE HAD PASSED.

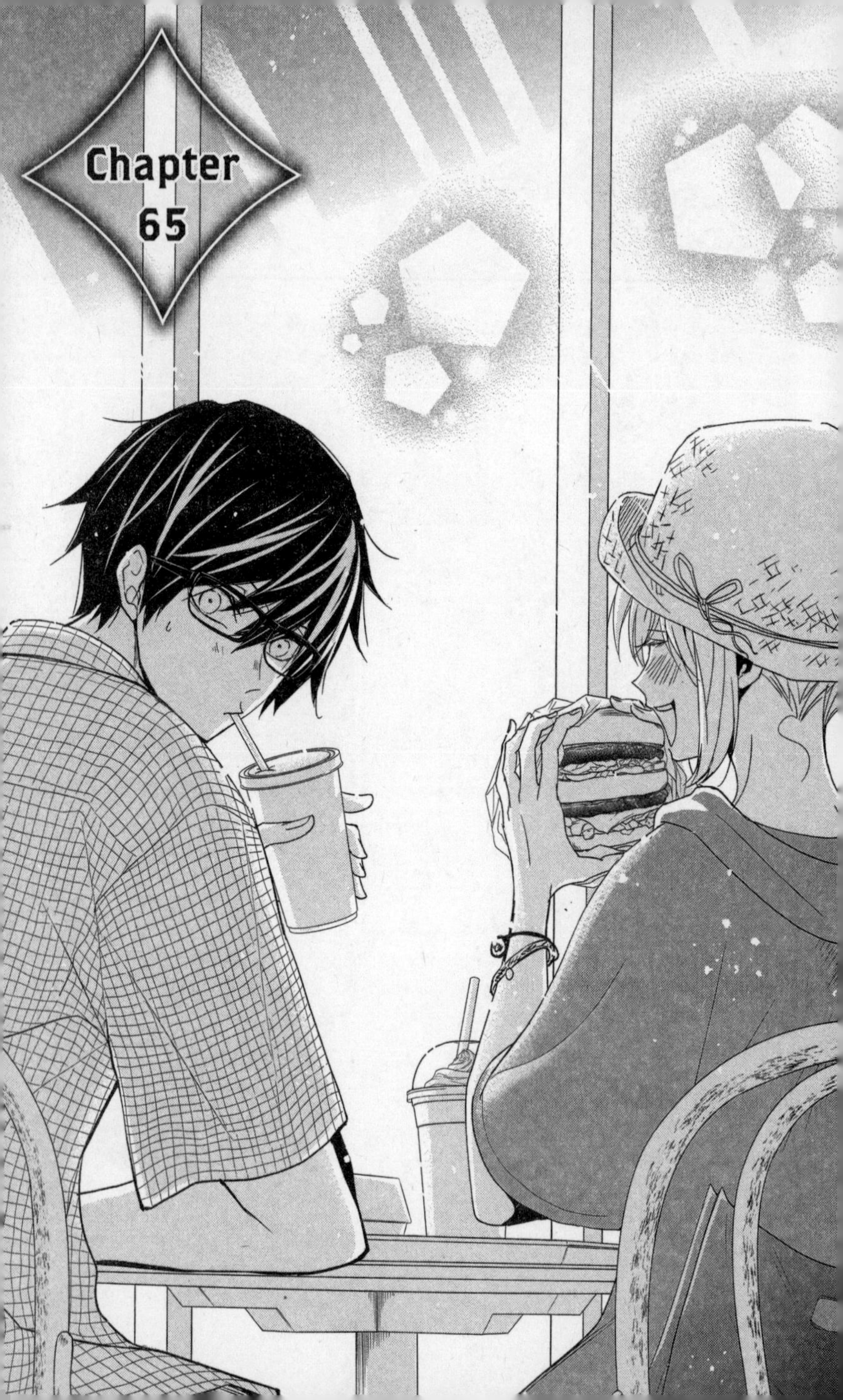
Chapter 65

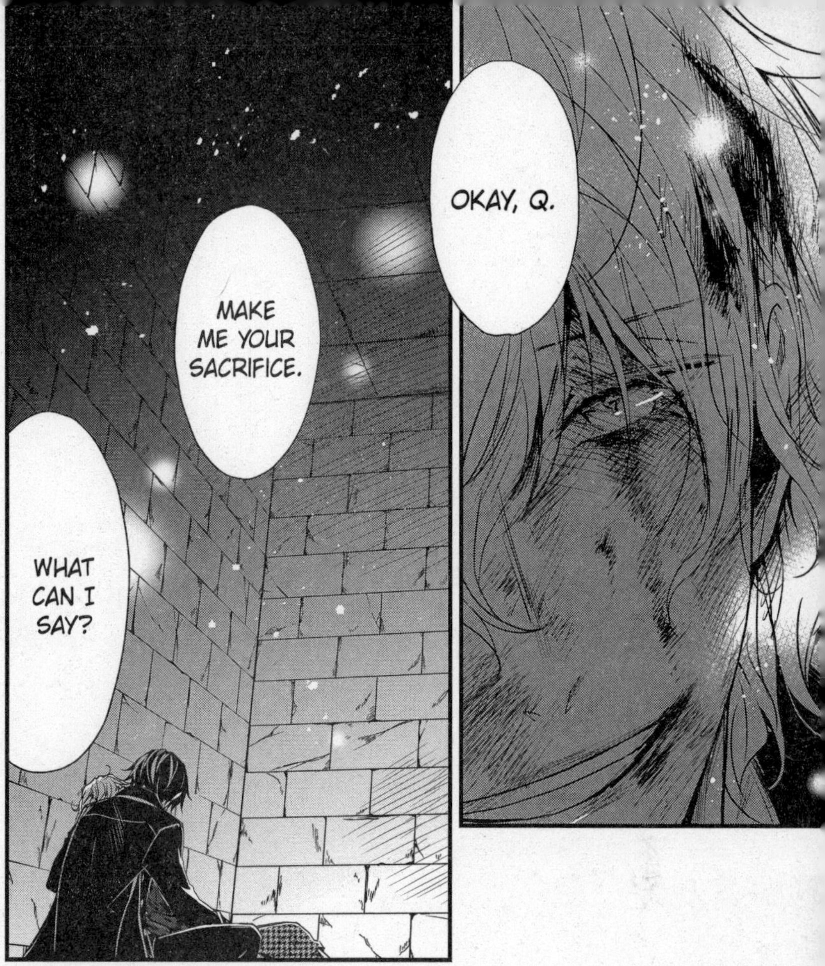
OKAY, Q.
MAKE ME YOUR SACRIFICE.
WHAT CAN I SAY?

I've been exercising and working out lately. If I keep it up, I think eventually I'll have well-defined abs.

This is completely unrelated, but my heels have been cracking. I've tried sanding them down and putting medicine on them, but the cracks keep returning, so I've decided to go back to basics and moisturize them. I'm hoping that by the time I have my six-pack, my heels will have healed. I just have to keep it up.

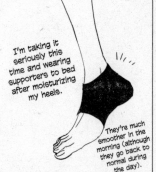

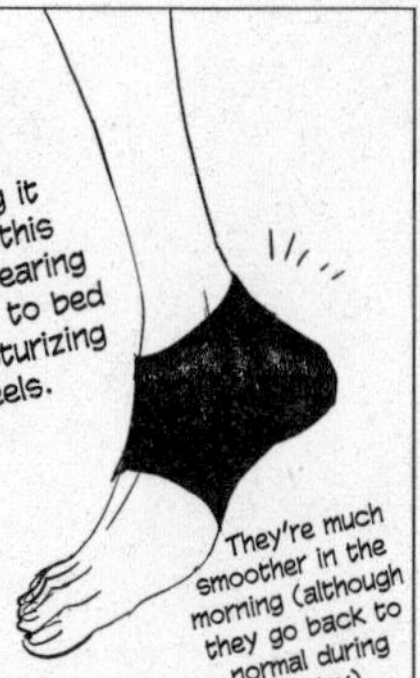
I'm taking it seriously this time and wearing supporters to bed after moisturizing my heels.
They're much smoother in the morning (although they go back to normal during the day).

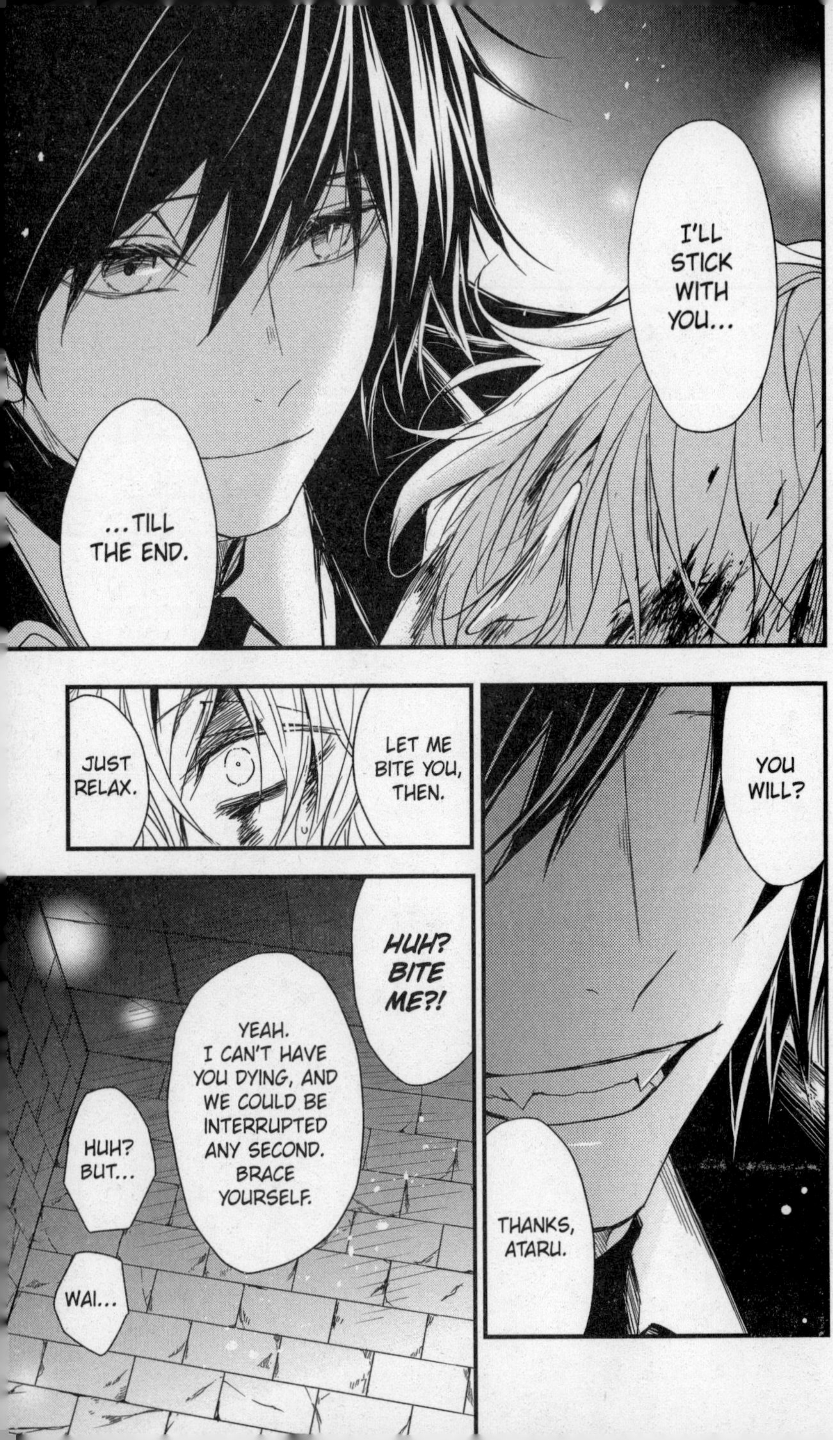
I'LL STICK WITH YOU...
...TILL THE END.
YOU WILL?
THANKS, ATARU.
LET ME BITE YOU, THEN.
JUST RELAX.
HUH? BITE ME?!
YEAH. I CAN'T HAVE YOU DYING, AND WE COULD BE INTERRUPTED ANY SECOND. BRACE YOURSELF.
HUH? BUT...
WAI...

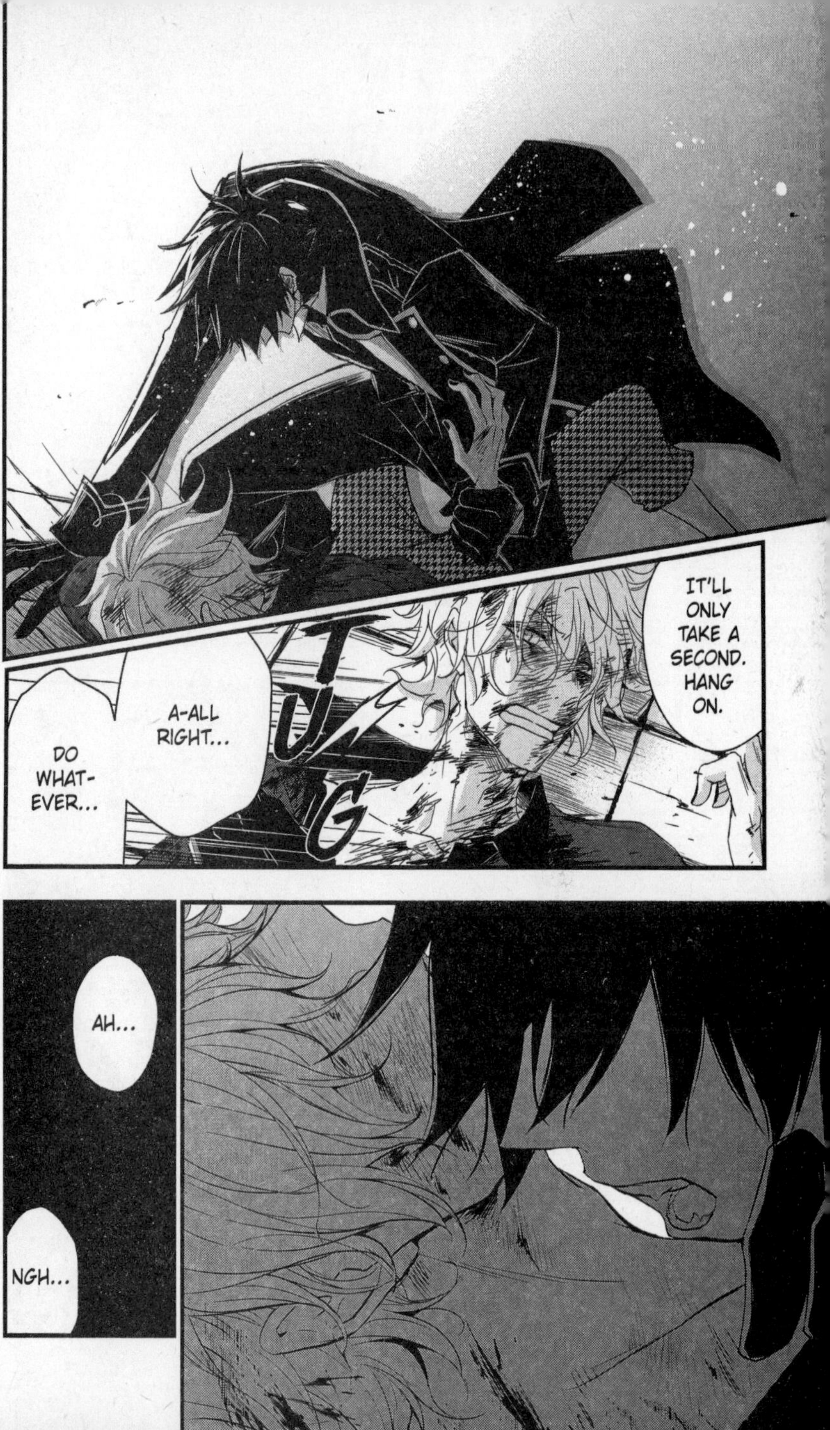
IT'LL ONLY TAKE A SECOND. HANG ON.
TUG
A-ALL RIGHT...
DO WHAT-EVER...
AH...
NGH...

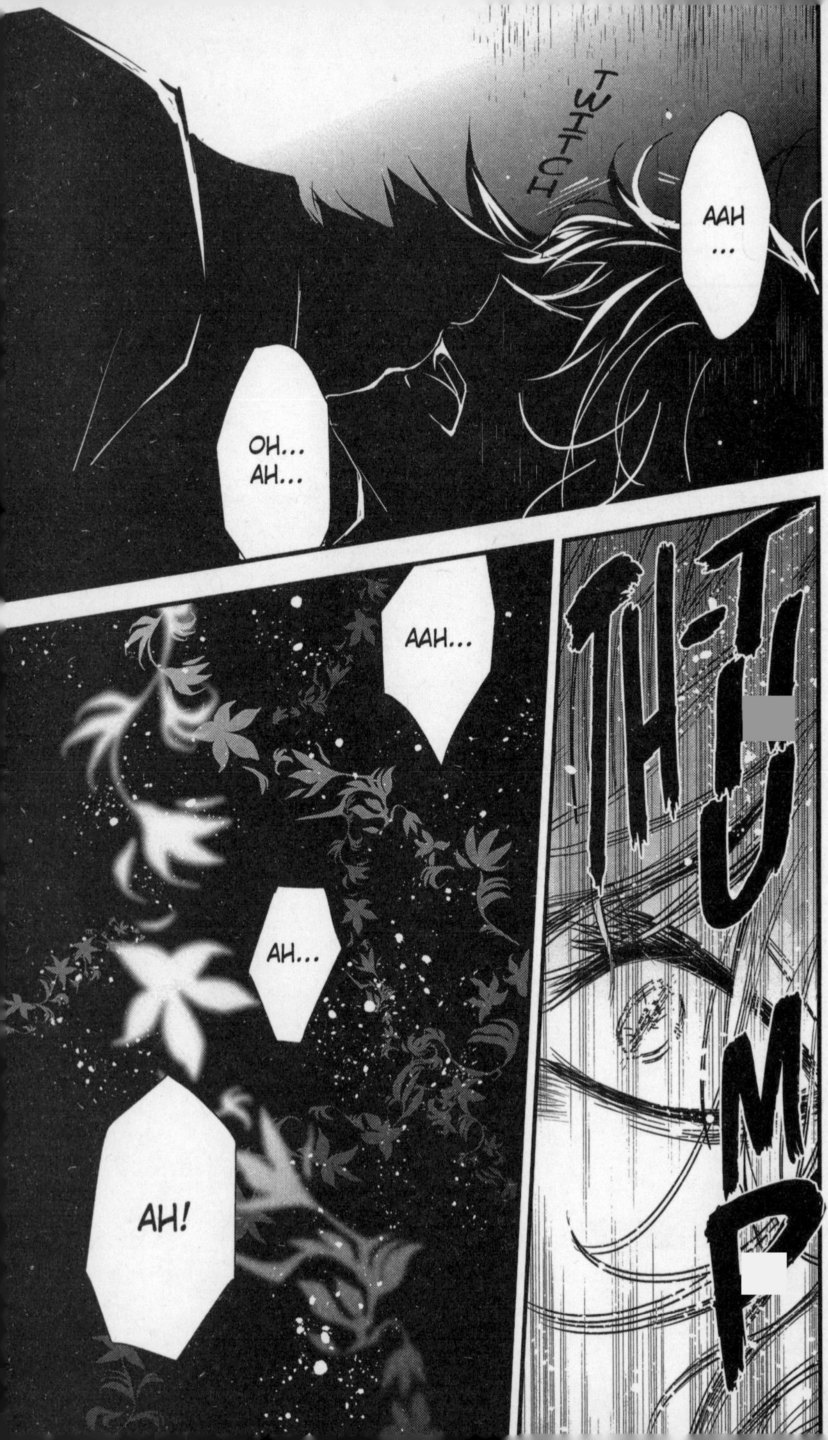
AAH ...
TWITCH
OH... AH...
TH-UMP
AAH...
AH...
AH!

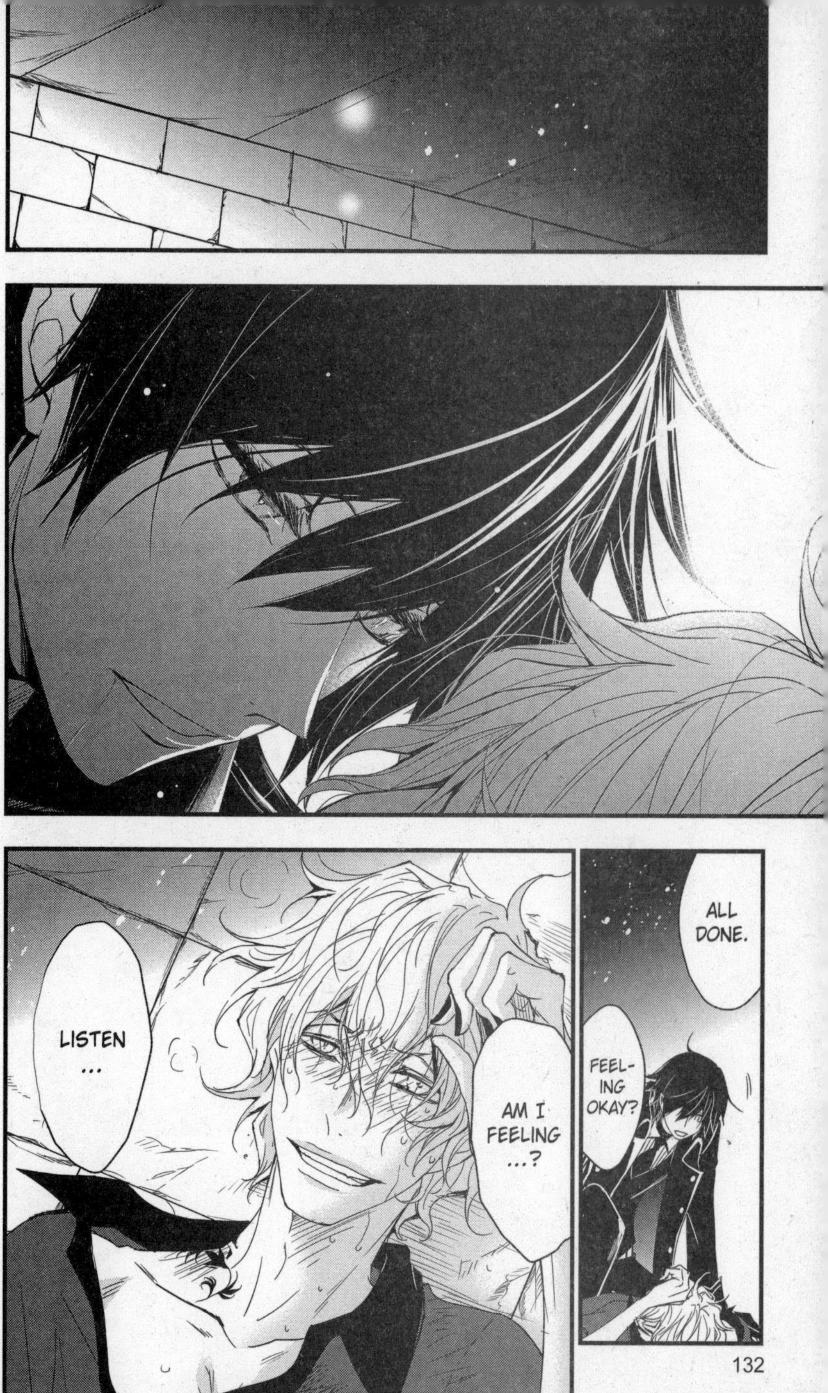
ALL DONE.
FEEL-ING OKAY?
AM I FEELING ...?
LISTEN ...

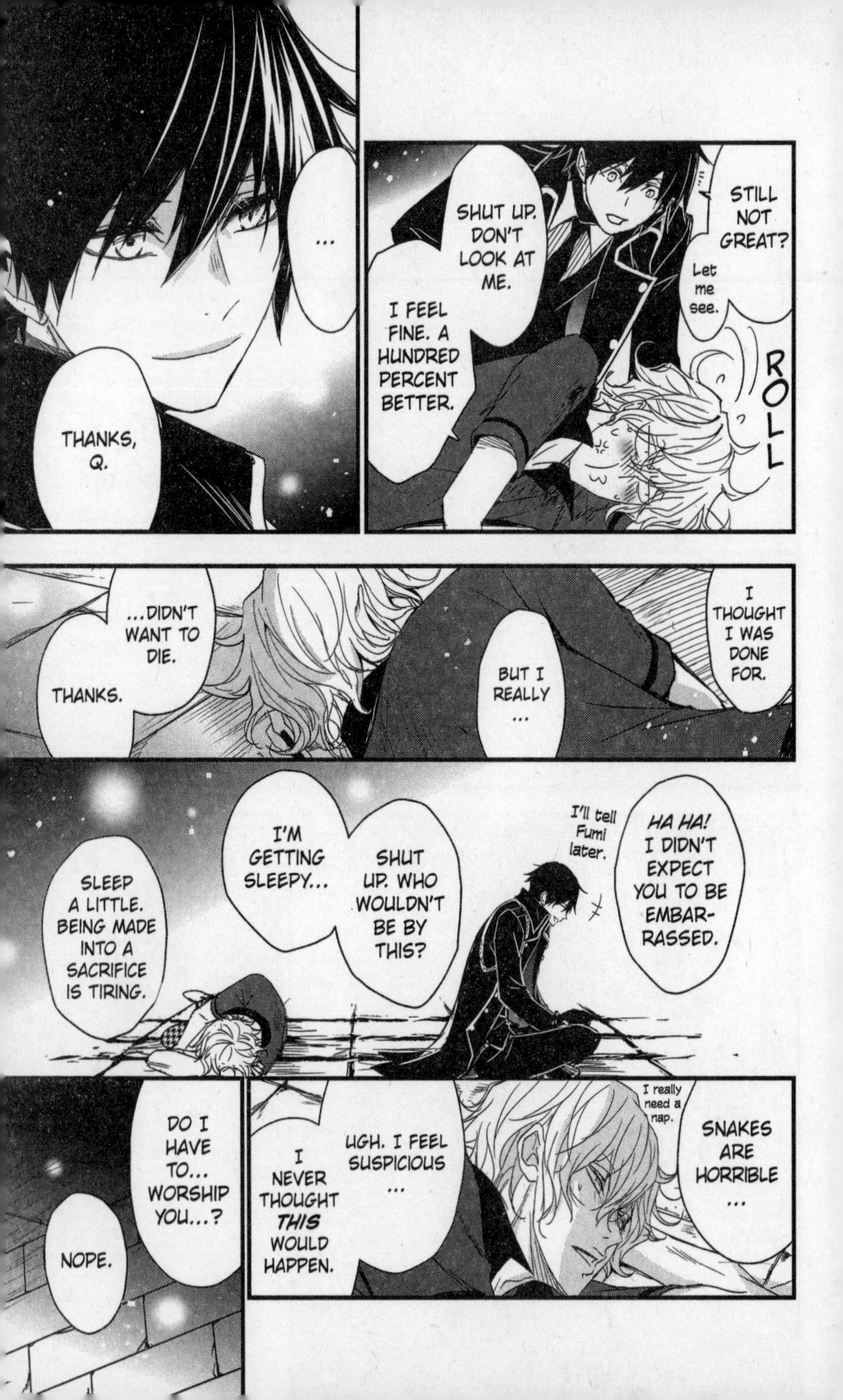
STILL NOT GREAT?
Let me see.
ROLL
SHUT UP. DON'T LOOK AT ME.
I FEEL FINE. A HUNDRED PERCENT BETTER.
...
THANKS, Q.
I THOUGHT I WAS DONE FOR.
BUT I REALLY ...
...DIDN'T WANT TO DIE.
THANKS.
HA HA! I DIDN'T EXPECT YOU TO BE EMBARRASSED.
I'll tell Fumi later.
SHUT UP. WHO WOULDN'T BE BY THIS?
I'M GETTING SLEEPY...
SLEEP A LITTLE. BEING MADE INTO A SACRIFICE IS TIRING.
SNAKES ARE HORRIBLE ...
I really need a nap.
UGH. I FEEL SUSPICIOUS ...
I NEVER THOUGHT *THIS* WOULD HAPPEN.
DO I HAVE TO... WORSHIP YOU...?
NOPE.

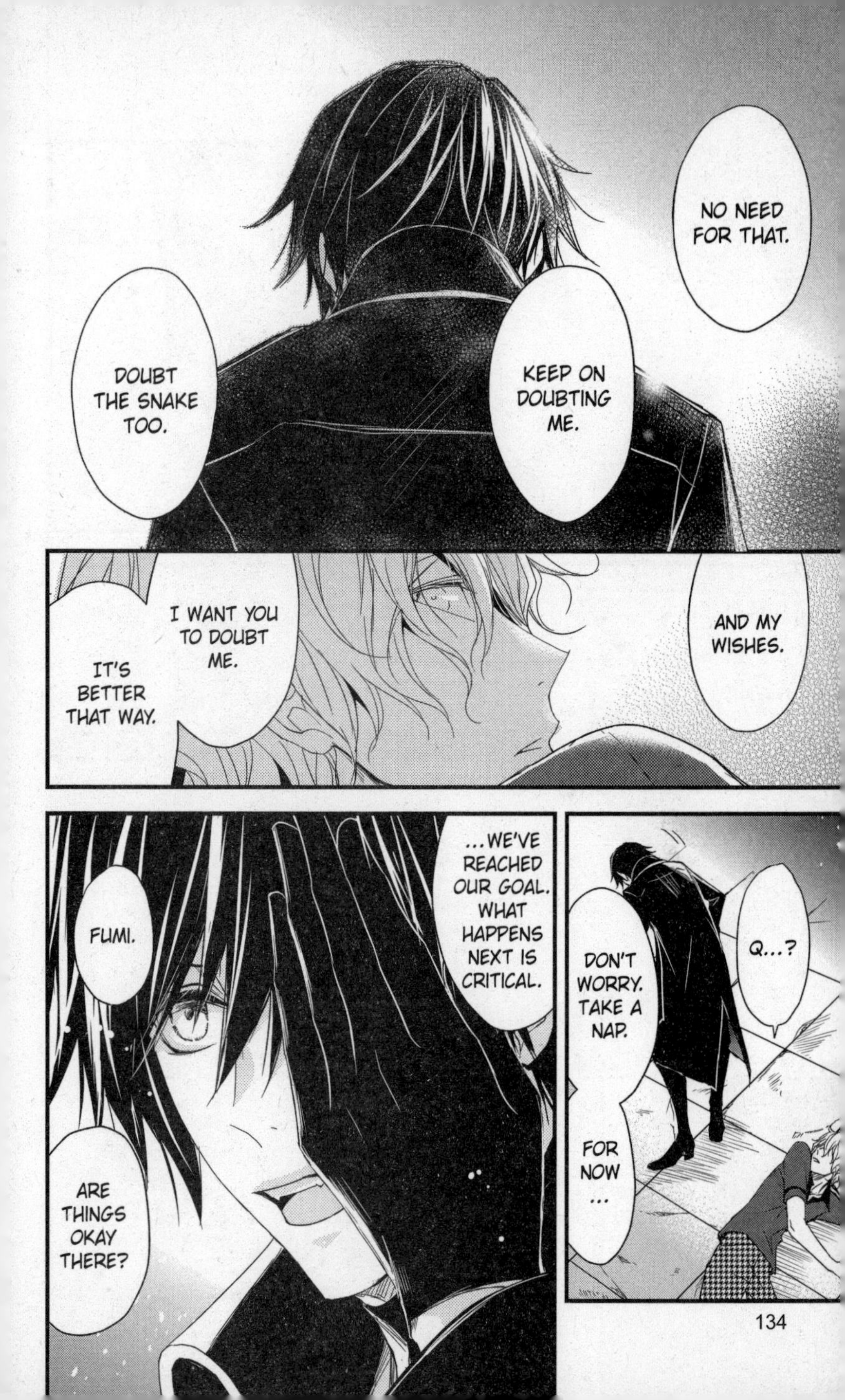
NO NEED FOR THAT.
KEEP ON DOUBTING ME.
DOUBT THE SNAKE TOO.
AND MY WISHES.
I WANT YOU TO DOUBT ME.
IT'S BETTER THAT WAY.
Q...?
DON'T WORRY. TAKE A NAP.
FOR NOW ...
...WE'VE REACHED OUR GOAL. WHAT HAPPENS NEXT IS CRITICAL.
FUMI.
ARE THINGS OKAY THERE?

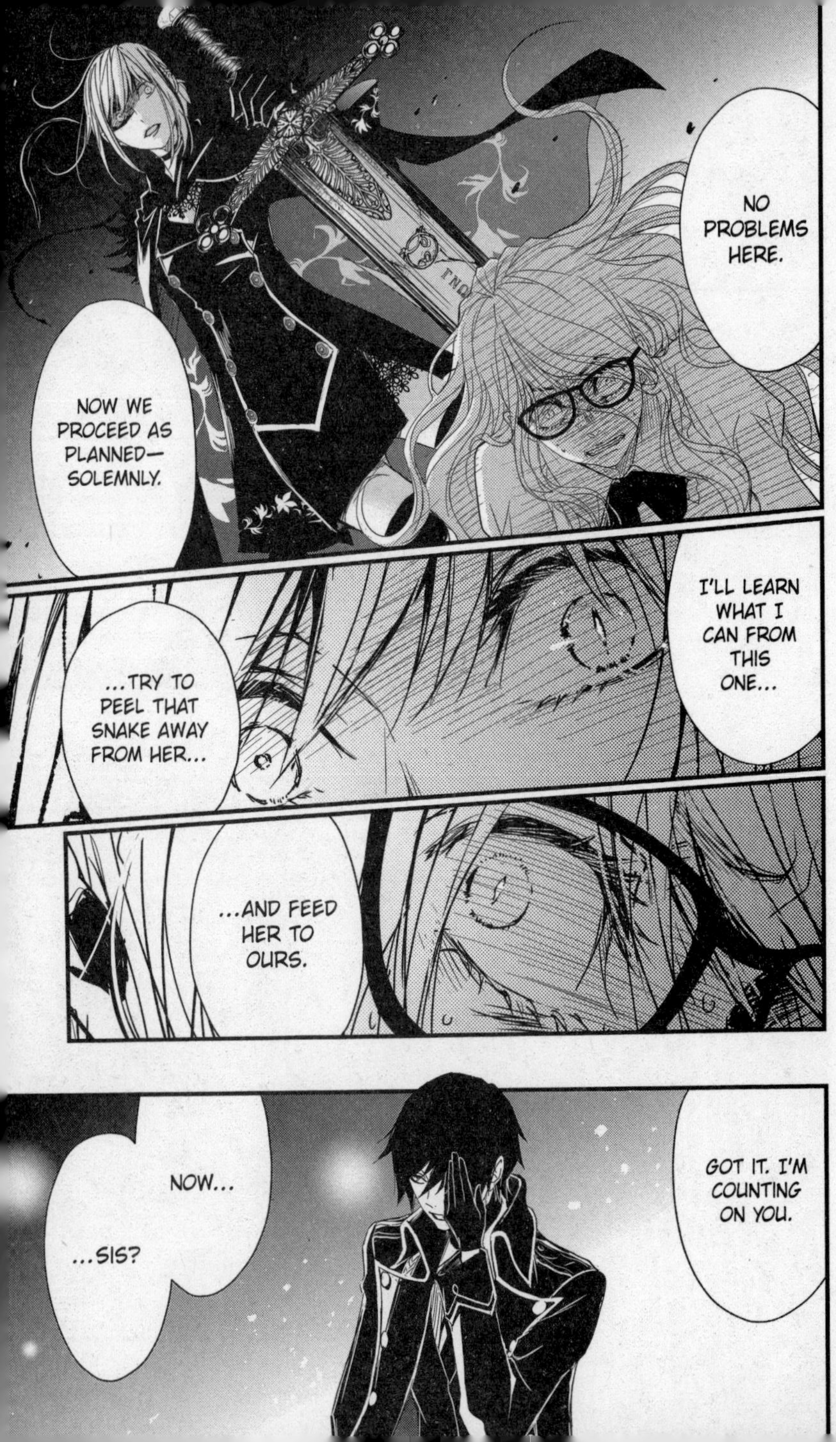
NO PROBLEMS HERE.
NOW WE PROCEED AS PLANNED—SOLEMNLY.
I'LL LEARN WHAT I CAN FROM THIS ONE...
...TRY TO PEEL THAT SNAKE AWAY FROM HER...
...AND FEED HER TO OURS.
GOT IT. I'M COUNTING ON YOU.
NOW...
...SIS?

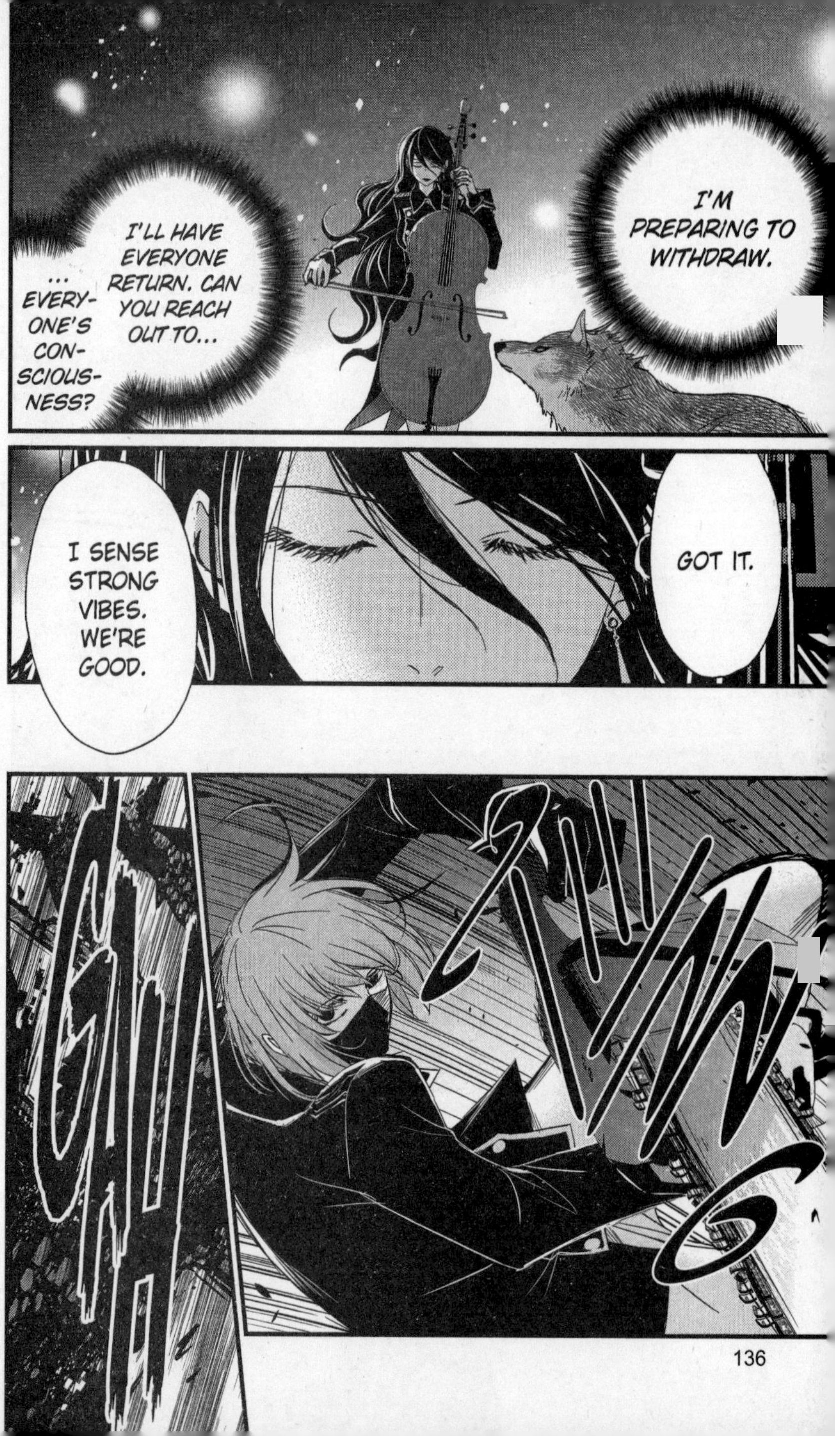
I'M PREPARING TO WITHDRAW.
I'LL HAVE EVERYONE RETURN. CAN YOU REACH OUT TO...
...EVERYONE'S CONSCIOUSNESS?
GOT IT.
I SENSE STRONG VIBES. WE'RE GOOD.

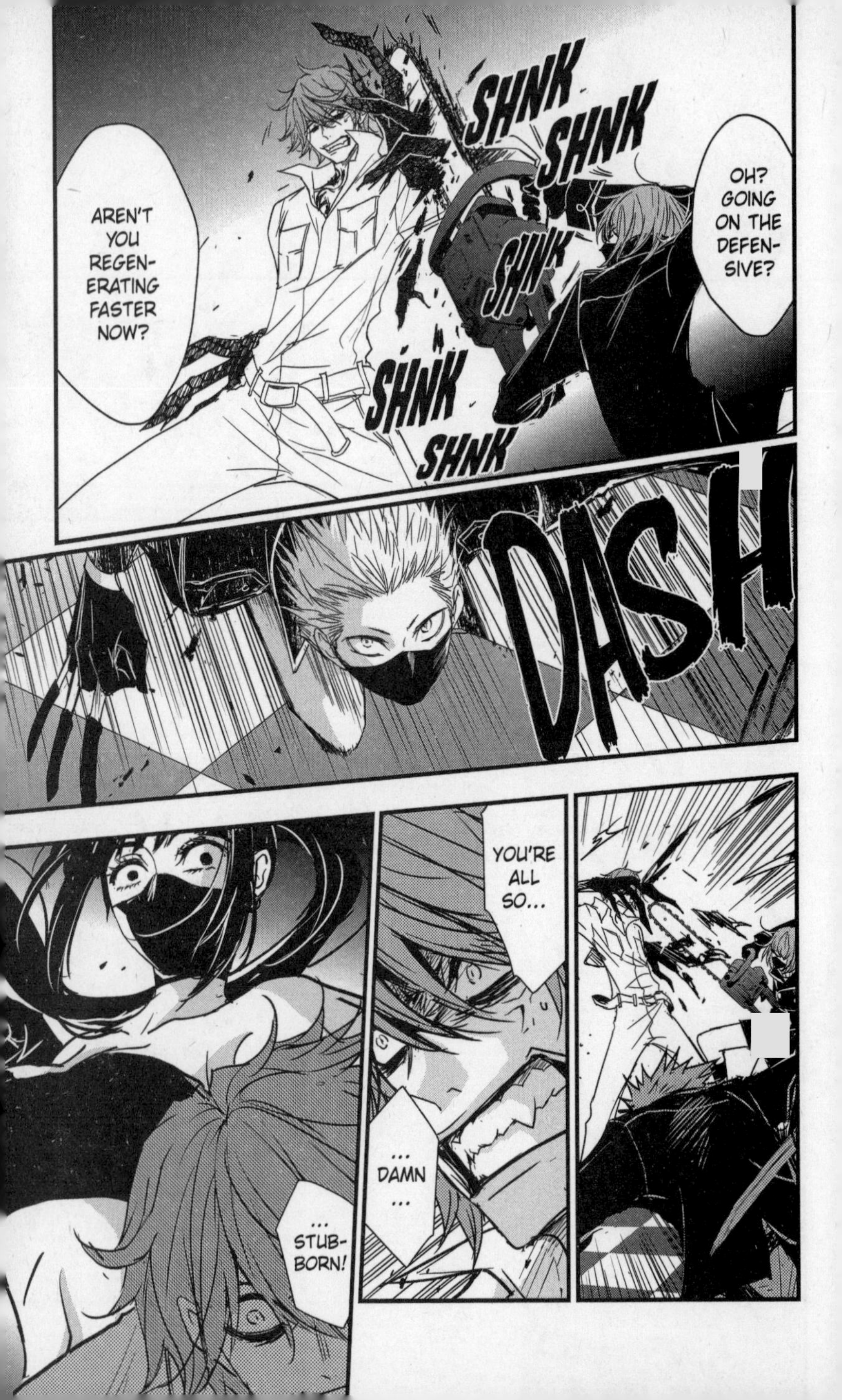
OH? GOING ON THE DEFEN-SIVE?
SHNK
SHNK
SHNK
SHNK
SHNK
AREN'T YOU REGEN-ERATING FASTER NOW?
DASH
YOU'RE ALL SO...
...DAMN...
...STUB-BORN!

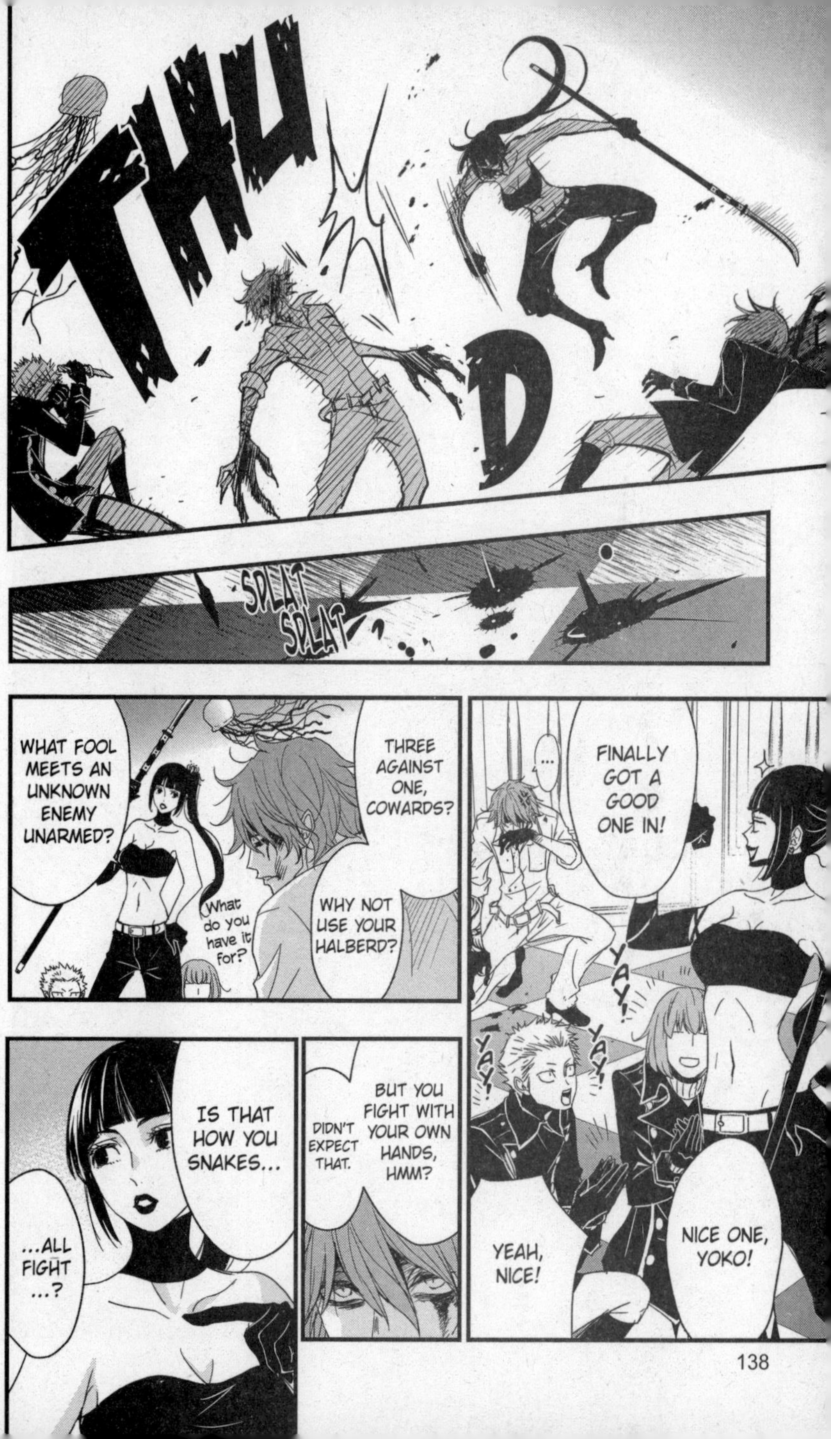
THUD
SPLAT
SPLAT
FINALLY GOT A GOOD ONE IN!
...
YAY!
YAY!
YAY!
NICE ONE, YOKO!
YEAH, NICE!
THREE AGAINST ONE, COWARDS?
WHY NOT USE YOUR HALBERD?
What do you have it for?
WHAT FOOL MEETS AN UNKNOWN ENEMY UNARMED?
BUT YOU FIGHT WITH YOUR OWN HANDS, HMM?
DIDN'T EXPECT THAT.
IS THAT HOW YOU SNAKES...
...ALL FIGHT ...?

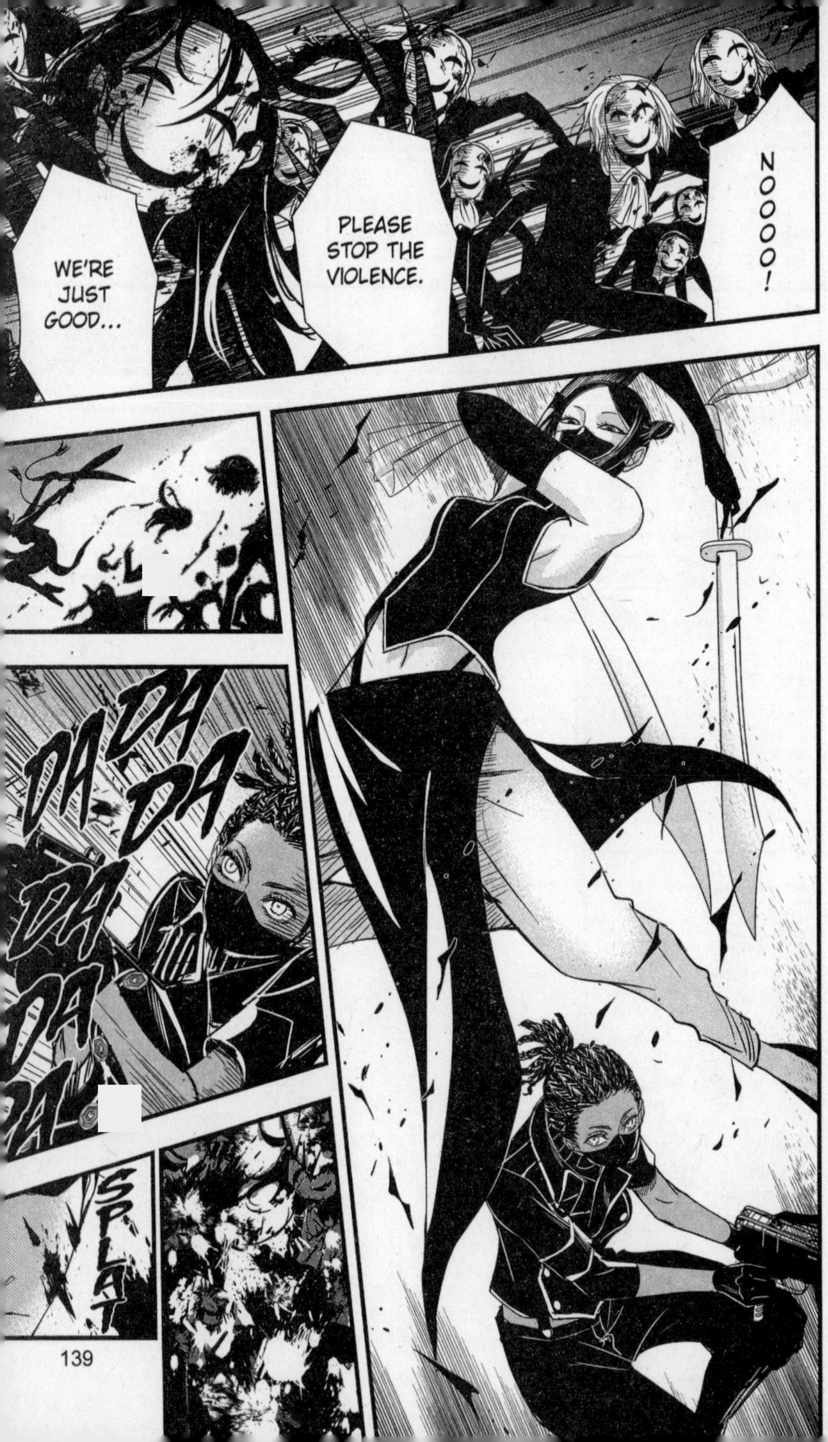

NOOOOO!
PLEASE STOP THE VIOLENCE.
WE'RE JUST GOOD...
DA DA DA DA DA DA DA
SPLAT

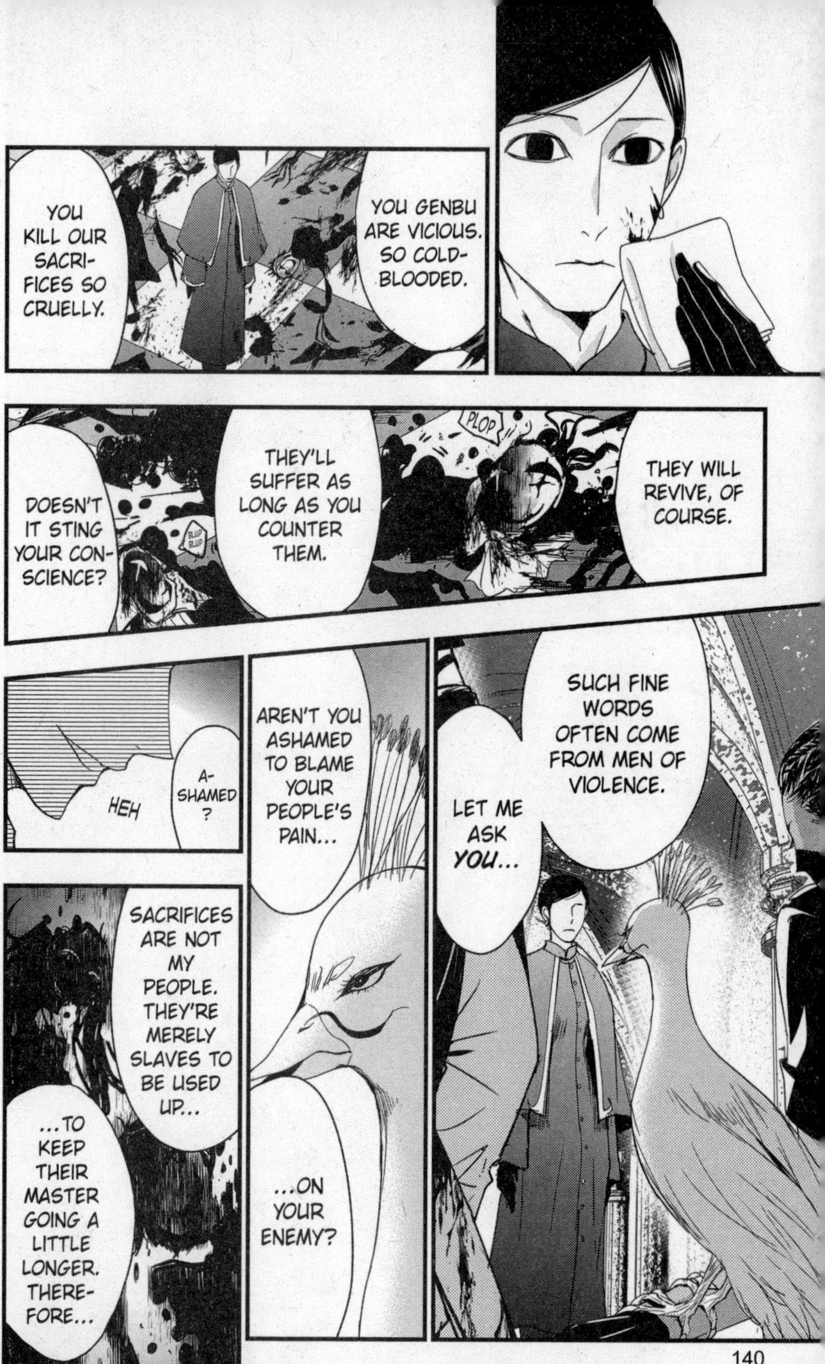
YOU GENBU ARE VICIOUS. SO COLD-BLOODED.
YOU KILL OUR SACRI-FICES SO CRUELLY.
THEY WILL REVIVE, OF COURSE.
PLOP
THEY'LL SUFFER AS LONG AS YOU COUNTER THEM.
BLUP BLUP
DOESN'T IT STING YOUR CON-SCIENCE?
SUCH FINE WORDS OFTEN COME FROM MEN OF VIOLENCE.
LET ME ASK *YOU*...
AREN'T YOU ASHAMED TO BLAME YOUR PEOPLE'S PAIN...
...ON YOUR ENEMY?
A-SHAMED?
HEH
SACRIFICES ARE NOT MY PEOPLE. THEY'RE MERELY SLAVES TO BE USED UP...
...TO KEEP THEIR MASTER GOING A LITTLE LONGER. THERE-FORE...

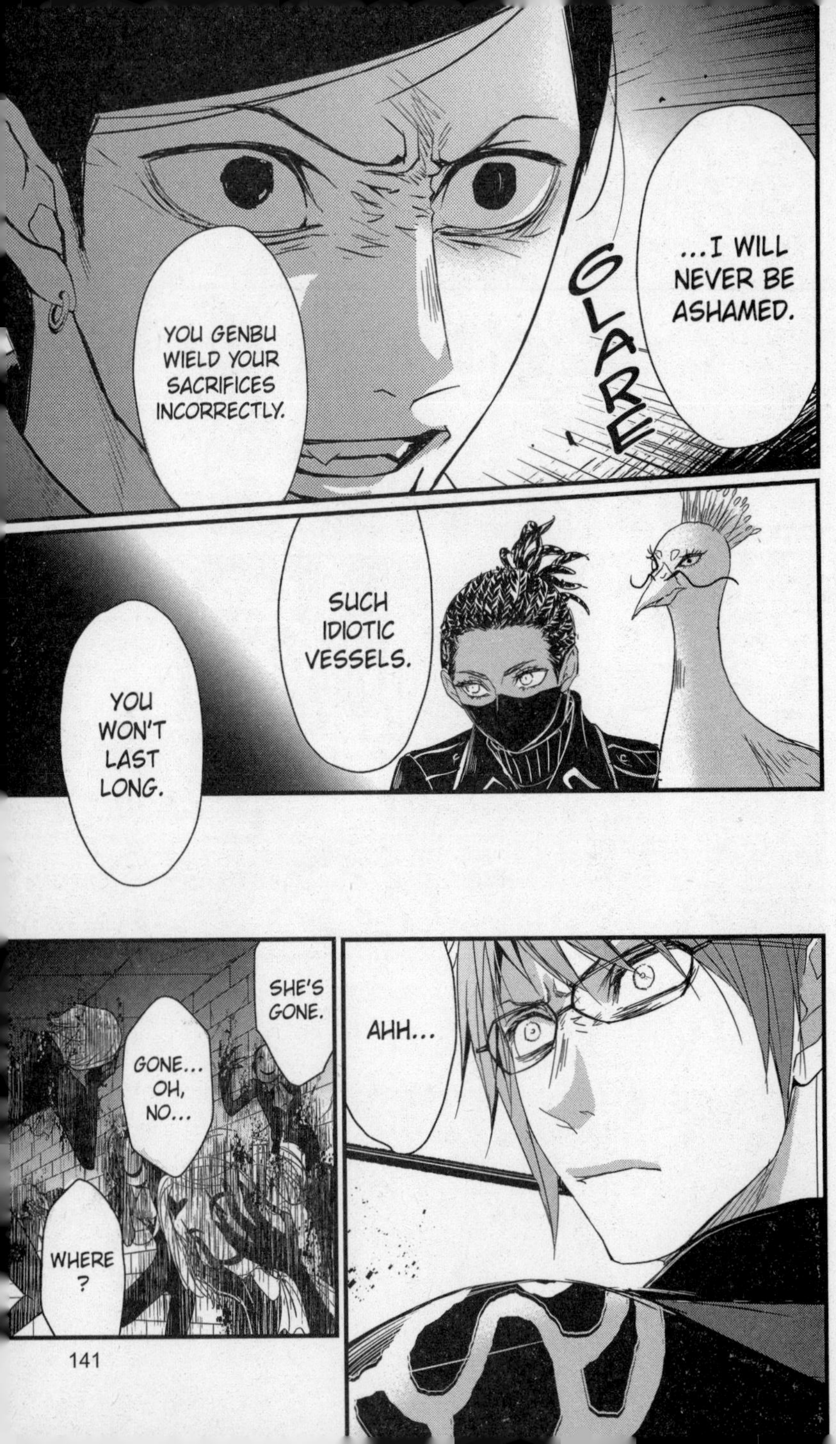
...I WILL NEVER BE ASHAMED.
GLARE
YOU GENBU WIELD YOUR SACRIFICES INCORRECTLY.
SUCH IDIOTIC VESSELS.
YOU WON'T LAST LONG.
AHH...
SHE'S GONE.
GONE... OH, NO...
WHERE?

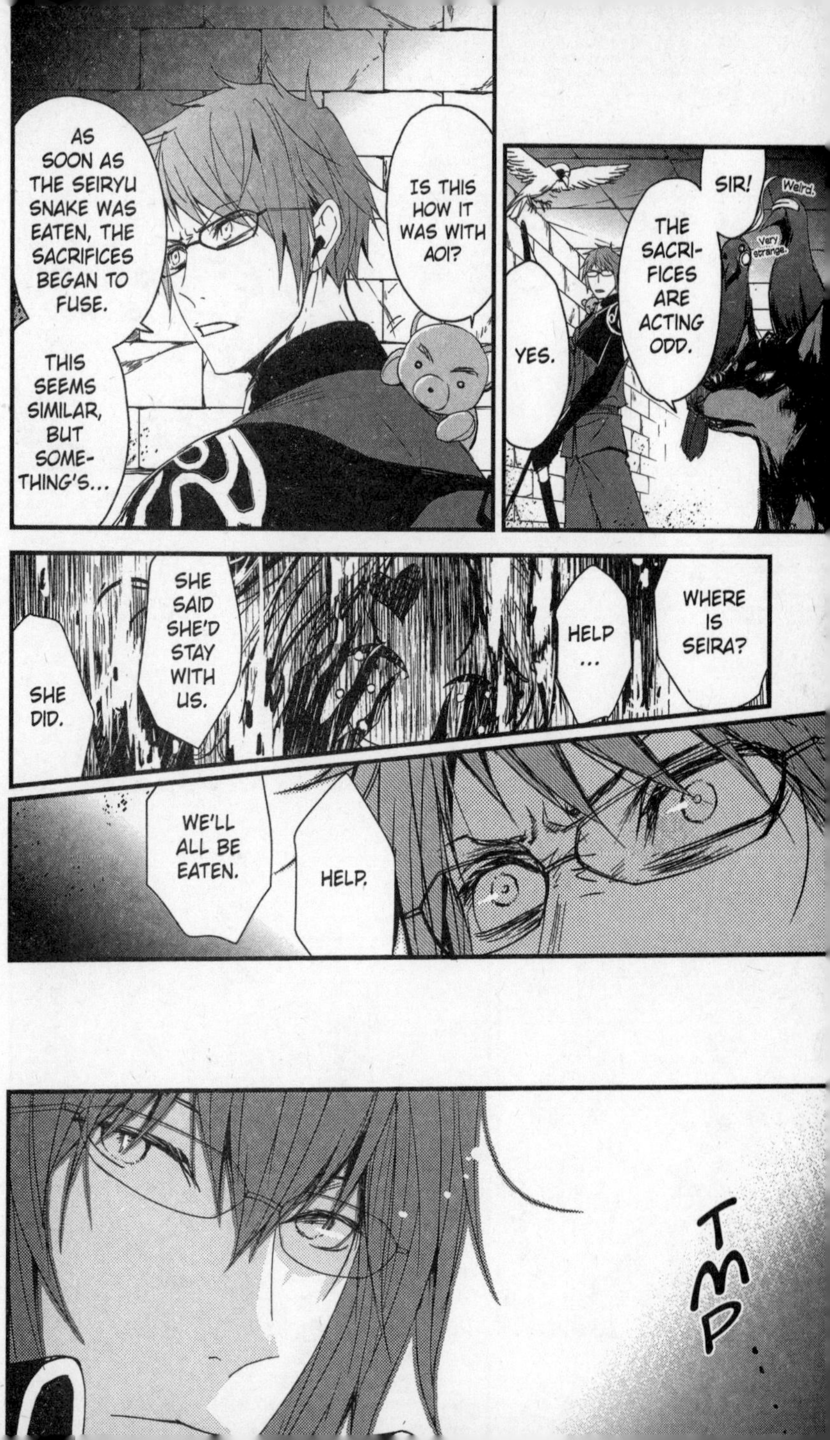
Weird.
Very strange.
SIR!
THE SACRI-FICES ARE ACTING ODD.
YES.
IS THIS HOW IT WAS WITH AOI?
AS SOON AS THE SEIRYU SNAKE WAS EATEN, THE SACRIFICES BEGAN TO FUSE.
THIS SEEMS SIMILAR, BUT SOME-THING'S...
WHERE IS SEIRA?
HELP...
SHE SAID SHE'D STAY WITH US.
SHE DID.
HELP.
WE'LL ALL BE EATEN.
TMP

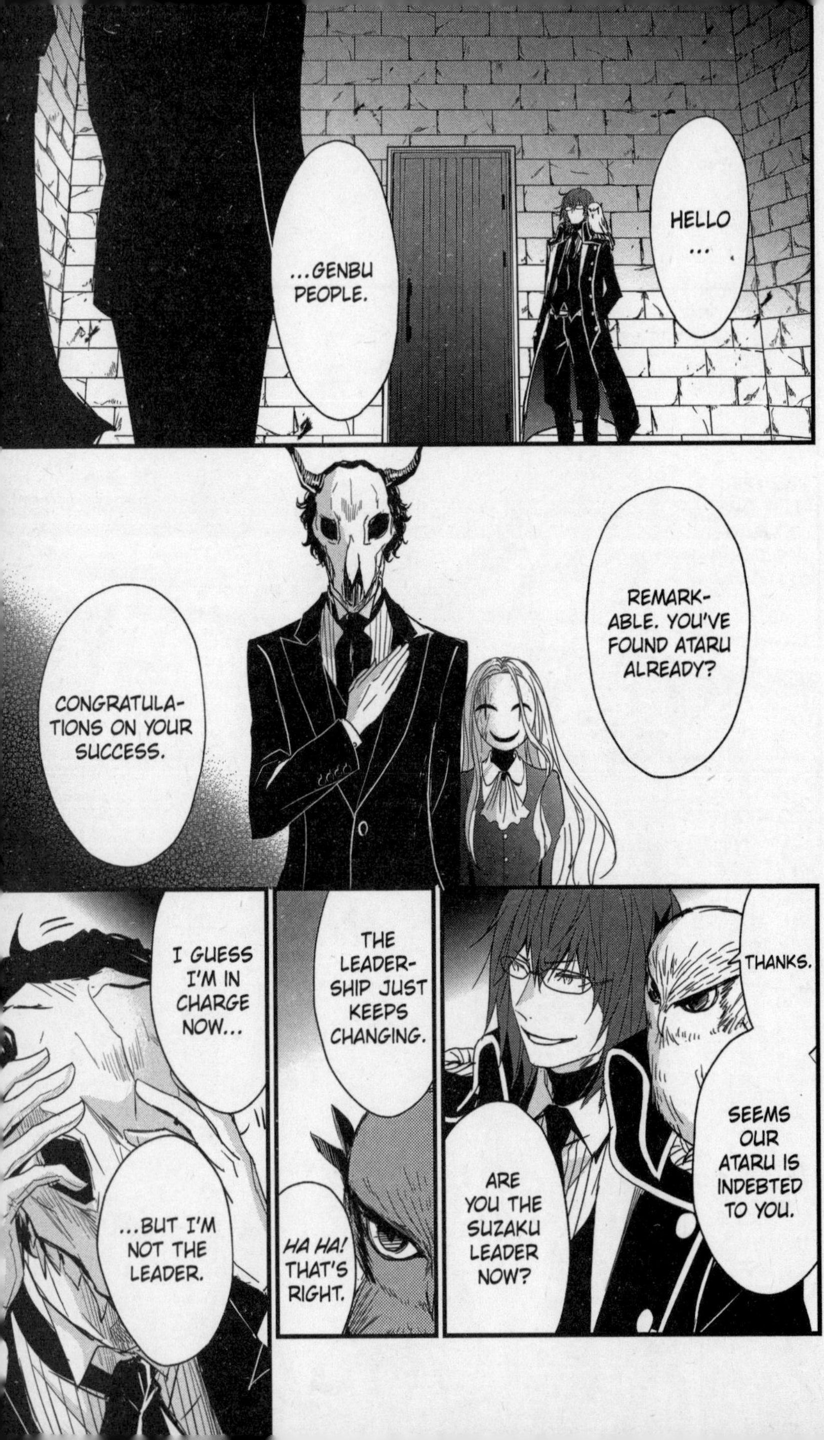
HELLO ...
...GENBU PEOPLE.
REMARKABLE. YOU'VE FOUND ATARU ALREADY?
CONGRATULATIONS ON YOUR SUCCESS.
THANKS.
SEEMS OUR ATARU IS INDEBTED TO YOU.
ARE YOU THE SUZAKU LEADER NOW?
THE LEADERSHIP JUST KEEPS CHANGING.
HA HA! THAT'S RIGHT.
I GUESS I'M IN CHARGE NOW...
...BUT I'M NOT THE LEADER.

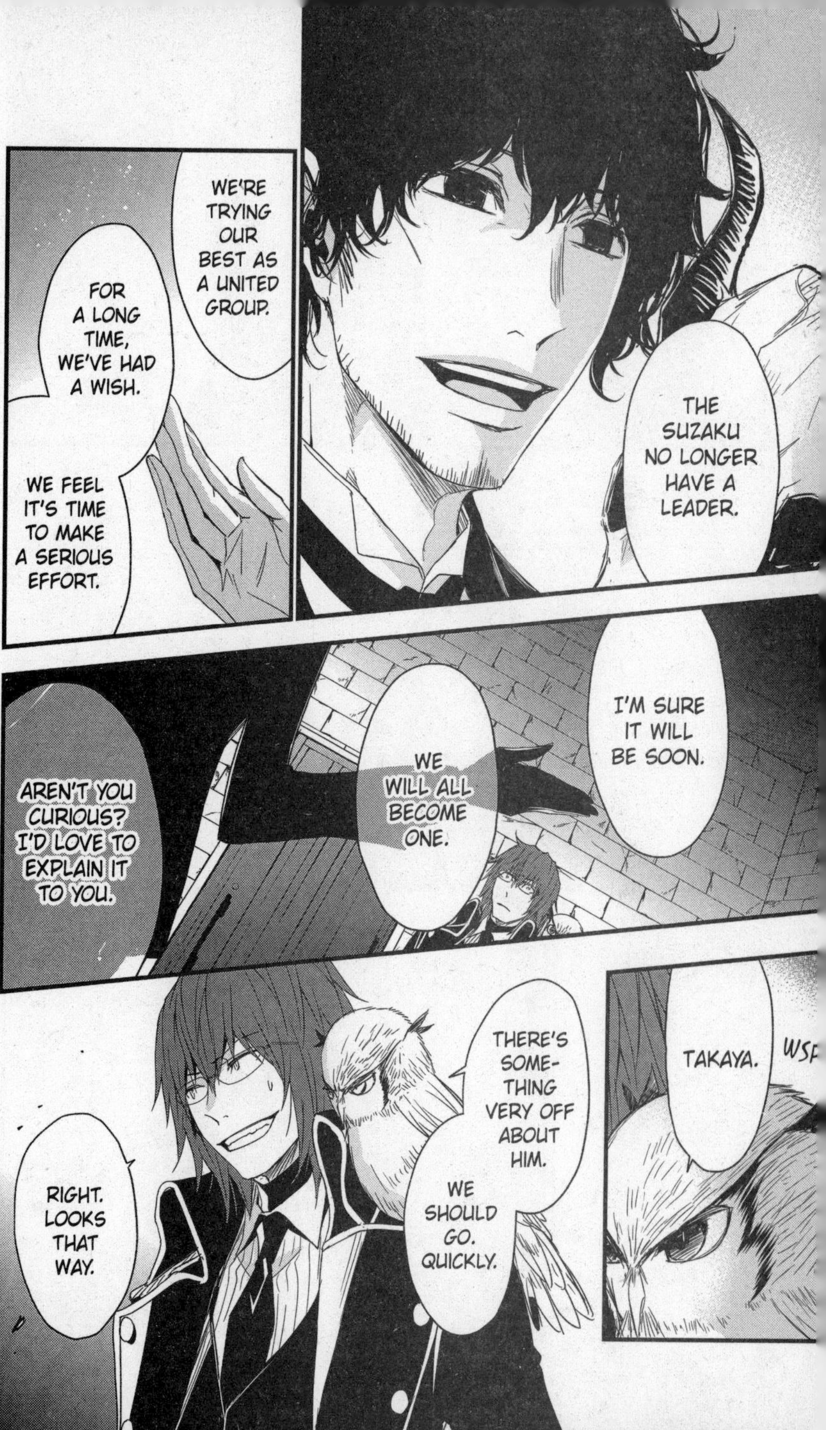
THE SUZAKU NO LONGER HAVE A LEADER.
WE'RE TRYING OUR BEST AS A UNITED GROUP.
FOR A LONG TIME, WE'VE HAD A WISH.
WE FEEL IT'S TIME TO MAKE A SERIOUS EFFORT.
I'M SURE IT WILL BE SOON.
WE WILL ALL BECOME ONE.
AREN'T YOU CURIOUS? I'D LOVE TO EXPLAIN IT TO YOU.
TAKAYA.
THERE'S SOME-THING VERY OFF ABOUT HIM.
WE SHOULD GO. QUICKLY.
RIGHT. LOOKS THAT WAY.

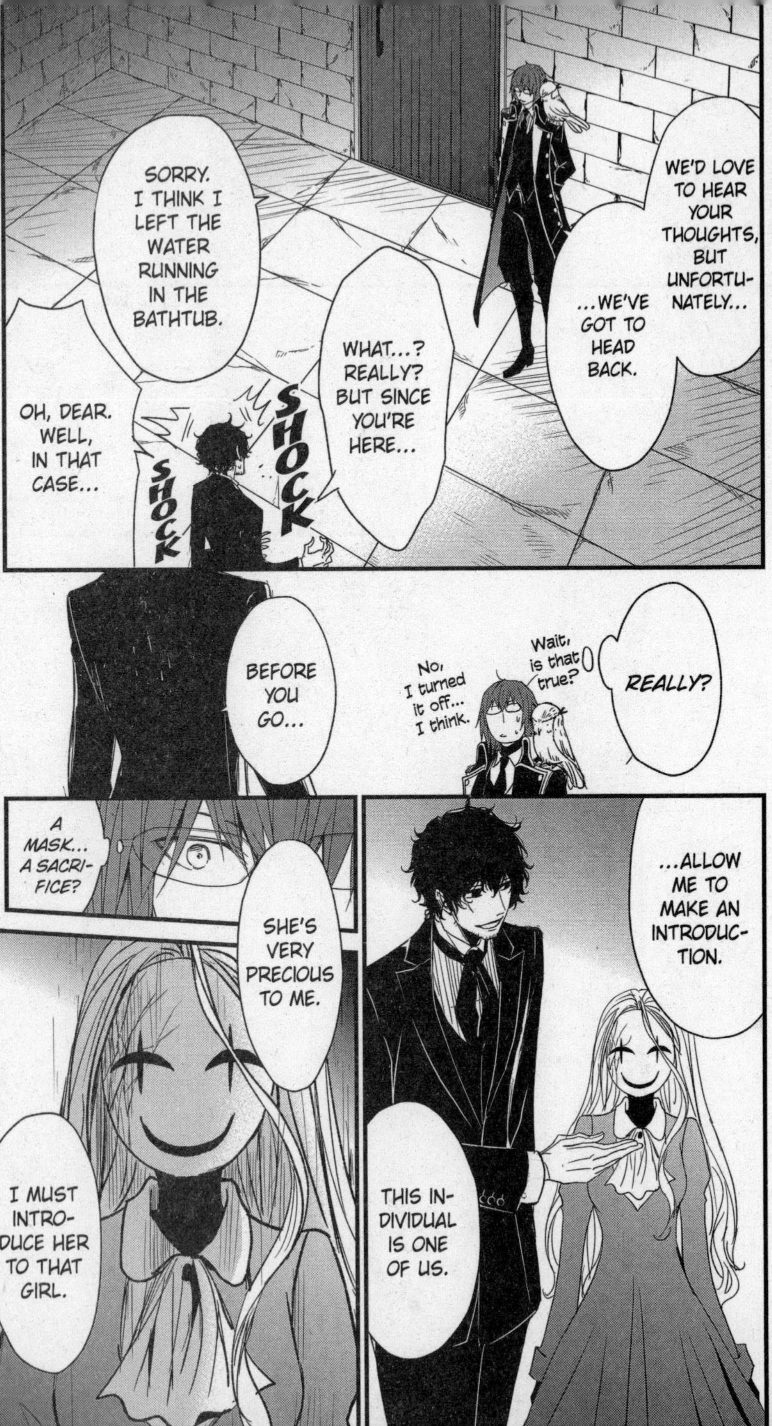
WE'D LOVE TO HEAR YOUR THOUGHTS, BUT UNFORTUNATELY...
...WE'VE GOT TO HEAD BACK.
WHAT...? REALLY? BUT SINCE YOU'RE HERE...
SHOCK
SHOCK
SORRY. I THINK I LEFT THE WATER RUNNING IN THE BATHTUB.
OH, DEAR. WELL, IN THAT CASE...
REALLY?
Wait, is that true?
No, I turned it off... I think.
BEFORE YOU GO...
...ALLOW ME TO MAKE AN INTRODUCTION.
THIS INDIVIDUAL IS ONE OF US.
A MASK... A SACRIFICE?
SHE'S VERY PRECIOUS TO ME.
I MUST INTRODUCE HER TO THAT GIRL.

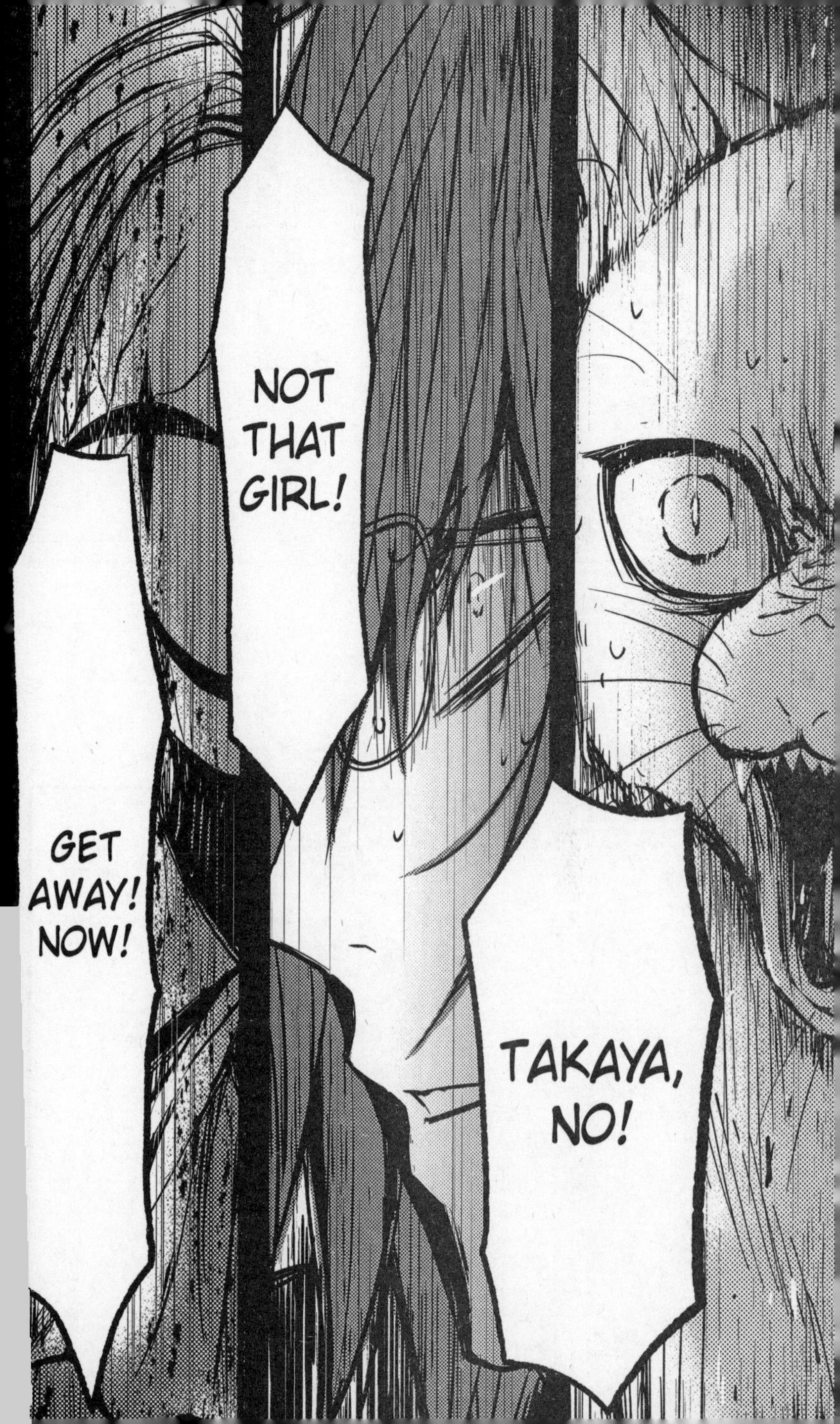
TAKAYA, NO!
NOT THAT GIRL!
GET AWAY! NOW!

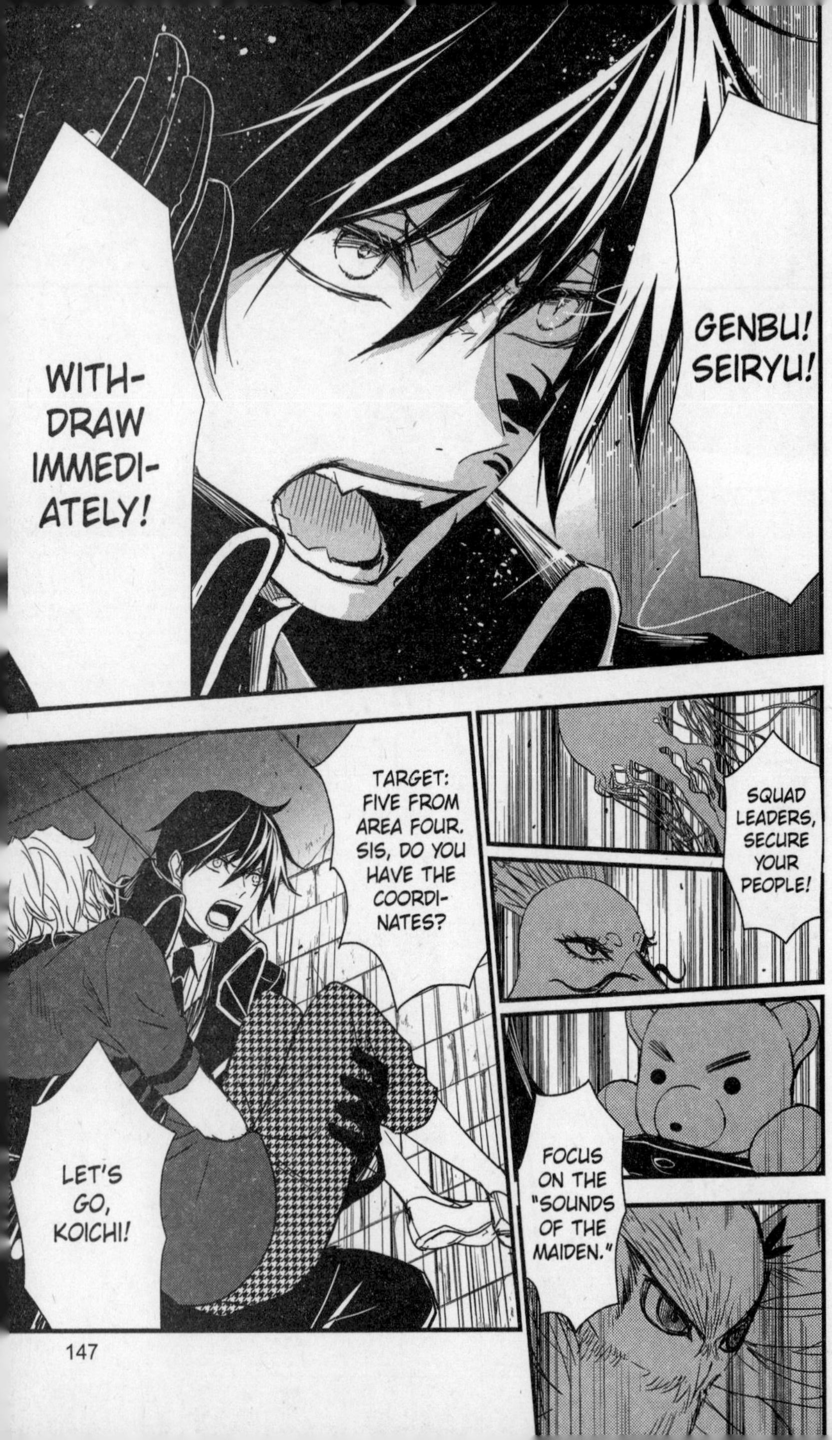
GENBU! SEIRYU!
WITH-DRAW IMMEDI-ATELY!
SQUAD LEADERS, SECURE YOUR PEOPLE!
FOCUS ON THE "SOUNDS OF THE MAIDEN."
TARGET: FIVE FROM AREA FOUR. SIS, DO YOU HAVE THE COORDI-NATES?
LET'S GO, KOICHI!

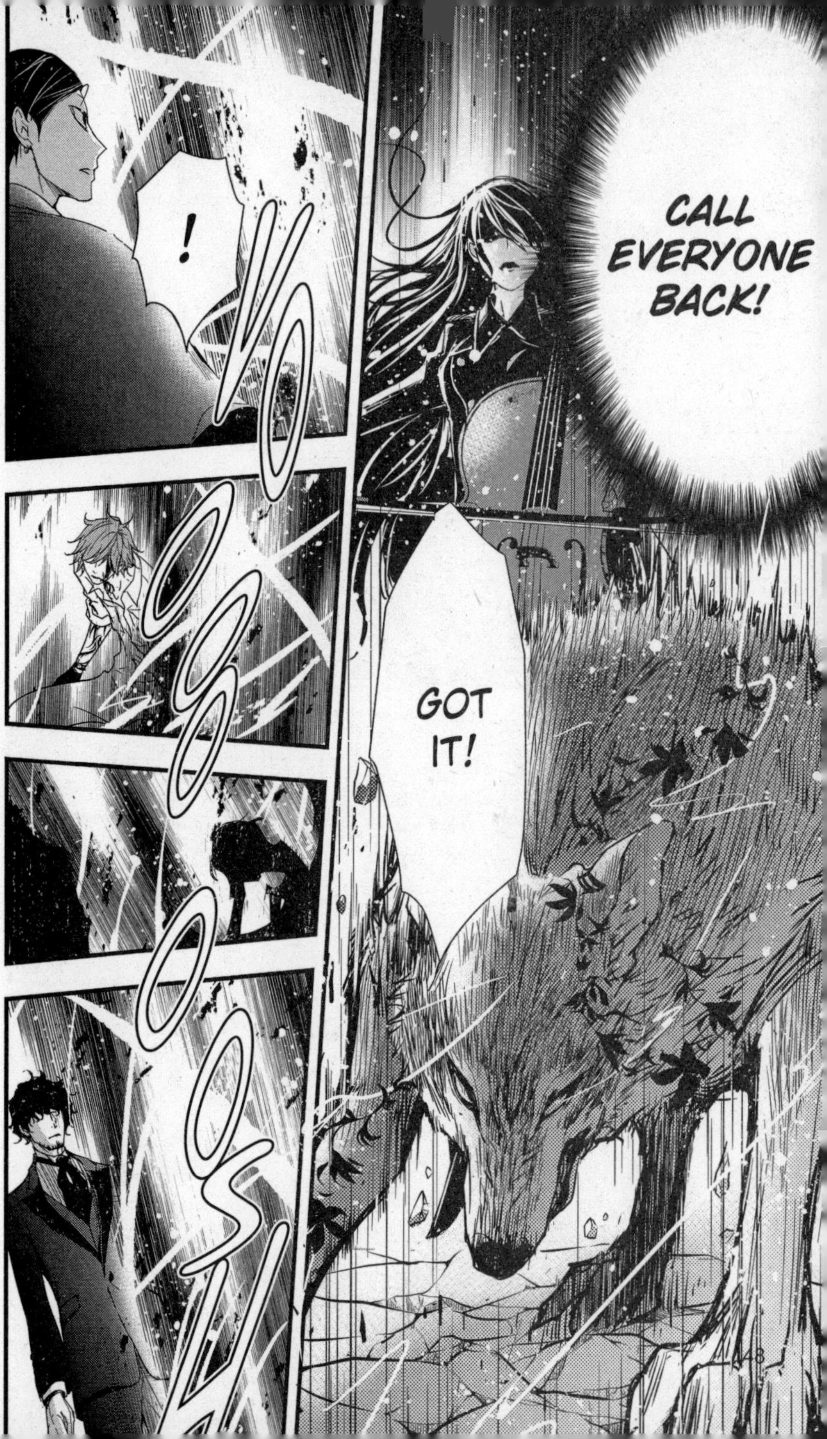
CALL EVERYONE BACK!
GOT IT!
!

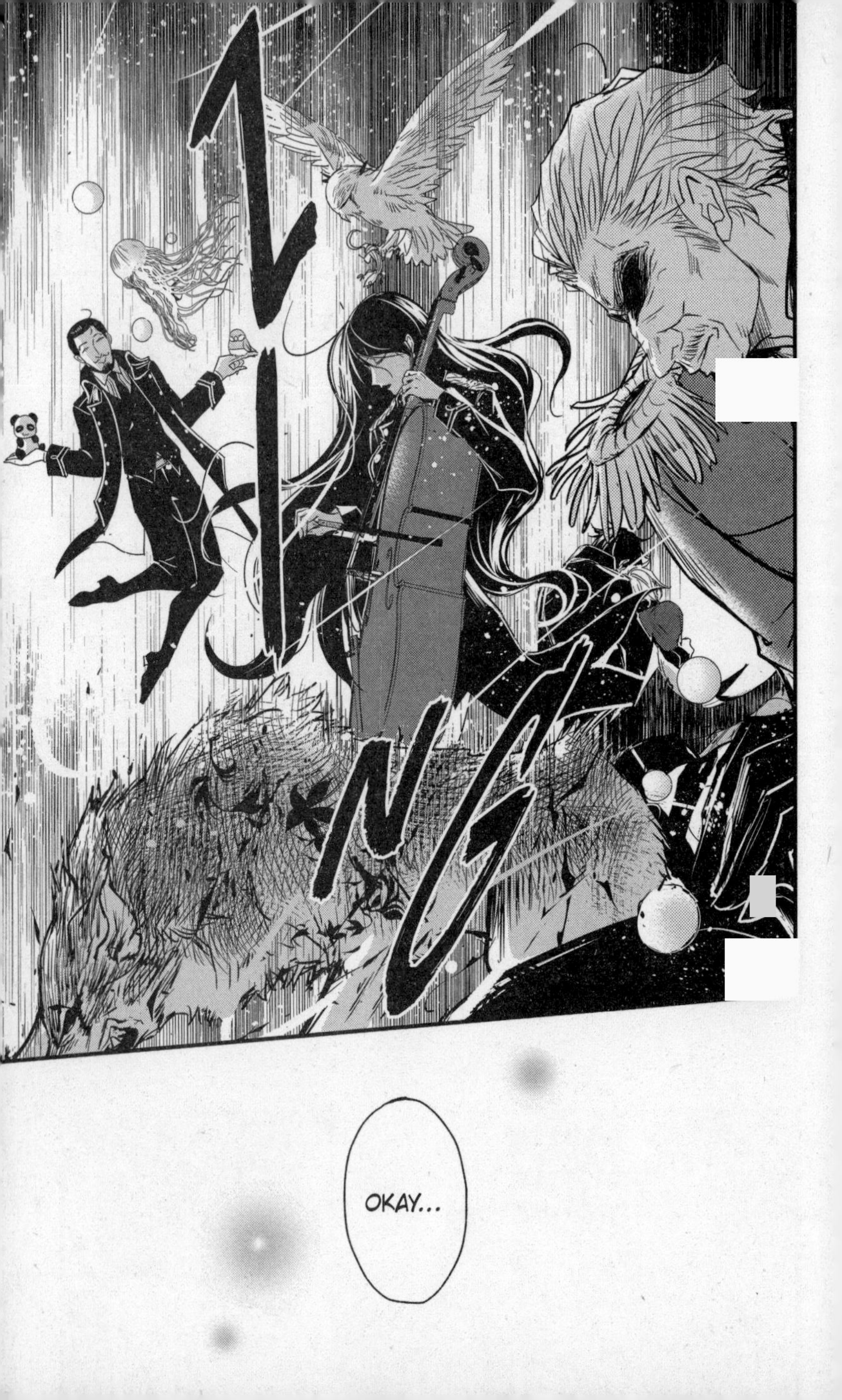
OKAY...

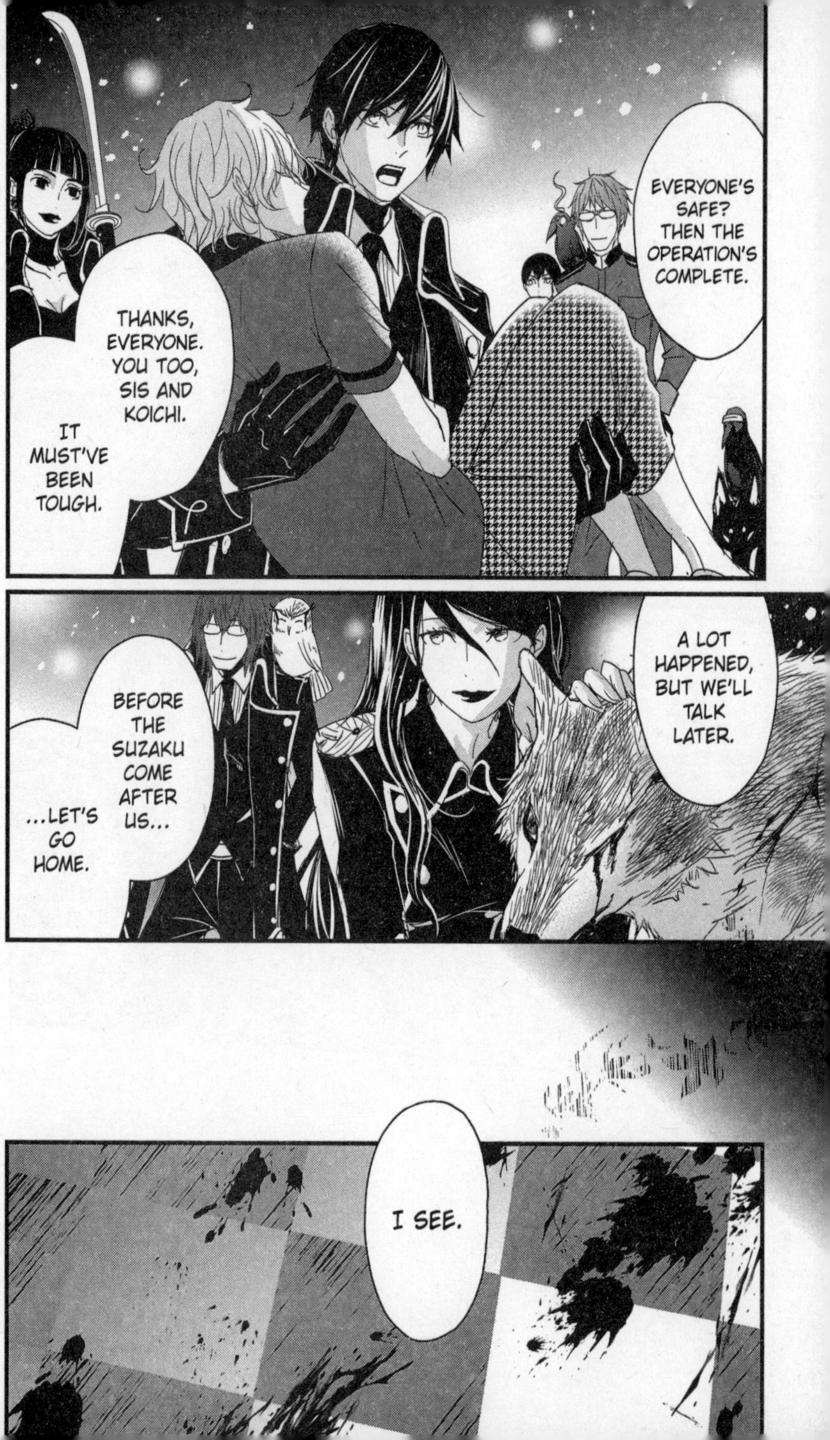
EVERYONE'S SAFE? THEN THE OPERATION'S COMPLETE.
THANKS, EVERYONE. YOU TOO, SIS AND KOICHI.
IT MUST'VE BEEN TOUGH.
A LOT HAPPENED, BUT WE'LL TALK LATER.
BEFORE THE SUZAKU COME AFTER US...
...LET'S GO HOME.
I SEE.

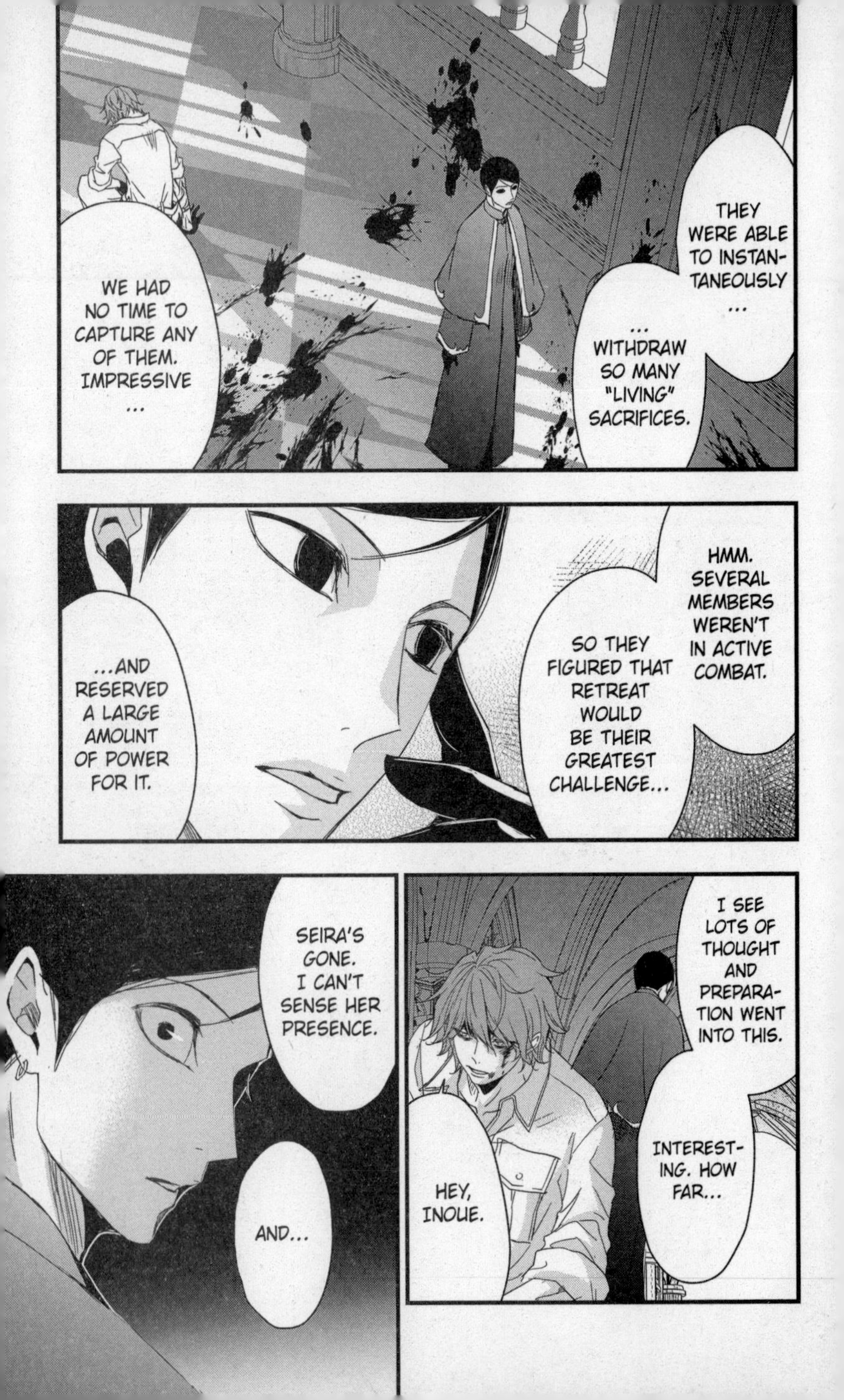
THEY WERE ABLE TO INSTANTANEOUSLY ...
... WITHDRAW SO MANY "LIVING" SACRIFICES.
WE HAD NO TIME TO CAPTURE ANY OF THEM. IMPRESSIVE ...
HMM. SEVERAL MEMBERS WEREN'T IN ACTIVE COMBAT.
SO THEY FIGURED THAT RETREAT WOULD BE THEIR GREATEST CHALLENGE...
...AND RESERVED A LARGE AMOUNT OF POWER FOR IT.
I SEE LOTS OF THOUGHT AND PREPARATION WENT INTO THIS.
INTEREST-ING. HOW FAR...
HEY, INOUE.
SEIRA'S GONE. I CAN'T SENSE HER PRESENCE.
AND...

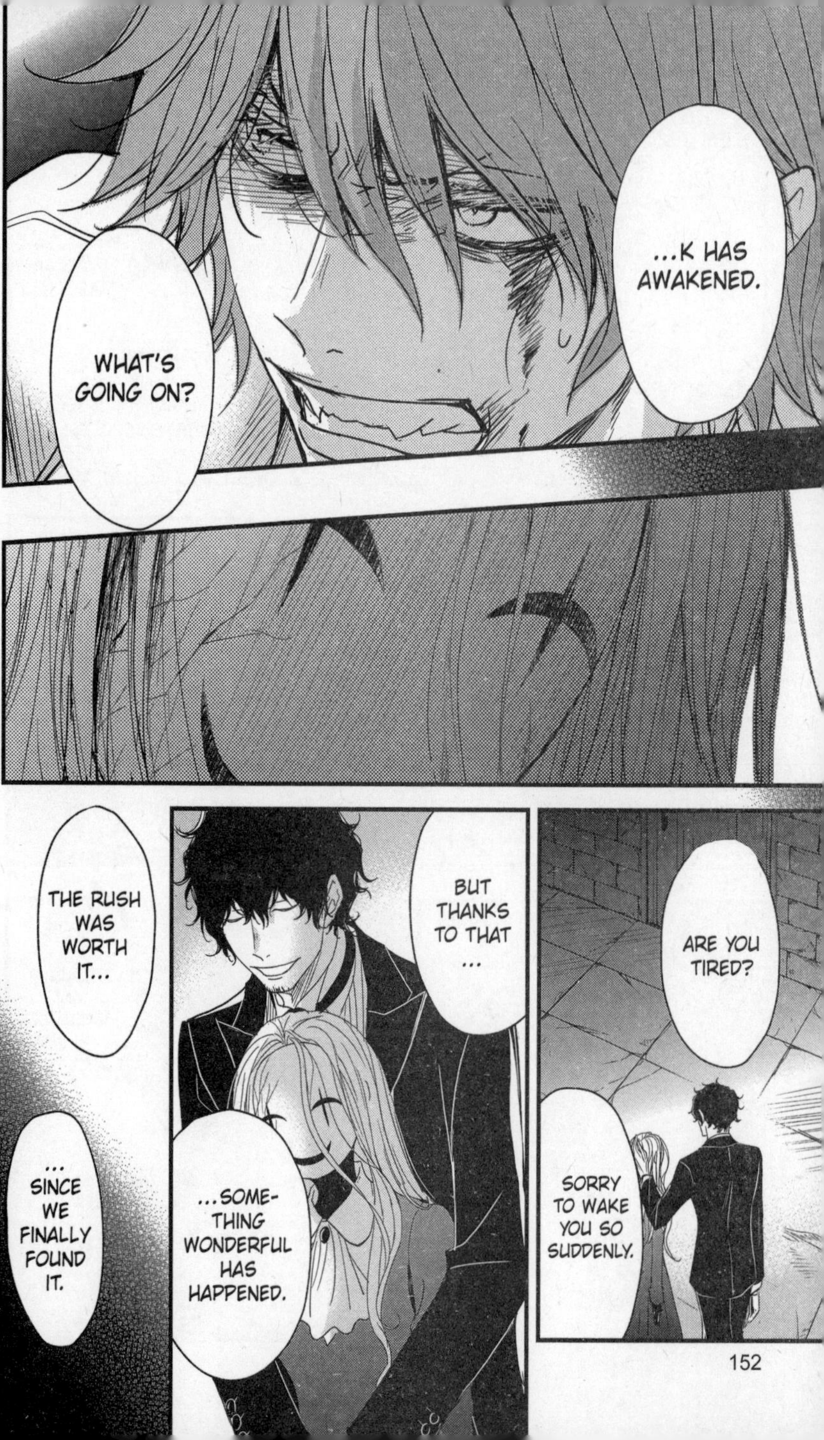
...K HAS AWAKENED.
WHAT'S GOING ON?
ARE YOU TIRED?
SORRY TO WAKE YOU SO SUDDENLY.
BUT THANKS TO THAT ...
...SOME-THING WONDERFUL HAS HAPPENED.
THE RUSH WAS WORTH IT...
... SINCE WE FINALLY FOUND IT.

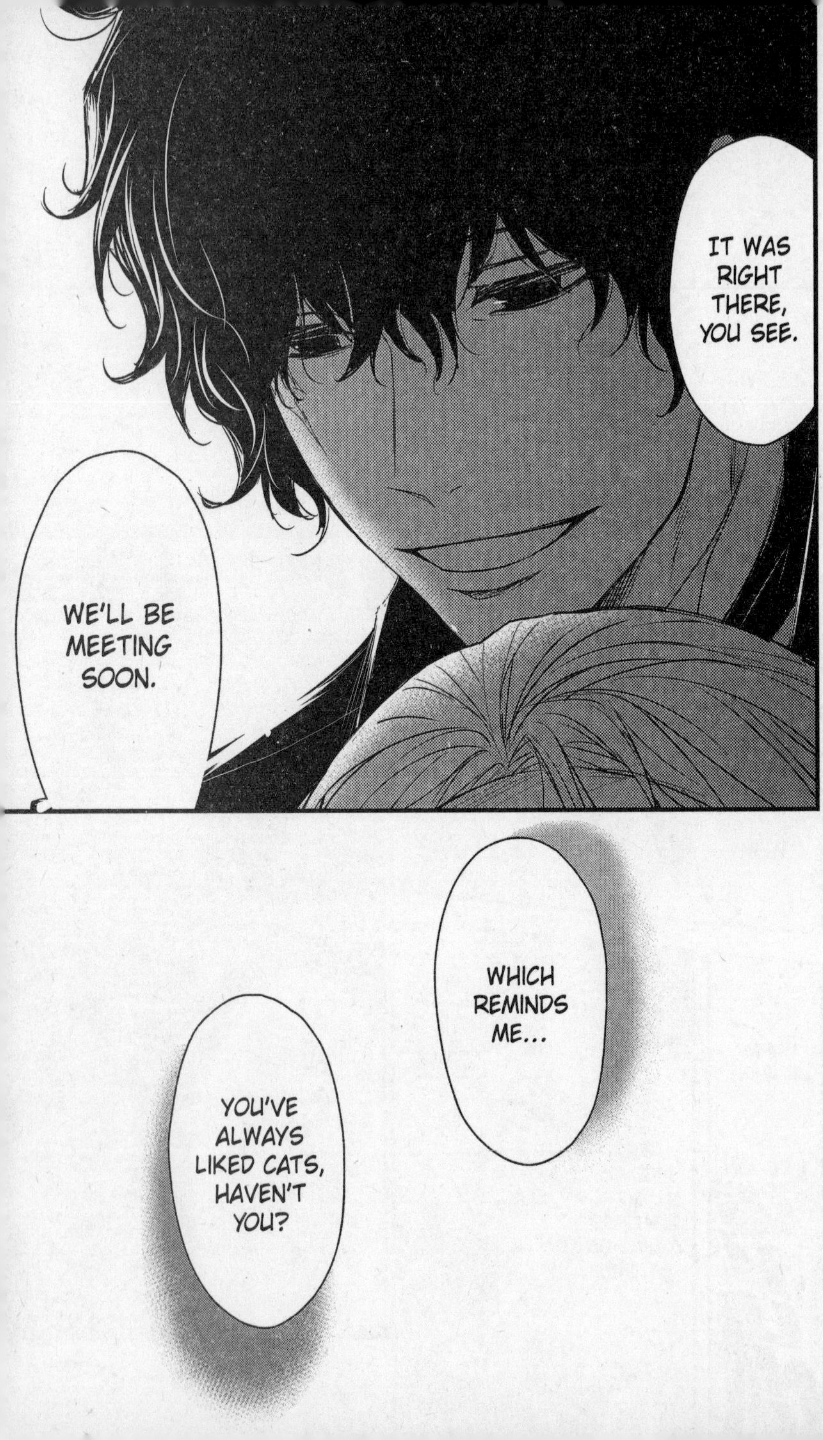
IT WAS RIGHT THERE, YOU SEE.
WE'LL BE MEETING SOON.
WHICH REMINDS ME...
YOU'VE ALWAYS LIKED CATS, HAVEN'T YOU?

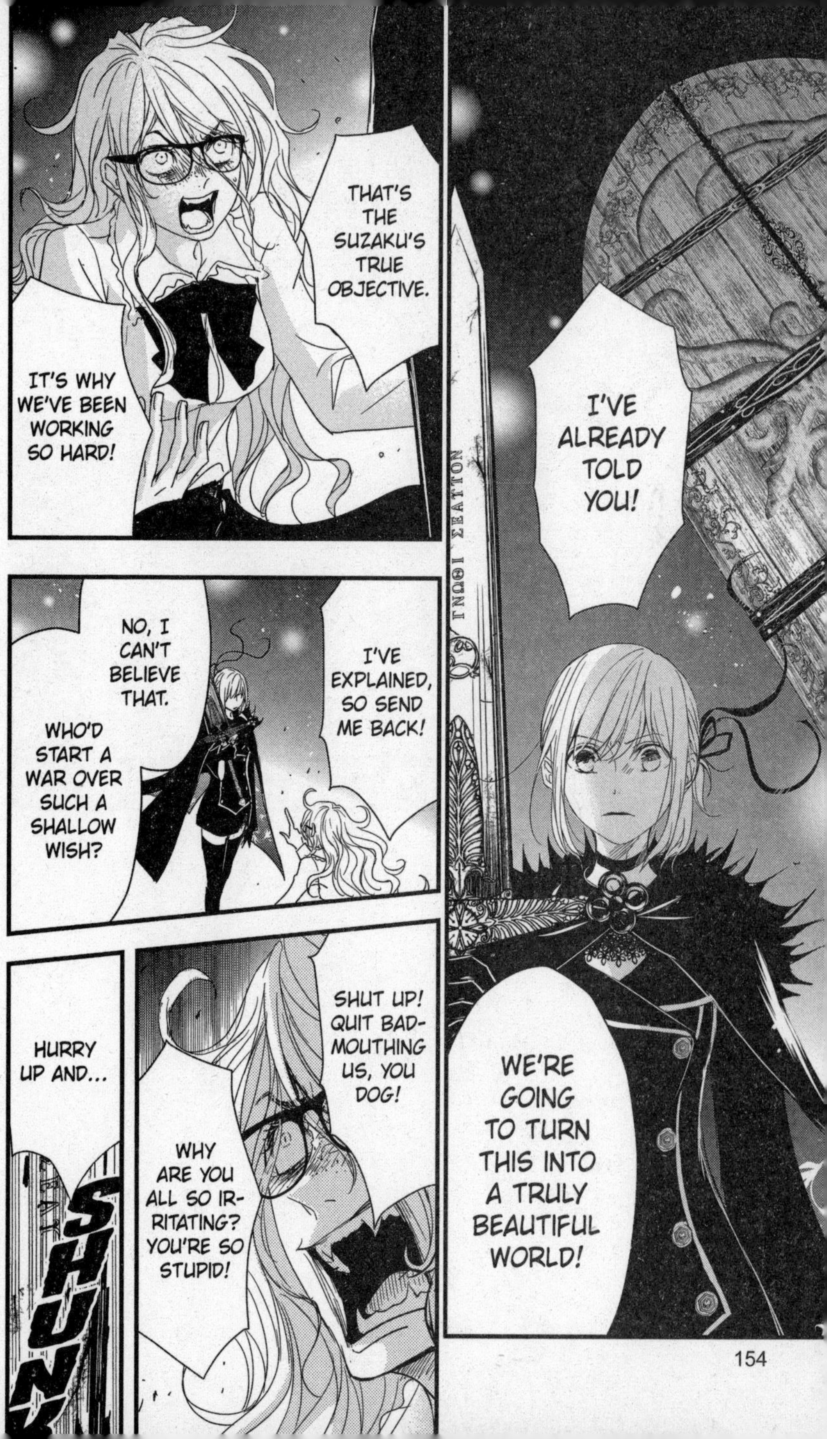
I'VE ALREADY TOLD YOU!
WE'RE GOING TO TURN THIS INTO A TRULY BEAUTIFUL WORLD!
THAT'S THE SUZAKU'S TRUE OBJECTIVE.
IT'S WHY WE'VE BEEN WORKING SO HARD!
I'VE EXPLAINED, SO SEND ME BACK!
NO, I CAN'T BELIEVE THAT.
WHO'D START A WAR OVER SUCH A SHALLOW WISH?
SHUT UP! QUIT BAD-MOUTHING US, YOU DOG!
WHY ARE YOU ALL SO IR-RITATING? YOU'RE SO STUPID!
HURRY UP AND...
SHUN

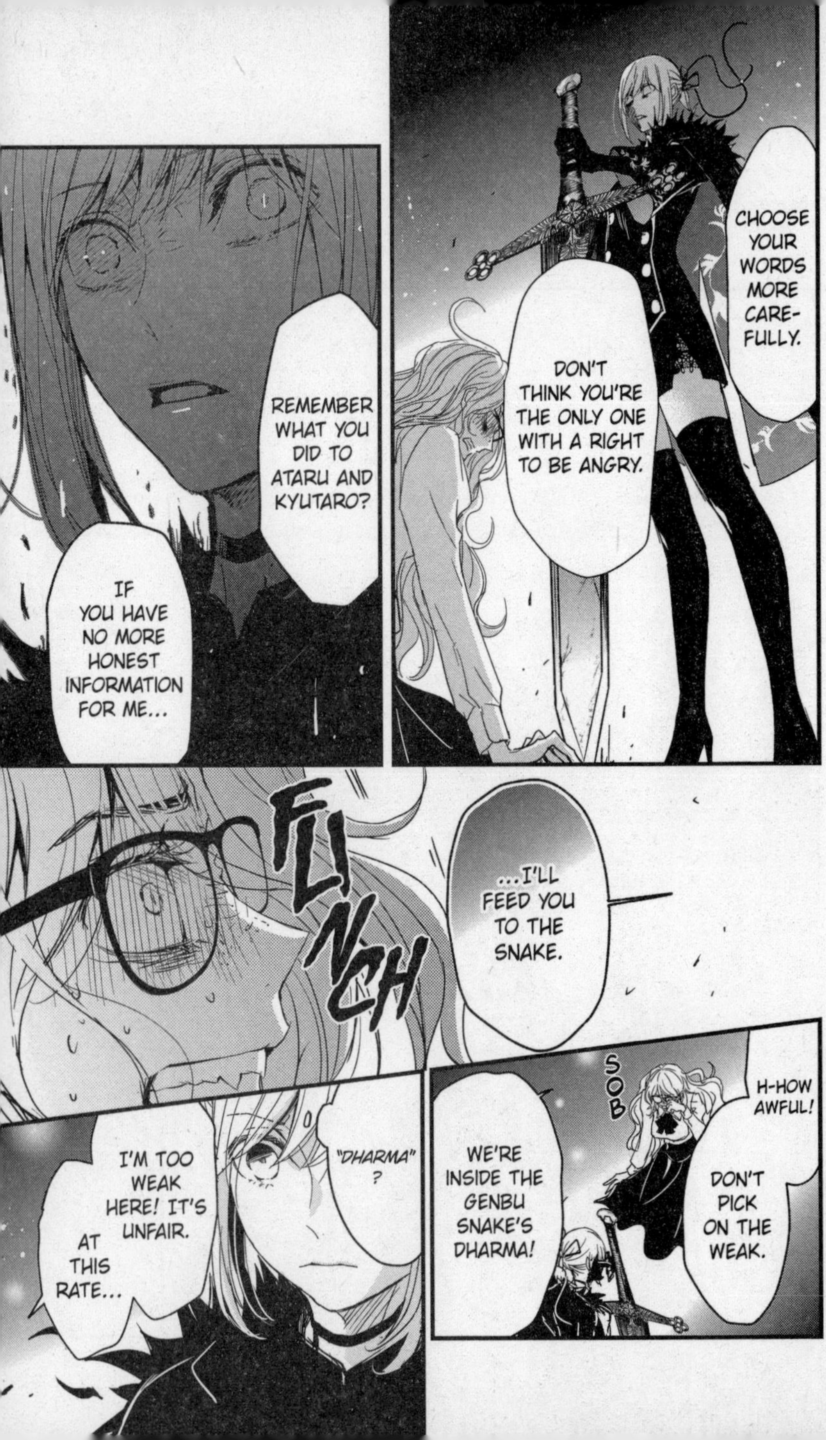
CHOOSE YOUR WORDS MORE CARE-FULLY.
DON'T THINK YOU'RE THE ONLY ONE WITH A RIGHT TO BE ANGRY.
REMEMBER WHAT YOU DID TO ATARU AND KYUTARO?
IF YOU HAVE NO MORE HONEST INFORMATION FOR ME...
...I'LL FEED YOU TO THE SNAKE.
FLINCH
SOB
H-HOW AWFUL!
DON'T PICK ON THE WEAK.
WE'RE INSIDE THE GENBU SNAKE'S DHARMA!
"DHARMA"?
I'M TOO WEAK HERE! IT'S UNFAIR.
AT THIS RATE...

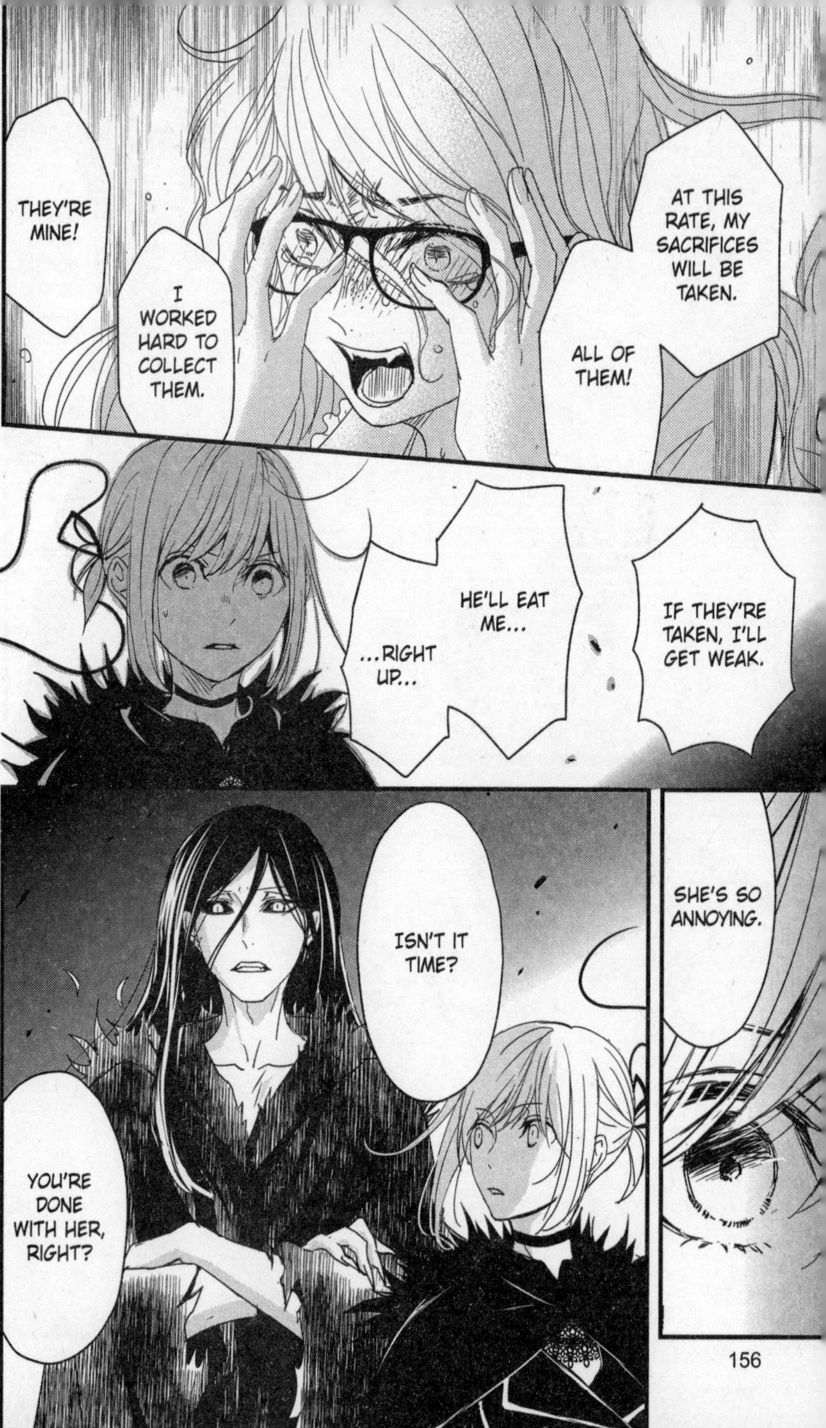
AT THIS RATE, MY SACRIFICES WILL BE TAKEN.
ALL OF THEM!
THEY'RE MINE!
I WORKED HARD TO COLLECT THEM.
IF THEY'RE TAKEN, I'LL GET WEAK.
HE'LL EAT ME...
...RIGHT UP...
SHE'S SO ANNOYING.
ISN'T IT TIME?
YOU'RE DONE WITH HER, RIGHT?

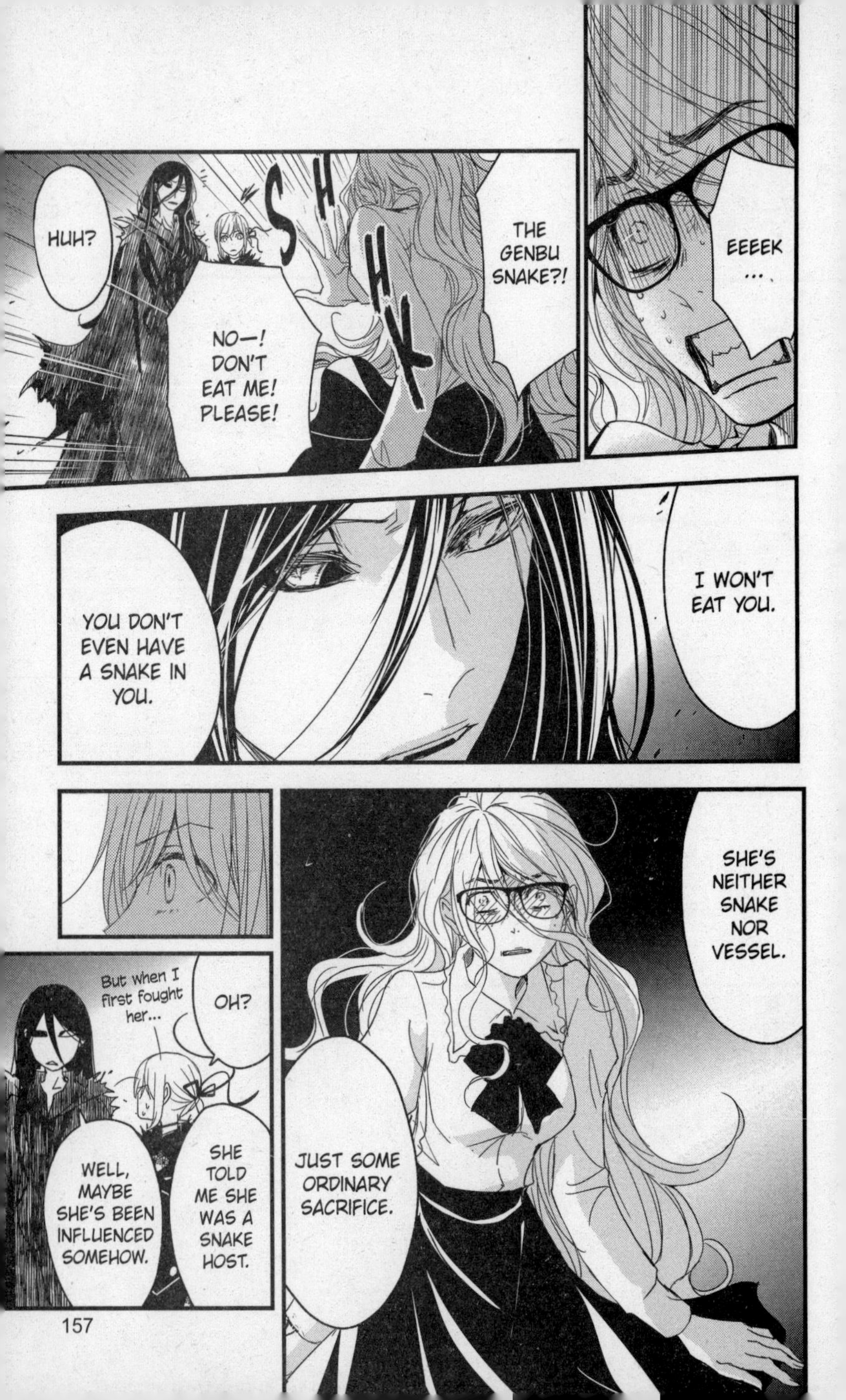
EEEEK ...
THE GENBU SNAKE?!
SHHK
NO—! DON'T EAT ME! PLEASE!
HUH?
I WON'T EAT YOU.
YOU DON'T EVEN HAVE A SNAKE IN YOU.
SHE'S NEITHER SNAKE NOR VESSEL.
JUST SOME ORDINARY SACRIFICE.
OH?
But when I first fought her...
SHE TOLD ME SHE WAS A SNAKE HOST.
WELL, MAYBE SHE'S BEEN INFLUENCED SOMEHOW.

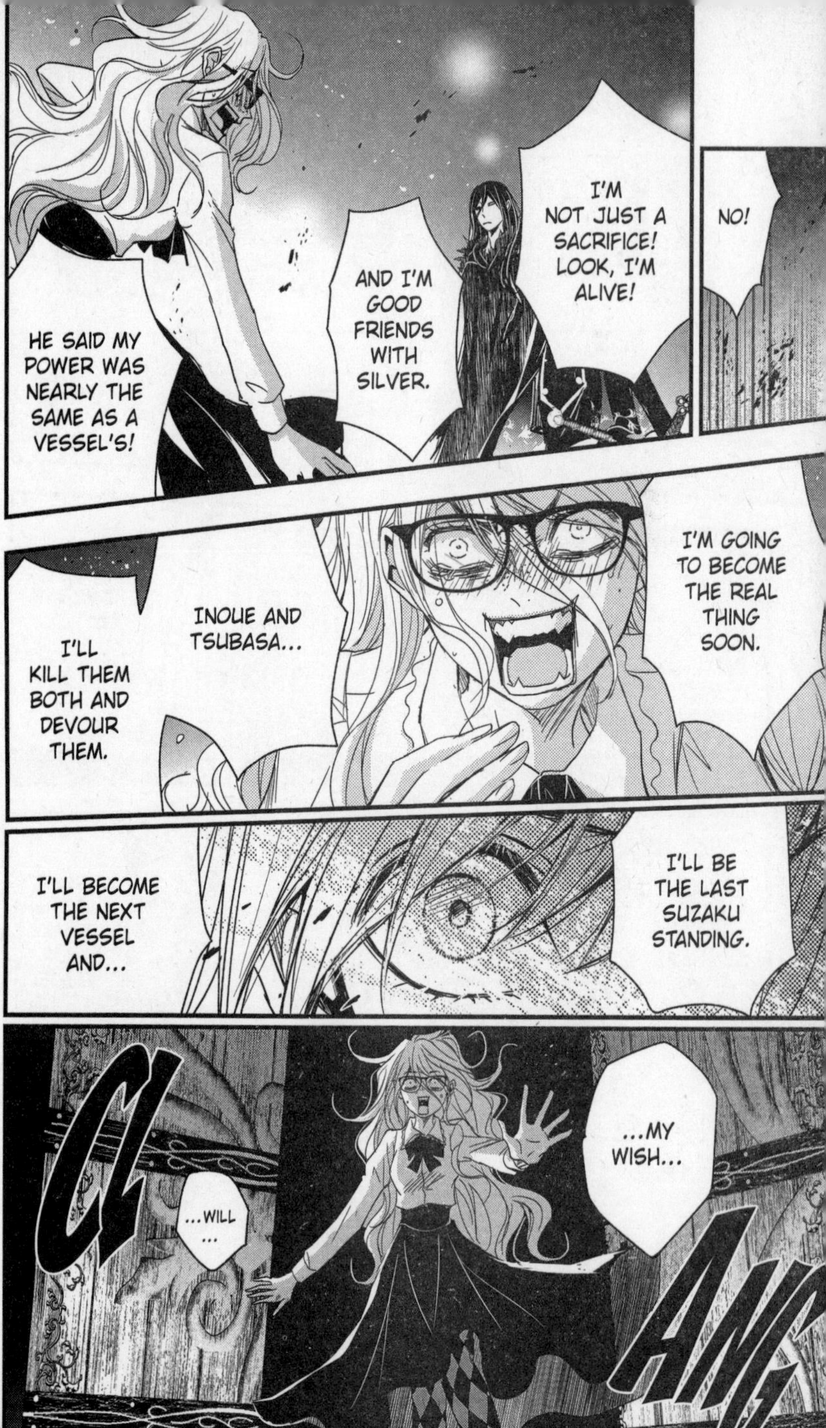
NO!
I'M NOT JUST A SACRIFICE! LOOK, I'M ALIVE!
AND I'M GOOD FRIENDS WITH SILVER.
HE SAID MY POWER WAS NEARLY THE SAME AS A VESSEL'S!
I'M GOING TO BECOME THE REAL THING SOON.
INOUE AND TSUBASA...
I'LL KILL THEM BOTH AND DEVOUR THEM.
I'LL BE THE LAST SUZAKU STANDING.
I'LL BECOME THE NEXT VESSEL AND...
...MY WISH...
...WILL ...
CL
ANK

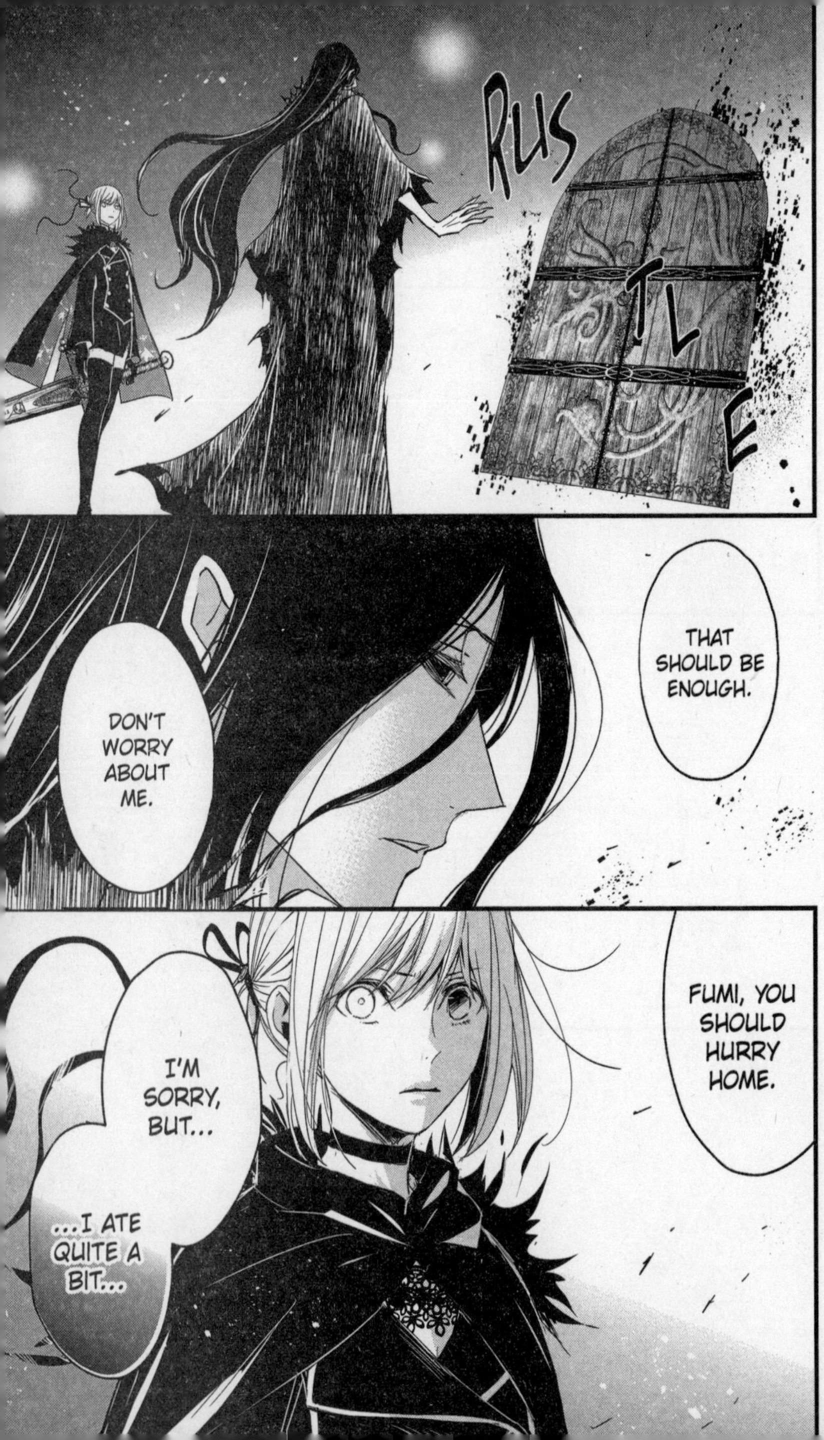
RUSTLE
THAT SHOULD BE ENOUGH.
DON'T WORRY ABOUT ME.
FUMI, YOU SHOULD HURRY HOME.
I'M SORRY, BUT...
...I ATE QUITE A BIT...

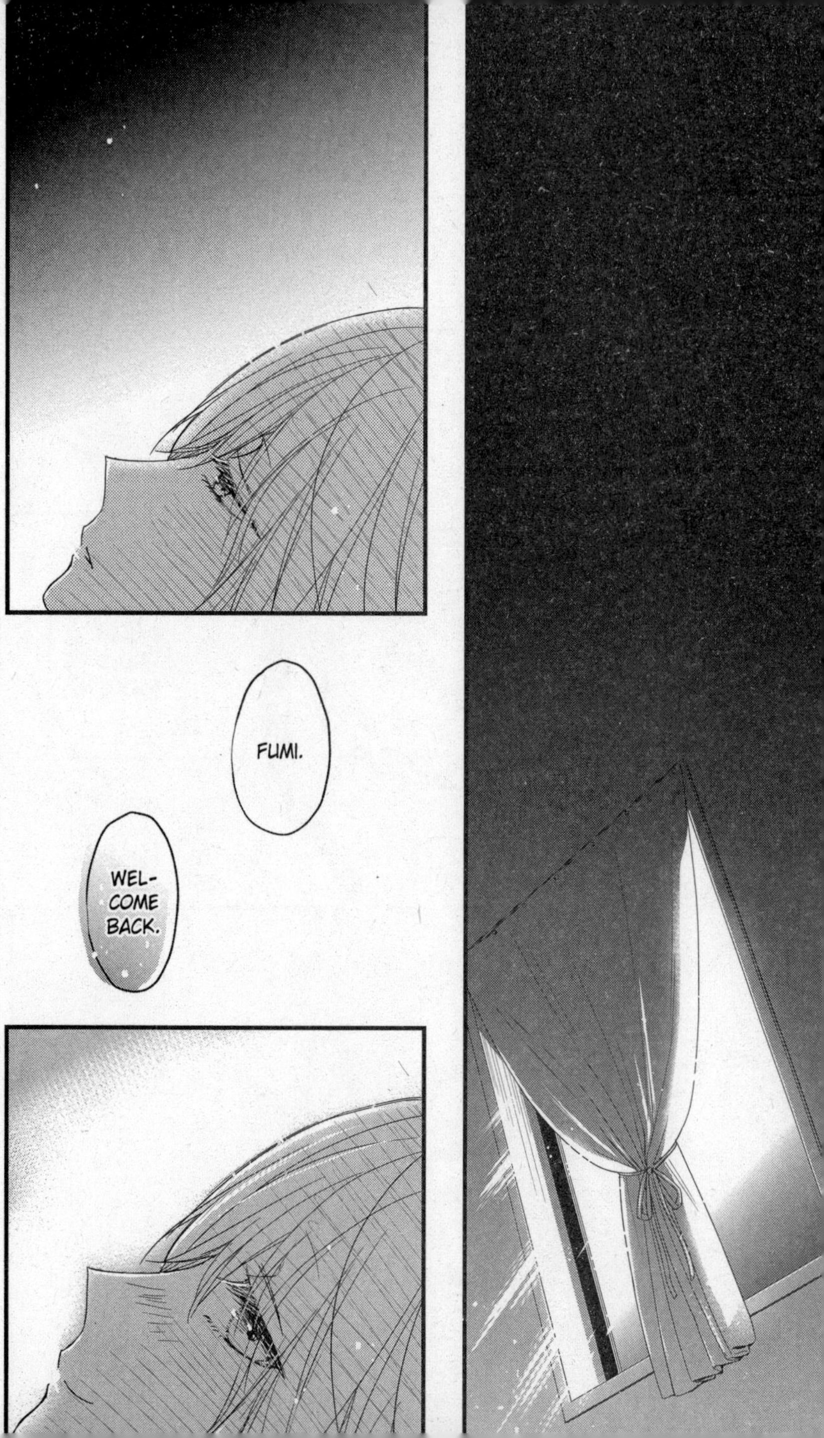
FUMI.
WEL-COME BACK.

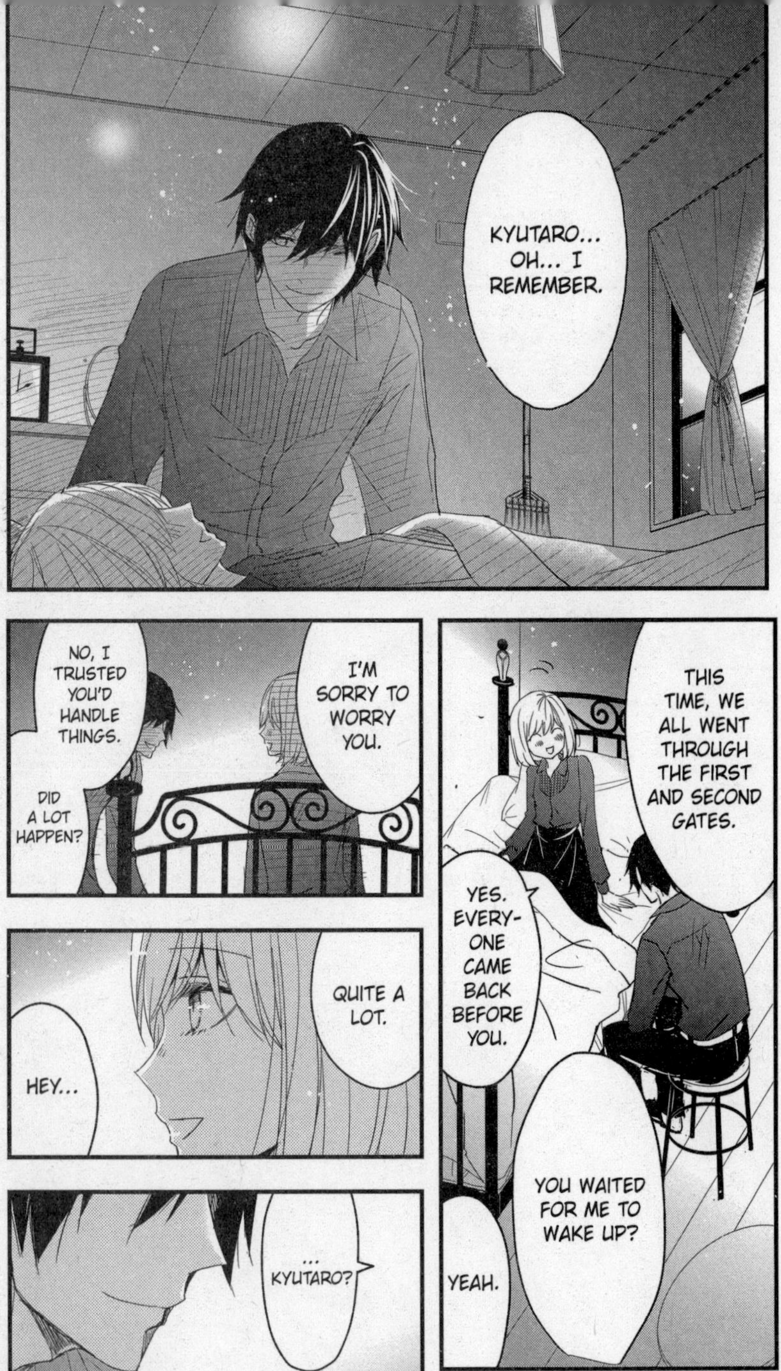
KYUTARO... OH... I REMEMBER.
THIS TIME, WE ALL WENT THROUGH THE FIRST AND SECOND GATES.
YES. EVERY-ONE CAME BACK BEFORE YOU.
YOU WAITED FOR ME TO WAKE UP?
YEAH.
I'M SORRY TO WORRY YOU.
NO, I TRUSTED YOU'D HANDLE THINGS.
DID A LOT HAPPEN?
QUITE A LOT.
HEY...
...KYUTARO?

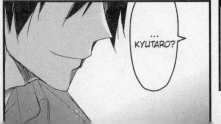

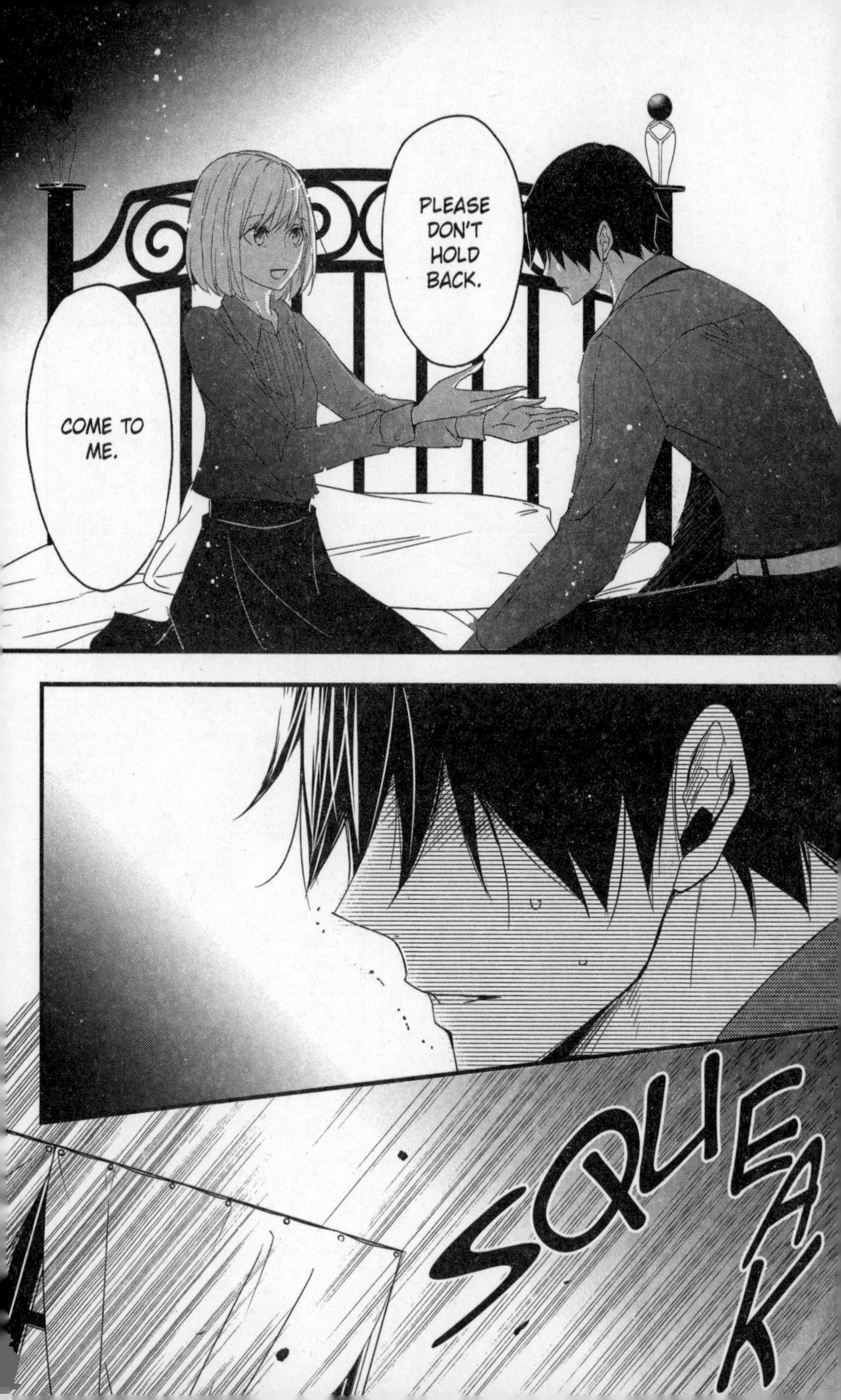
PLEASE DON'T HOLD BACK.
COME TO ME.
SQUEAK

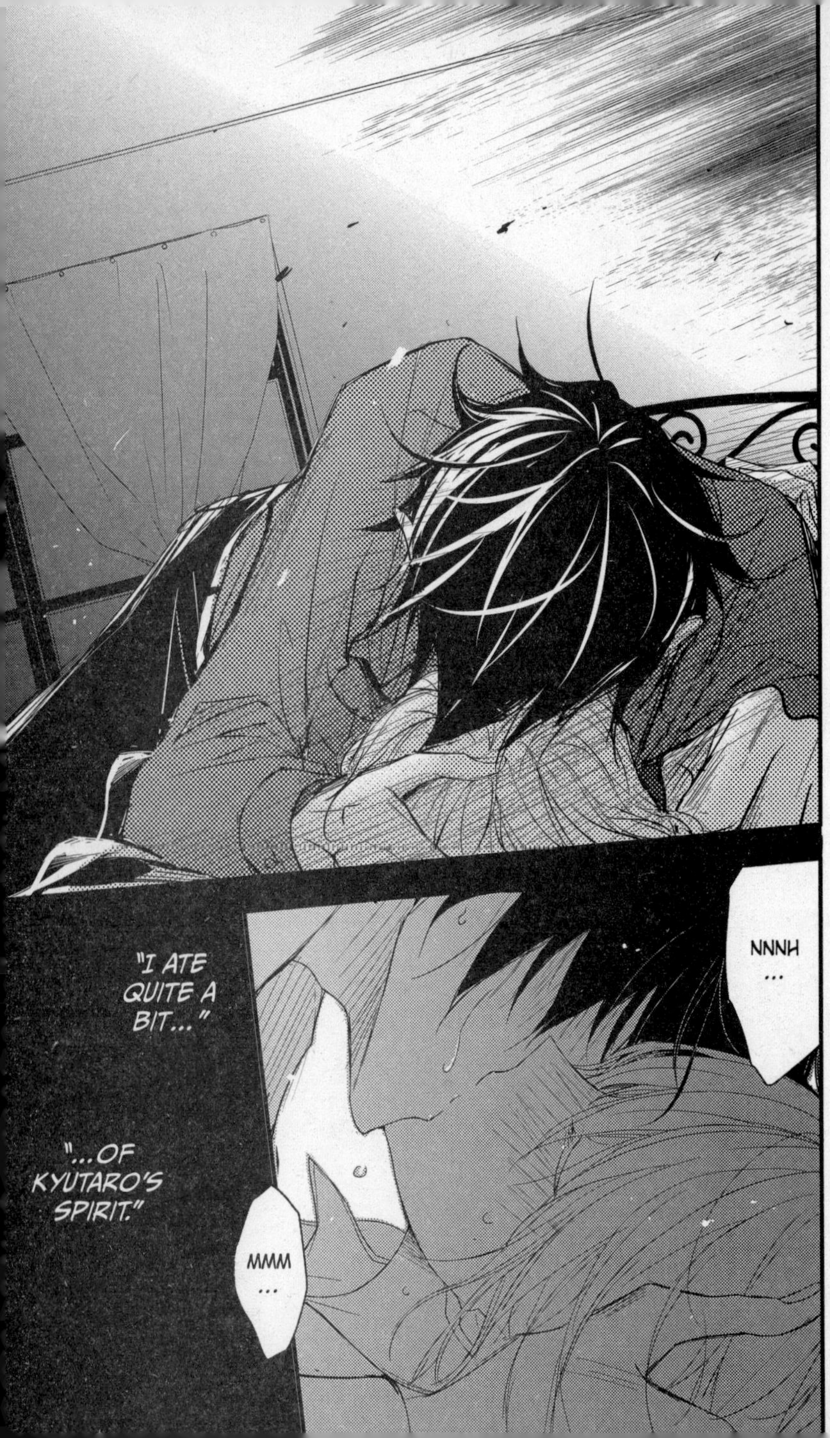
NNNH ...
"I ATE QUITE A BIT..."
"...OF KYUTARO'S SPIRIT."
MMM ...

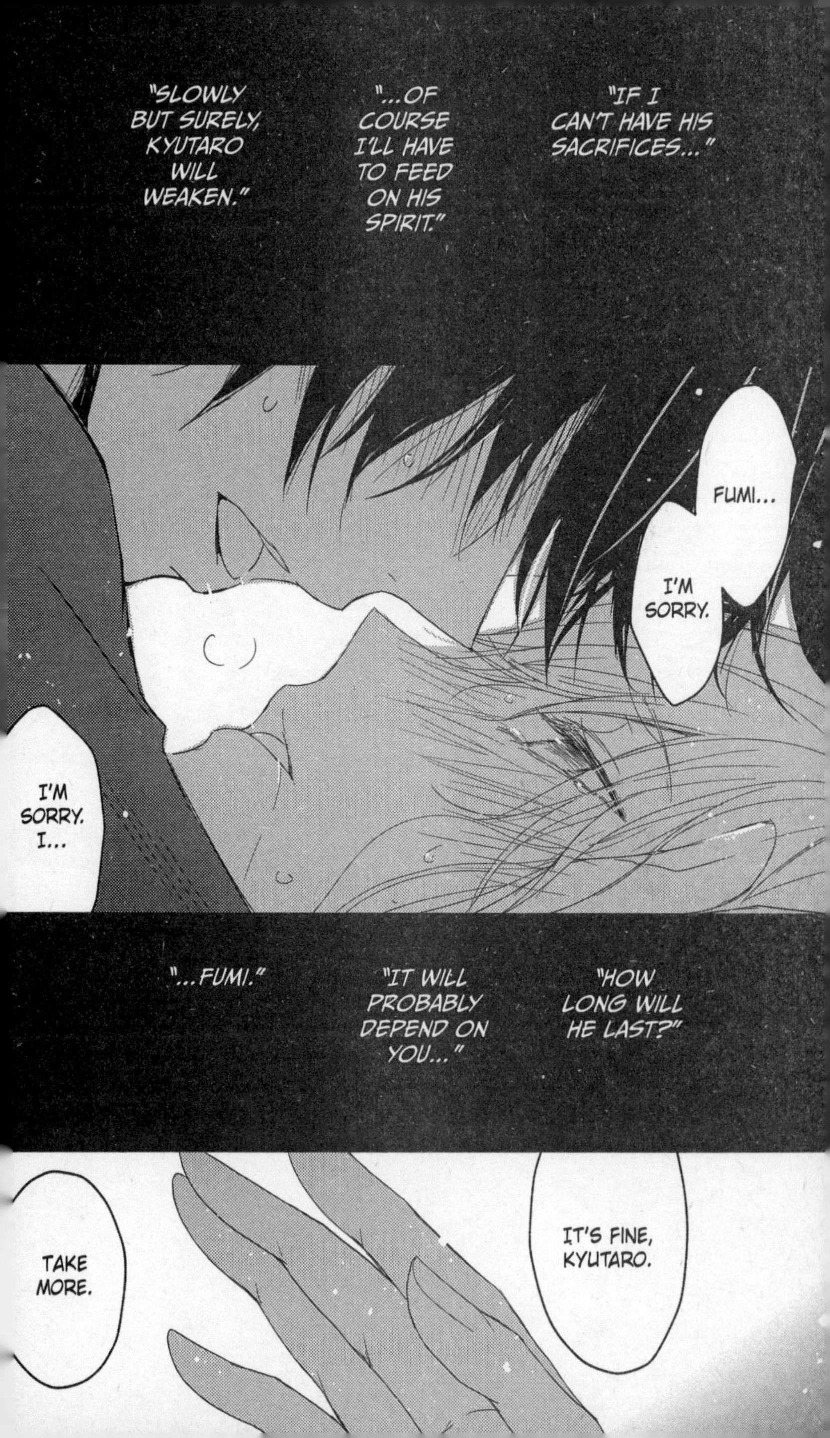
"IF I CAN'T HAVE HIS SACRIFICES..."
"...OF COURSE I'LL HAVE TO FEED ON HIS SPIRIT."
"SLOWLY BUT SURELY, KYUTARO WILL WEAKEN."
FUMI...
I'M SORRY.
I'M SORRY. I...
"HOW LONG WILL HE LAST?"
"IT WILL PROBABLY DEPEND ON YOU..."
"...FUMI."
IT'S FINE, KYUTARO.
TAKE MORE.

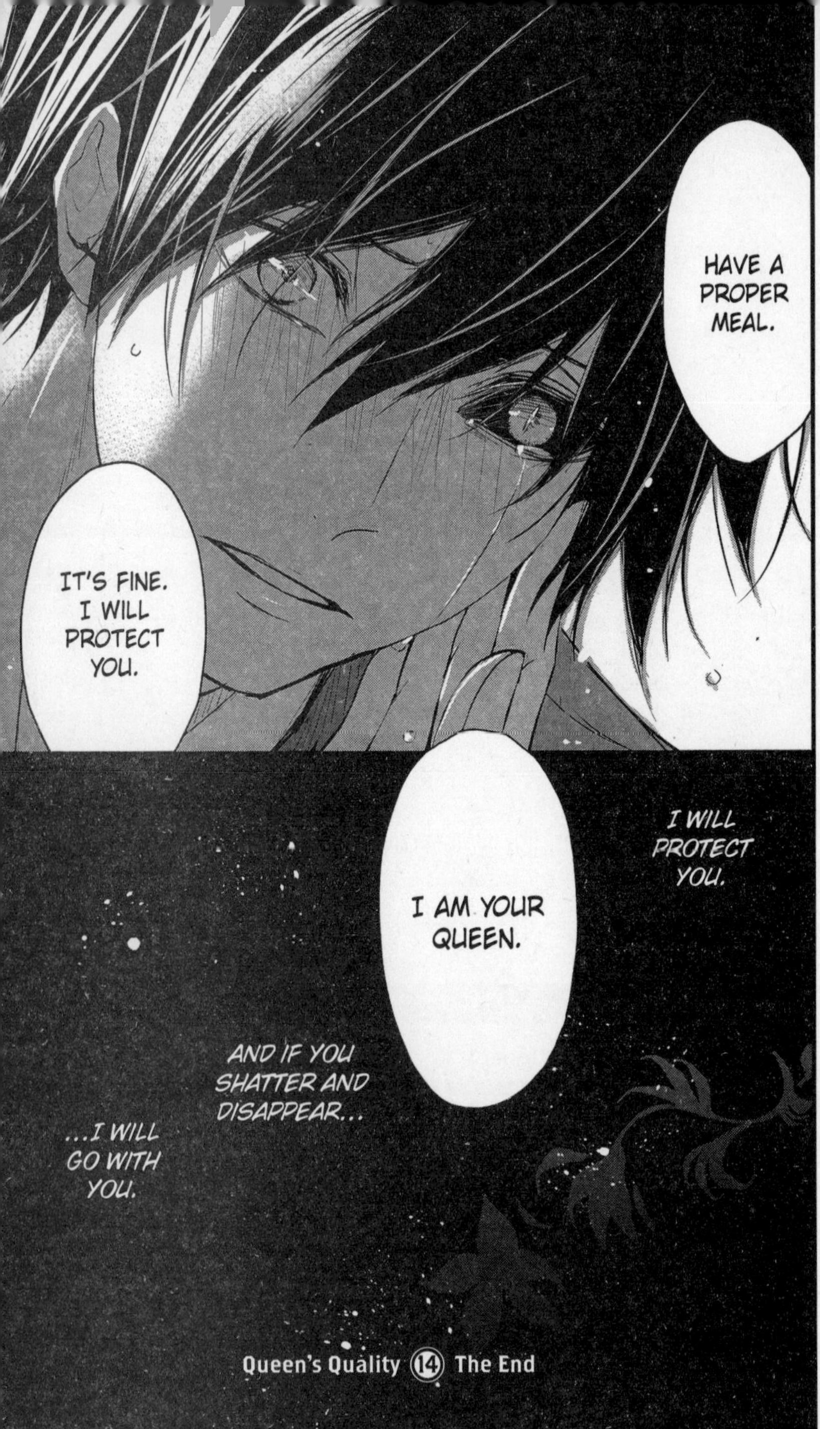
HAVE A PROPER MEAL.
IT'S FINE. I WILL PROTECT YOU.
I WILL PROTECT YOU.
I AM YOUR QUEEN.
AND IF YOU SHATTER AND DISAPPEAR...
...I WILL GO WITH YOU.

Queen's Quality ⑭ The End

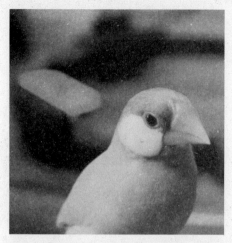

I've started the *Ring Fit* game as a way to build up my muscles. Kojiro is scared of it and won't go near, so I try keeping it at a distance.

—Kyousuke Motomi

Author Bio

Born on August 1, Kyousuke Motomi debuted in *Deluxe Betsucomi* with *Hetakuso Kyupiddo* (No Good Cupid) in 2002. She is the creator of *Dengeki Daisy*, *Beast Master*, and *QQ Sweeper*, all available in North America from VIZ Media. Motomi enjoys sleeping, tea ceremonies, and reading Haruki Murakami.

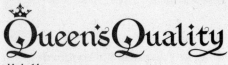

Queen's Quality

Vol. 14
Shojo Beat Edition

STORY AND ART BY
KYOUSUKE MOTOMI

QUEEN'S QUALITY Vol. 14
by Kyousuke MOTOMI
© 2016 Kyousuke MOTOMI
All rights reserved.
Original Japanese edition published by SHOGAKUKAN.
English translation rights in the United States of America, Canada, the United
Kingdom, Ireland, Australia and New Zealand arranged with SHOGAKUKAN.

ORIGINAL DESIGN/Chie SATO+Bay Bridge Studio

English Adaptation/Ysabet Reinhardt MacFarlane
Translation/JN Productions
Touch-Up Art & Lettering/Rina Mapa
Design/Julian [JR] Robinson
Editor/Amy Yu

Printed in the U.S.A.

Published by VIZ Media, LLC
P.O. Box 77010
San Francisco, CA 94107

10 9 8 7 6 5 4 3 2 1
First printing, April 2022

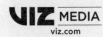

viz.com   shojobeat.com

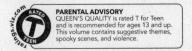

This is the Last Page!

It's true: In keeping with the original Japanese comic format, this book reads from right to left—so action, sound effects, and word balloons are completely reversed. This preserves the orientation of the original artwork—plus, it's fun! Check out the diagram shown here to get the hang of things, and then turn to the other side of the book to get started!

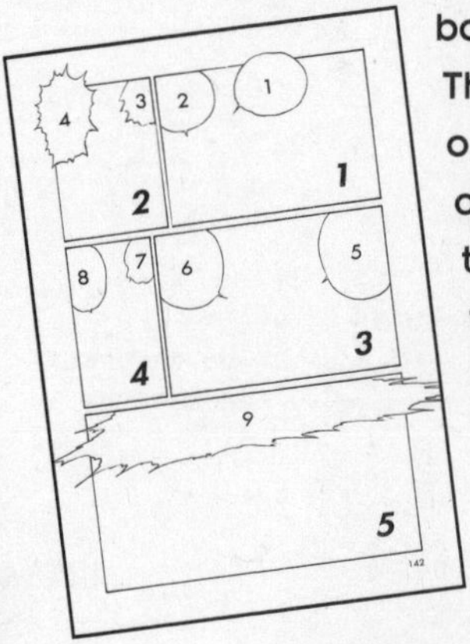
1
2
3
4
1
2
5
6
7
8
3
4
9
5
142

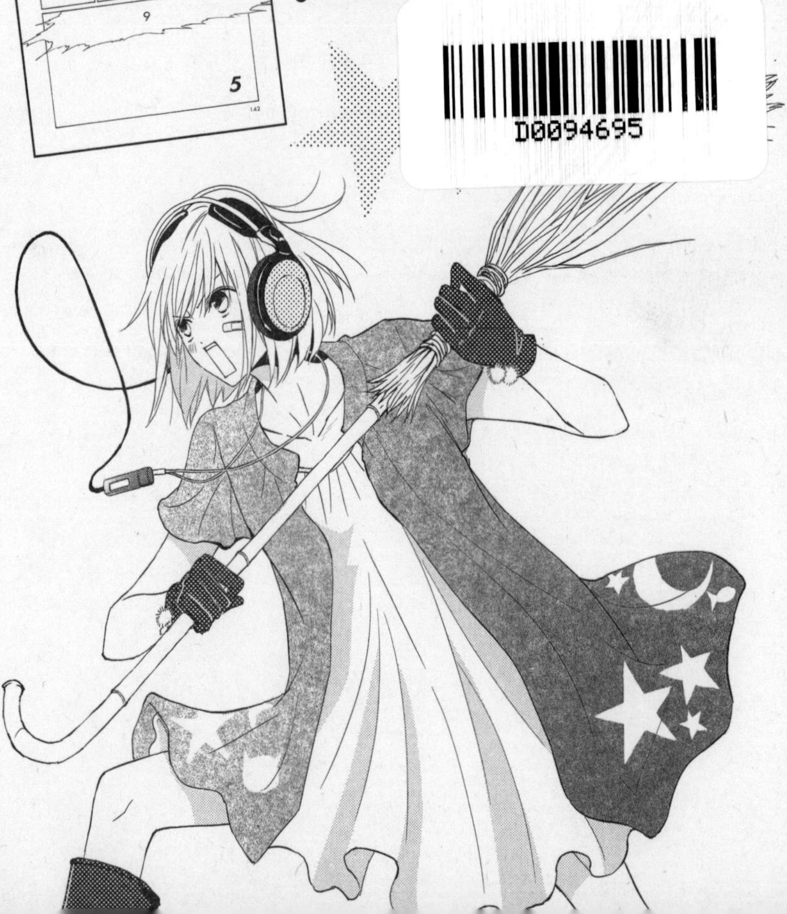
D0094695